Windows Me

THE MISSING MANUAL

*The book that
should have been
in the box*

Windows Me

THE MISSING MANUAL

David Pogue

POGUE PRESS™

O'REILLY®

Beijing • Cambridge • Farnham • Köln • Paris • Sebastopol • Taipei • Tokyo

Windows Me: The Missing Manual

by David Pogue

Copyright © 2000 Pogue Press, LLC. All rights reserved.
Printed in the United States of America.

Published by Pogue Press/O'Reilly & Associates, Inc., 101 Morris Street, Sebastopol, CA 95472.

September 2000: First Edition.
December 2000: Second printing.

This book is printed on acid-free paper with 85% recycled content, 15% post-consumer waste. O'Reilly & Associates is committed to using paper with the highest recycled content available consistent with high quality.

ISBN: 0-596-00009-X   [12/00]
[M]

Table of Contents

Part Two: The Components of Windows Me

The Missing Credits

About the Author

 David Pogue, creator of the Missing Manual series, is the computer columnist for the *New York Times*. He has written or co-written numerous computer, humor, and music books. They include the Computer Press Association award winner *PalmPilot: The Ultimate Guide;* six books in the ...*for Dummies* series (including *Macs, Magic, Opera,* and *Classical Music);* and *Mac OS 9: The Missing Manual.*

In his other life, David is a former Broadway show conductor, magician, and piano player. He and his wife Jennifer Pogue, MD, live in Connecticut with their young son and daughter. Photos, book information, and the whole life story await at *www.davidpogue.com.*

He welcomes feedback about this book and others in the Missing Manual series by email: *david@pogueman.com.* (If you're seeking technical help, however, please refer to the help sources listed in Chapter 15.)

About the Creative Team

Nan Barber (copy editor) works as a freelance writer and editor from her home near Boston. She majored in Japanese studies at Brown University and traveled throughout Asia and Europe as a jewelry buyer. Nan is the managing editor for *Salamander,* a magazine for poetry, fiction, and memoirs, and marketing writer for Whole Foods Market. On this book project, her pursuit of prose perfection was polished by proofreaders John Cacciatore, Danny Marcus, and Jennifer Barber.

Craig Zacker (technical editor) began his computing experience began in the halcyon days of teletypes and paper tape. After earning a master's degree in English and American Literature from New York University, he worked as a consultant and Windows NT integrator, and as a technical writer and webmaster for the online services group of a large software company. Craig has authored or contributed to many books on PC hardware, operating systems, and networking topics; he's a contributing editor for *Windows NT Magazine.* A complete résumé and writing samples await at *www.zacker.com,* or via email at *craig@zacker.com.*

David A. Freedman created the cover design for the Missing Manual series (with assistance from illustrator Marc Rosenthal, who drew the Missing Manual dog). From his studio in Carlisle, Massachusetts *(df301@aol.com),* David also designs logos and other graphics. Prior to establishing his design business, David worked for 20 years with Milton Glaser in New York City.

Rose Cassano (cover joystick illustration) has worked as an independent designer and illustrator for 20 years. Assignments have spanned the nonprofit sector to corporate clientele. She is lives in beautiful Southern Oregon, grateful for the miracles of modern technology that make living and working there a reality. Email: *cassano@cdsnet.net.* Web: *www.rosecassano.com.*

Phil Simpson (book design and layout) has been involved with computer graphics since 1977, when he worked with one of the first graphics-generating computers—an offspring of flight-simulation technology. He now works out of his office in Stamford, CT *(pmsimpson@earthlink.net),* where he has had his graphic design business for 18 years. He is experienced in many facets of graphic design, including corporate identity, publication design, corporate and medical communications.

Acknowledgments

The Missing Manual series is a joint venture between Pogue Press—the dream team introduced on these pages—and O'Reilly & Associates. In particular, this book owes its existence to Tim O'Reilly, Cathy Record, Edie Freedman, Allen Noren, Laura Schmier, Glenn Harden, Sue Willing, Mark Brokering, Dana Furby, and Sara Winge.

Larry Seltzer, Sharon Crawford, and Microsoft's PR firm, Waggener/Edstrom, also did great favors for this book. So did Elizabeth "Eagle Eye" Tonis, this book's beta reader, who pulled out every stop to exterminate lingering typos. Enthusiastic thanks also go to Microsoft product manager Tom Laemmel, who went out of his way to provide information that wasn't in the help files.

My agent, David Rogelberg, was this series' first believer. Finally, thanks to my wife, Jennifer, who makes the Missing Manual series—and everything else—possible.

The Missing Manual Series

Missing Manuals are designed to be authoritative, superbly written guides to popular computer products that don't come with printed manuals (which is just about all of them). Each book features a hand-crafted index; cross-references to specific page numbers (not just "See Chapter 14"); and RepKover, a detached-spine binding that lets the book lie perfectly flat without the assistance of weights or cinder blocks.

Recent and upcoming titles include:

- *Mac OS 9: The Missing Manual* by David Pogue
- *AppleWorks 6: The Missing Manual* by Jim Elferdink & David Reynolds
- *iMovie 2: The Missing Manual* by David Pogue
- *Windows 2000 Pro: The Missing Manual* by Sharon Crawford
- *DreamWeaver 4: The Missing Manual* by Dave McFarland
- *Office 2001 for Macintosh: The Missing Manual* by Nan Barber & David Reynolds
- *Mac OS X: The Missing Manual* by David Pogue

Introduction

As any PC magazine will tell you, Windows 95 was the Big One. That was the rock-star operating system, the technological leap forward that inspired hordes of anxious early birds to line up outside computer stores at midnight on the night of its release.

Most experts dismissed Windows 98, by contrast, as little more than warmed-over Windows 95, garnished with bug fixes that had long been available on the Web.

Now Microsoft brings us Windows Millennium Edition. (Microsoft has dubbed it Windows Me for short; evidently whoever named Microsoft Bob still works at Microsoft.) It's easy to see how veteran PC fans might be tempted to shrug off Windows Me as just another rehash.

But that would be a mistake. In Windows Me, Microsoft has made some impressive and worthwhile improvements to the most-used operating system in the world. As you can read in Chapter 1, most of these new features involve the *removal* of time-honored annoyances: silly error messages, poor installer design, fragile system files, vulnerability to conflicts, and so on. (Real Mode and the ability to boot into DOS are gone, too, for those who care.) The new programs included with Windows Me are a mixed bag, but some—the new Media Player and the Home Networking Wizard, in particular—are home runs.

If you bought a PC with Windows Me preinstalled, you're in for even better things; such PCs offer hardware features, such as a 30-second startup time and a Hibernation mode, that make the new Windows especially delectable. But even if you're upgrading an older machine (see Appendix A), you're likely to keep discovering Microsoft's sweet little nips and tucks for months to come.

About this Book

Despite the many improvements in Windows over the years, one feature hasn't improved a bit: Microsoft's documentation. With Windows Me, in fact, you get no printed user guide at all. To learn about the thousands of pieces of software that make up this operating system, you're expected to read the online help screens.

Unfortunately, as you'll quickly discover, these help screens are tersely written, offer very little technical depth, and lack examples and illustrations. You can't even mark your place, underline, or read them in the bathroom.

The purpose of this book, then, is to serve as the manual that should have accompanied Windows Me. In this book's pages, you'll find step-by-step instructions for using almost every Windows feature, including those you may not even have quite understood, let alone mastered: playing games via Internet, setting up a small office network, playing movie and sound files, using email, and so on.

Windows Me: The Missing Manual is designed to accommodate readers at every technical level. The primary discussions are written for advanced-beginner or intermediate PC users. But if you're a first-time Windows user, special sidebar articles called Up To Speed provide the introductory information you need to understand the topic at hand. If you're an advanced PC user, however, keep your eye out for similar shaded boxes called Power Users' Clinic. They offer more technical tips, tricks, and shortcuts for the veteran PC fan.

About the Outline

This book is divided into six parts, each containing several chapters:

• Part 1, **The Windows Me Desktop,** covers everything you see on the screen when you turn on a Windows Me computer: icons, windows, menus, scroll bars, the Recycle Bin, shortcuts, the Start menu, shortcut menus, and so on.

• Part 2, **The Components of Windows Me,** is dedicated to the proposition that an operating system is little more than a launch pad for *programs*—the actual applications you use in your everyday work, such as email programs, Web browsers, word processors, and so on. Chapter 6 describes how to work with applications in Windows—launch them, switch among them, swap data between them, use them to create and open files, and so on.

This part also offers an item-by-item discussion of the individual software nuggets that make up this operating system: not just the items in your Control Panel folder, but also the long list of free programs that Microsoft threw in, such as Windows Media Player, Movie Maker, Paint, WordPad, and so on.

• Part 3, **Windows Online,** covers all the special Internet-related features of Windows, including the wizards that set up your Internet account, Outlook Express (for email), Internet Explorer 5.5 (for Web browsing), chatting with MSN Messenger Service, videoconferencing with NetMeeting, and so on.

- Part 4, **Plugging Into Windows Me,** describes the operating system's relationship to equipment you can attach to your PC: scanners, cameras, disks, printers, and so on. Special chapters describe the Profiles (multiple users) feature, troubleshooting your PC, and preventing problems from arising to begin with.

- Part 5, **Building a Small Network,** honors the millions of households and offices that now contain more than one PC. It guides you through setting up, and making the most of, your own office network.

At the end of the book, two appendixes provide guidance in installing this operating system and a menu-by-menu explanation of the Windows Me desktop commands.

About→These→Arrows

Throughout this book, and throughout the Missing Manual series, you'll find sentences like this one: "Open the My Computer→C: drive→Windows folder." That's shorthand for a much longer instruction that directs you to open three nested icons in sequence, like this: "On your desktop, you'll find an icon called My Computer. Open that. Inside the My Computer window is a disk icon labeled C:; double-click it to open it. Inside *that* window is yet another one called Windows. Double-click to open it, too."

Similarly, this kind of arrow shorthand helps to simplify the business of choosing commands in menus, as shown in Figure I-1.

Figure I-1:
In this book, arrow notations help to simplify folder and menu instructions. For example, "Choose Start→ Programs→Accessories→ Notepad" is a more compact way of saying, "Click the Start button, then slide up to the Programs command; without clicking, now slide to the right onto the Accessories submenu; in that *submenu, click Notepad," as shown here.*

About MissingManual.com

You're invited and encouraged to submit corrections and updates on this book's Web page at *www.missingmanual.com*. In an effort to keep the book as up-to-date and accurate as possible, each time we print more copies of this book, we'll make any confirmed corrections you've suggested. We'll also note such changes on the Web site, so that other readers can mark important corrections into their own copies of the book, if they like.

In the meantime, we'd love to hear your suggestions for new books in the Missing Manual line. There's a place for that on the Web site, too, as well as a place to sign up for free email notification of new titles in the series.

Part One:
The Windows Me Desktop

1

A Welcome to Windows

Microsoft Windows Millennium Edition, or Windows Me if you're in a hurry, is the latest version of the most-used software in the world. If you recently bought a new PC, Windows Me probably came pre-installed on it. If you already own a computer (running, for example, Windows 95 or 98), you can buy Windows Me separately to upgrade your machine (see Appendix A).

No matter how you go about getting it on your PC, however, you'll be spending a lot of time with Windows Me. It's your computer's face; it's the first thing that greets you when you turn on the machine, and the last thing you see before it blinks off.

Windows: What It's For

Windows is an *operating system,* the software that controls your computer. It's designed to serve you in several ways:

- **It's a launching bay.** At its heart, Windows is a home base, a remote-control clicker that lets you call up the various *applications* (software programs) you'll use to get work done or time killed: email programs, word processors, and so on. When you get right down to it, applications are the real reason you bought a PC.

  Windows Me is a well-stocked software pantry unto itself; for example, it comes with such basic programs as a Web browser, an email program, a simple word processor, and a calculator. Windows Me comes with games, too—*lots* of games, several which you can play live against other people on the Internet. (Chapter 11 covers the free Internet programs; Chapter 7 describes the other freebie programs.)

  If you were stranded on a desert island, the built-in Windows Me programs could suffice for everyday operations. But if you're like most people, sooner or later you'll buy and install more software—perhaps a more powerful word processor like Microsoft Word, a spreadsheet program like Excel, slide-show software like PowerPoint, or a Web-design program like FrontPage or DreamWeaver. (Because the Microsoft Office programs are so popular in the business world, many PCs even come with them—Word, Excel, and PowerPoint—already installed.)

Microsoft Word   random notes   WinMe   New Folder

Figure 1-1:
Your Windows world revolves around icons, the tiny pictures that represent your programs, documents, and various Windows components. From left to right: the icons of a word processor program (Word), a word processing document, a CD-ROM inserted into your computer, and a folder into which you can organize other icons.

That's one of the luxuries of using Windows: You can choose from a staggering number of add-on programs. Whether you're a left-handed beekeeper or a German-speaking nun, some company somewhere is selling Windows software designed just for you, its target audience.

UP TO SPEED

When to Click Once, When to Click Twice

One of the most confusing aspects of Windows, both for beginners and for the occasional veteran, is knowing when to click something on the screen, and when to *double-click*.

When you read an instruction to *click* something on the screen, you're supposed to roll the mouse across your desk until the arrow pointer rests on the target—and then click and release the left mouse button once. When you click an icon, it darkens to indicate that you've *selected* it. Other things to click only once: a menu name (including the Start menu), a toolbar button (such as those in Microsoft Word or Excel), and a hyperlink (a blue underlined phrase like the ones you find on Web pages, on help screens, and so on).

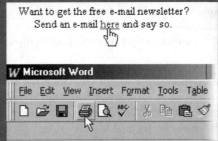

Double-clicking, on the other hand, involves keeping the mouse perfectly still and then clicking the left mouse button *twice* in rapid succession. On your desktop, double-clicking has only one meaning: *open this icon into a window.* Double-clicking a folder or disk icon opens a window that shows what's stored inside; double-clicking a word processor document opens a window that shows you what's written inside; and so on.

Double-clicking has one other useful function that has nothing to do with icons: You can double-click a word (in a word processor, in an email program, on the Web, and so on) to highlight exactly one word without having to drag precisely from one end of the word to the other.

- **It's a file cabinet.** Every application on your machine, as well as every file you've created by typing, "painting," or composing, is represented on the screen by an *icon* (see Figure 1-1). You can organize these icons into little on-screen file folders. You can make backups (safety copies) by dragging file icons onto a floppy disk, or send them by email to friends and co-workers. You can also get rid of icons you no longer need by dragging them onto the Recycle Bin icon.

- **It's your equipment headquarters.** You can only *see* a tiny portion of Windows. An enormous chunk of Windows is behind-the-scenes plumbing that controls the various functions of your computer—its modem, screen, keyboard, printer, and so on. In fact, many of the new features in Windows Millennium are improvements to exactly such invisible software components.

(At Microsoft, the slogan for Windows Me is, "It just works." Windows veterans take that slogan with a grain of salt the size of Miami; having anything as complex as Windows work perfectly on PCs from dozens of different manufacturers, each configured differently, is unattainable. But Windows Me certainly comes closer to that ideal than Windows 95 or 98.)

Getting Ready for Windows

To get the most out of Windows with the least frustration, it helps to become familiar with the following concepts and terms. You'll encounter them over and over again—in the built-in Windows help, in computer magazines, and in this book. For example:

The Right Mouse Button Is King

One of the most important features of Windows isn't on the screen—it's under your hand. The standard mouse has two mouse buttons. You use the left one to click buttons, highlight text, and drag things around on the screen.

When you click the right button, however, a *shortcut menu* appears on the screen, like the ones shown in Figure 1-2. Get into the habit of right-clicking things—icons, folders, disks, text in your word processor, buttons on your menu bar, pictures on a

Figure 1-2:
Shortcut menus (sometimes called context menus) *sometimes list commands that aren't in the menus at the top of the window. Here, for example, are the commands that appear when you right-click a disk icon (left), a folder (middle), and a date square in a calendar program (right). Left-click the command you want.*

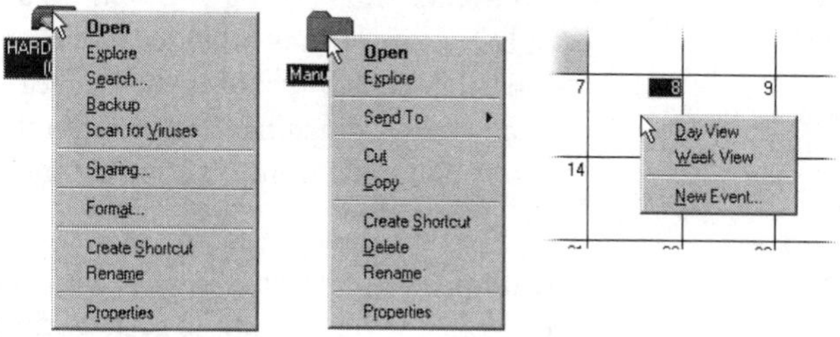

Web page, and so on. The commands that appear on the shortcut menu will make you much more productive and lead you to discover handy functions whose existence you never even suspected.

Tip: Microsoft doesn't discriminate against left-handers...much. You can swap the functions of the right and left mouse buttons easily enough. Click Start→Settings→Control Panel. Then double-click the Mouse icon.

When the Mouse Properties dialog box opens, click the Basics tab, and where it says "Select the mouse button you want to use for most tasks," click Right, then click OK. Windows automatically assumes that you therefore want to use the *left* mouse button as the one that produces shortcut menus.

Windows Wizards Ask a Lot of Questions

A *wizard* is a series of screens that walks you through the task you're trying to complete. Wizards make configuration and installation tasks easier by breaking them down into smaller, more easily digested steps. Figure 1-3 shows an example.

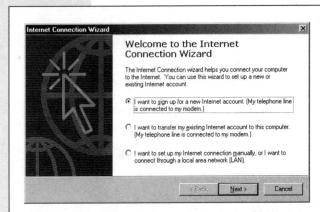

Figure 1-3:
Wizards—interview screens—are everywhere in Windows. On each of the screens, you answer a question about your computer or your preferences, and then click a Next button. When you click Finish on the final screen, Windows whirls into action, automatically completing the installation or setup.

There's More than One Way to Do Everything

No matter what setting you want to adjust, no matter what program you want to open, Microsoft has provided five or six different ways to do it. For example, you can delete a file by pressing the Delete key, choosing Delete from the menu at the top of a window, dragging the icon onto the Recycle Bin, or right-clicking the icon and choosing Delete from the shortcut menu.

Optimists point out that this abundance of approaches means that almost everyone will find, and settle on, a satisfying method for each task. Pessimists grumble that there are too many paths to each destination, making it much more difficult to learn Windows. Whenever you find a task becoming irksome, remember that you have other options.

You Can Use the Keyboard for Everything

Speaking of alternate methods of doing things: One of the first things a newcomer notices about Windows is the abundance of underlined letters in the names of menus and dialog boxes. These underlines are clues for people who find it faster to do something by pressing keys than by using the mouse.

The scheme is simple: You can open a menu by pressing the underlined letter along with the Alt key, which is next to your Space bar. (You can release the Alt key immediately after pressing it.) In this book, in help screens, and in computer magazines, you'll see this key combination indicated like this: Alt+S (for example).

Tip: The most frequently used menu of all, the Start menu, doesn't show an underline. To pop the Start menu open, press the Windows-logo key that's *next* to the Alt key on recent keyboards.

Once the menu is open, press the letter key that corresponds to the underlined letter in the menu command you want. Or press Esc to close the menu without doing anything. (In Windows, the Esc key always means *cancel* or *close this thing.*)

Pressing a letter key may trigger the command immediately, or it may open a dialog box (see Figure 1-4). Once a dialog box is open, you can trigger its options, too, by pressing Alt along with the underlined letters.

It's a rare task indeed that you can't perform entirely from the keyboard. For example, Figure 1-4 shows how you might print the first three pages of a document without using the mouse at all.

Figure 1-4:
Press Alt+F, which opens the File menu (left). Then press P, which triggers the Print command. (Or press Ctrl+P to bypass both steps.) When the Print box appears (right), press Alt+G to highlight the Pages box; type the page range you want; and then press Enter to "click" the OK button.

You Could Spend a Lifetime Changing Properties

You can't write an operating system that's all things to all people, but Microsoft has sure tried. It would be hard to imagine an operating system that's more flexible; you can change almost every aspect of the way Windows looks and works. For example, you can replace the gray backdrop of the screen with your favorite photograph, change the typeface used for the names of your icons, or set up a particular program to launch automatically every time you turn on the PC.

When you want to change some *general* behavior of your computer, such as how it connects to the Internet, how soon the screen goes black to save power, or how quickly a letter repeats on the screen when you hold down a key, you use the Control Panel window (see Chapter 9).

Many other times, however, you may want to adjust the settings of only one *particular* element of the machine, such as the hard drive, the Recycle Bin, or a particular application. In those cases, you right-click the corresponding icon. In the resulting shortcut menu, you'll often find a command called Properties. When you click it, a dialog box appears containing settings or information displays about that object, as shown in Figure 1-5.

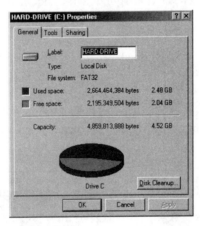

Figure 1-5:
One quick way to find out how much space is left on your hard drive is to right-click it and choose the Properties command (left). The Properties dialog box appears (right), featuring a handy graph that shows how much of the disk is full.

Keyboard-shortcut fans, take note: Pressing Ctrl+Tab takes you from one tab of the dialog box to the next.

It's also worth getting to know how to operate *tabbed dialog boxes,* like the one shown in Figure 1-5. These are configuration windows that contain so many options, Microsoft has had to split them up onto separate panels, or *tabs.* To reveal a new set of options, click a different tab (called General, Tools, and Sharing in Figure 1-5), which are designed to resemble the tabs at the top of file folders in a drawer.

Every piece of hardware requires software

You can't walk six feet into the room at a computer user group meeting without hearing people talk about their *drivers.* They're not talking about their chauffeurs (unless they're Bill Gates); they're talking about the controlling software required by every hardware component of a PC.

The *driver* is the translator between your PC's brain and the equipment attached to it. Windows requires a driver for anything you might attach to, or install inside, your computer: the mouse, keyboard, screen, floppy drive, CD-ROM drive, networking circuitry, modem, scanner, digital camera, and PalmPilot, among others. Without the driver software, the corresponding piece of equipment doesn't work at all.

When you buy one of these gadgets, you get a floppy disk or CD containing the driver software. If the included driver software works fine, great. If your gadget acts up, however, remember that equipment manufacturers regularly release improved or less buggy versions of these software chunks. (You can generally find such updates on the manufacturers' Web sites.)

You can read much more about drivers in Chapter 13. For now, it's worth noting that two of the most important improvements in Windows Me pertain to drivers:

- **Automatic Updates.** The new Automatic Updates feature checks the Internet for many kinds of updated drivers automatically, and even offers to install them for you (see page 186).

- **Plug and Play.** Your Windows Me CD-ROM comes with the drivers for thousands of products from hundreds of manufacturers, saving you the trouble of having to scavenge for them on a disk or on the Internet. This gigantic library is the heart of Microsoft's heavily advertised *Plug and Play* feature (Chapter 13), which lets you connect a new gadget to your PC without even having to think about the driver software. Windows Me locates and installs the appropriate software driver automatically.

What's New in Windows Me

There aren't any big-ticket new features in Windows Me, at least none as dramatic as the ones that distinguished, say, Windows 95 from Windows 3.1. Instead, this version of Windows is composed of dozens upon dozens of smaller fixes, tweaks, and upgrades. In a way, they add up to one *gigantic* big-ticket feature, because they let you spend a lot less time worrying about your PC and more time using it.

Microsoft puts all of these small- and medium-ticket improvements into the following categories:

PC Health

Microsoft eventually figured out that most PC troubles result from your attempts to install some new piece of software or hardware. After all, the PC probably worked fine the day you took it out of the box. Therefore, the PC Health features include:

- **System File Protection.** Before Windows Me, the installer for some new piece of software might have replaced some important Windows file with an older version, resulting in instability or crashes. System File Protection prevents software installers from doing that.

  Of course, if its installer is unable to replace the component it wants to replace, your new software might not run. However, thanks to System File Protection, you'll at least be no worse off than you were before the new installation. (This feature lets your PC run smoothly even if *you* delete a key system file, too.)

- **System Restore.** Windows Me memorizes the condition of its own system files before you perform any kind of installation. If you find your PC doesn't work properly after installing some new piece of software, you can use the new System Restore feature (page 323) to "roll back" your computer to its earlier, healthy condition. Once again, you've just undone the installation, so you can't start using that new piece of software or equipment—but you've also saved lots of time troubleshooting. System Restore is a quick alternative to trying to return your machine, step by step, to the way it was before things went wrong.

- **Unified Help Center.** Microsoft has gathered together the hodgepodge of on-screen help systems into a single program called the Help Center (Chapter 5). It contains not only the usual Windows help, but also direct links to helpful Web pages; the help modules of your applications may appear on this window, too.

- **Automatic Updates.** Like any software company, Microsoft regularly releases small fixes, patches, and updates to Windows. In the old days, it was your job to read the magazines or scan the Web sites for news about these updates. As noted earlier, Windows Me takes over that task for you: Whenever you're connected to the Internet, Windows invisibly sneaks over to the Microsoft Web site, checks for updates to your software components, downloads any that it thinks you need, and pops up a window offering to install the patch for you. (You can turn off this feature if it feels too much like Big Brother.) See page 186 for details.

FREQUENTLY ASKED QUESTION

Why don't they just fix it?

Even in Windows Me, I still get occasional error messages and system freezes. Microsoft has had all these years to perfect Windows—why don't they just get it right?

Each time Microsoft updates Windows, it's simply adding stories to a house whose foundation was built on sand. Underneath even this super-modern version of Windows still lies DOS, the ancient operating system that first put Microsoft on the map—25 years ago. Each version of Windows piles on more layers of software designed to further mask the limitations of this ancient infrastructure.

If Microsoft's programmers had their way, they'd write a new operating system from scratch—one that was rock solid, state-of-the-art, and crash-proof. So why don't they? Because of *backwards compatibility.* If Microsoft were to start fresh with a brand-new operating system, tens of thousands of Windows programs and add-on products wouldn't

work. 200 million people would have to buy all new software and equipment—and Microsoft would have a revolt on its hands.

As it is, Microsoft is trying as hard as it can to take steps in that direction without cutting your PC off from the mountain of Windows products. For example, Windows Me does away with "real mode," a memory mode required by certain ancient DOS programs. Furthermore, the next consumer version of Windows (code-named Whistler) will, according to rumor, jettison even more baggage. It will become much more like Windows 2000, the very stable corporate version of Windows, and will therefore be incompatible with hundreds of older games.

Whether it's Microsoft, Apple, or any other computer company, improving the operating system is always a balancing act.

- **Better utilities, troubleshooting, and error messages.** Some of the free, included Windows Me utilities, such as ScanDisk and Disk Defragmenter (see Chapter 15), have been improved for better speed and reliability. The Troubleshooter wizards described on page 110 have been enhanced and improved, too. And many Windows error messages, long ridiculed for their unhelpfulness, have been reworked by actual writers.

Pictures and Movies

As described in Chapter 8, Windows Me makes it easier to grab images from the next generation of digital cameras and scanners, thanks to a new technology standard called Windows Image Acquisition (WIA). Unfortunately, it's so new that, at this writing, few cameras and scanners work with it—but over time, that situation is likely to improve.

Eager to compete with the success of Apple's iMovie video-editing software, Microsoft also includes Movie Maker, which lets you grab certain shots from your camcorder or VCR, rearrange them, and edit out bad shots. This feature, too, requires special equipment: a compatible video-capture card or the combination of a digital camcorder and FireWire (IEEE-1394) card.

Finally, Windows Me comes with version 7 of Media Player, one of the new operating system's shining lights (Chapter 8). Media Player lets you play movies, listen to radio stations over the Internet, and transfer music files to your portable MP3 player.

Games

Microsoft is trying hard to distinguish its *corporate* version of Windows (Windows 2000) from its *home* version of Windows (Windows Me). To help drive home the point, Microsoft blessed Windows Me with a set of new and improved games that would be out of place in most workplaces (unless you've got a really great boss). You can even play some of these games (Backgammon, Checkers, Hearts, Reversi, and Spades) against other people on the Internet (see Chapter 7).

If your PC has speakers and a microphone, some of these games even let you *talk* to your opponent on the Internet as you play.

Better Connections

It's easier than ever to set up an Internet account in Windows Me (see Chapter 10 for details). The new operating system also comes with Internet Explorer 5.5, a faster version of Microsoft's famous Web browser. Its most important new feature: much better printing abilities, including a print preview.

And speaking of connections, Windows Me includes a vastly improved Home Networking Wizard, which walks you through the process of connecting two or more computers together. That's handy if you want to be able to play games over the network, share a single printer among several computers, drag files from machine to machine, or let all the PCs in your house connect to the Internet simultaneously over a single cable modem, DSL line, or phone line.

The Desktop and Start Menu

The first time you turn on a new Windows Me PC, you encounter some welcoming and setup screens from the PC company (Dell, Gateway, or whatever). This introductory slide show may let you register your new PC, watch a basic "how to use the mouse" tutorial, specify your time zone, sign up for a new Internet account, and so on. If you've just installed Windows Me yourself, a three-minute advertisement movie plays on the screen, courtesy of Microsoft. Once you're beyond these big hellos, however, you encounter the digital vista shown in Figure 2-1: the Windows *desktop*.

Some of the most useful components of the Windows world are the doodads that appear on this desktop. Some, such as the My Computer, My Documents, and Recycle Bin icons, are important to you. Others, such as MSN Network, are important to Microsoft.

At the lower-left corner of your screen, meanwhile, is a button labeled Start. When you click it, you open a menu that lists every significant command and software component on your PC.

This chapter covers each of these two important desktop elements—the desktop icons and the Start menu—in detail.

The Desktop Icons

The icons on your desktop may not exactly match those on someone else's Windows Me desktop; each PC manufacturer may offer a different assortment of them. But the standard Windows Me installation puts these icons on your desktop:

• **My Computer** is the trunk lid, the doorway to every single shred of software on your machine. When you double-click My Computer, a window opens to reveal icons that represent each disk drive in your machine, as shown in Figure 2-2. (Note to power users: Technically, My Computer shows a different icon for each hard drive *partition*.)

By double-clicking, for example, your hard drive icon, and then the various folders on it, you can eventually see the icons for every single file and folder on your computer. No matter which version of Windows you have, the importance of this icon is reflected by its location in the upper-left corner of the screen.

Note: The My Computer window shows you an icon for each disk drive in your machine—floppy drive, Zip drive, CD-ROM drive, and so on—whether or not there's actually a disk in that drive. If you try to double-click one of these icons when the corresponding drive is empty, you'll get nothing but a confusing error message. (It tells you that the drive "isn't ready," which isn't the problem at all.)

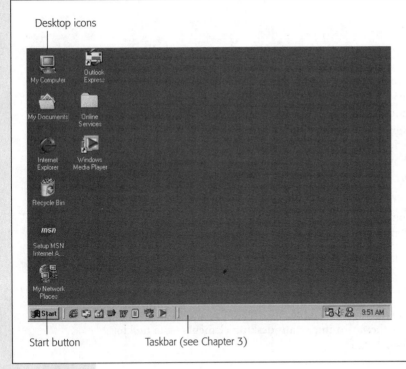

Desktop icons

Start button

Taskbar (see Chapter 3)

Figure 2-1:
A brand-new Windows Me computer screen looks like this. Everything you'll ever do on the computer will begin with a click on one of these three elements: The desktop icon, the Start button, or the Taskbar, which is described in Chapter 3. Some people find this opening desktop too cluttered, and promptly delete some of the icons they'll never use. Others place even more icons on the desktop—favorite programs and documents—for quicker access. Let your personality be your guide.

• **My Documents** is a special folder that's designed to hold the *documents* (data files) you create when you're working in your application programs. Most programs propose this folder as the target location for newly created documents. (You're welcome to rename this folder, by the way, exactly the way you'd rename any folder; see page 90.) More about My Documents in Chapter 6.

- **Internet Explorer** opens the Internet browser that comes with Windows Me (see Chapter 11).

- **Recycle Bin** is your trash can: You delete a file from your hard drive by dragging it onto this icon. (So why isn't it *called* the Trash Can? First, because you can recover files from the Recycle Bin, just as you can from a real recycle bin that hasn't yet been taken out. And second, because it's called Trash on Macintosh computers.) You can read more about this special icon on page 98.

Figure 2-2:
This computer has one floppy drive, one hard drive, and one CD-ROM drive. For your convenience, you also get a link to the Control Panel folder (see Chapter 9). If you click an icon to select it, Windows politely shows you a description on the left side of the window. If there's a disk in the CD-ROM drive, you get to see its name, not just its drive letter.

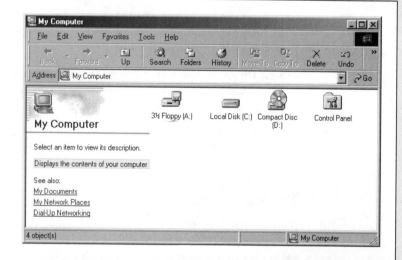

My Documents Is a Shifty Character

As described on page 101, a Windows *shortcut* is like a duplicate icon for a file. When you double-click the shortcut icon, you open the original file (the *target* file) from which it was made. The My Documents icon on the desktop, however, is unique: it's a shortcut that can *change* its target depending on who's using the PC at the moment.

If you haven't set up your copy of Windows Me to accommodate multiple users as described in Chapter 14, never mind; the My Documents desktop icon always opens the My Documents folder on your hard drive. You can skip the rest of this sidebar.

But if you do use the multiple-user feature, when you log on, you get your own My Documents folder, which sits in the My Computer→Windows→Profiles→*YourName*

folder. In other words, double-clicking the My Documents icon on the desktop opens your own personal documents folder.

This feature can be confusing if you're not expecting it. For example, if you stop by the computer after somebody else has logged in, none of your stuff is where you expect to find it, in the My Documents folder. That's because the computer no longer opens *your* documents folder when you double-click My Documents.

If this happens to you, right-click the My Documents desktop icon and choose Properties from the shortcut menu. By reading the path revealed there (see page 26), you'll be able to see whose documents are currently showing up in the My Documents window.

- **My Network Places** shows you the names of other computers to which yours is connected on an office network. If your PC *isn't* on a network, this icon doesn't serve much purpose, although there's no easy way to delete it. For more on networking and using this icon, see Chapter 17.

- **Outlook Express** is an email program you can use to send and receive email and to read the messages on Internet *newsgroups* (bulletin boards). See Chapter 11 for more on Outlook Express.

- **Windows Media Player** is the movie-playing software described in Chapter 8.

- **Online Services** is a folder containing the setup software for several Internet services: America Online, Prodigy, EarthLink, AT&T, and so on. You can read more about them in Chapter 10.

- **Sign Up for MSN Internet Access.** If you'd rather sign up for Microsoft's own online service, this is the icon to double-click. Feel free to drag it to the Recycle Bin if you don't intend to sign up.

- **My Briefcase.** This icon generally appears only on laptops. It's designed to help you keep your laptop documents synchronized with those on your desktop PC; see Chapter 15 for details.

The Start Menu

If you're willing to double-click 65 times in succession, opening folder after folder, the disk icons in the My Computer window can eventually lead you to every single file in your computer. But the vast majority of the files and folders you'll encounter are utterly useless to you personally; they're support files, there for behind-the-scenes use by Windows and your applications.

Figure 2-3:
Thin etched lines divide the Start Menu into three sections. The top section offers Windows Update, a link to a Web page that lists new or updated Windows Me components. This top section may also contain commands added by certain software installers, such as those for Microsoft Office or Corel Suite. The center section lists the commands you'll use most. The bottom section is conveniently located close to the Start button for a quick log off or shut down.

That's why the Start menu is so important—it lists every *useful* piece of software on your computer, including commands, programs, and files you've been working on recently. You can use the Start menu to open your applications, install new software, configure hardware, get help, find files, and much more.

To open the Start menu, click the Start button at the lower-left corner of your screen. The Start menu pops open, shooting upward. Its contents depend on which options you (or your computer's manufacturer) selected when installing Windows, but Figure 2-3 shows a representative example.

Tip: If you're a keyboard-shortcut lover, you can open the Start menu by pressing the Windows-logo key on the bottom row of your keyboard. (If you're using one of those antique, kerosene-operated keyboards that lack a Windows key, press Ctrl+Esc instead.)

In fact, if your mouse ever stops working, you can always use one of these keyboard methods to get to the Shut Down command on the Start menu. Then press the up or down arrow keys to highlight the Start-menu commands; press Enter to "click" that command.

Start menu items graced by a right-pointing triangle arrow (such as Settings in Figure 2-3) have *submenus,* also known as *cascading menus.* As you move your mouse pointer over an item that has such an arrow, the submenu, listing additional options, pops out to the right (you don't have to click). It's not unusual for submenu items to have arrows of their own, indicating *additional* submenus.

This discussion describes the items in the Start menu from the bottom up, the way your mouse encounters them as it moves up from the Start button.

FREQUENTLY ASKED QUESTION

Shut Down in the Start Menu

Could someone explain why the Shut Down command is in a menu called Start?

The Name-the-Button committee at Microsoft probably thought that you'd interpret *Start* to mean, "Start here to get something accomplished."

But if you find it illogical that you have to click Start when you want to shut down, you wouldn't be the first. Microsoft probably should have named the button "Menu," saving all of us a lot of confusion.

Start→Shut Down

The Shut Down menu item is more powerful than its name implies. Choosing it opens a dialog box that offers several variations on "off" (see Figure 2-4).

- **Shut Down** quits all open programs, offers you the opportunity to save any unsaved documents, and then exits Windows. Most modern PCs then turn off automatically.

If your older model requires you to press the Power button manually, you must wait until a message appears on the screen telling you that it's safe to turn off the computer, which may take more than a few seconds.

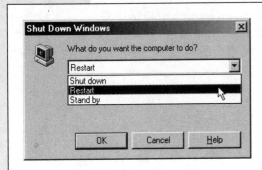

Figure 2-4:
Click the drop-down menu (the black, downward-pointing triangle) to see the choices available in the Shut Down Windows dialog box. When you select an option, you get to read an explanation of the command you've selected.

You can also choose an option by typing its first initial: S for "Shut down," R for Restart, S a second time for "Stand by," and so on.

- **Restart** quits all open programs, and then starts Windows again automatically. The computer doesn't turn off. (You might do this to "refresh" your computer when you notice that it's responding sluggishly, for example.)

- **Stand by** puts your computer to "sleep." This special state of PC consciousness reduces the amount of electricity the computer uses. The machine remains in suspended animation until you use the mouse or keyboard to begin working again.

  How the PC sleeps depends on its power-saving features. Usually, the hard drive stops spinning and the monitor goes dark. Whatever program or document you were working on remains in memory. (It's a good idea to save your work before going into standby mode, just to be safe.)

  If you're using a laptop computer and working on battery power, the standby mode is a real boon. When the flight attendant hands over your microwaved bowl of chicken teriyaki, you can take a food break without closing all your programs and shutting down the computer—and still avoid running down the battery.

  Use the "Stand by" option in the Shut Down dialog box when you want to put your computer to sleep on cue. It's worth noting, however, that you can set the computer to go into standby automatically if you haven't used the mouse or keyboard for a while. You can even make it so that the computer won't wake up again unless you type in a certain password. Page 208 has the details on these extra features.

- **Hibernate,** a new feature in Windows Me, shuts down the machine after it *memorizes* the state of your software, including all open operating system files, applications, and documents. Behind the scenes, it saves all this memorized information into a file on your hard disk. (As a result, the Hibernate command doesn't work unless you have a lot of free disk space. The more RAM your computer has, the more disk space you'll need.)

As with the Standby feature, you can configure your computer to hibernate automatically after a period of inactivity, or require a password to bring it out of hibernation. See page 208.

The beauty of this feature is that when you start the computer again, everything returns to the way it was when you shut down—*fast*. The same documents appear, the same programs are running, and so on. Hibernate, in other words, offers the speed and convenience of Standby, with the safety of Shut Down.

Note: Some older computers don't come with the necessary circuitry (technically, *BIOS support*) for the Hibernate command. In that case, the Hibernate choice doesn't appear in the list.

GEM IN THE ROUGH

Hibernation as a Shutdown Technique

When you shut down the computer in hibernation mode, the next startup is lightning-fast. As soon as the startup procedure begins, Windows notices the hibernation file on the hard drive, says, "Hey, everything's in place," and loads the file into memory. After you push the power button, everything reappears on the screen faster than you can say, "Redmond, Washington." After you've enjoyed the speed of a power up from hibernation mode, the normal startup seems interminably, unbearably slow.

This instant-on characteristic makes it tempting to use the hibernation feature *every* time you shut down your computer. But before adopting hibernation as your standard shutdown procedure, there are a few things to consider. When your PC hibernates, Windows doesn't have a chance to quit and then restart, as it would if you use the Restart command or shut the computer down. As a result, Win-

dows never gets the opportunity to flush your computer's memory or perform the other domestic chores of a modern operating system. As a result, Windows may seem to slow down over time.

Furthermore, the Plug and Play feature described in Chapter 13 might not work when you plug in some new piece of equipment. That's because Windows ordinarily recognizes such new arrivals during the startup process—and when your computer hibernates, there *is* no startup process.

The solution is to compromise. Use Hibernate most of the time, but shut the computer down or restart it every now and then. (If you bought your PC with Windows Millennium pre-installed, you may have noticed that it starts up remarkably fast anyway.) And always shut the computer down after installing new hardware or software.

Start→Log Off

This command is at the heart of Windows Me's *multiple-users* feature, in which each person who uses this PC gets to see his own setup, files, and so on (see Chapter 14). Use this command to close all open programs and present a new Logon dialog box—which asks for a name and password—so that the next person can sign in. If you haven't saved your work, each application gives you an opportunity to do so before closing.

This command usually says *Log Off [your name]*. But if, when signing *on*, you'd skipped the Logon dialog box by clicking the Cancel button, the command just says *Log Off* or *Log Off Default*.

If you're using Windows Me on a network, the Logon feature is a necessary security feature. If you share your *home* computer with someone else, the logon feature just keeps your stuff separate from hers (see Chapter 14). But if you're the only one who uses this PC, you can take the Log Off command completely off your Start menu, if you like, as described on page 46.

Start→Run

Use the Run menu item to get to a *command line*, as shown in Figure 2-5. A command line is a text-based method of performing a task. You type a command, click OK, and something happens as a result.

Working at the command line is becoming a lost art in the world of Windows, because most people prefer to issue commands by choosing from menus using the mouse. However, some old-timers still love the command line, and even mouse-lovers encounter situations where a typed command is the *only* way to do something. The Run dialog box presents what's called a *command-line interface*, as shown in Figure 2-5.

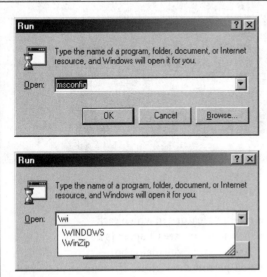

Figure 2-5:
Top: The last Run command you entered appears automatically in the Open text box. You can use the drop-down list to see a list of commands you've previously entered.

Bottom: The Run command knows the names of all of your folders. As you type, you're shown the best match for the characters you're typing. When the name of the folder you're trying to open appears in the list, click it (or press the down-arrow key to highlight it, and then press Enter) to avoid having to type the rest of the entry.

If you're an old-time PC veteran, your head probably teems with neat Run commands you've picked up over the years. If you're new to this idea, however, here are a few of the useful and time-saving things you can do with the Run box.

Launch a Program

As noted later in this discussion, one of the most important Start menu commands is the Programs submenu, where you'll find the name of almost every application on your computer. You can open each of these programs by typing its *program file name* in the Open box and then pressing Enter. That's an extremely useful shortcut for both pros and novices alike, because it's frequently faster to launch a program this way than it is to launch one using the Start→Programs menu.

Unfortunately, the program file name isn't the same as its plain-English name; it's a cryptic, abbreviated version. For example, if you want to open Microsoft Word, you must type *winword*. That's the actual name of the Word program icon as it sits in your My Computer→C: drive→Program Files→Microsoft Office→Office folder. (If your Program Files window shows up empty, click the "View the entire contents of this folder" button.) Some other common program-file names are shown here:

Program's real name	Program's familiar name
iexplore	Internet Explorer
msworks	Microsoft Works
msinm	Outlook Express
wmplayer	Windows Media Player
palm	Palm Desktop
sol	Solitaire
regedit	The Registry Editor
calc	Calculator

Tip: To discover the program file name of a favorite program, see "Which One's the Program?" on page 48.

If, like efficiency freaks worldwide, you believe that it's generally faster and more efficient to do something using the keyboard than using the mouse, get this: You can perform this entire application-launching stunt without using the mouse at all. Just follow these steps in rapid succession:

1. **Press the Windows-logo key on the bottom row of your keyboard.**

    Doing so makes the Start menu pop open. (Ctrl+Esc does the same thing.)

2. **Press the letter R key.**

    That's the underlined letter for the Run command, whose box now opens.

3. **Type the program file's name.**

    If you've typed it before, just type a couple of letters; Windows Me fills in the rest of the name automatically.

4. **Press Enter.**

Windows opens the requested program instantly. Keystrokes: 4, Mouse: 0.

Launch any Program or Document

Using the Run dialog box is handy for launching favorite applications, because it requires so few keystrokes. But you can also use the Run dialog box to open *any* file on the computer—if you're willing to do some additional typing.

The trick here is to type in the entire *path* of the program or document you want. (See the sidebar box below if you're new to the idea of file paths.) For example, to open your family budget spreadsheet that's in your My Documents folder, you might type *c:\my documents\familybudget)*.

Tip: Typing the path in this way is also useful for launching applications that don't appear in the Start→Programs menu. (If a program doesn't appear there, you must type its entire path name.)

For example, some advanced Windows Me utilities (including the *registry editor,* an advanced program described at the end of Chapter 15) are accessible only through the command line. You also need to use the Run command to open some older DOS programs that aren't listed in the Programs menu.

UP TO SPEED

The Path to Enlightenment about Paths

Windows is too busy to think of a particular file as "that family album program in the Program Files folder, which is in the My Programs folder on the C: drive." Instead, it uses shorthand to specify each icon's location on your hard drive—a series of disk and folder names separated by backslashes, like this: *C:\program files\my programs\familyalbum.exe.* Similarly, if a document named NoteToMom.doc sits in the folder called Personal, which is in the My Documents folder on drive C, Windows thinks of that file as *C:\my documents\personal\notetomom.doc.*

This kind of location code is that icon's *path.* (Capitalization doesn't matter, even though you may see capital letters in Microsoft's examples.)

You'll encounter file paths when using several important Windows features. The Run dialog box described in this section is one. The Search command is another; as you'll see in the next chapter, when you choose the Search command, Windows identifies the location of each file it finds for you by displaying its path.

Open a Drive Window

When you double-click the My Computer icon on your desktop, you'll discover something interesting: Windows assigns a letter of the alphabet to each disk drive attached to your machine—the hard drive, CD-ROM drive, floppy drive, and so on. The floppy drive is almost always A:, the hard drive is almost always C:, and so on. (There hasn't been a drive B since the demise of the two-floppy computer.)

By typing a drive letter followed by a colon (for example, *c:*) into the Run box and pressing Enter, you make a window pop open, displaying the contents of that drive.

Open a Folder Window

You can also use the Run dialog box to open the window for any folder on your machine. To do so, type a backslash followed by the name of a folder (see Figure 2-5, bottom). You might type, for example, *Program Files* to see your complete software collection.

Note: The Run command assumes that you're opening a folder on drive C:. If you want to open a folder on a different drive, add the drive letter and a colon before the name of the folder (for example, *d:\data*).

If you're on a network, you can even open a folder that's sitting on some other computer on the network. To do so, type two backslashes, the computer's name, a single backslash, and the shared folder's name. For instance, to access a shared folder called Budgets on a computer named Admin, enter *admin\budgets.* (See Chapter 17 for more on sharing folders over the network.)

It might make you feel extra proficient to know that you've just used the *Universal Naming Convention,* or UNC, for the shared folder. The UNC is simply the two-backslash, computer name\folder name format—like this: *computername\ foldername.*

Tip: In any of these cases, if you don't remember the precise name of a file or folder you want to open in the Run dialog box, click the Browse button to display the Browse dialog box, as shown in Figure 2-6.

Figure 2-6:
The Browse dialog box, which makes frequent appearances in Windows Me, lets you navigate the folders on your computer to find a file. The five icons at the left side make it easy to jump to places you're most likely to find the document you want. If you enter a drive letter and a colon in the Run dialog box before clicking the Browse button (such as c:), the Browse dialog box opens with a display of that drive's contents.

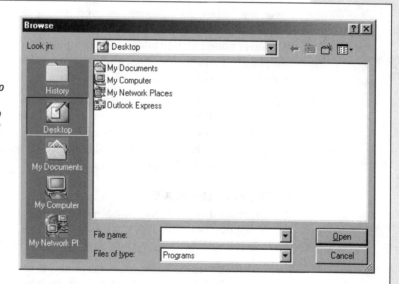

Connect to a Web Page

You can launch your Web browser (such as Internet Explorer) and jump directly to a specific Web page by typing its Web address (URL), such as *www.realbigcompany.com*, and then pressing Enter.

Once again, you may not have to type very much; the pop-up list in the Run box lists every URL you've previously entered. Click one (or press the down arrow to highlight the one you want, and then press Enter) to go there.

Note: This trick only works if you're already connected to the Internet—or if you've configured your browser to dial the Internet automatically, as described on page 230.

Start→Help

Choosing Start→Help opens the new, improved Windows Help and Support window, which is described in Chapter 5.

Tip: Once again, speed fans have an alternative to using the mouse to open the Help window—just press the F1 key. You get help screens for the program you're in; if you're at the desktop, you get Windows help.

Start→Search

The humble Search command looks no more special than anything else on the Start menu. But in fact, it's a powerhouse, and you'll probably use it often. The Search function (which was called Find in Windows 95 and 98) can quickly find all kinds of computery things: file and folder icons, computers on your network, email addresses and phone numbers, Web sites, and even maps that pinpoint any address in the United States and Canada.

If the Search program looks vaguely familiar, that's because it's actually Internet Explorer, the Web browser. Microsoft has disguised it to resemble a specialized searching program, but it's the same old program. You can read more about Internet Explorer in Chapter 10. (You can find out how it's interwoven throughout Windows in any of various Justice Department documents.)

Finding Files and Folders

If you save the files you create exclusively in the My Documents folder on the desktop, as described on page 120, you'll have little need to use the Search function to locate your files. You'll always know where they are—right there in that folder.

Every now and then, however, you won't be able to remember where you filed something, or you'll download something from the Internet and not be able to find it again, or you'll install something and not know where to look for it. In those situations, the Search command is just what you need. It lets you look for a particular file or folder based on its description—by its name, size, date stamp, and so on.

Tip: The Search command can also look for the words *inside* your files. That's a powerful feature if you remember having typed or read something, but can't remember what you named the file.

Figure 2-7:
When you're looking for files, the Search feature is like having a bloodhound available. You can use as much information as you manage to remember to initiate a search, and it doesn't matter if you can't remember the exact name of the file that's gone missing. The Search feature ordinarily finds both folder titles and filenames; to search only for files, add . to the end of the name you're looking for (for example,* memo.*).

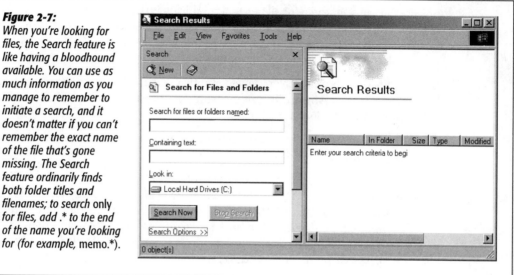

Setting up the search

A typical search goes like this:

1. **Choose Start→Search→For Files and Folders.**

   The Search window appears, as shown in Figure 2-7.

2. **Specify what disk you want to search, using the "Look in" drop-down menu.**

   Every disk attached to your PC at the moment—your hard drive, Zip disk, CD-ROM, and so on—shows up here in this list. Most of the time, you just want to search your C: hard drive; ensure that "Local Hard Drives (C:)" appears in the "Look in:" box, and then proceed.

Tip: Here's a fantastic time-saver. If you know that the file or folder you're looking for is on a particular disk or in a certain folder, open that disk's or folder's icon *first,* and *then* press F3. Doing so splits the disk or folder window in half–the left half now contains the Search controls, which are already set up to search only inside that disk or folder window. In other words, you're spared the first two steps of this search setup business. (Press F3 again to remove the Search panel.)

Also, you can limit your search to a specific folder on your hard drive by typing its path into the "Look in:" blank.

---

3. **To find a file whose name you know, type its name into the top blank.**

You don't have to type the entire filename—only enough of it to distinguish it from the other files on your computer. Capitals don't matter, and neither does the position of the letters you type—if you type *John,* Windows will find files with the names Johnson, Peterjohn, and DiJohnson.

You can also search for all files of a specific type, such as all Word files, by typing **.doc*—that is, an asterisk, a period, and then the three-letter extension of the kind of file you want. (See page 133 for more on filename extensions.) The asterisk is a wildcard meaning, "any text at all."

To narrow the search, you can enter both a partial name *and* an extension, such as *mom*.doc,* which will turn up Word files named Mom's Finances.doc, Moment of Truth.doc, and so on.

4. **If you can't remember the file's name, type some of the words that were in it into the "Containing text:" box.**

Sooner or later, it happens to everyone: A file's name doesn't match what's inside it. Maybe a marauding toddler pressed the keys, inadvertently renaming your doctoral thesis "xggrjpO#$5%////." Maybe, in a Saturday afternoon organizing binge, your spouse helpfully changed the name of your "ATM Instructions" document to "Cash Machine Info," little realizing that it was a help file for Adobe Type Manager. Or maybe you just can't remember what you called something.

The "Containing text" option searches for words *inside* your files, regardless of their names. It's extremely slow—Windows has to read every single file, which it does only slightly faster than you could—and it works only if you can remember an *exact* word or phrase in the missing document. (Even punctuation has to be an exact match.) Also, the text you enter should be unique enough to assume it only exists in the file you're looking for; if you search for, say, *good,* Windows will find so many files that the search will be pointless.

5. **Restrict the search even more by clicking Search Options, if you like.**

Searching for a file by typing in a few letters of its name is by far the most frequently used Search function. But in certain circumstances, you may want to narrow the search by confining it to only files you created yesterday, for example.

When you click Search Options, you get the panel shown in Figure 2-8. The **Date** controls let you find only files or folders you created or changed in a certain date range; the **Type** checkbox restricts your search to a particular *type* of file (Acrobat documents, applications, JPG images, and so on); and the **Size** checkbox lets you screen out files larger or smaller than a number of KB you specify.

Finally, if you turn on the Advanced Options checkbox, you're offered two final choices. **Search subfolders** makes Windows look inside all folders *inside* the disk or folder you've specified. Turn this option off only when you know for sure that the file you need is in the disk or folder you're starting with, but *not* within any subfolders there. Skipping the subfolders makes the search process much faster. **Case sensitive** instructs the Search program to match the capitalization of the characters you enter; searching for files containing "dentist appointment" won't find files containing "Dentist appointment" (with a capital D).

Windows uses the criteria you enter in these fields *in addition* to any data you entered into the basic search fields.

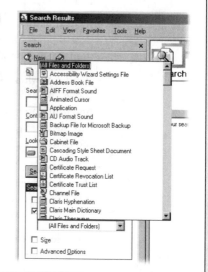

Figure 2-8:
Left: You can use the drop-down arrow to specify the date the file was created or the date the file was last accessed. Specify the specific dates by clicking the drop-down arrow to produce a little calendar, which you can adjust by clicking the arrow buttons and the calendar dates. Right: You can confine the search to a certain kind of document, which you can choose from the list that appears when you click the Type checkbox.

6. Finally, click Search Now (or press Enter).

A couple of seconds later, the screen changes. On the right side of the screen, you now see a list of files and folders whose names contain what you typed in the blank. (Figure 2-9 shows this list.)

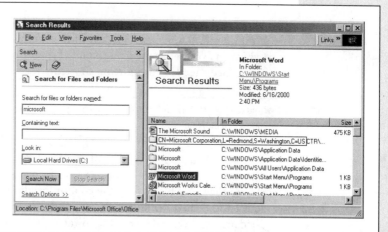

Figure 2-9:
You can manipulate the list of found files much the way you'd approach a list of files in a standard folder window. For example, you can highlight one file by typing the first couple letters of its name. You can also highlight individual items by clicking them while pressing Ctrl, drag vertically over the list to enclose a cluster of them, and so on.

Using your search results

Figure 2-9 shows the splendor of the Search Results window. At this point, you can proceed in many different ways:

- **Read the complete name.** If the Name column is too narrow to show the entire name of a file, use your arrow cursor to point to it without clicking. As shown in Figure 2-9, a pop-up *tooltip* appears, showing the complete name.

- **Read all about it.** If you click the name of a found icon, the top part of the window displays a little paragraph identifying the file's path, full name, and modification date and time. (Once again, this feature is shown in Figure 2-9.)

- **Find out where something is.** The column just to the right of an icon's name shows you exactly where it is on your machine, using the standard Windows path notation described on page 26. (You may have to widen the column to see the complete path name; to do so, drag the dividing line at the top of the column, to the right of the "In Folder" column heading.)

- **Open the file.** If one of the found files is the one you were looking for, double-click it to open it. This, in fact, is what most people do most of the time when using the Search program. In many cases, you'll never even know or care *where* the file was—you just want to get into it.

- **Jump to an icon in its home folder.** If you want to get your mouse on the icon itself, without opening it yet, you can use a new Windows Me feature. Right-click the icon in the Search window and choose Open Containing Folder from the shortcut menu. The Search window instantly retreats to the background, as Windows highlights the actual icon in question, sitting there in its window wherever it happens to be on your hard drive.

- **Move or delete the file.** You can drag an item directly out of the found-files list onto the desktop, directly onto the Recycle Bin icon, or into a different folder, window, or disk. (For more on moving icons, and the hazards thereof, see Chapter 4.)

- **Send To, Rename, or Create Shortcut.** After highlighting an icon (or icons) in the list of found files, you can use any of the commands in the File menu: Send To (which lets you move the icon to one of several standard folders), Rename, and so on. (See page 101 for more on shortcuts.)

Tip: You can right-click a found icon to copy, move, rename, or create a shortcut of it. Just choose from the resulting shortcut menu.

- **Adjust the list.** By clicking the column headings of the results window, you can sort the list of found files in various ways: by name, size, date, and so on. (You can reverse the order by clicking the column heading a second time.) You can also adjust the relative widths of the columns, just by dragging the column-name dividers. (You can also drag the lower-right corner of the window to make it bigger or smaller.)

Tip: Press the F3 key to hide the search-criteria panel that occupies the left part of the window. The results portion of the window now fills the screen, making it easier for you to see what you've got. Press F3 a second time to restore the criteria panel.

- **Save the search setup.** By choosing File→Save Search, you can immortalize the search you've just set up. You might use this feature if you perform the same search each day—if, for example, you like to round up all the documents you created yesterday for backing up.

  Windows Me automatically names the search file with a description it derives from the criteria you entered into the search fields, and adds the extension *.fnd* (for example, *files called@doc.fnd*). You can save the resulting search icon anywhere you like.

  To use the search criteria again, double-click the saved *.fnd* file. The Search window opens, with your data already entered. Click Search Now to get the canned search underway.

GEM IN THE ROUGH

Using Search to Clean Up Your Drive

You don't have to restrict your use of the Search feature to finding files you can't locate on your own. You can use its power to gather files for general hard-drive housekeeping.

If you have files about the same subject scattered in a variety of folders, you can use the Search command to gather them together. For example, search for all files with the word "budget" in the filename. Create a new folder, select all the found files in the Search Results window (documents, spread-sheets, accounting reports, and so on), and drag any *one* of them into the new folder to move them en masse.

You can also search for the backup files your software creates, such as files with the extensions *.xlk* (Microsoft Excel) or *.wbk* (Microsoft Word). They take up disk space, and you'll probably never use them. You can round them up using the Search command, and then delete them as a group from the Search Results window.

Searching for Computers

If you type in the name of a computer, the Search program tries to find it on the network (if you're on one). If you enter *part* of the computer's name, the search function locates all matching characters; for example, if you search for *ac*, the search will turn up *accounts, packages,* and so on. There's no browse function; you have to know at least part of the name of the computer you want to find.

Of course, if you're trying to find another PC on the network, you can simply double-click the desktop icon named My Network Places, which shows you icons representing all the computers on your network. So why would you ever use the Search function to find a computer? Because it sometimes finds computers that My Network Places can't. Every Windows veteran has lost count of the number of times computers have been missing from My Network Places or Network Neighborhood. In such cases, the search function is the reliable way to locate the computer and thus access its contents.

Searching for People

This tantalizing option lets you type in somebody's name; the Search program can consult any of several "White Pages" Web sites online in an attempt to track down that person's email address and telephone number. It can also search your own Windows address book when you want to check someone's phone number or other information.

To try out this feature, choose Start→Search→People. The dialog box shown in Figure 2-10 appears.

WORKAROUND WORKSHOP

Finding Missing Network Computers

When My Network Places doesn't see all the computers on the network, it's usually because the missing computer had a problem and left, then rejoined, the network. Furthermore, refreshing My Network Places by pressing the F5 key doesn't always work to bring it back to the screen.

Rebooting your own computer, the one that doesn't see all the machines on the network, usually fixes the problem, but that seems an extreme measure to correct a recalcitrant refresh feature. The search function, which uses a different method to locate computers, usually gets you to the computer you want to open.

Even Microsoft's support staff can't provide the technical explanation for this quirk. But the point is clear: When a computer fails to appear in My Network Places, head for the search feature; it almost always finds the quarry. If the search yields no results, you can confidently call the user of the missing computer, and tell him that the problem is on that end. You'll always be right: The computer is off or the cable is detached.

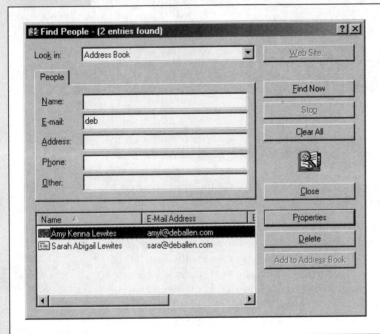

Figure 2-10:
Fill in whatever you know about the person you want to find (top). You can use partial words. The Search command produces a list of all matches (bottom). As shown here, if you're trying to find an email address for somebody at a company, you don't even have to know the company's full domain name. Select the entry that matches your quest, and then click Properties to see all the information you've collected about that person.

Searching your address book

As one of the bonus freebie programs that comes with Windows Me, you get a program called Address Book. (It's an address book.) You can look at yours by choosing Start→Programs→Accessories→Address Book, although the place you're likely to use it the most is when you're in the email program Outlook Express, which is described in Chapter 11.

In any case, the Start→Search→People command brings up the dialog box shown in Figure 2-10. Windows assumes that you want to search your Address Book for a certain name or phone number. Enter information in one or more fields, and then click Find Now. All matching entries appear at the bottom of the window, as shown in Figure 2-10.

Searching phone books on the Internet

No matter how social a person you are, it's theoretically possible somebody out there has managed to elude your Address Book. There may be times that you want to look up the phone number or email address of someone who's not only not in your Address Book, but not even in your local phone book. Fortunately, you live in the Internet age, where a number of Web sites serve as worldwide White Pages. The Search→People command can access these Web sites automatically.

Use the Look In drop-down menu (see Figure 2-11) to display a list of these people-finding Web sites. Choose a search service to try; as a little experimentation will quickly demonstrate, some of these sites work better than others.

You must be connected to the Internet to use this feature (or your browser must be configured to start your Internet connection automatically when it opens; see page 230). The dialog box that appears has two tabs:

- The **People** tab provides a place to enter a name, email address, or both. Use this tab if you know that information, and need a street address or a telephone number.

- The **Advanced** tab lets you narrow your search. As you can see in Figure 2-11, you can make some very fine distinctions as you describe the person you're trying to find.

When you're finished setting up your search, click Find Now. The Search program uses your existing Internet connection to send the query off to the chosen Web site. After a few minutes, you'll get a response, even if it's "No response."

Unfortunately, the technology gods don't smile on this feature. You'll probably discover that Internet phone book sites fail to find someone more often than they succeed. Sometimes you get outdated email addresses. Sometimes you get no results at all—the search Web sites do one quick pass of their databases and then return an error message. That message might say simply that the person couldn't be found, or it might say, "The search could not be completed within the time specified for this directory service." (In other words, the search engine took a quick look, didn't find an exact match, and doesn't want to take the time to keep looking.)

Tip: Instead of using the Find People dialog box, it's frequently more productive to work directly on the directory Web page. After choosing the search engine you want to use from the drop-down list, click Web Site. In a flash (or in a few minutes, depending on the speed of your Internet connection), you're on the Internet; the browser window displays the search engine you selected. Working directly on the Web, instead of using the Search feature as an intermediary, offers more powerful choices for searching.

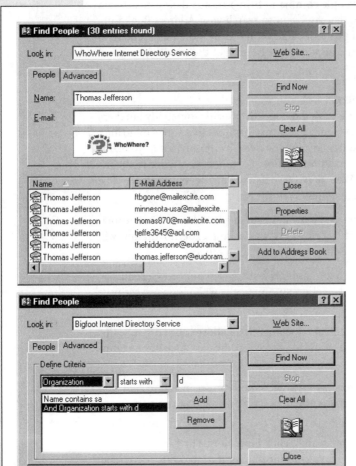

Figure 2-11:
Top: A straight-ahead name search by no means turns up every one of the 200 million Internet citizens, but it's occasionally successful in turning up a few matches for the name you specify.

Bottom: On the Advanced tab, you can use the categories and choices in the drop-down lists to provide as many details as possible to the Internet search engine. Here, for example, you're looking for a company whose name, you vaguely remember, begins with a D and contains sa. Delessa, Dilessa, or something like that; if you're lucky, the Web site will find it.

Searching the Internet

Because the Search feature is, behind the scenes, Internet Explorer, it's already set up to search for information on the World Wide Web (if you have an Internet account). See Chapter 10 for much more about the Internet and surfing the Web.

If the Search window is open, click the Internet link (which would appear in Figure 2-12 if you scrolled down one line). If not, choose Start→Search→On the Internet.

Either way, there's once again an area to type what you're looking for on the left side of the window, as shown in Figure 2-12. If you click Customize, you see a list of popular *search engines*—Web pages that search the Internet, such as Yahoo or AltaVista. And if you turn on the "Use the Search Assistant for smart searching" button at the top of the Customize dialog box, you can even set up a search of more than one search engine simultaneously. That's especially handy when you realize that each Internet search engine actually "knows about" only 30 percent of the world's Web pages.

To conduct a search, first select the kind of search you want. The list at the top left corner of this window offers several options (see Figure 2-12), as described next.

Figure 2-12:
Left: Windows Me is prepared to search the entire Web for a phrase you specify—in this case, "space shuttle." Right: The results window. Point to one without clicking to view the first paragraph of text that appears on that Web page, or click the name of a Web page to view the actual Web site on the right side of the window.

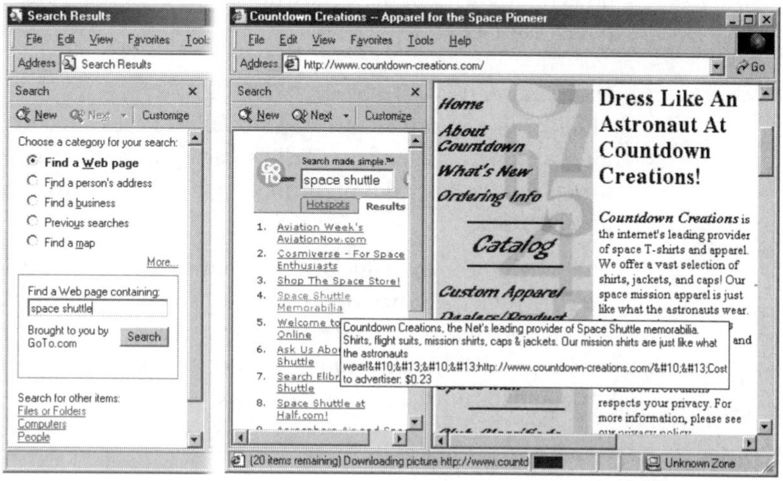

Find a Web page

This is the function you might expect when you choose Start→Search→Internet. It lets you search the World Wide Web for a particular phrase, such as *space shuttle* or *Harry Potter*. Then click Search Now (or press Enter).

If you're online (or have set up your PC to dial the Internet automatically, as described on page 230), Windows now sends your search request to the selected Web pages. After a moment, you get a list of results on the left side of the window (Figure 2-12, right). Here's what you can do with one of these results:

• **Read the first paragraph.** Using your arrow cursor, point to one of the Web pages listed in the search results; as shown in Figure 2-12, Windows shows you the first paragraph or so of text that appears on that Web page. This blurb is a useful preview that can save you the effort of opening (and waiting for) that Web page, only to find that it's not what you were looking for.

• **Go to the Web page.** Click one of the listings to view the actual page in the larger right portion of the window.

Find a person's address

This function makes Windows send your search request to an Internet "White Pages" Web site, exactly as described in the previous section. This time, however, you can search several of these sites simultaneously, which greatly increases the odds that you'll find the person you're looking for.

To do so, click the Customize button. The Customize dialog box appears, as shown in Figure 2-13. Scroll down to see the checkboxes for the "Find a person's address" category; turn on as many as you'd like. Click OK.

From the Search For drop-down menu, specify what you're looking for—"mailing address" or "email address"—and then type in the first name, last name, and (if you know it) city and state or province. When you click Search (or press Enter), Windows returns a list of matches. Click one to view that person's complete address and phone number.

Find a business

Think of this option as a worldwide Yellow Pages directory. Once again, click Customize to view a list of the "Yellow Pages" Web sites that Windows is prepared to search. For the best odds of turning up the company you want to find, turn on *all* of the checkboxes.

This time, type in the name of a company or the kind of business (depending on your selection from the Search By drop-down list), such as *auto glass* or *pediatricians*. Specify the city and state or province you want to search, and then press Enter. This function works remarkably well; it comes in especially handy when you're traveling in a strange city and find yourself in desperate need of a drugstore, hospital, or bowling alley.

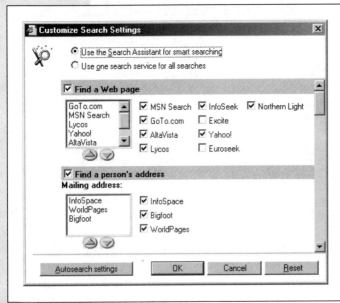

Figure 2-13:
When you use the Search command to find Internet-based information, you're actually searching several Web sites simultaneously. The Customize dialog box lets you specify which ones you want the command to search. If you scroll down far enough, you'll see similar checkboxes for the other kinds of Web searches, such as "Find a business" and "Find a map."

Previous searches

Click this button to view a tidy list of the Internet searches you've most recently performed. Click a recent search to repeat it; the Internet is constantly changing, and you're likely to turn up different results each time you search.

Find a map

It's one of the miracles of the Internet: You can type in almost any street address in the United States or Canada, and get a map, as detailed as you want it (see Figure 2-14). It's all free, and it's all built right into the Windows Me search function.

Tip: As great as the Search feature is, invoking it is a lot of work. You have to click, for example, Start→Search→Internet; by Windows standards, that's a colossal expenditure of energy.

Fortunately, there are faster ways to summon the Search feature. While holding down the Windows-logo key, you can press the letter F key. You can also click the Search button on the toolbar of any folder or disk window—or, if there's no toolbar, you can choose File→Search.

Figure 2-14:
Once Windows shows you the map of the address you specified, click the Zoom Level controls to magnify or reduce the scale the map. You can also view adjacent chunks of the map by clicking the Map Mover arrow buttons at right.

Start→Settings

The Start→Settings command offers four commands: Control Panel (see Chapter 9), Dial-Up Networking (Chapter 10); Printers (Chapter 12); and Taskbar and Start menu (later in this chapter). These last three items are actually Control Panel programs; that is, you can also see them represented as icons by choosing Start→Settings→Control Panel. But most people use them so frequently that Microsoft put them on the Settings submenu to save a step.

Start→Documents

The Documents submenu lists the My Documents folder (which is also represented by an icon on the desktop) and a cascading list of the last fifteen documents you've opened. Using the My Documents command can be useful when your desktop is covered up by other windows, thus blocking the My Documents folder icon. And using the list of recent documents can save you time when you want to reopen something you've been working on recently, but you're not in the mood to go burrowing through desktop folders to find its icon.

Note, however, that:

• Documents appear on the "recently used" list only if your applications are smart enough to update it. Most modern programs (including all Microsoft programs) perform this administrative task, but not all do.

• The Documents list doesn't know when you've deleted a document or moved it to another folder or disk; it continues to list the file even after it's gone. In that event, clicking the document's listing produces an error message.

Tip: There's another easy way to open a document you've recently worked on: Start by launching the program you used to create it. Many programs maintain a list of recent documents at the bottom of the File menu; choose one of these names to open the corresponding file.

Start→Programs

For most people, the Start→Programs command is the most important function of the Start menu. It's the master list of every program on your computer. You can jump directly to your word processor, calendar, or favorite game, for example, just by choosing its name from the Start→Programs menu.

When you install a software program, it usually installs either a *program item* or a *program group* on the Start→Programs menu, as shown in Figure 2-15.

The StartUp folder

The Start→Programs menu also lists the *StartUp folder,* a folder (program group) of programs that loads automatically every time you start Windows Me. This can be a very useful feature; if you check your email every morning, you may as well save yourself a few mouse clicks by putting your own email program into the Startup folder. If you spend all day long word processing, you may as well put Microsoft Word or Corel WordPerfect in there.

In fact, although few PC users suspect it, what you put into the StartUp folder doesn't have to be an application. It can just as well be a certain document you have to consult, or work on, every day. It can even be a folder or disk icon whose window you'd like to find open and waiting each time you turn on the PC. (The My Documents folder is a natural example.)

Of course, you may be interested in the StartUp folder for different reason: to *stop* some program from launching itself. This is a particularly common syndrome if somebody else set up your PC for you. Some program seems to launch itself, unbidden, every time you turn the machine on.

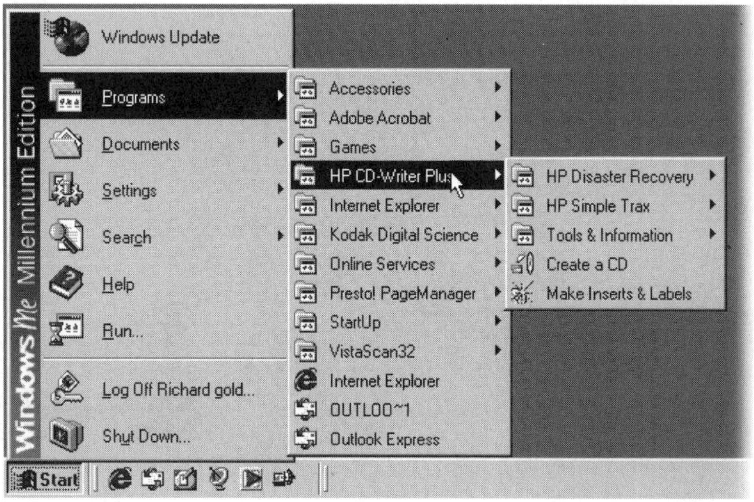

Figure 2-15:
The submenu of Start→ Programs may list the actual application (such as Microsoft Word), which you can click to launch the program. But it may also list a program group, a submenu that lists everything in a particular application folder. Some programs offer commands for launching the software, uninstalling the software, running specific utilities, opening the help files, and so on.

Fortunately, it's easy to either add or remove items from the StartUp folder:

1. **Click the Start button. Slide the cursor up to Programs. Right-click StartUp, and choose Open from the shortcut menu.**

   (If nothing happened when you right-clicked, then you may have turned off "Enable dragging and dropping," as described on page 46. Turn it back on and then restart the computer before proceeding.)

   The StartUp window opens, revealing whatever is inside it at the moment.

   To delete an icon from this folder, just right-click it and choose Delete from the shortcut menu. The deed is done; close all the windows you've opened and enjoy your newfound freedom from self-launching software.

   To add a new icon to the startup folder, on the other hand, read on.

2. **Navigate to the disk, folder, application, or document icon you want to add to the StartUp folder.**

   Doing so requires familiarity with one of two folder-navigation schemes: My Computer or Windows Explorer. Both are fully described in the next chapter.

3. **Using the right mouse button, drag the icon directly into the StartUp window, as shown in Figure 2-16.**

When you release the button, a shortcut menu appears.

4. **Choose Create Shortcut(s) Here from the shortcut menu.**

Close all the windows you've opened. For now on, each time you turn on or restart your computer, the program, file, disk, or folder you dragged will open by itself.

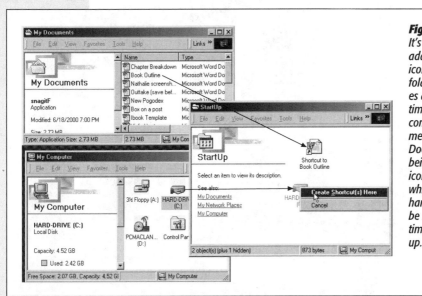

Figure 2-16:
It's easy—and useful—to add a program or file icon to your StartUp folder, so that it launches automatically every time you turn on the computer. Here, a document from the My Documents folder is being added. So is the icon for the hard drive, which ensures that the hard drive window will be ready and open each time the computer starts up.

WORKAROUND WORKSHOP

When Programs Dump Their Things into the StartUp Folder

Some programs dump icons into your Startup folder without asking you. Often, the unfamiliar icon represents a background utility that's required by an application. Two of the most notorious practitioners of this scheme are Microsoft Office and Quicken. Office installs a utility named Office Startup into the Startup folder, and Quicken adds the Quicken Startup and Billminder utilities.

Some people find this practice annoying, especially because these little utility stubs consume some of your computer's memory all day long, and they're not technically required by Word and Quicken. Fortunately, it's easy to get rid of them, as described in step 1 on page 41.

Customizing the Start Menu

As millions of Windows users illustrate, it's perfectly possible to live a long and happy life without ever tampering with the Start menu; for many people, the idea of making it look or work differently comes dangerously close to nerd territory. (It's true that listing your favorite files there gives you quicker access to them—but it's even easier to use the Quick Launch toolbar, as described on page 79.)

Still, knowing how to manipulate the Start menu listings may come in handy some-day. It also provides an interesting glimpse into the way Windows works.

Note: If you use the Multiple Users feature described in Chapter 14, any Start menu changes you make apply only to you. Each person can have her own, customized Start menu. When you sign onto the machine using your name and password, Windows Me loads *your* customized Start menu.

Changing the Basic Start Menu Settings

Microsoft offers a fascinating set of Start menu customization options. It's hard to tell whether these options were selected by a scientific usability study or by a dart board, but you're likely to find something that suits you.

To view and change the basic options, right-click a blank spot on the Taskbar; choose Properties from the shortcut menu. Alternatively, choose Start→Settings→Taskbar and Start Menu. Either way, the Taskbar and Start Menu Properties dialog box opens, as seen in Figure 2-17.

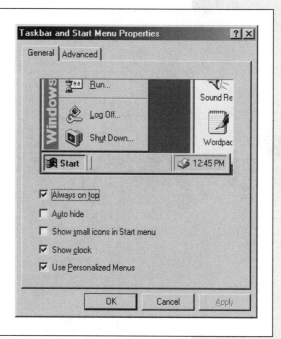

Figure 2-17:
Only two of the options on the General tab apply to the Start menu; the rest are for configuring the Taskbar. The two Start menu items, "Show small icons on Start menu" and "Use Personalized Menus," have a great deal of influence over the way the Start menu looks and behaves. Because of their impor-tance, you should try changing the settings for each before deciding on a final configuration for the Start menu.

Only two of the checkboxes in this dialog box pertain to the Start menu: "Show small icons in Start menu" and "Use Personalized Menus."

- **Show small icons in Start menu.** Turning on this checkbox gives you smaller icons next to the commands in the Start menu. As a result, the Start menu is more compact, requiring less mouse travel.

• **Use Personalized Menus.** When the Use Personalized Menus checkbox is on, Windows watches you and studies your behavior (that is, even more than usual). If it notices that you haven't been using certain Start menu commands, Windows hides them, making the menu listing shorter. Figure 2-18 shows the idea.

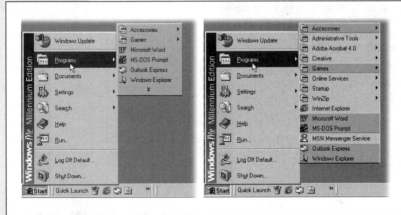

Figure 2-18:
Left: A truncated Programs menu, displaying only recently used commands. Click the double arrow to see the full menu, as shown at right. The previously displayed items announce their favored status by appearing in a darker shade of gray.

Some people find it disconcerting that Personalized Menus makes the Start menu *change* frequently, making it difficult to get used to the positions of familiar items. Other people find that this feature makes the Programs menu and its submenus easier to use, because it frees them from hunting through commands that they don't use much.

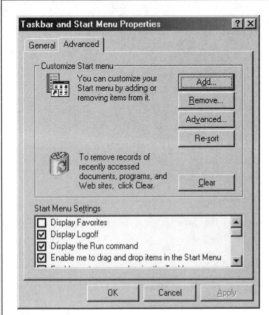

Figure 2-19:
The bottom of the Advanced tab contains a list of on/off options for the Start menu. The list is about five times the height of the tiny scrolling window Microsoft allotted in this dialog box; that may be something for the programmers to fix in, say, Windows Me 2.

The Advanced tab

Click the Advanced tab (Figure 2-17) to see the dialog box shown in Figure 2-19. At the bottom of the dialog box, you'll find a long scrolling list of checkboxes. Some affect the Taskbar, and are described in the next chapter; the rest affect the Start menu in interesting ways:

- **Display Favorites.** This option adds a Favorites command to the Start menu, which then lists your favorite Web sites, the same ones you've "bookmarked" when using Internet Explorer (see page 250). Thereafter, you can use the Start Menu to launch Internet Explorer and travel directly to the selected site.

Figure 2-20:
When Expand Control Panel is turned off (see page 46), you, like generations of Windows users before you, can't open a particular Control panel directly from the Start menu. Instead, you must choose Start→ Settings→Control Panel (top), which opens the Control Panel window, where it's up to you to open the individual control panel you want.

Expanding the Control Panel saves you a step; as shown at bottom, you now get a submenu that lists each program in the Control Panel folder. By clicking one, you can open it directly, without ever having to open the Control Panel window.

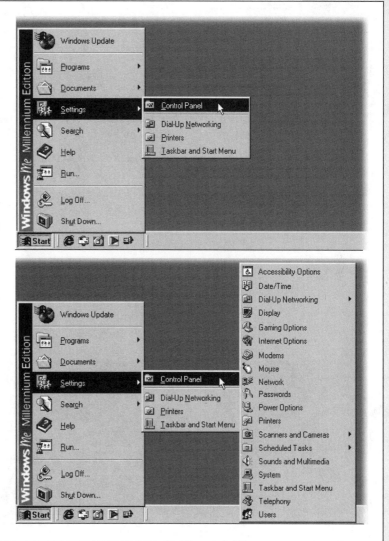

- **Display Logoff.** This option hides or shows the Logoff item on the Start menu. If you're not on a network (Chapter 16) or sharing your PC with other people (Chapter 14), you don't need the Logoff command; turn this off.

- **Display Run.** If you never use the Run command (see page 24), you might as well remove it from the Start menu, which makes the Start menu less crowded. To do so, turn off this checkbox.

- **Enable dragging and dropping.** This delicious option lets you rename and rearrange files on, add files to, or remove files from your Start menu by dragging them with the mouse. These techniques are described on the following pages.

Note: After turning "Enable dragging and dropping" on or off, you must restart your computer to make the change take effect.

- **Expand Options.** *Expanding* means that instead of simply listing the name of a folder (such as Control Panel), your Start menu sprouts a submenu listing the *contents* of that folder. As illustrated in Figure 2-20, this feature saves you the trouble of having to open a folder window (such as Control Panel or My Documents), double-click an icon inside it, and then close the window again.

  If you scroll down in the Taskbar and Start Menu Properties dialog box (Figure 2-19), you'll find individual checkboxes for expanding these Start menu items:

  - Control Panel

  - My Documents

  - My Pictures (a folder inside My Documents)

  - Network and Dial-Up Connections

  - Printers

  There's no downside to turning on the Expand checkboxes of the folders you access frequently; the time you save could be your own.

FREQUENTLY ASKED QUESTION

Opening the Control Panel Window When You Can't

OK, I'm with you—I turned on the Expand Control Panel checkbox, so now I can open any control panel directly from my Start menu. Trouble is, now I can't open the Control Panel window! Nothing happens when I click the Start→Settings→Control Panel command. How do I open the Control Panel window?

Ah, there's a troublemaker in every class.

Click the Start button to open the menu, slide up to Settings, and then *right-click* Control Panel. Choose Open from the shortcut menu. You're back in business.

- **Scroll Programs.** This option changes how the Start→Programs menu looks when there are too many programs listed there to fit on the screen. Ordinarily when this situation arises, a second Programs menu appears to the right of the first one, continuing the list. But if you turn on this checkbox, all your programs appear instead on one massive, scrolling Programs list. As you scroll down past the last visible name, the top of the Programs menu scrolls off the screen.

Adding Icons to the Start Menu

Usually, when you install a new program, its installer inserts the program's name and icon in your Start→Programs menu automatically. There may be times, however, when you want to add something to the Start menu yourself, such as a folder, a document, or even a disk—not to mention applications whose installers don't add their names automatically.

Note: You're not allowed to touch the body of the Start menu—the list of commands between Shut Down and Documents. You can move things, remove things, or add things only in the listings *above* the Programs command—and among the items in the Programs submenu. (The two legal areas are highlighted in Figure 2-21.) In other words, Windows won't let you drag, say, the Shut Down or Help commands into oblivion.

Microsoft wouldn't be Microsoft if it didn't provide at least 437 different ways to do this job. Here are three of the world's favorites.

Drag an icon directly onto the Start menu

Nothing could be easier:

1. **Locate the icon you want to add to your Start menu.**

   It can be an application (see the sidebar on page 48), a document you've created, a folder you frequently access, one of the programs in your Control Panels folder, or even your hard drive or floppy-drive icon. (Adding disks and folders to the Start menu is especially handy, because it lets you dive directly into their contents without having to drill down through the My Computer window.)

Tip: Adding an application name to your Programs menu requires that you find the program *file*, as described on page 48. To do so, either use the Search command described earlier in this chapter, or use the Windows Explorer window described in Chapter 4. You'll find your program files in the My Computer→C: drive→Program Files folder.

---

2. **Drag it directly onto the Start button.**

   If you release the mouse now, Windows adds the name of the icon you've just dragged to the top of the menu, as shown at right in Figure 2-21.

   But if you've turned on "Enable dragging and dropping," as described in the previous section, you gain some additional control over the placement of the icon.

For example, if you continue the drag upward to the top section of the menu (above the Programs command), you're free to drop it exactly where you want it among the items listed there (Figure 2-21, left).

Similarly, if you drag to the Start button and then up to the Programs command without releasing the mouse, you can place it exactly where you want it in the Start→Program submenu.

Tip: After making a mess of your Start→Programs menu by dragging icons onto it, you may want to restore some order—specifically, alphabetical. That's easy: Just right-click anywhere on the Programs menu and choose Sort By Name from the shortcut menu.

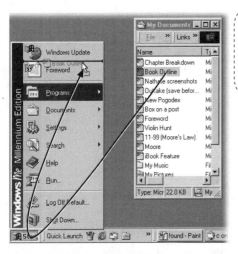 

Figure 2-21:
Left: You can add something to the top of your Start menu by dragging it, from whatever folder it's in, onto the Start button to open the Start menu, and then directly up into position. When you release the mouse, you'll find that it's been happily ensconced where you dropped it (right). Once the menu is open, you can drag commands up or down in the circled area of the menu at right.

Which One's the Program?

I want to add a program to my Start menu like you said. But where is its icon?

To discover the program file name of a favorite program, open your My Computer→C: drive→Program Files folder. Inside you'll find folders containing all of your applications—and inside each of *these* folders, you'll find icons for each application's components. Right-click the window, choose View→Details from the shortcut menu, and look for an icon whose Type column says "application."

OK, I did that. But in the program's folder, there are 15 million little files that all say they're applications. How do I know which is the actual application file?

First, you can usually recognize which application is the primary one both by its short-form name and by its icon. *WinWord* is probably a good hint that you've found Word for Windows, for example.

Second, the instructions from the software company may tell you which file to click.

Use the Add Listing wizard

If dragging icons around isn't your thing, you can use one of Microsoft's famous wizards for the same purpose, like this:

1. **Choose Start→Settings→Taskbar and Start Menu.**

   Alternatively, right-click a blank spot on the Taskbar and choose Properties from the shortcut menu. Either way, the Taskbar and Start Menu Properties dialog box appears.

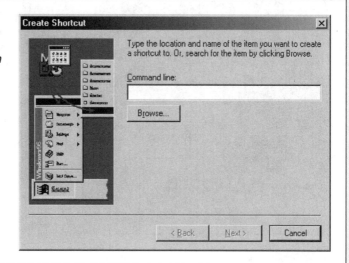

Figure 2-22:
The Create Shortcut wizard needs the name of the item you want to add. The wizard has the word "shortcut" in its name because, in fact, everything you add to your Start menu is just a shortcut, not the actual program, document, folder, or disk. (As described on page 101, a shortcut is an icon that serves as a pointer to a real file or folder.)

2. **Click the Advanced tab, then the Add button.**

   The Create Shortcut wizard opens, as shown in Figure 2-22.

3. **Enter the path (see page 26) and filename of the item you want to add.**

   If you don't know the path and filename, click the Browse button to open the Browse dialog box. Find the file, highlight it, and then click Open.

4. **Click Next to open the Select Program Folder window (see Figure 2-23).**

5. **Select a location for your new item (usually the Programs menu); click Next.**

6. **Change the name for the new shortcut, if you like, and then click Finish.**

   Now check out your Start menu: Sure enough, the new icon is listed there.

Tip: If there's a program you want to launch every time you turn on your computer, put it in the Start→Programs→StartUp folder.

Use the Start Menu folder

Everything in your Start menu is represented by an icon in the My Computer→C: drive→Windows→Start Menu folder. Instead of the fancy icon-adding wizards and drag-and-drop schemes described in this section, you may prefer to fine-tune your Start menu the low-tech way. Just open the Start Menu folder. You can add shortcut icons to, remove them from, or rename them in your Start menu just by manipulating the shortcuts in this folder.

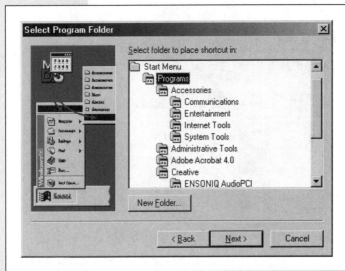

Figure 2-23:
You can select any submenu on your Start menu as the location of your new menu item—the Programs menu is usually the best choice. Notice that the arrangement of folders in this window is indented to indicate submenus and even sub-submenus. This pattern matches the way the menus appear when you click the Start button to open the Start menu.

Removing Icons from the Programs Menu

It's easy to delete most applications from your PC—at least those whose programmers have read the Emily Post Big Book of Programming Etiquette. Just choose Start→Settings→Control Panel, and then open the Add/Remove Programs control panel ; you get a list of every program on your machine, from which you can make a selection and then click Add/Remove to delete the software from your life. (More on Add/Remove Programs in Chapter 9.)

However, doing so rarely removes the program's name from the Start→Programs menu. Over time, the Programs submenu becomes extremely crowded, and therefore harder to navigate. Error messages become increasingly frequent as you choose the names of these dearly departed applications, perhaps forgetting that you've sent them to the great CompUSA in the sky.

Fortunately, you can remove such programs' names—or any other program, file, folder, or disk name—from your Start menu, using one of these two methods.

Note: When you delete an item from one of the menus on the Start menu, you're only deleting the *shortcut* that appears on the menu. You're not deleting the real file that that shortcut opens. In other words, deleting items from the Start menu doesn't actually uninstall any software.

Drag it off the menu

If you've turned on "Enable dragging and dropping," as described on page 46, you can use the world's easiest method for ditching a file, program, folder, or disk name from your Start menu. Click the Start menu to open it, and then simply *drag* the name in question off of the menu—onto the desktop, for example, or even directly onto the Recycle Bin icon.

Use the shortcut menu

Here's the second easiest way to clean up the Start menu: Click the Start menu to open it. Then right-click the file, folder, program, or disk name and choose Delete from the shortcut menu. It disappears instantly. (This method, too, requires the "Enable dragging and dropping" feature, as described on page 46.)

Tip: Speaking of the shortcut menu, you can also *rename* something you've added to your Start or Start→Programs menu. Click the Start menu to open it, right-click the name of the item you want to rename, and choose Rename from the shortcut menu. You'll be offered the Rename dialog box, where you can edit the name and then click OK.

Use the Delete Item wizard

If "Enable dragging and dropping" is turned off, you can also delete a Start-menu item using a Microsoft wizard.

1. Click Start→Settings→Taskbar and Start Menu.

    The Taskbar and Start Menu Properties dialog box appears.

2. Click the Advanced tab, then click Remove.

    Now find the item you want to remove by scrolling through the Programs menu, or by clicking the + sign next to a submenu to see its entries.

3. Select the item and click Remove; click OK.

Tip: If you delete a menu item by mistake, you can correct the error if you act quickly. Just after screaming "Oh no," press Ctrl-Z. The menu item immediately reappears on the menu. (You can also right-click any blank spot on your desktop and choose Undo Delete from the shortcut menu.)

Reorganizing the Programs Menu

To change the order of the Start→Programs listings, make sure "Enable dragging and dropping" is turned on. Then click the Start menu to open it, slide up to the word Programs, and simply drag the folder, document, disk, or program name up or down as you see fit. As you drag an item through the list of programs, a black line appears to show you the resulting location of your dragging action. Release the mouse when the black line is where you want the relocated icon to appear.

Tip: If you change your mind while you're dragging, press the Esc key to leave everything as it was.

Add folders to hold submenus

Many listings on the Start→Programs menu represent folders (those accompanied
by a right-facing triangle arrow). For example, clicking Start→Programs→Games
reveals a submenu that lists all the Windows Me games (see Figure 2-24).

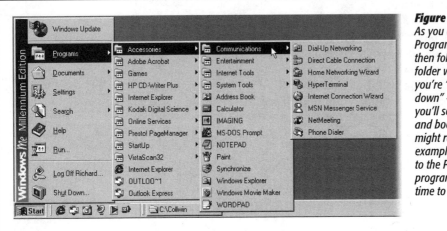

Figure 2-24:
*As you open the
Programs menu and
then folder after
folder within it,
you're "drilling
down" – a phrase
you'll see in manuals
and books. (You
might read, for
example, "Drill down
to the Phone Dialer
program when it's
time to call Mom.")*

Without all these folders consolidating the Start→Programs menu, you'd need one
of those very expensive 95-inch monitors to see the entire list of applications. Fortunately, you can create Programs-menu folders of your own, and stock them with
whatever icons you like. For instance, you may want to create a folder for CD-ROM-
based games, eliminating those long lists from the Programs menu. You may even
want to create multiple folders for those games, perhaps making a folder for each
family member's game selections.

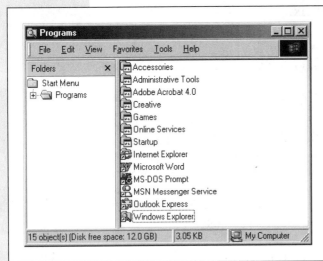

Figure 2-25:
*The contents of the Programs menu
appear in the right pane. Notice that some
of the items have folder icons. These are
the folders that, in the Start menu, turn
into submenus.*

To add a folder to the Programs menu, follow these steps:

1. **Choose Settings→Taskbar and Start Menu.**

   The Taskbar and Start Menu Properties dialog box opens.

2. **Click the Advanced Tab, then click Advanced.**

   The Start menu's Explorer window appears. (See page 88 for more on the Windows Explorer folder-navigation system.)

3. **Click the Programs folder.**

   Its contents are listed in the right pane, as shown in Figure 2-25.

4. **Choose File→New→Folder.**

   Or, if your right mouse button hasn't been getting enough exercise, right-click a blank spot in the right pane, and then choose New→Folder from the shortcut menu.

5. **When the new folder icon appears, type a folder name and then press Enter.**

6. **Close the Start Menu window. Click OK to close the dialog box.**

Your new folder appears at the bottom of the Start→Programs menu. Feel free to drag your new folder to the location you choose on the menu.

Now you can put your favorite file, folder, disk, or application icons *into* this new folder. To do so, drag an icon onto the Start→Programs menu, and then onto the new folder/submenu you created. Of course, the first time you do this, your newly created folder submenu just says "Empty"; drag the icon onto that "Empty" notation to install it into your submenu. Then drag as many other icons as you like into this new folder.

You can even create folders *within* folders in your Start→Programs menu. Just repeat the instructions above—but following step 3, click the + sign next to the first folder you added. Then continue with step 4.

Windows, Folders, and the Taskbar

Windows got its name from the rectangles on the screen—the *windows*—in which every computer activity takes place. You look at a Web page in a window, type short stories in a window, read email in a window, and look at the contents of a folder in a window—sometimes all at once.

This overlapping-windows scheme makes using a computer much easier than windowless operating systems like DOS. But it has a downside of its own, as any Windows veteran can tell you: As you create more files, stash them in more folders, and launch more programs, it's easy to wind up paralyzed before a screen awash with cluttered, overlapping rectangles.

Fortunately, Windows is crawling with icons, buttons, and other inventions to help you keep these windows under control.

Windows in Windows

There are two categories of windows in Windows: *desktop* windows (which open when you double-click a disk or folder icon) and *application* windows (which appear when you're working on a document or in a program, such as Word or Internet Explorer). Nonetheless, all of these windows have certain components in common. Figure 3-1 shows a representative example: the window that appears when you double-click the My Documents icon on your desktop.

- **Title bar.** This top strip displays the name of the window. It's also the "handle" that you drag when you want to *move* the window on the screen.

- **Minimize button.** Click this box to temporarily hide a window; it shrinks down into the form of a button on your *Taskbar* (see page 74). You can open it again by clicking that icon. *Keyboard shortcut:* Press Alt+Space bar, then N.

- **Maximize button.** Click this button to enlarge the window so that it fills the screen. At this point, the Maximize button turns into a Restore button (whose icon shows two overlapping rectangles), which you can click to return the window to its previous size. *Keyboard shortcut:* Press Alt+Space bar, then X.

Tip: You can also maximize a window by double-clicking its title bar. Double-clicking the title bar again takes it back to its original *(restored)* sized and shape.

- **Close button.** Click the X to close the window. *Keyboard shortcut:* Press Alt+F4, or press Alt+Space bar, then C.

- **Menu bar.** Click one of these words (such as File or Edit) to open a menu, which shows a list of commands available in this window.

- **Toolbar.** Some windows have these special strips that hold one-click shortcut buttons—equivalents for menu commands Microsoft thinks you'll use frequently. (More on toolbars at the end of this chapter.)

- **Scroll bar.** A scroll bar appears on the right side or bottom of the window if it isn't large enough to show all its contents, as described in the sidebar box below.

- **Address bar.** This bar lets you type in a Web address, or even the address of a folder on your PC. When you press Enter, that Web page or a list of the contents

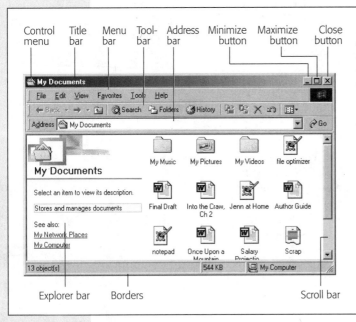

Figure 3-1:
All windows have the same basic ingredients, making it easy to become an expert in window manipulation. This figure shows a desktop window—a disk or folder window; but you'll encounter the same elements in application windows.

of the folder appears on the screen. (This bar shows up in desktop windows and Web browsers, not in application windows. See page 70 for details.)

- **Control menu.** The icon next to the title is actually a menu that offers commands for sizing, moving, and closing the window. You can double-click it to close a window; otherwise, it's not very useful, because its commands duplicate the other doodads described here.

- **Borders.** You can change the size of a window by dragging these borders. Position your pointer over any border until the pointer turns into a double-headed arrow. Then drag inward or outward to reshape the window. (To resize a full-screen window, click the Restore button first.)

Tip: If you drag the corner of a window, you can resize it in both dimensions at once. The diagonally striped ribs of the lower-right corner may suggest that that's the *only* corner you can drag, but it's not; all four corners work the same way.

- **Explorer bar.** This special left-side-of-the-window panel shows information about the window, or about whatever icon you click.

But using the View→Explorer Bar command, you can fill this half of the window with your choice of several other kinds of information: the Search pane described in Chapter 2, your list of Favorite icons and Web sites, the History list (folders you've opened recently), or Folders (the Windows Explorer-like folder tree described on page 70). You can even choose Tip of the Day (to see a helpful Windows trick at the bottom of the window), or if you're online, Discuss (to open a chat window).

Windows in Windows

UP TO SPEED

Scroll-Bar Crash Course

Scroll bars are the strips at the right side and bottom of a window. Some windows have both, some have only one, and a few have none. The scroll bar signals you that the window isn't big enough to show you all of its contents.

Click the arrows at each end of a scroll bar to move slowly through the window, or drag the square handle (called the *thumb*) to move faster. (The position of the thumb relative to the entire scroll bar reflects your relative position in the entire window or document.) You can quickly move to a specific part of the window by holding the mouse button down on the scroll bar where you want the thumb to be.

The scroll bar rapidly scrolls to the desired location and then stops.

If you have a mouse that's equipped with a wheel, such as the Microsoft IntelliMouse, you can scroll (in most programs) just by turning the wheel with your finger, even if your cursor is nowhere near the scroll bar. You can turbo-scroll by dragging the mouse upward or downward while keeping the wheel pressed down inside the window.

Finally, you can scroll without using the mouse. The Page Up or Page Down keys scroll the window by one window-full; the up- and down-arrow keys scroll one line at a time.

Sizing, Moving, and Closing Windows

There are three sizes for a window:

- **Maximized** means that the window fills the screen; its edges are glued to the boundaries of your monitor, and you can't see anything behind it. It gets that way when you click its Maximize button (see Figure 3-1). Maximizing your window is a great idea when you're surfing the Web or working on a document for hours at a stretch, because the largest possible window means the least possible scrolling.

Tip: When a window is maximized, you can *restore* it (as described below) by pressing Alt+Space bar, then R.

- When you click a window's **Minimize** button (Figure 3-1), the window disappears from sight. It hasn't actually closed, however; it's simply reincarnated as a button on the Taskbar strip at the bottom of the screen. You can bring the window back by clicking the Taskbar button that bears the window's name. Minimizing a window is a great tactic when you want to see what's in the window behind it.

- A **restored** window is neither maximized nor minimized; it's a loose cannon, floating around on your screen as an independent rectangle. Because its edges aren't attached to the walls of your monitor like a maximized window, you can make it any size you like by dragging its borders.

Tip: As noted earlier, double-clicking the title bar makes a window alternate between its maximized (full-screen) and restored conditions.

Moving a window

Moving a window is easy—just drag the title bar.

Most of the time, you move a window to get it out of the way when you're trying to see what's *behind* it. However, moving windows around is also handy if you're moving or copying data between programs, or moving or copying files between drives or folders, as shown in Figure 3-2.

Closing a window

You can close a window in any of several ways:

- Click the Close button (the X in the upper-right corner of the window).

- Click the Control-menu icon in the upper-left corner, and then choose Close from the drop-down menu. Or just double-click the Control-menu icon.

- Press Alt+F4.

- Right-click the window's Taskbar button (see page 74), and then choose Close from the shortcut menu.

- In application windows, choose File→Exit.

- In desktop windows, choose File→Close.

When you close a document window in one of your programs, no matter which action you use, you're given an opportunity to save your work before the window closes. Be careful, though—in many programs, including Internet Explorer, closing the window also quits the program entirely.

Tip: If you see *two* sets of window controls in the upper-right corner of your screen, then you're probably using a program like Microsoft Word. It's what Microsoft calls a *multiple document interface* program (see page 116). It gives you a window-within-a-window. The outer window represents the application itself; the inner one represents the particular *document* you're working on.

If you want to close one document before working on another, in other words, be careful to click the *inner* Close button. If you click the outer one, you'll exit the entire application.

Figure 3-2:
Creating two restored (free-floating) windows is a convenient preparation for copying information between them. Make both windows small and put them side-by-side, scroll if necessary, and then drag the highlighted material from one into the other. This works either with icons in desktop windows (top) or text in a word processor like Microsoft Word (bottom). If you press Ctrl as you drag text in this way, you make a copy of the original passage instead of moving it.

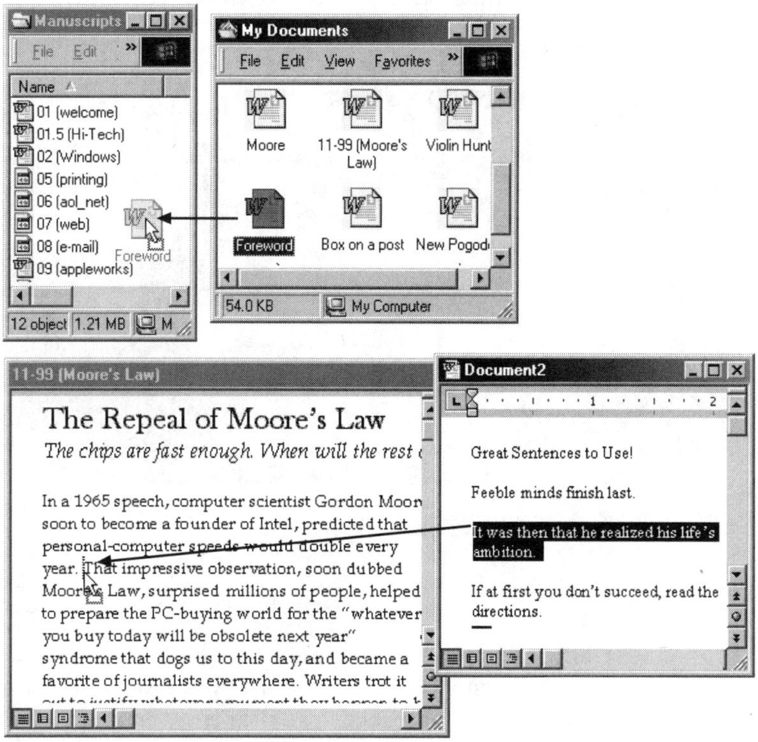

Working with Multiple Windows

Many people routinely keep four or five programs open at once—a calendar, word processor, Web browser, and email program, for example. Others (such as computer book authors) regularly work in just one program, but have several document windows open at once (representing several chapters, for example). Clearly, learning how to manage and navigate among a flurry of overlapping windows is an essential Windows survival skill.

Active and inactive windows

When you have multiple windows open on your screen, only one window is *active*, which means that:

- It's in the foreground, *in front* of all other windows.

- It's the window that "hears" your keystrokes and mouse clicks.

- The title bar is blue; the background (inactive) window title bars are gray. (You can change this color scheme, as described on page 191.

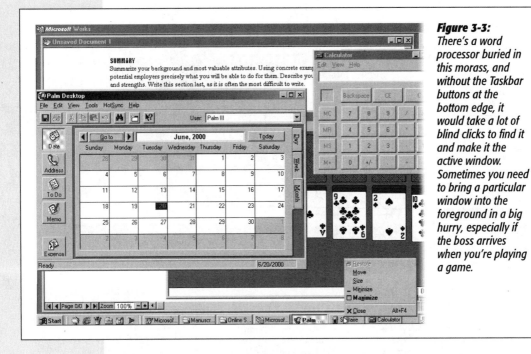

Figure 3-3:
There's a word processor buried in this morass, and without the Taskbar buttons at the bottom edge, it would take a lot of blind clicks to find it and make it the active window. Sometimes you need to bring a particular window into the foreground in a big hurry, especially if the boss arrives when you're playing a game.

Just because a window is in the background, by the way, doesn't mean that it can't continue with whatever assignment you gave it. For example, when your word processor is printing a document, your email program may be collecting mail, or your Web browser can be loading a Web page. If a background program needs to pass a message up to you (such as an error message), it automatically pops to the foreground, becoming the active program. When you respond to the message (usually by clicking OK), Windows Me sends the program *back* to the background and returns you to the window you were using before the message appeared.

Tip: To make a background window active, click anywhere on it. If you can't see it because too many other windows are in the way, click the name of the window you want on the corresponding Taskbar button (as described in the next section).

You can also rotate through all the open windows and programs by pressing Alt+Tab. A little panel appears in the center of your screen, filled with the icons of open folders and programs; each press of Alt+Tab highlights the next in sequence. (Alt+*Shift*+Tab moves you one *backwards* through the sequence.) When you release the keys, you jump to the highlighted window.

Manipulating Windows with the Taskbar

The *Taskbar* is a nifty assistant when you're working with multiple windows. It provides one-click window-manipulation commands. As you can see in Figure 3-3, it's not always easy to find a particular window.

• To bring a window to the foreground, making it the active window, click its button on the Taskbar.

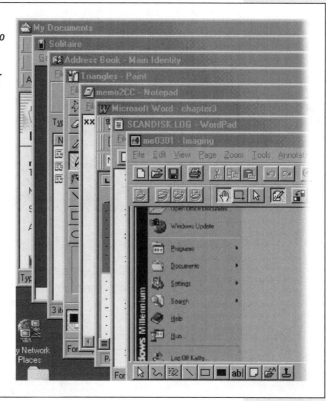

Figure 3-4:
Cascading windows are neatly arranged so you can see the title bar for each window. Click any title bar to bring that window to the foreground as the active window. After you've clicked a few title bars and worked in several windows, you'll have to choose the Cascade Windows command again to rearrange all your open windows.

- To minimize, maximize, restore, or close a window, even if you can't see it on the screen, right-click its button on the Taskbar and choose the appropriate command from the shortcut menu (Figure 3-3, bottom).

- To arrange all open windows in an overlapping pattern (except those you've minimized), as shown in Figure 3-4, right-click a blank spot on the Taskbar and choose Cascade Windows from the shortcut menu.

- To arrange all non-minimized windows in neat little boxes, each getting an equal rectangular chunk of your screen, right-click a blank spot on the Taskbar and choose Tile Vertically or Tile Horizontally from the shortcut menu.

- To minimize all the windows in one fell swoop, right-click a blank spot on the Taskbar and choose Minimize All Windows from the shortcut menu.

If you change your mind, the Taskbar shortcut menu always includes an Undo command for the last Taskbar command you invoked. Its wording changes to reflect your most recent action—"Undo Minimize All," for example."

Tip: To close all windows—actually, there *is* no command to close all windows.

There is, however, a trick to closing multiple *desktop* windows: While pressing the Shift key, click the X in the upper-right corner of the last window you opened.

Doing so doesn't close all open desktop windows, but it closes all the ones that sprang from a single "parent" disk or folder. For example, if you opened My Computer, then your C: drive, then your Program Files folder, the Shift trick closes all those windows. But if you had also opened the My Documents folder on the desktop, it stays open, because it wasn't part of the My Computer→C: drive→Program Files series.

UP TO SPEED

When There's No Blank Space on the Taskbar

When the Taskbar is crowded with buttons, it may not be easy to find a blank spot to click to bring up the Taskbar shortcut menu. Usually there's some space just to the left of the Taskbar Tray (see page 75); but you can make it easier to find some blank space by *enlarging* the Taskbar, as described on page 78.

Configuring Desktop Windows

Windows windows look just fine as they come from the factory; all the edges are straight, and the text is perfectly legible. Still, if you're going to stare at this computer screen for half of your waking hours, you may as well investigate some of the ways these windows can be enhanced for better looks and greater efficiency. As it turns out, there's virtually no end to the tweaks Microsoft lets you perform.

Icon and List Views

You can view the files and folders in a desktop window in any of several ways: as small icons, as jumbo icons, as a tidy list, and so on. Each window remembers its view settings independently.

To change the view setting for a particular open window, choose one of these commands from its View menu: Large Icons, Small Icons, List, Details, or Thumbnails. (Figure 3-5 illustrates each of these options.)

Figure 3-5:
*The five ways you can view the contents of a folder window. In **Large Icons** view (top), a large icon, with its label beneath, represents each file or folder. This is the default view. In **Small Icons** view (middle left, shown without its left-side panel), a small icon (label to the right) represents each file or folder; the icons are arranged in rows. (The alphabetical progression goes from left to right, rather than top to bottom.) The **List** view is similar, except the contents are arranged in columns (middle right). **Details** view (lower left) is the same as List view, except that you get additional columns that reveal the size, icon type, and the date and time the object was last modified. (This view, a familiar one to Macintosh fans, is growing in popularity.) Finally, in **Thumbnails** view (lower right), each icon is enclosed in a tiny picture frame, bearing a miniature picture of the graphic itself. This view is primarily useful, therefore, for windows that contain graphics files. (Thumbnails view isn't available in the My Computer window.)*

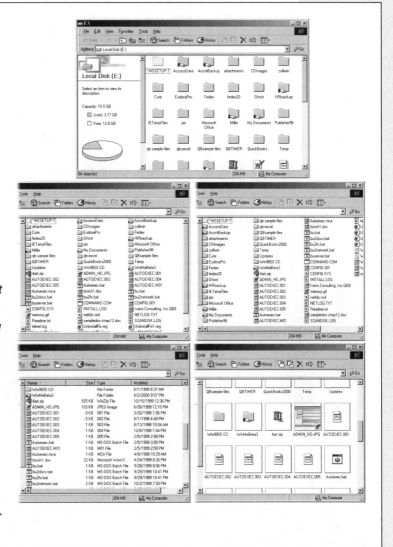

Changing the sorting order

Windows Me starts out arranging the icons alphabetically, with folders in one A-to-Z group followed by the list of loose files in a second group. To change the sorting method, choose View→Arrange Icons, and then select one of these options:

• **By Name** arranges the icons alphabetically by name. This setup is useful when you're scanning the list for a file or folder whose name you know.

• **By Type** arranges the files in the window alphabetically by file *type,* such as Word documents, applications, JPEG files, and so on. This option sorts files by their filename extensions (see page 133).

• **By Size** arranges the files in the window by size, starting with the smallest file. (Folders are unaffected; Windows never shows you the sizes of folders.)

• **By date** sorts the files in the window by creation date (not modified date), starting with the oldest file.

• **Auto Arrange,** which is available only in icon views, isn't actually a sorting method; it's a straightening-up method. It rearranges the icons so they're equally spaced and neatly positioned. (You can use this command on the desktop, too, which is one way to avoid Cluttered Windows Desktop Syndrome.)

Note: You can't reverse the sort *order* of your icons (from Z to A, for example) except in Details view, described next.

Manipulating the Details view

The Details view provides some unique characteristics that make it more powerful than the other views.

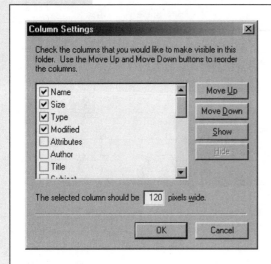

Figure 3-6:
The range of information you can display about objects in the window is robust enough to satisfy even the terminally curious. Some of the characteristics listed here are for specific types of files; you won't need a column for Audio Format, for example, in a folder that holds word processing documents.

First, there's the obvious advantage of being able to see the size and date of the objects in neat columns, as shown in Figure 3-5. Second, you can sort the contents by file size, type, or date simply by clicking the appropriate column heading.

Tip: If you click the same column heading again, the sorting order is reversed. For instance, clicking the Modified column once places your files into oldest-files-first sequence; a second click arranges the files with the *newest* file first. A small arrow appears on the column heading that points up or down to indicate the current sorting order.

Finally, you can add more columns to the window, providing even more information about each icon. Start by choosing View→Choose Columns, which opens the Column Settings dialog box shown in Figure 3-6. Click the checkboxes to turn the columns on or off. To rearrange the sequence of columns, click the name of a checked column and use the Move Up and Move Down buttons. The top-to-bottom list in the dialog box becomes the left-to-right display in the window.

Tip: You can change the width of a column by editing the number at the bottom of the Column Settings window (Figure 3-6). But that's much too unnatural. Instead, position your cursor on the vertical line between column headings in a Details-view window. When the pointer turns into a double-headed arrow, drag the vertical line horizontally.

Figure 3-7:
*Opening My
Documents reveals a
graphical display of
contents and a Web-
like layout, including
underlined links, an
address bar, and
Back/Forward buttons
on the toolbar. If you
wish, you can even
add a background
graphic like the ones
that sometimes lurk
as the backdrops of
Web pages, which
adds nothing to the
features of the
window but may
satisfy some artistic
yearning in you.*

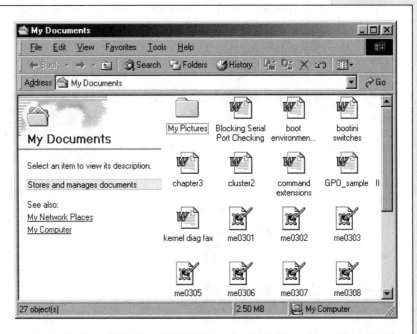

Tip: After you've twiddled and tweaked your system windows into a perfectly beautiful and efficient configuration, you don't have to go through all of that work for each folder. Windows Me can establish your changes as the new default for *all* your desktop windows.

Choose Tools→Folder Options→View tab. Click the Like Current Folder button. Windows Me asks if you're sure you know what you're doing. Click Yes.

Web View vs. Classic View

When you first run Windows Me, desktop windows feature many visual attributes similar to Web page, as shown in Figure 3-7.

The *classic* view, on the other hand, simply displays the contents of the folder, omitting the graphics (the Explorer bar) on the left side of the Web-type window. It packs a lot more info into your window (see Figure 3-8). Switching to the classic view is a system-wide alteration, affecting all desktop windows. To accomplish this change, take these steps:

1. **Double-click the My Computer icon (or any folder icon).**

   It opens into a window.

2. **Choose Tools→Folder Options from the menu bar.**

   The Folder Options dialog box appears.

3. **Turn on "Use Windows classic folders," and then click OK.**

Now your windows look more like Figure 3-8, which shows the same folder that appears in Figure 3-7.

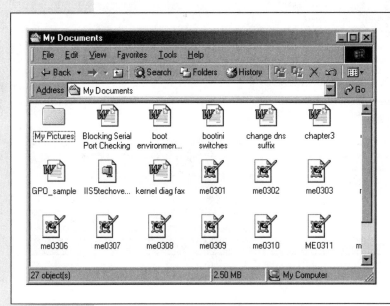

Figure 3-8:
Microsoft dubs this the "classic" view, meaning the way folders looked before the Web-type display was built into desktop windows. That should mean that folder windows look like Windows 95 or Windows NT 4 windows. However, a "classic" window is actually a melding of the classic Windows design and the newer Web style; it can still incorporate an address bar and Back/Forward buttons.

The Four Window Toolbars

On the day it's born, every Windows Me desktop window has two *toolbars* across the top (see Figure 3-9). This total doesn't include the strip that says File, Edit, View, and so on. (That's not a toolbar; it's the *menu bar*.)

By choosing View→Toolbars, or right-clicking a blank spot on a toolbar and choosing toolbar names from the shortcut menu, you can add or hide whichever toolbars you like, on a window-by-window basis. There are a total of four toolbars from which to choose: the Standard Buttons, Address Bar, Links, and Radio toolbars. (Only the first two appear when you first open a window in Windows Me.)

The Standard Buttons toolbar

This toolbar helps you navigate your desktop. It contains buttons like these:

- **Back, Forward.** These buttons resemble those in a Web browser that let you return to Web pages you've just seen. This time, however, they show you the contents of a disk or folder you've just seen. If you're using one-window-at-a-time mode (see "Uni-window vs. Multi-Window" in the next section), these buttons are your sole means of getting around as you burrow through your folders.

- **Search.** Opens the Search panel described on page 28. (Keyboard shortcut: F3, or press the Windows logo-key+F.)

POWER USERS' CLINIC

Customizing and Decorating Web-Style Windows

As you may have noticed, the desktop windows in Windows Me look a bit like a Web page, complete with a colorful graphic and links at the left side (see Figure 3-7). Using a special wizard, you can change the look of this left-side window portion. You can change the picture that appears here, the color of the background or the icon labels, the message that appears that describes the folder contents, and so on. (No, this feature is nothing to write home about, but some lucky Microsoft intern worked very hard on it.)

To get started, choose View→Customize This Folder from any desktop window (except the My Computer window). When the wizard appears, click Next. The wizard offers to help you do any of the following tasks:

- Choose a different *HTML template* for the window. This option, for people who know the HTML

Web-programming language, lets you specify the font, color, size, and other characteristics of the design of the left-side pane. If you click "I want to edit this template," the wizard opens the actual HTML code in the Notepad (see page 150), where you can go to town changing its look.

- Choose a new background color for the window, as well as a contrasting color for the text inside.

- Add a comment to explain the folder's purpose and what's inside.

After you use the wizard to customize your Web-based windows, the next time you launch the wizard, you'll be offered a new option: Remove Customizations. The wizard lists the customizations you've made, so that you can remove one or all of them.

- **Folders.** Hides or shows the master map of disks and folders at the left side of the window, in effect re-creating the two-panel Windows Explorer navigational display described in the next chapter.

- **History.** Opens a new panel at the left side of the window that shows every Web site and network computer you've visited recently.

Tip: If you can't exactly see the logic of having a list of Web sites in the window that contains, say, your word processing documents, it's easy enough to remove this button, as described in the next section.

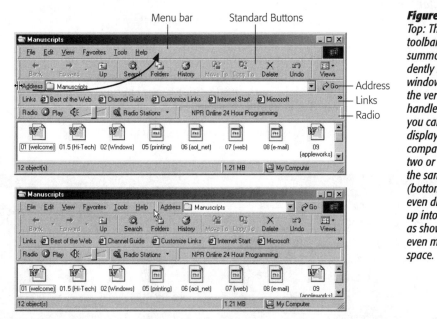

Menu bar   Standard Buttons

Figure 3-9:
Top: The four basic toolbars that you can summon independently for any desktop window. By dragging the vertical left-side handle of a toolbar, you can make the displays more compact by placing two or more bars on the same row (bottom). You can even drag one directly up into the menu bar, as shown here, saving even more vertical space.

GEM IN THE ROUGH

Eliminating Double-Clicks

If you like the Web-like window display shown in Figure 3-7, you can take the Web paradigm a step further so that *one* click, not two, opens an icon.

To accomplish this setup, choose Tools→Folder Options. Select "Single-click to open an item" on the General tab to enable single clicks to open folders and files. (A single click, of course, is faster and easier than a double click.) Then turn the icon names into links by selecting "Underline all

icon titles" or "Underline an icon title when I point to it."

If a single click opens an icon, you're entitled to wonder: Then how does one *select* an icon (which you'd normally do with a single click)? Answer: Just point to it, letting the mouse hover over the listing without clicking. To make multiple selections, press the Ctrl key as you point to additional icons.

- **Move To, Copy To.** These buttons are available only when you've highlighted an icon or icons in a folder or disk window. Clicking the Move To or Copy To button summons a "Browse for Folder" window that lets you choose a different folder or disk on your computer. If you then click OK, you move or copy the highlighted icons to the specified location.

- **Delete.** Gives the highlighted icons an instantaneous trip into the Recycle Bin. (The icons may not disappear until you close and re-open the window you were looking at.)

- **Undo.** Takes back the last thing you did, such as clicking the Move To, Copy To, or Delete button.

- **Views.** Opens a short menu listing the five basic ways a window can display its icon contents—as large icons, small icons, and so on. You can also use the View menu on the menu bar for the same purpose. For details on these window views, see page 63.

These are just the buttons that Microsoft proposes; you're free to add any of several other buttons to the toolbar, or hide the ones you never use. You can also change the size of these buttons—a useful feature, considering that the factory settings give you gigantic icons with both pictures and text labels.

To begin the customizing process, right-click a blank spot on the toolbar. Choose Customize from the shortcut menu to open the Customize Toolbar dialog box (Figure 3-10).

- To remove a button from the toolbar, click its name in the right pane and click Remove.

Figure 3-10:
The Customize Toolbar dialog box opens in front of the window you were viewing, so you can see the relationship between the window and the dialog box settings. For instance, notice that the right pane of the dialog box lists the current toolbar buttons. (The top-to-bottom listing matches the left-to-right arrangement of the toolbar on the window.) A Separator is the thin vertical line on the toolbar.

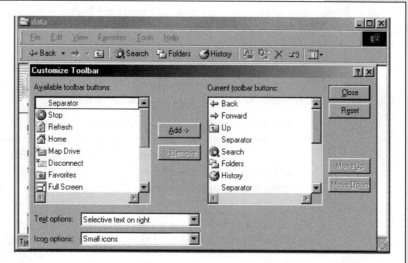

- To change the position of a button, select it in the right pane and click Move Up (to move the button to the left on the toolbar) or Move Down (to move the button to the right on the toolbar).

- To add a button to the toolbar, select it in the left pane and click Add.

Tip: Some of the useful buttons available to your toolbar include Properties (which saves you a right-click whenever you want to examine an icon) and Full Screen (which expands the window to fill the entire monitor, in the process replacing all of the toolbars with a single, tiny-iconned control strip at the very top of the screen). To recover from Full Screen view, click the (shrunken) Full Screen icon a second time.

- To add a separator (a vertical divider line) between buttons, click Separator in the left pane and then click Add. Use the Move Up and Move Down buttons at the right of the dialog box to position it.

- To place each button's text label to the right of its button instead of underneath, choose Text Options→Selected text on right. (As is implied by the name, Windows doesn't put a label next to *every* icon—just the ones it likes.)

- If you'd like only icons for buttons (no labels), choose Text Options→No Text Labels. (There's no way to display *only* labels without the pictures.)

- To enlarge the icons on the buttons, choose Icon Options→Large Icons.

- To put everything back the way it was when you first started using Windows Me, click Reset.

Click Close when you're finished customizing your Standard Buttons toolbar.

The Address bar toolbar

The Address bar may confuse you at first: Isn't this the white strip at the top of your Web browser, where you type the URL (Web address) of a Web site you want to visit?

Yes indeed; yet again, Microsoft has buried an Internet function into everyday, non-Internet features. But the Address bar actually accepts more than just Web addresses. Here are some of the things you can type there:

- **A Web address.** You can leave off the *http://* portion. Just type the body of a Web address, such as *www.sony.com,* into this strip. When you click Go or press Enter, the icons in your desktop window vanish, having been replaced by the actual Web page you specified. (See page 230 if you'd like your PC to dial the Internet automatically on occasions like this.)

Tip: By pressing Ctrl+Enter, you can surround whatever you've just typed into the Address bar with *http://www.* and *.com.* See Chapter 11 for even more typing shortcuts along these lines.

- **A search phrase.** If you type some text into this strip that isn't obviously a Web address, Windows assumes that you're telling it, "Go onto the Internet and search for this phrase." From here, it works exactly as though you've used the Internet search feature described on page 36.

- **A folder name.** You can also type one of several important folder names into this strip, such as *My Computer, My Documents, My Briefcase, My Music, My Network Places, My Pictures,* and so on. When you click Go or press Enter, you open that folder window.

- **A program or path name.** In these regards, the Address bar works just like the Run command described on page 24.

In each case, as soon as you begin to type, a pop-up list of recently visited Web sites, files, or folders appears below the Address bar. Windows Me is trying to save you some typing. If you see what you're looking for, click it with the mouse, or press the down arrow key to highlight the one you want and then press Enter.

The Links toolbar

This toolbar offers buttons representing your favorite Web sites—the ones you've added to your Favorites→Links folder in the Internet Explorer Web browser (see page 250).

Tip: You can drag these links around on the toolbar to put them into a different order.

When you're viewing a Web page, you can also drag a link directly into the Address bar to jump to that particular Web page. But when you're viewing a folder window, dragging one of these links to the Address bar creates an Internet shortcut file, a special document that, when double-clicked, connects to the Internet and opens the specified Web page.

The Radio toolbar

If you've been looking for a rationale for Microsoft's yearnings to incorporate Internet features into everyday windows, this one may be it. If you have a full-time connection to the Internet (such as a corporate network, cable modem, or DSL connection), or if you've signed onto the Internet with your modem, you can listen to the radio while you work, courtesy of your computer speakers. This toolbar offers a pop-up menu of radio stations you enjoy, along with a volume control and a play/stop button. Configuring these controls in such a way that you don't drive other people in your house or office crazy is left up to you. (The radio playing stops as soon as you close the window that contains the Radio toolbar, but it'll keep playing if you just minimize the window.)

For instructions on adding radio stations to your list of favorites, see Chapter 8.

Uni-window vs. Multi-Window

When you double-click a folder, Windows can react in one of two ways:

- **It can open a new window.** Now you've got two windows on the screen, one over-lapping the other. Moving or copying an icon from one into the other is a piece of cake, as shown in Figure 3-2. Trouble is, if your double-clicking craze contin-ues much longer, your screen will eventually be overrun with windows, which you must then painstakingly close again.

- **It can replace the original window with a new one.** This only-one-window-at-all-times behavior keeps your desktop from becoming crowded with windows. If you need to return to the previous window, the Back button takes you there. Of course, you'll have a harder time moving or copying icons from one folder to another using this method.

Which system you adopt is a matter of preference and experience. Whatever you decide, here's how you tell Windows which behavior you'd like:

1. **Choose Tools→Folder Options in any desktop window.**

   It doesn't matter what window you start in; the change you're about to make affects every window. The Folder Options dialog box appears.

2. **On the General tab, click "Open each folder in the same window" or "Open each folder in its own window," as suits your fancy, and then click OK.**

Tip: You can override whatever choice you just made on a case-by-case basis by pressing *Shift* as you open a folder. Doing so reverses the status of the setting described in step 2 above.

The "Folder Options" Options

If you choose Tools→Folder Options from any folder window, and then click the View tab (see Figure 3-11), you see an array of options that affect all of the folder windows on your PC. When assessing the impact of these controls, *earth-shattering* isn't the adjective that springs to mind; still, you may find one or two of them useful:

- **Automatically search for network folders and printers.** When this checkbox is turned on, Windows explores your network (if you have one) every few seconds in hopes of detecting PCs that have been recently turned on or off. That way, your Network Places window will be up to date when you open it.

- **Display all Control Panel options and all folder contents.** When you open the My Computer, C: drive, or Start→Settings→Control Panel windows, you may notice that Windows Me hides some or all of the icons inside them. Windows Me thinks it's doing you a favor by hiding important controls whose deletion or set-tings changes could get your PC in trouble. This checkbox is responsible for that safety feature.

- **Display the full path in the address bar.** When this option is on, Windows shows the exact location of the current window in the Address bar (if it's showing)—for example, *C:\My Documents\My Pictures*.

- **Display the full path in the title bar.** Same idea, but this time the path of the open folder or file shows up in the *title bar* of the window. Seeing the path can be useful when you're not sure which disk a folder is on, for example.

- **Hide protected operating system files.** Windows Me hides certain files and information that, if deleted or changed by mistake, could damage the operating system and cause you hours of troubleshooting grief. Yes, Big Brother is watching you, but he means well.

You'll have the smoothest possible computing career if you leave these options untouched.

- **Hide file extensions for known file types.** Windows Me normally hides the three-letter *filename extension* on standard kinds of files and documents (Word files, Photoshop files, and so on), in an effort to make Windows seem less technical and intimidating. If you prefer, however, you can make these extensions reappear by turning this option off.; see page 133 for more on this topic.

Figure 3-11:
Use the list in this dialog box to choose what you want to see and how you want to see it. Don't make important system files visible unless you're confident that you'd never accidentally delete them during a cleaning frenzy.

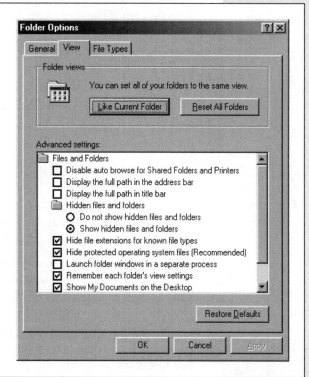

- **Launch folder windows in a separate process.** This geekily worded setting makes each folder open into a different chunk of memory (RAM). In theory, this setup is more stable, but slightly slows down your machine.

- **Remember each folder's view settings.** Ordinarily, Windows memorizes the changes you make to your folder view settings (such as your choice of List, Details, and Icon views). It also lets you create different view settings for each folder window.

  But if you turn *off* this checkbox, all folders use the same view settings. Furthermore, you'll see the changes only while the window remains open. The next time you open the folder, it will have forgotten the changes you made.

- **Show My Documents on the Desktop.** The My Documents folder is a handy gathering place for all of the documents you create. It's a shortcut of the *actual* My Documents folder, which is on your C: drive.

  You're not allowed to throw away the My Documents desktop icon, but you can make it disappear by turning off this checkbox.

- **Show pop-up description for folder and desktop items.** If you point to (but don't click) an icon, Taskbar button, and so on, a pop-up tooltip appears: a floating yellow label that helps identify what you're pointing to. If you find tooltips distracting, turn off this checkbox.

Note: The changes you make in the Folder Options settings are global; they affect *all* desktop windows.

The Taskbar

The permanent gray stripe across the bottom of your screen is the famous Taskbar, one of the most prominent and important elements of the Windows interface (see Figure 3-12).

The Taskbar has several important functions:

- **It shows you what's happening.** The right end of the Taskbar—the *Tray*—contains little status icons that show you the time, whether or not you're online, whether or not your laptop's plugged in, and so on.

- **It lists every open window and program.** Each time you launch an application or open a desktop window, a new button appears on this Taskbar. A single click makes that window pop to the front—a terrific tool in your fight against window clutter.

- **It gives you quick access to buried functions.** The left end of the Taskbar—the Quick Launch toolbar—lists the icons of frequently used programs, folders, disks, and files.

This section covers each of these features in turn.

The Tray

The Tray (see Figure 3-12) displays several icons, many of which represent quick-access buttons for corresponding control panel programs (see Chapter 9 for more on control panels). For example, yours may display:

- The current **time,** which, when double-clicked, opens to display the Date/Time control panel programs.

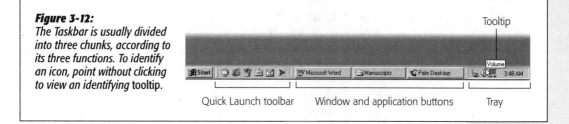

Figure 3-12:
The Taskbar is usually divided into three chunks, according to its three functions. To identify an icon, point without clicking to view an identifying tooltip.

Tooltip

Quick Launch toolbar   Window and application buttons   Tray

Tip: If you point to the time and wait a moment without clicking, a pop-up balloon appears that tells you the day of the week and today's date.

- A **speaker** icon, which reveals a slider that you can use to adjust the volume of your speakers. Double-click the icon to open a dialog box that controls all sound properties, including speaker balance.

- A **display** icon, which you can use to change the resolution of your screen.

- A **battery meter** icon, which shows how much battery power your laptop has left.

- A **modem** icon, which appears while you're connected to the Internet.

- A **printer** icon, which appears while you're printing something.

- A **fax** icon, which appears while you're sending or receiving a fax.

Window Buttons

When you open a program or a folder, the Taskbar sprouts a button bearing that window's name and icon. Buttons make it easy to switch between open programs and windows: Just click one to bring its associated window into the foreground, even if it had been minimized.

Figure 3-13:
If the name is too long for the button, a tooltip can show you the full name of the document.

Some programs, such as Microsoft Word, also display the name of the document. However, the button is almost always too small to rarely show the full document name. Figure 3-13 shows the solution.

You can also manipulate windows directly from the Taskbar button. Right-click the button to see a shortcut menu containing Minimize, Maximize, Close, and other useful window-control functions. It's a real time-saver to be able to close a window without having to first bring it into the foreground.

The Quick Launch Toolbar

The left end of the Taskbar shows little icons that represent your favorite files, programs, and windows (see Figure 3-12). One click does the trick. For details on this toolbar and the others in Windows Me, see page 79.

Customizing the Taskbar

You're not stuck with the Taskbar as it came from Microsoft. You can resize it, move it, or hide it completely.

Moving the Taskbar

You can move the Taskbar to the top of your monitor, or, if you're a true rebel, to either side. To do so, just drag it there using any blank spot in the central section as a handle. Release the mouse when you see a red line appear near the edge.

When the Taskbar is on the left or right edge of the screen, Windows Me widens it automatically. That's because the Taskbar buttons are horizontal; if you're expected to read their names, you need the added width.

Tip: No matter which edge of the screen holds your Taskbar, applications written for Windows adjust their own windows to make sure the Taskbar is visible. In other words, your Word document will shift sideways so that it doesn't overlap the Taskbar you've dragged to the side of the screen.

Resizing the Taskbar

When the Taskbar accumulates a lot of buttons and icons, you may want to enlarge it so you can see what's what.

GEM IN THE ROUGH

The Taskbar Shortcut Menu

The Taskbar has its own, very useful shortcut menu, which you can summon by right-clicking any blank spot on the Taskbar. It offers several commands for organizing swarms of open windows (see "Manipulating Windows with the Taskbar" on page 61), as well as a Toolbars command that lets you show and hide the four Windows Me Taskbar tool-

bars. (See page 79 for more on these toolbars.)

Furthermore, in some applications, you'll see additional commands on the Taskbar button shortcut menu. For example, the Taskbar button shortcut menu for Eudora (an email program) offers a command to check for new mail.

Of course, the larger the Taskbar, the less room is available for your application windows, which shrink to get out of the way. On the other hand, if you work with a larger Taskbar and then *remove* icons or toolbars, you can make the Taskbar smaller. Here's how to adjust the size of the Taskbar:

1. **Position your pointer on the inside edge of the Taskbar.**

   That is, use the edge that's closest to the desktop.

2. **When the pointer turns into a double-headed arrow, drag the edge of the Taskbar in the appropriate direction.**

   Drag it toward the desktop to enlarge the Taskbar, or toward the edge of your monitor to make it smaller.

Note: If you're resizing a Taskbar that's on the top or bottom of the screen, the Taskbar automatically changes its size in increments of its original size. You can't fine-tune the height; you can only double or triple it, for example.

If it's on the left or right edge of your screen, however, you can resize the Taskbar freely.

Setting Taskbar Properties

You can further adjust the Taskbar's behavior in some interesting ways; for example, you can make it invisible until you request it. To do so, choose Start→Settings→ Taskbar and Start Menu. (Or right-click a blank spot on the Taskbar, and then choose Properties from the shortcut menu.)

The Taskbar and Start Menu Properties dialog box appears, offering these options:

- **Always on top.** This option makes sure that no other window can cover up the Taskbar. Your programs automatically shrink their own windows as necessary to accommodate the screen bulk of the Taskbar. This is the standard Windows behavior. (If you deselect this option, full-screen application windows don't make room for the Taskbar; they overlap it.)

  You may find it useful to turn this option off when you need extra screen space, such as when you're running games and graphics programs. Some people also like the additional lines they gain in a word processing window, or the additional Web-page space they can see in a Web browser.

Tip: To open the Taskbar when it's not visible, just press Ctrl+Esc, or press the Windows-logo key on your keyboard.

- **Auto hide.** This feature makes the Taskbar disappear whenever you're not using it. This is a clever way to devote the entire screen to application windows, and yet have the Taskbar at your cursor-tip when you need it.

When Auto hide is enabled, the Taskbar disappears when you click anywhere else, or when your cursor has moved a short distance from the Taskbar. You can see a thin black line along the edge of your screen, which represents the edge of the Taskbar. As soon as your pointer moves close to that black line, the Taskbar reappears.

- **Show clock.** This option makes a tiny digital clock readout appear (or disappear) in the Taskbar Tray.

Caution: Computer clocks are notoriously bad timekeepers. They gain or lose time capriciously, so don't rely on the display for meeting trains or planes or any other time-sensitive activity.

Hiding the Taskbar manually

You may occasionally want to dedicate all your desktop space to an application window. Perhaps you're designing a complicated set of graphics, or you need to see more rows in a spreadsheet.

In these situations, you don't have to change the configuration options to hide the Taskbar and give that space to the window. There's a quicker way to hide the Taskbar when the need arises:

1. **Position your mouse pointer on the inside edge of the Taskbar.**

   When you reach the right spot, the pointer turns into a double-headed arrow.

TROUBLESHOOTING MOMENT

Retrieving a Lost Hidden Taskbar

Sometimes, after manually hiding the Taskbar (or going too far when you're trying to make it smaller), you can't get it back. The thin black line disappears, or your mouse pointer won't turn into a double-headed arrow when you position it on the thin line. Here's how to fix the problem:

1. Press Ctrl+Esc. This keystroke selects the Taskbar, even though you can't see it (although you can now see the Start menu).

2. Now press Esc to make the Start menu disappear. (The Taskbar is *still* selected, even though you still can't see it.)

3. Press Alt+Space bar to bring up a shortcut menu.

4. Choose Size from the shortcut menu, which changes your mouse pointer into a four-sided shape. Don't click anything.

5. Use the arrow keys on your keyboard to resize the Taskbar. If the Taskbar is on the bottom of your screen, use the Up arrow; if it's on the left edge of the screen, use the Right arrow; and so on.

6. As you use the arrow keys, your cursor turns into a double-headed arrow. It moves away from the edge of the screen each time you press an arrow key.

7. Watch for a red line that moves along with your pointer; it represents the new position for the inside edge of your Taskbar. When the red line is a good distance away from the edge of your monitor, press Enter to display the Taskbar.

8. Resize the Taskbar very carefully so you don't have to do all this again.

---

2. **Drag the Taskbar edge toward the edge of the monitor.**

   When the Taskbar disappears, you can see a thin black line representing the hidden edge. To bring the Taskbar back, move your mouse toward the line until the usual cursor turns into a double-headed arrow, then drag the Taskbar back onto the screen.

Taskbar Toolbars

Windows Me offers four canned Taskbar *toolbars*: separate, recessed-looking areas on the Taskbar containing special-function features. You can add icons to any toolbar, and you can also create your own toolbars (see page 82).

To make these toolbars appear or disappear, right-click a blank spot on the Taskbar and choose from the list of toolbars that appears. The ones with checkmarks are the ones you're seeing now; choose a toolbar name *with* a checkmark to make that toolbar disappear.

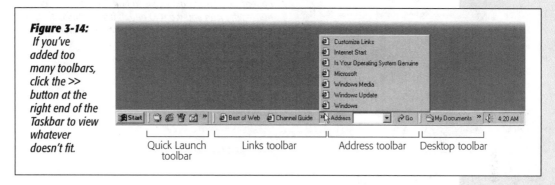

Figure 3-14:
If you've added too many toolbars, click the >> button at the right end of the Taskbar to view whatever doesn't fit.

Quick Launch toolbar   Links toolbar   Address toolbar   Desktop toolbar

Quick Launch Toolbar

The Quick Launch toolbar is fantastically useful. In fact, for sheer convenience, it puts the Start menu to shame. Maybe that's why it's the only toolbar that appears on your Taskbar automatically. It contains icons for functions that Microsoft assumes you'll use most often:

- **Show Desktop.** A one-click way to minimize (hide) *all* the windows on your screen to make your desktop visible. Don't forget about this button the next time you need to burrow through some folders, put something in the Recycle Bin, or perform some other activity in your desktop folders. (*Keyboard shortcut:* Windows key+D.)

- **Launch Internet Explorer.** Provides one-click access to the Web browser included with Windows Me.

- **Launch Outlook Express.** Used for one-click access to the email program included with Windows Me (see Chapter 10).

But you should consider those buttons as only hints of this toolbar's power. What makes it great is how easy it is to add your *own* icons, those you use frequently. There's no faster or easier way to get them open, no matter what you're doing on your PC—the Taskbar is always visible and showing your favorite icons.

To add an icon there, simply drag it from whatever desktop window it's in onto the Quick Launch toolbar area, as shown in Figure 3-15. To remove an icon, right-click it and choose Delete from the shortcut menu. (You're removing only its image from the Quick Launch toolbar; you're not actually removing any software from your computer.) If you don't use Outlook Express for email, for example, remove it from the Quick Launch toolbar.

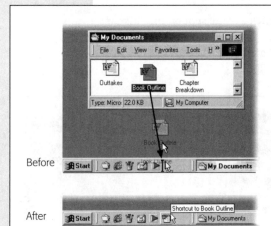

Figure 3-15:
You can add almost any kind of icon to the Quick Launch toolbar (an application, document file, disk, folder, control panel, or whatever) just by dragging it there (top); the thick vertical bar shows you where it'll appear. The only challenge is to find the window that houses the icon you want to add. If it's an application, see page 48 for hints on finding the actual icon of the program in question.

Before

After

Desktop Toolbar

The Desktop toolbar (Figure 3-14) is a row of icons representing the icons sitting on your desktop: My Computer, My Documents, and so on. This toolbar makes your Taskbar very crowded—so much, in fact, that you have to *scroll* to see the icons that don't fit.

Consider avoiding this space-hungry toolbar. Instead, when you need to access one of the icons on your desktop, click the Show Desktop icon on the Quick Launch toolbar.

Address Toolbar, Links Toolbar

These toolbars are exactly the same as the window toolbars described on page 70-71. Those toolbars, however, appear only in the windows in which you've summoned them; this one appears on the Taskbar at all times.

Redesigning Your Toolbars

To change the look of a toolbar, right-click a blank spot on that toolbar to display its shortcut menu.

Tip: If you have difficulty finding a blank spot, position your cursor over either end of the toolbar (if you look carefully, you can see an etched vertical bar). When your pointer turns into a double-headed arrow, drag to enlarge the toolbar, thus creating some blank space.

The shortcut menu offers these choices:

- **View** lets you change the size of the icons on the toolbar.

- **Show Text** identifies each toolbar icon with a text label.

- **Refresh** re-draws the Links or Desktop toolbar if it needs updating. For example, suppose you drag an icon onto your desktop. The Desktop toolbar doesn't change to list the new icon until you use this Refresh command.

- **Open** works only with the Quick Launch and Links toolbars. It opens a window that lists what's in the toolbar, so that you can conveniently delete or rename the icons. (Of course, you can also delete or rename something on these toolbars by right-clicking an icon and choosing Delete or Rename from the shortcut menu. But using the Open command can be useful when you're performing extensive changes to the toolbar, since it opens a window, where the icons are larger and you have more working room.)

- **Show Title** makes the toolbar's name (such as "Quick Launch" or "Desktop") appear on the toolbar.

Tip: You can enlarge the toolbar by placing your mouse pointer on either edge of it. When the pointer changes to a double-headed arrow, drag to the right to make the toolbar wider. (Doing so may make the other toolbars smaller, however.)

Moving toolbars

You don't have to keep toolbars on the Taskbar; you can move them anywhere on your screen (see Figure 3-16). To return a toolbar to its original location, drag its title bar back onto the Taskbar.

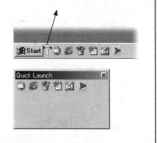

Figure 3-16:
To park a toolbar in a different location, drag upward on the ridge at the left edge (top). What you get is a strange sort of floating toolbar (bottom); it's now an on-screen, perpetually available launcher. (Use tooltips, or choose Show Text from its shortcut menu, to identify the icons.) If you drag the toolbar to an edge of the screen, it becomes glued there like a second Taskbar.

The disadvantage to moving a toolbar off the Taskbar is that you're using screen real estate that might be better used by your document windows. In addition, any windows you open *cover* the on-screen toolbar, rendering it useless. Of course, you can minimize all the windows to get to the toolbar, but that seems more like work than convenience.

Creating Toolbars

The Quick Launch area of the Taskbar is such a delight that you may actually develop a syndrome called Quick Launch Envy—you'll find that having only one of it isn't enough. You might wish you could create several different Quick Launch toolbars, each stocked with the icons for a different project or person. One could contain icons for all the chapters of a book you're writing; another could list only your games.

Fortunately, Microsoft has anticipated your craving. It's easy to create as many different custom toolbars as you like, each of which behaves exactly like the Quick Launch toolbar.

Windows Me creates toolbars from *folders*. Therefore, during the process of creating a toolbar, you must create a folder (unless you have an existing folder filled with the stuff you want to toolbar-ize). Here are the steps you need to take to create a toolbar:

1. **Right-click a blank spot on the Taskbar. From the shortcut menu, choose Toolbars→New Toolbar.**

   The New Toolbar dialog box appears, as shown in Figure 3-17.

2. **If the icons you want on your toolbar are already in a folder, click the appropriate + button to find and select it.**

   For example, if the folder you created is in the My Documents folder, click the + next to My Documents to reveal its contents.

Figure 3-17:
The major folders of your computer are displayed in the New Toolbar dialog box. You can click the + button to expand an element and continue to expand its sub-elements until you find the folder you're looking for. Or you can create a new folder for your toolbar anywhere on your hard drive.

If your toolbar-to-be candidates aren't already in a folder, you can create a new one at this point. Highlight the appropriate location (usually a hard drive, which you can see by clicking the + button next to the My Computer icon). Then click New Folder, and give the folder a name.

3. **Click OK.**

Your new toolbar is on the Taskbar. As mentioned earlier, you should feel free to tailor it—by changing its icon sizes, hiding or showing the icon labels, or adding new icons to it by dragging them from other desktop windows.

FREQUENTLY ASKED QUESTION

The Not-So-Amazing Disappearing Toolbar

Hey, what's going on? I made a custom toolbar, and spent quite a lot of time on it. And then, when I needed more space on my Taskbar, I right-clicked it and chose Close from shortcut menu.

And now I want it back. But when I right-click a blank area on the Taskbar and choose Toolbars, my custom toolbar isn't listed there! How do I get it back?

You've discovered an unfortunate little quirk of custom

toolbars: They don't really exist. All you've done is added a folder listing to your Taskbar, as fleeting as the morning dew. If you close a custom toolbar, it no longer appears on that shortcut menu; it's gone forever.

The folder from which you created it, however, is still hanging around. If you want your toolbar back, you must create it all over again as described in this section; but at least you don't have to create its folder from scratch.

Icons, Shortcuts, and the Recycle Bin

A s mentioned in Chapter 1, every disk, folder, file, application, printer, and networked computer, on or attached to your PC, is represented on your screen by an icon and a name. The icon helps you identify what kind of object something is at a glance.

To avoid spraying your screen with hundreds of thousands of overlapping icons, seething like snakes in a pit, Windows organizes them into folders. It then puts those folders into *other* folders, and so on, until only a handful of icons actually appears on your screen.

This folder-in-a-folder-in-a-folder scheme works beautifully at reducing screen clutter, but it means that you've got some hunting to do whenever you want to open a particular icon. You've got to *open* folder after folder until you corner your quarry.

Making this navigation process easy and understandable is one of the primary design goals of Windows—and of this chapter.

UP TO SPEED

Two Folder Notes

To create a new folder to hold your own icons, right-click where you want the folder to appear (on the desktop, or in any desktop window except My Computer) and choose New→Folder from shortcut menu. The new folder appears with its temporary "New Folder" name highlighted. Type a new name for the folder and then press Enter.

And by the way: Before Windows took over the universe, folders were called *directories*, and folders inside them were called *subdirectories*. Keep that in mind the next time you're reading some user guide, magazine article, or computer book written by an old-timer.

Two Ways to Navigate

Windows Me offers two key ways to begin your folder quest:

- **My Computer.** Using this scheme, you double-click one folder after another, leaving a trail of open windows behind you, burrowing ever deeper into the folders-within-folders.

- **Windows Explorer.** You do all of your navigating in a single window, where all the folders appear in a vertical list that looks something like an outline.

Each method has its advantages, which you can read about in this section; you'll probably settle on using one or the other most of the time.

Navigating the My Computer Icon

You can't miss the My Computer icon. It's in the upper-left corner of the screen, where your eye naturally falls. You never *will* miss the My Computer icon, either—you can't remove it or rename it.

When you double-click this icon, you see icons that represent the disk drives attached to, or installed inside, your computer (see Figure 4-1, top). By double-clicking one of these icons, you open a window that lists the folders and files on it (see Figure 4-1, bottom). Frequently, you have to open folders *within* folders (subfolders) to find the actual icon you're looking for. (You can save yourself the trouble of having to individually close all the windows you've opened if you use the tip described on page 62.)

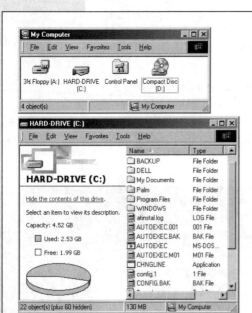

Figure 4-1:
Top: The My Computer window is the starting point for any folder-digging you want to do. It shows the "top-level" folders—the disk drives of your PC. If you double-click the icon of a removable-disk drive, such as your CD-ROM drive, Zip drive, or Jaz drive, you get only an error message unless there's actually a disk in the drive.

Bottom: The contents of a typical hard drive (C: drive) after you've clicked the "View the entire contents of this drive" link (not shown).

Here are three of the most important standard folders you'll find in your hard drive window:

- **My Documents.** "But wait a minute," you're entitled to protest. "Isn't the My Documents folder on the *desktop*?" The answer is no, not really. What's on the desktop is only a *shortcut* of the real My Documents folder. (See page 101 for more on shortcuts.) Put another way, you can double-click *either* My Documents folder; you'll see exactly the same files inside.

Note: If you're using the multiple-user feature described in Chapter 14, your My Documents folder isn't in the hard drive window. It's in the folder that contains your profile information.

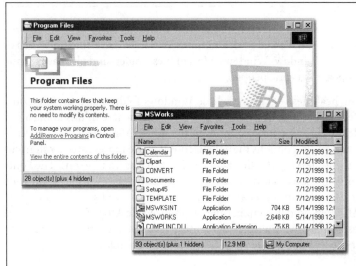

Figure 4-2:
Top left: The Program Files folder may start out looking empty.

Lower right: Here's what Microsoft Works actually looks like—93 little software crumbs in your Program Files→MSWorks folder. Only one of these icons (the one called MSWORKS) is the actual program. But don't try to move it, or any of its support files, out of this folder. (The exceptions: It's OK, and even encouraged, to drag the program icon onto your Start menu or Quick Launch toolbar, where it turns into a shortcut.)

- **Program Files.** This folder contains all of your applications—Word, Excel, Internet Explorer, your games, and so on. But that isn't the impression you get when you first open the folder (see Figure 4-2). You might stare in horror as this window opens up, completely empty. Your software folders appear only when you click "View the entire contents of this folder" on the panel at the left side of the window. (As shown in Figure 4-1, the C: drive window works the same way.)

This peculiar behavior requires some explanation. A Windows program isn't a single, self-contained icon. Instead, each is accompanied by a phalanx of support files and folders, as shown at lower right in Figure 4-2. Nestled among all of these auxiliary files is the actual application icon, which can't even run if it's separated from its support group.

Microsoft and other software companies grew weary of taking tech-support calls from people whose programs stopped working because they moved some of these programs around. Finally, as a preemptive strike, Microsoft simply made them invisible. The initially empty Program Files window is meant to say: "Nothing to see here, folks. Move along."

So how are you supposed to launch your programs if you can't see them in the Program Files folder? You can take your pick from a half-dozen ways, all of which are described in the beginning of Chapter 6.

Note: A typical software installer puts pieces of a new program all over your hard drive; the little chunks you see in the Program Files folder are only the beginning. Therefore, if you decide that you don't like having most of your software in the Program Files folder, don't just move the files to a different folder. Instead, uninstall the software (using the Add/Remove Programs control panel described in Chapter 9) and then reinstall it, taking advantage of the option to choose an installation folder of your own choice.

• **Windows.** This is another folder that Microsoft wishes its customers would simply ignore. This most hallowed folder contains Windows itself, the thousands of little files that make Windows Windows. Most of these folders and files have cryptic names that appeal to cryptic people.

In general, the healthiest PC is one whose Windows folder has been left alone. There are a few exceptions, however. As you'll read elsewhere in this book, a few of these folders hold some interest for even the non-NASA scientist. The Desktop folder, for example, contains the actual icons that are represented by shortcut icons lying on your desktop (Online Services, My Briefcase, and so on). The Fonts folder contains the icons that represent the various typefaces installed on your machine; the Start Menu folder houses the icons that are listed in your Start menu; the All Users folder contains the customized desktop, Start menu, and other settings used by the multiple-user feature described in Chapter 14; and so on. You're free to add or remove icons from any of these folders.

Tip: As you navigate your folders, keep in mind the power of the Backspace key. Each time you press it, you jump to the parent window of the one you're now looking at—the one that contains it. For example, if you're perusing the My Pictures folder inside My Documents, pressing Backspace opens the My Documents window.

Likewise, the Alt key, pressed with the right and left arrow keys, serves as a Back and Forward button. Use this powerful shortcut to "walk" backward or forward through the list of windows you've most recently opened.

Navigating With Windows Explorer

Windows Explorer is another method of navigating the folders on your PC. Explorer gives you a single window that shows every folder on the machine at once. You're less likely to lose your bearings using Windows Explorer than when simply burrowing through folder after folder; many Windows veterans navigate using the Explorer window exclusively.

To give Explorer a try, right-click a disk or folder icon and choose Explore from the shortcut menu. (You can also find the Explore command in the My Computer and Start button shortcut menus; you can even get to it by choosing Start→Programs→ Accessories→Windows Explorer.) You get a window like the one in Figure 4-3.

As you can see, this hierarchical display splits the window into two panes. The left pane displays only disks and folders; the right pane displays the contents of any disk or folder you click. You can manipulate the icons on either side much as you would any icons. For example, you can double-click one to open it, drag it to the Recycle Bin to get rid of it, or drag it into another folder in the folder list to move it elsewhere on your machine.

When the panel is too narrow

As shown in Figure 4-3, clicking the + button to expand a folder gives you a new indented list of folders inside it. If you expand folders within folders to a deep enough level, the indentation may push the folder names so far to the right that you can't read them. You can remedy this problem with any of the following actions:

- Adjust the relative sizes of the window halves by dragging the vertical bar between them.

- Position your mouse pointer over a folder whose name is being chopped off. A tooltip appears to display the full name of the folder.

- Use the horizontal scroll bar at the bottom of the left pane to shift the contents.

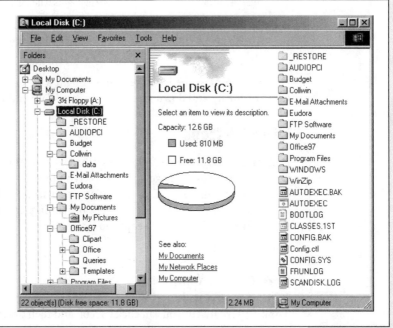

Figure 4-3:
Windows Explorer offers a treetop view of your computer's hierarchy. When you click a disk or folder in the left pane, the right pane displays its contents, including files and folders. Click the + button to "expand" a disk or folder, opening a new indented list of what's inside it; click the – button to "collapse" the folder list again. The dotted vertical and horizontal lines in the left pane help you keep track of the hierarchical levels.

Viewing folder contents

To see what's in one of the disks or folders listed at the left side of the Explorer window, you can use any of these techniques:

- Click a folder in the left pane of the Explorer; the contents appear in the right pane.

- Double-click a folder in the left pane, or click the + button next to its name. The branch expands in the left pane.

- Right-click a folder in the left pane and select Open from the shortcut menu. A new window opens, displaying the contents of the folder you clicked. (To open a *program or document* that appears in either side of the window, double-click it as usual.)

Keyboard shortcuts

If you arrive home one day to discover that your mouse has been stolen, or if you just like doing things with the keyboard, you'll enjoy the shortcuts that work in the Explorer window:

left-arrow key	Collapses the highlighted folder—or, if it's already collapsed, highlights its "parent" folder
right-arrow key	Expands a highlighted folder, or if it's already expanded, highlights the first folder inside it
F6 or Tab	Highlights the other half of the window
Alt+left arrow	Highlights whatever folder you last highlighted
Ctrl+Z	Undoes whatever you just did.
Backspace	Highlights the "parent" disk or folder of whatever you'got highlighted

You can also press the letter keys to highlight a folder or file that begins with that letter, or the up and down arrow keys to "walk" up and down the list.

Life with Icons

Both of the navigational schemes described so far in this chapter have only one goal in life: to help you manage your icons. Windows displays every shred of software and hardware on your PC as an independent icon. You could spend your entire workday just mastering the techniques of naming, copying, moving, and deleting these icons—and plenty of people do.

Here's the crash course.

How to Name Your Icons

To rename a file, folder, printer, or disk icon, click carefully, just once, on the icon's name. (Alternatively, you can click its icon and then press F2, or right-click the icon and choose Rename from the shortcut menu.) Either way, a "renaming rectangle" appears around the current name; simply type the new name you want, and then press Enter. You can use all the usual text-editing tricks: Press Backspace to fix a typo, press the arrow keys to move the insertion point, and so on. When you're finished editing the name, press Enter to make it stick. (If another icon in the folder has the same name, Windows beeps and makes you choose another name.)

A folder or file name can be up to 255 characters long, including spaces and the *file extension* (the three-letter suffix that identifies the type of file). Windows won't let you use the following symbols in a filename, however, because they're reserved for behind-the-scenes use by Windows itself: \ / : * ? " < > |

POWER USERS' CLINIC

Long Names and DOS Names

The capability to use up to 255 characters in a filename or folder name is a feature cleverly called *long filenames*. Windows Me supports long filenames, but DOS—the ancient operating system that underlies Windows—doesn't.

PC pros refer to the folder DOS naming system as the *8.3* ("eight dot three") system, because the actual name of the folder or file can't be any longer than eight characters, and it requires a file suffix that's up to three letters long. To accommodate the DOS rules, Windows Me creates an 8.3 version of every long filename. As a result, every file on your computer actually has two *different* names—a long one and a short one.

Every now and then, you'll run up against DOS filename limitations. For example, this quirk explains why the actual name of an application is a cryptic, shortened form of its full name (WINWORD instead of Microsoft Word, for example).

Windows creates the shortened version by inserting the tilde character (~), followed by sequential numbers, after the sixth character of the filename, plus the original extension. For example, the *My Documents* folder shows up as

My Docu ~ 1 when you view it in a DOS window. If you name a file *letter to mom.doc,* it appears in DOS as *letter ~ 1.doc.* If you then name a file *letter to dad.doc,* it appears in DOS as *letter ~ 2.doc,* and so on.

This naming convention only becomes important if you work in DOS, or you exchange files with someone who uses Windows 3.1 or DOS.

If you're working in DOS, however, you can still use the long filenames of Windows Me if you want to. The trick is to enclose it in quotation marks. For example, if you want to move to the My Documents folder, type *cd\"my documents" (cd* is the command to change folders). (You need quotation marks if there's a space in the file or folder name.)

If you want to copy, delete, or rename files from the DOS command line, you can use the same trick. (Renaming files is usually much easier in DOS than in Windows because you can change batches of files at once.) When you enter the *dir* command, you see *both* the DOS filename and the long filename, making it easy to use either the 8.3 or long filename (using quotes, of course).

Even so, it's not a good idea to create names that approach the 255-character maximum length, because you'll have trouble reading their names in Windows Explorer and in dialog boxes. Furthermore, some of your applications may not be able to open files with extremely long filenames.

You can give more than one file or folder the same name, as long as they're not in the same folder. For example, you can have as many files named "Letter to Smith" as you wish, as long as each is in a different folder.

Icon Properties

As you may have read in Chapter 1, *properties* are a big deal in Windows. Properties are preference settings, and you can change them independently for every icon on your machine.

To view the Properties dialog box for an icon, choose your favorite technique:

- Right-click the icon, and then choose Properties from the shortcut menu.

- While pressing Alt, double-click the icon.

- Highlight the icon, and then press Alt+Enter.

- Highlight the icon, and then click the Properties button on the Standard Buttons window toolbar (if you see it).

But these settings aren't the same for every kind of icon. Here's what you can expect from opening the Properties dialog boxes for various kinds of desktop icons (see Figure 4-4).

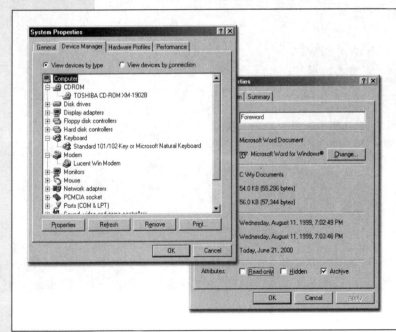

Figure 4-4:
The Properties dialog boxes are different for every kind of icon. In the months and years to come, you may find many occasions when adjusting the behavior of an icon has big benefits in simplicity and productivity.

Left: the System Properties dialog box (which appears when you check the properties of your My Computer icon).

Right: the Properties dialog box for a document.

- **My Computer.** This Properties dialog box is packed with useful information about your machine. For example, the **General** tab tells you what kind of processor is inside, how much memory (RAM) your PC has, and what version of Windows you've got. The **Device Manager** tab (shown in Figure 4-4) breaks down your equipment even more specifically, providing the manufacturer and model name of each component on your machine: modem, monitor, mouse, and so on. (It's here that you discover how little your computer's manufacturer, such as Dell or Gateway, actually produces; almost every component of your computer came from other companies.)

  The **Hardware Profiles** feature isn't something you'll use much unless you have a laptop; see page 308 for details. Finally, the **Performance** tab provides some very technical information about the computer's speed. For best results, change these settings only on the advice of a technical-help expert.

- **Disks.** You get to see the disk's name (which you can change), its capacity (which you can't change), and how much of it is full. A second tab in the dialog box, called **Tools,** offers quick access to such disk-maintenance tools as ScanDisk and Defrag (see Chapter 15), and the **Sharing** tab controls who can access this disk over the network (Chapter 17).

- **Data files.** The Properties for a plain old file, such as one of your documents, offers a few interesting-looking checkboxes. These options control special file-system properties known as *attributes.* For example, the *read-only* attribute locks the document; you can open it and read it, but you can't make any changes to it. *Hidden* makes the icon invisible. (This is a great way to prevent something from being deleted; on the other hand, because the icon becomes invisible, you may find it a bit difficult to open it *yourself.*)

  Archive means, "Back me up." This message is intended for the Windows Backup program described in Chapter 15, and indicates that this document has been changed since the last time it was backed up (or that it has never been backed up).

Tip: Depending on the kind of document you've highlighted, the Properties dialog box may have other tabs that give you reams of information about what's in the file. The Summary tab, for example, tells you how many words, lines, and paragraphs are in a particular Word document. For a graphics document, the Summary tab tells you the graphic's dimensions, resolution, and color settings.

- **Folders.** Here you get the same checkbox options described for data files. But now you get a separate tab called **Sharing,** which lets you make this folder available for invasion by other people on your office network (see Chapter 17).

- **Program files.** There's not much here that you can change yourself (only the three checkboxes described above), but you certainly get a lot to look at: The **Version** tab offers a considerable wealth of detail about the program's version number, corporate parent, language, and so on.

- **Shortcuts.** You can read about these useful controls at the end of this chapter.

Copying and Moving Folders and Files

Moving folders and files from one disk or folder to another is a snap. Windows Me offers two different techniques: dragging icons, and using the Copy and Paste commands.

No matter which method you use, however, you start by showing Windows which icons you want to copy or move. And you do that by *highlighting* them.

Highlighting Icons

To highlight one icon, you just click it once. But you don't have to move or copy one icon at a time; you can select multiple icons in the same folder or disk window. For example, you can move a bunch of documents from one folder in your My Documents folder to another, or copy a group of them onto a backup disk.

Tip: It's easier to work with multiple icons in Details view (page 64), where every icon is displayed in a single column.

To highlight multiple files in preparation for moving or copying, use one of these techniques:

To highlight all the icons

To select all the icons in a window, press Ctrl+A (the keyboard equivalent of the Edit→Select All command).

To highlight several icons in a list

If you're looking at the contents of a window in Details view, you can drag vertically over the file and folder names to highlight a group of consecutive icons.

Alternatively, click the first icon you want to highlight, and then press Shift as you click the last file. All the files in between are automatically selected, along with the two icons you clicked.

To highlight several icons in Icon view

If you're looking at the contents of a window in Large or Small icon view, you can highlight a group of neighboring icons just by dragging across them. Start with your cursor above and to one side of the icons, and then drag diagonally. As you drag, you create a temporary dotted-line rectangle. Any icon that falls within this rectangle darkens to show that it's selected.

Tip: If you include a particular icon in your diagonally dragged group by mistake, click it while pressing Ctrl. That removes it from the selected cluster.

To highlight only specific icons

If you want to highlight only, for example, the first, third, and seventh icons in the list, start by clicking icon No. 1. Then, while pressing the Ctrl key, click each of the others. (If you click a selected icon *again* while pressing Ctrl, you *de*select it. You can use this trick when you've just highlighted an icon by accident.)

Tip: The Ctrl-key trick is especially handy if you want to select *almost* all the icons in a window. Press Ctrl+A to select everything in the folder, then hold down the Ctrl key while you click any unwanted icons to deselect them.

Copying by Dragging Icons

You can drag icons from one folder to another, from one drive to another, from a drive to a folder on another drive, and so on. (When you've selected several icons, drag any *one* of them; the others go along for the ride.)

Here's what happens when you drag icons in the usual way (using the left mouse button):

- Dragging to another folder on the same disk *moves* the icon.

- Holding down the Ctrl key while dragging to another folder on the same disk *copies* the icon. (If you do so within a single window, you get a duplicate of the file called "Copy of [whatever its name was].")

- Dragging an icon from one disk to another *copies* the folder or file.

- Pressing Shift while dragging from one disk to another *moves* the folder or file (without leaving a copy behind).

Figure 4-5:
Right-dragging icons is much easier, and much safer, than left-dragging when you want to move or copy something, thanks to this shortcut menu.

Tip: You can move or copy icons by dragging them either into an open window or directly onto a disk or folder *icon*.

The right-mouse button trick

Think you'll remember all of those possibilities every time you drag an icon? Probably not. Fortunately, Windows Me is prepared to offer you a menu of these choices each time you drag. The trick is to use the *right* mouse button as you drag. When you release the button, the menu shown in Figure 4-5 appears.

Tip: You can cancel a dragging operation at any time by pressing the Esc key.

Dragging icons in Windows Explorer

You may find it easier to copy or move icons in Windows Explorer, because the two-pane display format makes it easier to see where your files are and where they're going. (Remember, you can add the Explorer-like folder-list hierarchy to *any* window by choosing View→Explorer Bar→Folders.)

1. **If necessary, click the + button next to the appropriate icon in the left pane to make the destination folder visible.**

   For example, if you want to copy an icon into a certain folder, expand the drive (by clicking the + button) so that you can see its list of folders. If the destination is a folder *within* that folder, expand its parent folder as necessary.

2. **Click the *icon* (not the + button) of the disk or folder that contains the icon you want to manipulate.**

   Its contents appear in the right pane.

3. **Locate the icon you want to move in the right pane, then drag it to the appropriate folder in the left pane (see Figure 4-6).**

   When you release the mouse, Windows moves the icons as you've directed.

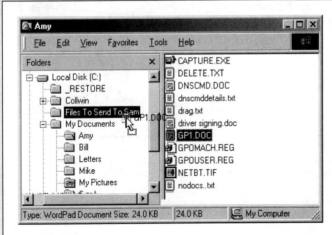

Figure 4-6:
The file GP1.DOC, located in My Documents→Amy, is being dragged to the folder named Files to Send to Sam. As the mouse pointer moves over any folder in the left pane, that folder's name is highlighted automatically. When you arrive at the correct target folder, release the mouse button.

Copying by Using Copy and Paste

Dragging icons to copy or move them may feel good, because it's so direct: You actually see your arrow cursor pushing the icons into the new location.

But you pay a price for this satisfying illusion: You may have to spend a moment or two fiddling with your windows, or clicking buttons in the Explorer folder hierarchy, so that you have a clear "line of drag" between the icon to be moved and the destination folder.

Fortunately, there's a better way: You can use the Cut, Copy, and Paste commands to move icons from one window into another. The routine goes like this:

1. **Highlight the icon or icons you want to move.**

2. **Right-click one of the icons. Choose Cut or Copy from the shortcut menu.**

   Alternatively, you can choose Edit→Cut or Edit→Copy, using the menu bar at the top of the window. (Eventually, you may want to learn the keyboard shortcuts for these commands: Ctrl+C for Copy, Ctrl+X for Cut.)

   The Cut command makes the highlighted icons disappear from the window. You've stashed them on the invisible Windows Clipboard, as described in Chapter 6.

   The Copy command also places copies of the files on the Clipboard, but doesn't disturb the originals.

3. **Right-click the window, folder icon, or disk icon where you want to put the icons. Choose Paste from the shortcut menu.**

   Once again, you may prefer to use the menu bar: Choose Edit→Paste. (*Keyboard equivalent:* Ctrl+V.)

   Either way, you've successfully transferred the icons. If you pasted into an open window, you'll see the icons appear there. If you pasted onto a closed folder or disk icon, you have to open the icon's window to see the results. And if you pasted right back into the same window, you get a duplicate of the file called "Copy of [whatever its name was]."

The Recycle Bin

The Recycle Bin is your desktop trash basket. This is where files and folders go when they've outlived their usefulness; it's the waiting room for data oblivion. There they stay, waiting to be rescued by being dragged out again, until you *empty* the Recycle Bin.

You can drop highlighted folders or files into the Recycle Bin in any of several ways:

- Press the Delete key.
- Click the Delete icon on the Standard Buttons toolbar.
- Choose File→Delete.

• Right-click a highlighted icon and choose Delete from the shortcut menu.

Windows Me asks you if you're sure you want to send the item to the Recycle Bin. (Click Yes; as noted below, it's easy enough to change your mind.) Now the Recycle Bin icon changes: The container appears to be brimming over with paper.

Tip: You can turn off the confirmation message that appears when you send files to the Recycle Bin. Just right-click the Recycle Bin, choose Properties from the shortcut menu, and turn off "Display delete confirmation dialog." Turning off the warning isn't much of a safety risk; after all, files aren't really being removed from your drive when you put them in the Recycle Bin.

You can put unwanted files or folders into the Recycle Bin from any folder window, from within Windows Explorer, or even inside the Open File dialog box of Windows applications (see Chapter 6).

Note: All of these methods put icons from your *hard drive* into the Recycle Bin. But deleting an icon from a removable drive (floppy, Jaz, or Zip drives, for example), or other computers on the network, does *not* involve the Recycle Bin, giving you no opportunity to retrieve them. (Deleting anything with the DOS del or erase commands bypasses the Recycle Bin, too.)

Restoring Deleted Files and Folders

If you change your mind about sending something to the software graveyard, open the Recycle Bin by double-clicking. A window like the one in Figure 4-7 opens.

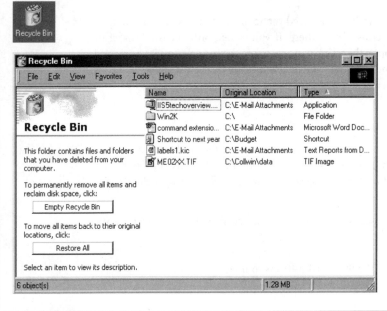

Figure 4-7:
When you double-click the Recycle Bin (top), the Recycle Bin window (bottom) displays information about each folder and file it holds. You can sort the contents, making it easier to find a deleted icon, by clicking the gray column heading for the type of sort you need.

To restore a file or a folder, right-click its icon and choose Restore from the shortcut menu. To restore multiple files, select them using any of the techniques described on page 94. Then right-click any *one* selected file and choose Restore from the shortcut menu. And to put *everything* back, of course, just click the Restore All button (Figure 4-7).

Restored, in this case, means returned to the folder from whence it came, wherever on your hard drive it was when you deleted it. If you restore an icon whose original folder has been deleted in the meantime, Windows Me re-creates that folder to hold the restored file(s).

POWER USERS' CLINIC

Secrets of the Send To Command

If you find yourself copying or moving certain icons to certain folders or disks with regularity, it's time to exploit the File→Send To command that lurks in every folder window (and in the shortcut menu for almost every icon).

This command's submenus offer a quick way to copy and move highlighted icons to popular destinations. For example, you can teleport a copy of a highlighted file directly to a floppy disk by choosing File→Send To→3 1/2 Floppy. You're spared the tedium of choosing Copy, selecting the floppy drive, and choosing Paste. Another useful command is "Send To→Desktop (create shortcut)," which dumps a shortcut icon onto your desktop background. Then there's the Send To→Mail Recipient, which bundles the highlighted icon as an email attachment that's ready to send.

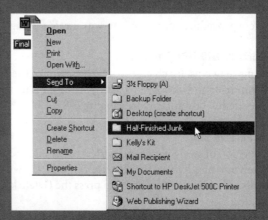

But the real power of the Send To command is its ability to accommodate your *own* favorite or frequently used folders. Lurking in your My Computer→C: drive→Windows folder is a folder called SendTo. Any shortcut icon you place here shows up instantly in the File→Send To menus (and shortcut menus) of your desktop folders (and icons).

This folder, alas, is among those that Microsoft considers inappropriate for inspection by novices. As a result, the SendTo folder comes hidden in Windows Me. To make it appear, open any folder window; choose Tools→Folder Options; click the View menu; and turn on "Show hidden files and folders." Click OK. Now, when you open My Computer→C: drive→Windows, you'll see the SendTo folder.

Most people create shortcuts here for folders and disks (such as your favorite backup disk). When you highlight an icon and then choose Send To→My Documents, for example, Windows Me copies that icon to the My Documents folder. (If you press Shift while you do so, you *move* the icon to the other disk or folder.)

But you can even add shortcuts of applications (program files) to the SendTo folder. By adding WinZip to this Send To menu, for example, you'll be able to drop-kick a highlighted icon onto the WinZip icon (for decompressing) just by choosing Send To→WinZip. You can even create shortcuts of your printer or fax modem; thereafter, you can print or fax a document just by highlighting its icon and choosing File→Send To→[your printer or fax modem's name].

Tip: You don't have to put icons back into their original folders. If you *drag* them out of the Recycle Bin window, you can put them back into any folder you like.

Emptying the Recycle Bin

While there's an advantage in the Recycle Bin (you get to undo your mistakes), there's also a downside: The files in the Recycle Bin occupy as much disk space as they did when they were stored in folders. Deleting files doesn't gain you any additional disk space until you *empty* the Recycle Bin.

That's why most people, sooner or later, follow up an icon's journey to the Recycle Bin with one of these cleanup operations:

- Right-click the Recycle Bin icon and choose Empty Recycle Bin from the short-cut menu.

- Choose File→Empty Recycle Bin, or click the Empty Recycle Bin button in the window.

- Open the Recycle Bin window. Highlight only the icons you want to get rid of. Click the Delete button on the toolbar (if it's there), or press the Delete key. (This method lets you empty only *part* of the Recycle Bin.)

- Wait. When the Recycle Bin accumulates so much stuff that it occupies a significant percentage of your hard drive space, Windows empties it automatically, as described in the next section.

All of these procedures produce "Are you sure?" messages.

Customizing the Recycle Bin

You can make two useful changes to the behavior of the Recycle Bin. Right-click the Recycle Bin icon and choose Properties from the shortcut menu. The Recycle Bin Properties dialog box appears (see Figure 4-8).

Skip the Recycle Bin

If you, a person of steely nerve and perfect judgment, never delete a file in error, you can make your files bypass the Recycle Bin entirely when you delete them. You'll reclaim disk space instantly when you press the Delete key to vaporize a highlighted file or folder.

To set this up, turn on the "Do not move files to the Recycle Bin" checkbox (Figure 4-8). And voilà: Your safety net is gone. (Especially if you *also* turn off the confirmation dialog box shown in Figure 4-8. Then you're *really* living dangerously.)

If that suggestion seems too extreme, consider this safety/convenience compromise: Leave the Recycle Bin safety net in place most of the time, but bypass the Recycle Bin on command only when it seems appropriate.

The trick to skipping the Recycle Bin on a one-shot basis is to press the Shift key while you delete a file. Doing so—and then clicking Yes in the confirmation box—

deletes the file permanently, skipping its layover in the Recycle Bin. (The Shift-key trick works for every method of deleting a file: pressing the Delete key, choosing Delete from the shortcut menu, and so on.)

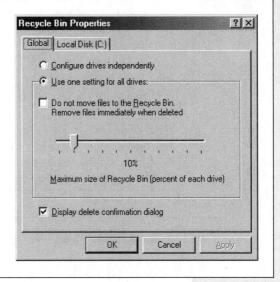

Figure 4-8:
Use the Recycle Bin Properties dialog box to govern the way the Recycle Bin works, or even if it works at all. If you have multiple hard drives, the dialog box has a tab for each of them, so that you can configure a separate and independent Recycle Bin on each drive.

Auto-emptying the Recycle Bin

The Recycle Bin has two advantages over the physical trash cans behind your house: First, you don't have to buy liners for it. Second, when it's full, it can empty itself automatically.

You configure this self-emptying feature by specifying a certain fullness limit, as a percentage of the hard drive capacity. When the Bin contents reach that level, Windows begins permanently deleting files as new files arrive in the Bin. Files that arrived in the Recycle Bin first are deleted first.

Unless you tell it otherwise, Windows Me makes 10% of your drive available to hold Recycle Bin contents. You can change that percentage by moving the slider on the Properties dialog box (see Figure 4-8). Keeping the percentage low means you're less likely to run out of the disk space you need to install software and create documents. On the other hand, raising the percentage means you'll have more opportunity to restore files you later want to retrieve.

Creating Shortcuts

A *shortcut* is a link to a folder, disk, program, or document (see Figure 4-9). You might think of it as a duplicate of the item's icon—but not a duplicate of that item itself; a shortcut takes up almost no disk space. When you double-click the shortcut icon, the original folder, disk, program, or document opens. You can also set up a keystroke for a shortcut icon, so that, in effect, you can open any program or document just by pressing a certain key combination.

Shortcuts provide quick access to things you use a lot. Because you can make as many shortcuts of a file as you want, and put them anywhere on your PC, you can effectively keep an important program or document in more than one folder. Just create a shortcut of each to leave on the desktop in plain sight. Or drag their icons onto the Start button or the Quick Launch toolbar (see page 79), which also works by creating shortcuts. In fact, everything listed in the Start→Programs menu is also a shortcut; even the My Documents folder on the desktop is a shortcut (to the actual My Documents folder).

Tip: Resist the confusion that may arise from the Microsoft term *shortcut,* which refers to one of these duplicate-icon pointers, and *shortcut menu,* the context-sensitive menu that appears when you right-click almost anything in Windows. The shortcut *menu* has nothing to do with the shortcut icons feature. (Maybe that's why it's sometimes called the *context* menu.)

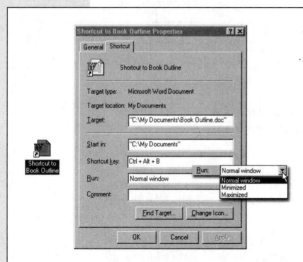

Figure 4-9:
You can tell a desktop shortcut (left) apart from its original in two ways. First, the tiny arrow "badge" identifies it as a shortcut; second, its name contains the word "shortcut."

Right: The Properties dialog box for a shortcut tells you which actual file or folder this one "points" to. The Run drop-down menu (inset) lets you control how the window opens when you double-click the shortcut icon.

Creating and Deleting Shortcuts

To create a shortcut, right-drag an icon from its current location (Windows Explorer, a folder window, or even the Search window described on page 28) to the desktop. When you release the mouse button, choose Create Shortcut(s) Here from the menu that appears.

Tip: If you're not in the mood to use a shortcut menu, just left-drag an icon while pressing Ctrl and Shift. A shortcut appears instantly.

You can delete a shortcut just as you'd delete any icon, as described in the Recycle Bin discussion earlier in this chapter. Deleting a shortcut doesn't delete the file it points to.

Note: As you may have read earlier in this book, applications in Windows are location-sensitive. If you drag them out of their original home folders in the Program Files folder, they stop working.

That's why dragging an application's icon to the desktop creates a shortcut instead of moving the real icon. But if you're determined to move an application icon out of the Program Files folder, you can do so by *right*-dragging its icon. When you finish dragging, choose Move Here from the shortcut menu.

Unveiling a Shortcut's True Identity

To locate the original icon from which a shortcut was made, right-click the shortcut icon and choose Properties from the shortcut menu. As shown in Figure 4-9, the resulting box shows you where to find the "real" icon.

Assigning a Keyboard Shortcut

Even after reading all of this gushing prose about the virtues of shortcuts, efficiency experts may still remain skeptical. Sure, shortcuts let you put favored icons everywhere you want to be, such as your Start menu, Quick Launch toolbar, the desktop, and so on. But they still require clicking to open, and that still means taking your hands off the keyboard, and that, in the scheme of things, means slowing down.

But lurking within the Shortcut Properties dialog box (Figure 4-9) is a feature with immense ramifications: the Shortcut Key box. By clicking here and then pressing a key combination, you can assign a personalized keystroke for the shortcut's file, program, folder, printer, networked computer, or disk. Thereafter, you can summon the corresponding window to your screen, no matter what you're doing on the PC, by pressing that simple keystroke.

Two rules apply as you're trying to choose keystrokes to open your favorite icons:

- They can't incorporate the Backspace, Delete, Esc, Print Screen, Tab keys, or the Space bar.

- There are no one- or two-key combinations available here. Your combination must include either Ctrl+Alt or Ctrl+Shift *and* another key.

   You'll see Windows enforce this rule rigidly. For example, if you type a single letter key into the box (such as *E*), Windows automatically adds the Ctrl and Alt keys to your combination *(Ctrl+Alt+E)*. The only permissible variation is Ctrl+*Shift* with another key. All of this is the operating system's attempt to prevent you from inadvertently duplicating one of the built-in Windows keyboard shortcuts, thus thoroughly confusing both you and your computer.

Tip: If you've ever wondered what it's like to be a programmer, try this. In the Shortcut Properties dialog box (Figure 4-9), use the Run drop-down menu at the bottom of the dialog box to choose "Normal window," "Minimized," or "Maximized." When you click OK, you've just told Windows what kind of window you want to appear when you open this particular shortcut. (See page 56 for a discussion of these window types.)

Controlling your Windows in this way isn't exactly the same as programming Microsoft Excel, but you are, in your own small way, telling Windows what to do, for a change.

UP TO SPEED

Meet the Explorer Bar

The primary difference between Windows Explorer and standard folder-opening is the split-window effect. Every now and then, you may wish you could see your entire folder hierarchy in an Explorer-type left panel, even while browsing a standard window.

Fortunately, you can. You can summon this left-side panel by choosing View→Explorer Bar→Folders, or by clicking the Folders button on the Standard Buttons toolbar (page 67). You've just turned your standard window into an Explorer-style window.

The folder hierarchy isn't the only thing you can display in the left side of a split-screen window, either. This special left-side panel is called the *Explorer bar,* and it can take on several different personalities. Using the other commands in the View→Explorer Bar, for example, you can fill this left-side pane with the Search panel, a Favorites list (Web sites or folders you've "bookmarked"), or a History list (Web sites and folders you've recently opened). To restore the default Explorer bar again, choose the same checkmarked item in the View→Explorer menu.

Getting Help

A s you may have noticed, each version of Windows seems to get bigger and more capable, but seems to come with even fewer pages of printed instructions. In Windows Me, Microsoft has relegated more of its wisdom than ever to online help screens.

If you've earlier versions of Windows, you may notice some big changes in the Windows Me help system, which is now called Help and Support. The chief change is that now, the Windows help text, help pages from Microsoft's Web site, and many applications' Help mechanisms all show up in a single, unified window, using the same organizational structure. The influence of the Internet is apparent: like a Web page, the new Help system uses hyperlinks, has a Home page, and loads slowly.

Navigating the Help System

To open the help system, choose Start→Help, or press F1. The Help and Support window appears, as shown in Figure 5-1. From here, you can home in on the help screen you want using any of three methods: clicking your way from the Help and Support home page, using the index, or using the Search command.

Help Home Page

The home page shown in Figure 5-1 contains a list of broad topics, such as "Printing, Scanning, & Photos" and "Email, Messaging, & Faxing." Click any topic to see a list of subtopics, each of which leads you to another, more focused list, which in turn leads you to a still more narrowed-down list. Eventually you arrive at a list that actually produces a help page.

Tip: As you burrow deeper into the Help system, don't overlook the Back button (the left-pointing arrow) at the top left corner of the window. It takes you back, screen by screen, to the starting page.

Burrowing around this way can be educational, but it's almost always faster and easier to use the index or the search feature to find the help page that contains the instructions you need.

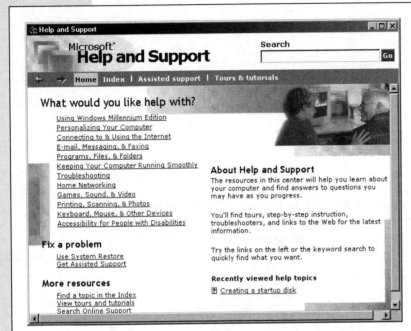

Figure 5-1:
As on a Web page, links on the Help and Support window let you move among topics. Back and Forward buttons on the toolbar let you return to pages you've already seen— and then come back to your most recent page. Other links on the toolbar open an index (an alphabetical listing of topics), a page for assisted support (mostly links to help pages on MSN.com), and tours and tutorials that work like story-books about particular topics.

Help Index

The index is a quick way to find a help topic. Click the Index link in the toolbar to open the index (see Figure 5-2), which lists all of the help topics in the Windows repertoire alphabetically. In the keyword box, type the topic you're investigating, such as *keyboard shortcuts*; as you type, Windows Me matches each character, highlighting successive index listings to match the characters you've typed so far. Just double-click a topic's name to see its corresponding help page.

If your typing doesn't produce a matching entry, you can scroll through the index to see what's available. When you find a listing you think might be helpful, double-click it to see its help page in the right pane.

Search the Help Pages

If the index doesn't provide the topic you're looking for, it's probably because you and Windows Me are referring to it using different topic names. For example, suppose you want information on the little menu that appears when you right-click something, which you've heard people call *context menus*. You'll quickly discover that the index doesn't contain any such entry.

Here's where the Search function is valuable: Windows Me can search all important words found *in* the help pages, not just the topic titles. Because the words you use to describe the topic are probably contained within a help page, searching for the words should yield the information you need. If you search for *context menus*, the list of results (in the left half of the Help window) includes "Using shortcut menus"—which is how Microsoft refers to this kind of menu.

When you enter multiple words, Windows Me assumes that you're looking for help screens that contain *all* of those words. For example, if you search for *video settings*, you'll be shown help screens that contain both the words *video* and *setting* (although not necessarily next to each other).

If you want to find pages containing any *one* of the words you've specified, separate your search terms with the word *or*. For example, if you type *video or settings,* you'll find all help pages that have *either* one of those words. Using "or" can produce a very long list; use it with discretion.

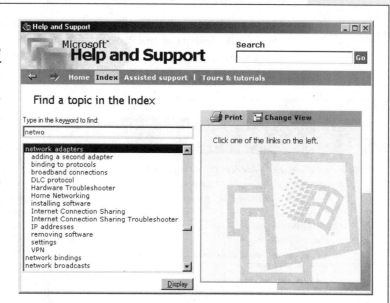

Figure 5-2:
As you type, Windows Me automatically highlights the topic title that matches your entry. Most of the entries in the index are indented; these are the links to actual help pages. Entries that aren't indented are either category headings (which have indented entries beneath them) or topic headings (which don't have indented entries beneath them). Category headings don't do anything when double-clicked; you're supposed to open one of the indented sub-entries.)

Tip: You can also precede a search phrase with the word *not,* which tells Windows Me to eliminate any pages that also contain the second word. For example, entering *video not settings* yields all help pages about video that *don't* discuss settings.

Using Help Pages

Whether you use the index or the Search box, eventually you'll click or double-click a topic in the left pane that actually produces a help page in the right pane.

Tip: Some of the help screens in the Help system are "local" (stored on your hard drive). Others are online (stored on Microsoft's Web site). Fortunately for people who can't stand it when the PC dials the Internet without warning, you can tell in advance which kind of help page is which: A symbol appears next to each listing in the left pane. If it's a question-mark symbol, the help page is on your hard drive; if it's a blue "e" (the Internet Explorer logo), the help page is on the Internet.

If you click a blue "e" topic, you get the Connect To box (see page 229). If you click Connect, your modem dials the Internet, your Web browser opens, and the help page from the Web eventually appears. (If you've set up your PC to dial the Internet automatically, you save a step; see page 230.)

Not every help page contains instructional prose. Some serve as electronic coaches, walking you through configuration tasks one step at a time; sometimes they point you to sources of further help, as shown in Figure 5-3.

Here's how to use the information and features on help pages:

- Links marked by a shortcut arrow (such as the first topic in Figure 5-3) are links that open relevant Control Panel or utility programs, which you'll need for whatever steps are described on the help page. (The help page stays on the screen so that you can refer to it as you work.)

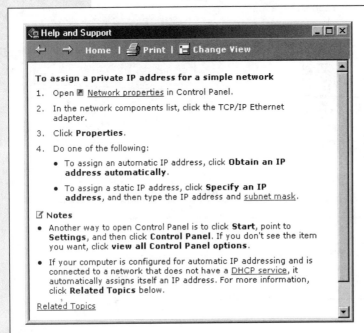

Figure 5-3:
You can't see the colors here, but help pages have color-coded underlining to help you get to all the information that's available. Underlined blue text is a link to another help page, a Control Panel applet, or a utility. Underlined green text is a definition. Click the link's text to see the definition in a pop-up box. To remove the pop-up box, click anywhere within its boundaries.

- The Related Topics link at the bottom of many help pages opens a list of similar help topics. Click one to open that help page.

- Ordinarily, the Help window fills most of your screen, so it may cover up whatever steps you're trying to follow. But if you click Change View (above the help text, as shown in Figure 5-3), you hide the list of topics, shrinking the help page so it fills a much smaller window. Click the button again to return to the two-pane view.

- Click Print to print the entire help page.

- After dragging diagonally to highlight some text in the help page, you can press Ctrl+C to copy it to the Clipboard. Then you can paste the data into a word processor, email message, and so on.

"What's This?": Help for Dialog Boxes

Whenever you find yourself facing some dialog box (like the one shown in Figure 5-4), scanning a cluster of oddly worded options, Windows Me's "What's This?" feature can come to the rescue. It makes tooltips (pop-up captions) appear for text boxes, checkboxes, option buttons, and other dialog box elements.

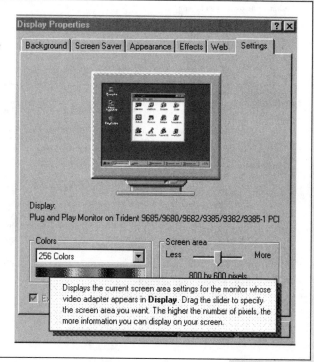

Figure 5-4:
After clicking the question-mark icon at the upper-right corner of the dialog box, you can click any control in the dialog box—in this case, the Screen Area slider—to read about its function. To make the pop-up box go away, click anywhere within its border.

You can summon these pop-up identifiers (see Figure 5-4) in either of three ways:

- Right-click something in the dialog box; in the world's shortest shortcut menu that now appears, click What's This?.

- Click the question mark in the upper-right corner of the dialog, then click the element you want identified.

- Click the object and then press F1.

Troubleshooters

When some PC feature isn't working the way you'd hope—or isn't working at all—Windows Me offers a special kind of wizard called a *troubleshooter,* a series of help screens designed to help you solve a problem.

You can find links to troubleshooters in the main Help and Support window. To see the list of them, type *troubleshooter* in the Search box and then click Go. Then, in the resulting list, double-click the name of the troubleshooter you need.

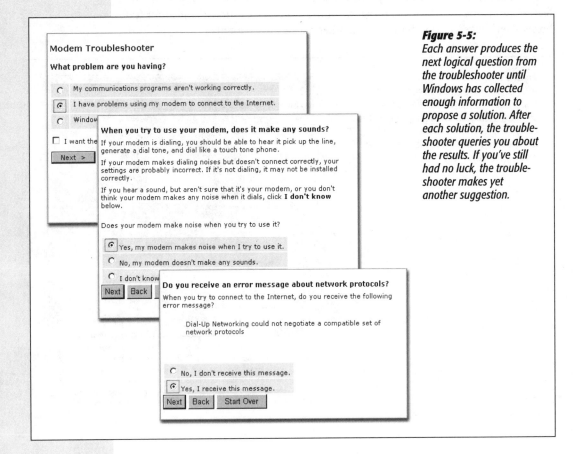

Figure 5-5:
Each answer produces the next logical question from the troubleshooter until Windows has collected enough information to propose a solution. After each solution, the trouble-shooter queries you about the results. If you've still had no luck, the trouble-shooter makes yet another suggestion.

Like a wizard, a troubleshooter asks one question per screen, and then follows up your replies with further suggestions. In Figure 5-5, for example, you can see the progression you see when you're trying to solve an Internet dialing problem.

If you follow all the steps suggested by the troubleshooter, and you're unable to fix your problem, the troubleshooter apologizes and suggests you find another resource for more help.

Tip: There are four buttons at the top of the Help and Support window. **Home** returns you to the main Help and Support screen; Index is described at the beginning of this chapter.

The remaining two buttons aren't nearly as useful as the Index, but are worth poking through. **Assisted support** offers links to bulletin-board and email sources of help from Microsoft. **Tours & tutorials** takes you to a list of new features in Windows Me; click one to read a few paragraphs extolling that feature's virtues.

TROUBLESHOOTING MOMENT

Following Troubleshooter Suggestions That Involve A Reboot

Some of the remedies offered by Windows Me trouble-shooters require you to change settings on your PC. If making those changes requires you to restart the computer, then, needless to say, you'll lose your place in the trouble-shooter.

Fortunately, it's easy to pick up where you left off: After your computer restarts, open the Help and Support window again (by pressing F1, for example). The trouble-shooter you were using appears in the Recently Viewed Help Topics section of the home page.

Sometimes the troubleshooter's instructions include an additional task you must perform *during* the restart process, such as booting your computer into Safe Mode or performing a task immediately after Windows loads. In that case, print the troubleshooter's instructions before you begin the configuration changes.

Tip: If Windows Me came installed on your computer, and the Help system doesn't get you out of whatever jam you're experiencing, call your *computer's* manufacturer, not Microsoft, for help. (Microsoft sells copies of Windows to computer makers on the condition that Microsoft won't have to answer all the technical-support calls.)

WINDOWS ME: THE MISSING MANUAL

2

Part Two:
The Components of
Windows Me

Chapter 6: Programs and Documents

Chapter 7: The Freebie Software

Chapter 8: Sound and Movies

Chapter 9: The Control Panel

Programs and Documents

When you get right down to it, an operating system like Windows is nothing more than a home base from which to launch *applications* (software programs). And you, as a Windows person, are particularly fortunate: More programs are available for Windows than for any other operating system on earth.

But when you launch a program, you're no longer necessarily in the world Microsoft designed for you. Each application from each software company may work a bit differently. And each must communicate with Windows itself using such onscreen conventions as the Save File dialog box.

This chapter covers everything you need to know about launching and managing programs, using them to generate documents (data files), and understanding how Windows and applications communicate.

Launching Programs

Windows Me lets you launch (open) programs in many different ways:

- Choose a program's name from the Start→Programs menu (page 40).

- Choose a program's name from the Quick Launch toolbar (page 79).

- Double-click an application's program-file icon in the My Computer→C: drive→Program Files→application folder, or highlight its icon and then press Enter.

- Press a key combination you've assigned to the program's shortcut (page 103).

- Choose Start→Run, then type the program file's name (page 48), and then press Enter.

- Type the program file's name into the Address bar of any folder window (page 70), and then press Enter.

- Open a document. You can do so in any of several ways, such as double-clicking its icon, typing its name in the Run or Address toolbar, or choosing its name from the Start→Documents command (if it's one you had opened recently). The program required for that document opens automatically. (For example, if you used Microsoft Word to write a file called Last Will and Testament.doc, choosing its name from the Start→Documents menu launches Word and opens that file.)

- Let Windows launch the program for you, at a time you've specified. For details on the Task Scheduler, see page 332.

When you launch a program, the PC reads its computer code, which lies on your hard disk's surface, and feeds it quickly into RAM (memory).

What happens next depends on the program you're using. Most present you with a new, blank, untitled document. Some welcome you instead with a question: Do you want to open an existing document or create a new one? And a few oddball programs, such as Photoshop, don't open *any* window when first launched. The appearance of tool palettes is your only evidence that you've even opened a program.

UP TO SPEED

"Multiple Document Interface" Programs

The world of Windows programs is divided into two camps. First, there are *single-document interface* programs, where the entire program runs in a single window. If you close that window, you also exit the application. Write, Notepad, Internet Explorer, and Palm Desktop work this way.

Then there are *multiple-document interface* (MDI) programs, where the application itself is a mother ship, a shell, that can contain lots of different document windows. Word 97, Excel, and Outlook Express work like this. As shown here, you may see two sets of upper-right window controls, one just beneath the other. The top one belongs to the *application*. The one below it belongs to the *document*. If you close a document window, you don't also quit the program.

To help you navigate your various open windows, MDI

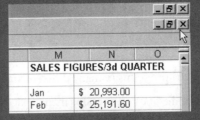

programs usually offer commands that arrange all open windows to fit neatly on the screen, each occupying an even fraction of the screen space. (These commands work much like the Tile and Cascade commands in desktop windows.) In Word 97, for example, the Windows menu offers a command called Arrange All that serves this purpose.

Getting to know which way a program deals with windows is important for a couple of reasons. First, it explains why the Taskbar sometimes shows only one button for an entire *program* (such as Word 97), but sometimes shows a button for each open *window* in a program (such as Word 2000). Second, it explains why closing a window sometimes exits the application (because it was an SDI program), and sometimes doesn't (because it's an MDI program).

Switching Programs

In these days of 64- or 128-megabyte RAM installations, it's the rare PC user who doesn't regularly run several programs *simultaneously.*

When you run applications simultaneously, however, the road gets bumpy. You may have a screen-management problem, because each program occupies its own windows, covering up your desktop and sometimes making it difficult to know what program you're in at that moment. You may also sometimes have a stability problem. Operating systems like Windows Me maintain a single bubble of memory for all open programs—if one of them crashes or freezes, it can wipe out the entire bubble, usually forcing you to restart the machine.

The key to juggling open programs is the Taskbar. It lists all open programs. As you can read at the end of Chapter 2, the Taskbar also offers controls for arranging all the windows on your screen, closing them via shortcut menu, and so on.

Only one window—the one whose Taskbar button looks "pushed in" and lighter than the others—can be in front, or *active,* at a time, as shown in Figure 6-1. To bring a different program to the front, you can use any of four tricks:

- **The relaunch technique.** Repeat whatever technique you used to launch the program to begin with: Choose its name from the Start→Programs menu, double-click its icon, press its keystroke, and so on.

- **Click the window.** You can also switch to another program by clicking whatever part of its window you can see peeking out from behind the frontmost window. Any window you click pops to the foreground.

- **Use the Taskbar.** Clicking a button on the Taskbar makes the corresponding program pop to the front, along with any of its floating toolbars, palettes, and so on.

- **Alt+Tab.** Finally, you can bring a different program to the front without using the mouse. If you press Alt+Tab, you summon a floating palette that displays the icons of all running programs, as shown in Figure 6-1. Each time you press Alt+Tab, you highlight the next icon; when you release the keys, the highlighted program jumps to the front, as though in a high-tech game of duck-duck-goose.

To move *backward* through the open programs, press *Shift*+Alt+Tab.

Figure 6-1:
The Taskbar reveals which programs are running and which is frontmost. Bottom: You can press Alt+Tab to highlight successive icons in the application list. When you release the Alt key, the highlighted program jumps to the front.

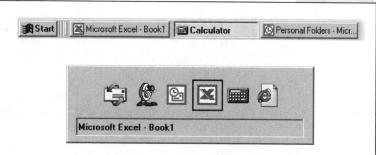

Exiting Programs

When you exit, or quit, an application, the memory it was using gets returned to the Windows pot for use by other programs and PC functions.

If you use a particular program several times a day, such as a word processor or calendar program, you'll save time in the long run by keeping it open all day long. (Remember that you can always minimize its window to get it out of the way when you're not using it.)

But if you're done using a program for the day, exit it, especially if it's a memory-hungry one such as, say, Photoshop. Do so using one of these techniques:

- Choose File→Exit.

- Press Alt+F, then X.

- Click the program window's Close box, or double-click its Control-menu icon (at the upper-left corner of the window).

- Right-click the program's Taskbar button and choose Close from the shortcut menu.

If you haven't saved the changes you've made to your document, you'll be offered the chance to do so before the program shuts down all the way.

Finally, the program's windows, menus, and toolbars disappear; you fall "down a layer" into whatever window was behind it.

Saving Documents

In a few programs, such as the Calculator or Solitaire, you spend your time working (or playing) in the lone application window. But when you close the window, no trace of your work remains.

Most programs, however, are designed to create *documents*—data files, represented on your hard drive as individual icons, which you can re-open for further editing, send to other people, back up on another disk, and so on. These programs, when first launched, present you with a new, blank, empty document: a word processor screen, spreadsheet, slide-show template, piece of sheet music, piece of electronic canvas, and so on. Now you set to work typing, painting, composing, designing, or whatever you do.

But until you use the File→Save command, any work you've done remains only in memory, kept alive by a tenuous strand of electricity. If the power goes out—or a system crash takes it out for you—before you've saved your work, it's gone forever.

That's why these programs offer File→Save and File→Open commands, which let you preserve the work you've done and return to it later.

The Save File dialog box

When you choose File→Save for the first time, the computer shows you the dialog box shown in Figure 6-2, in which you're supposed to type a name, choose a folder location, and specify the file format for the file you're saving.

This dialog box lets you access any folder on your PC. It's a miniature version of the desktop described in Chapter 2. Using the controls in this dialog box, you can specify exactly where you want to file your newly created document.

Tip: For reference, Windows Me shows you the names of both folders and your *documents* in this list (documents that match the kind you're about to save, that is). It's easy to understand why folders appear here: so that you can double-click one if you want to save your document inside it. But why do documents appear here? After all, you can't save a document into another document.

Documents are listed here so that you can perform one fairly obscure stunt: If you click a document's name, Windows Me copies its name into the "File name:" box at the bottom of the window. That's a useful shortcut if you want to *replace* an existing document with the new one you're saving. By saving a new file with the same name as the existing one, you force Windows Me to overwrite it (after asking your permission, of course).

You can also use this trick to save yourself typing when saving a document that you want to have a different version number, to keep it separate from earlier drafts. For example, if you click the Thesis Draft 3.1 document in the list, Windows copies that name into the "File name:" box; to save your new document as *Thesis Draft 3.2,* you have to change only one character (change the 2 to a 3) before clicking Save.

Saving into the My Documents Folder

If you prefer simplicity to complexity, you're in luck; the My Documents feature of Windows Me lets you avoid confronting the teeming swarms of features presented by the Save File box. Every time you use the File→Save command, in almost every program, Windows proposes this folder as the new home of whatever document you've just created (Figure 6-2). You're free to navigate to some other folder location, as described in the next section. But the My Documents folder will suggest itself as the new-document receptacle every time.

What's the benefit? First, using the My Documents folder ensures that your file won't fall accidentally into some deeply nested folder where you'll never see it again (a common occurrence among first-time computer users). Instead, the newly minted document will be waiting for you in the My Documents folder, whose icon has been sitting on your desktop since the first time Windows Me started up.

Second, it's now very easy to make a backup copy of your important documents, because they're all in a single folder, which you can drag onto a backup disk in one swift move.

Finally, whenever you use the File→Open command from within any program, Windows once again shows you the contents of the My Documents folder. All of your documents are now staring you in the face; you don't have to navigate through hard drive folders to locate the one you want. Not only does the My Documents folder save you time when creating a new file, but also when retrieving it.

Tip: If the contents of the My Documents folder becomes cluttered, feel free to make subfolders inside it to hold your various projects. In fact, some programs let you specify a different folder as the *default* (proposed) one. This feature gives you the freedom to create a different default folder in My Documents for each program.

Navigating in the Save File Dialog Box

If the My Documents method doesn't strike your fancy, you can use the Save dialog box's various controls to navigate your way into any folder on your PC. (You may have to learn this navigational scheme even if you *do* use the My Documents folder, such as when you've created project or topic folders *inside* the My Documents folder, for example.)

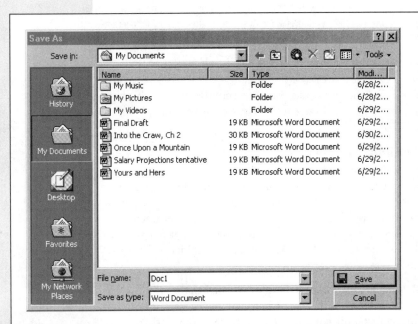

Figure 6-2:
The buttons at the left side of the Save As dialog box give you quick access to the folders where you're most likely to want to stash newly created documents: the My Documents folder, the desktop itself, the Favorites folder, and so on. But using the "Save in:" drop-down menu at the top of the screen, you can choose any folder you like.

What makes the Save dialog box confusing is that, unlike folder windows on the desktop, this listing shows the contents of only one folder at a time. As you survey the list of folders and files shown in Figure 6-2, for example, you can't tell at a glance where you are in your ladder of nested disks and folders.

The solution is the "Save in:" drop-down menu at the top of the dialog box. It lists, and lets you jump to, any disk or desktop folder on your PC—or to the My Computer level, if that's a more familiar landscape. To save a new document onto, say, a Zip disk or floppy, you'd choose the disk's drive letter from this drop-down list before clicking Save. To save it into a *folder* within a disk, simply double-click successive nested folders until you reach the one you want.

Tip: If you choose a removable-disk drive (such as floppy or Zip) from this menu, Windows won't let you save a document there unless a disk is actually in the drive.

Use the toolbar icons shown in Figure 6-3 to help you navigate:

- **Back button.** Click to move back to the last folder you browsed.

Tip: If you point to this button without clicking, a tooltip identifies the previous folder by name.

- **Up One Level.** Click to move up one level in your folder hierarchy (from seeing the My Documents contents to the hard drive's contents, for example).

- **Search the Web.** Closes the Save As dialog box, opens your browser, connects to the Internet, and prepares to search the Internet. (Next assignment: To figure out *why* you'd want to search the Web at the moment of saving your document.)

- **Delete.** If you click a file or folder name in the list before you, this button becomes active. Click it to fling the highlighted icon into the Recycle Bin.

- **New Folder.** Click to create a new folder in the current list of files and folders. You'll be asked to name it.

- **Views.** Click to change the way file listings look in this dialog box. Each time you click the icon, you get a different view: **List, Details, Properties, Preview, Thumbnail,** and so on (see Figure 6-4). These views vary by application, but in general, they closely correspond to the View menu options described on page 63. (You can also use the drop-down menu to choose one of these views by name, rather than clicking the icon repeatedly.)

Figure 6-3:
The toolbar icons (top) in the Save As dialog box (bottom) help you navigate your PC from within this window. Note to keyboard nuts: You can shift the focus from one of these buttons (circled) to the next by pressing the left and right arrow keys; when the one you want is highlighted, press the Enter key.

Back   Search the Web   New Folder

Up One Level   Delete   Views

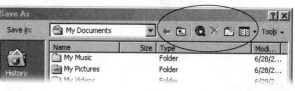

• **Tools.** This drop-down menu appears only in the Save boxes of enlightened programs, like those in the Microsoft Office suite. It offers some very useful commands, including **Delete** and **Rename**, that let you manage your files right from within this dialog box. **Add to Favorites** creates a shortcut of the highlighted disk, server, folder, or file in your Favorites folder, so that you don't have to go burrowing through your folders every time you want access; you can click the Favorites folder icon shown in Figure 6-2 to see everything you've stashed there. The **Properties** command lets you see an icon's description and stats.

Map Network Drive lets you assign a drive letter (such as *G:*) to a folder that's on another PC of your network. Having that folder show up on your screen as just another disk makes it much easier to find, open, and manage. (See Chapter 17 for more on sharing networked folders.)

Navigating the List by Keyboard

When the Save dialog box first appears, the "File name:" box is generally highlighted, so that you can type a name for the newly created document. At first glance, then, you might suppose that the Save dialog box isn't set up to be controlled without the mouse; after all, if typing types the file's name, how can it control the list of folders?

But as noted earlier in this chapter, a Windows dialog box is elaborately rigged for keyboard control. In addition to the standard Tab/Space bar controls described earlier, a few special keys work only within the list of files and folders:

Figure 6-4:
Left: The Preview mode is most useful for looking at folders full of graphics.

Right: The Properties view shows you statistics about the file that's currently highlighted in the list. Not all programs offer all of these views.

- Press letter keys to highlight the corresponding file and folder icons. To highlight the Program Files folder, for example, you could type *PR*. (If you type too slowly, your key presses will be interpreted as separate initiatives—highlighting first the People folder and then the Rodents folder, for example.)

- Press the Page Up or Page Down keys to scroll the list up or down. Press Home or End to highlight the top or bottom item of the list.

- Press the arrow keys (up or down) to highlight successive icons in the list.

- When a folder is highlighted, you can open it by pressing the Enter key (the equivalent of clicking the Open button).

- After opening a folder, you can back out of it by pressing Backspace. Doing so takes you one step closer to the desktop level. For example, if you're viewing the contents of your My Documents folder, Delete shows you the list of folders in the hard drive window.

UP TO SPEED

Dialog Box Basics

To the joy of the powerful Computer Keyboard lobby, you can manipulate almost every element of a Windows Me dialog box by pressing keys on the keyboard. If you're among those who feel that using the mouse takes longer to do something, you're in luck.

The rule for navigating a dialog box is simple: Press Tab to jump from one set of options to another, or Shift+Tab to move backward. (If the dialog box has multiple *tabs,* like the one shown here, press Ctrl+Tab to "click" the next tab, or Ctrl+*Shift*+Tab to "click" the previous one.)

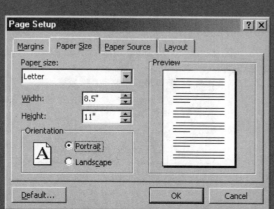

Each time you press Tab, you shift the PC's *focus* to a different control or set of controls. Windows shows you what element has the focus using text highlighting (if it's a text box or drop-down menu) or a dotted-line outline (if it's a button). In the illustration shown here, the Portrait button has the focus.

Once you've highlighted a button or checkbox, you can press the Space bar or Enter key to "click" it. If you've highlighted a drop-down menu or set of mutually exclusive *radio buttons* (like the Orientation buttons shown here), press the up or down arrow key.

Finally, remember that you can jump to a particular control or area of the dialog box by pressing Alt along with the underlined letter.

The File Format Pop-up Menu

Although it's by no means universal, the Save dialog box in many programs offers a pop-up menu of file formats below the "File name:" blank. Use this pop-up menu when you want to prepare a document for use by somebody else, somebody whose computer doesn't have the same software.

For example, if you've typed something in Microsoft Word, you use this drop-down menu to generate a Web-page document or a Rich Text Format document that can be opened by almost any standard word processor or page-layout program, on Windows or Macintosh. If you've used Photoshop to prepare a photograph for use on the Web, this pop-up menu is where you specify JPEG format (the standard Web format for photos), and so on.

Closing Documents

You close a document window just as you'd close any window as described in Chapter 3: by clicking the close box (marked by an X) in the upper-right corner of the window, by double-clicking the Control-menu icon just to the left of the File menu, or by pressing Alt+F4. If you've done some work in that document since the last time you used the Save command, Windows offers you a variation on the dialog box shown in Figure 6-5.

As described on page 117, sometimes closing the window also exits the application, and sometimes the application remains running, even with no document windows open. And in a few *really* bizarre cases, it's possible to exit an application (such as Outlook Express) while a document window (an email message) remains open on the screen, lingering and abandoned!

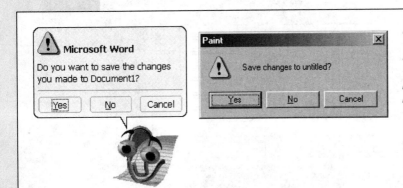

Figure 6-5:
When you close a file, you may be offered a box like one of these. Click Yes (or press Enter) if you want to preserve your work. Click No to abandon all of the changes you've made since the last time you used the Save command. Click Cancel if you don't want to close the window after all.

The Open File Dialog Box

When you want to re-open a document you've already saved and named, you can pursue an avenue like one of these:

• Open your My Documents folder (or whatever folder contains the saved file).

Double-click the file's icon.

- If the document was one you've had open recently, choose its name from the Start→Documents menu.

- If you're already in the program that created the document, check the File menu. Many programs add a list of recently opened files to the File menu, so that you can choose one's name to re-open it.

- Choose File→Open.

- Type the document's path and name into the Start→Run box or into a folder window's Address toolbar.

The dialog box that appears when you choose File→Open looks almost identical to the Save File dialog box (see Figure 6-3). The big change: The navigational drop-down menu at the top of the window now says "Look in:" instead of "Save in:".

Once again, you start out perusing the contents of your My Documents folder. Again, you may find that beginning your navigation by choosing Look In→My Computer gives you a useful overview of your PC when you're beginning to search for a par-ticular file. Here, too, you can open a folder or disk by double-clicking its name in the list, or navigate the list by pressing the keystrokes described in the previous sec-tion. And once again, you can use the pop-up menu above the list to back *out* of a folder that you've opened.

When you've finally located the file you want to open, do so by double-clicking it or by highlighting it (which you can do from the keyboard) and then pressing Enter.

In general, most people don't encounter the Open File dialog box nearly as often as they do the Save File dialog box. That's because Windows offers many more conve-nient ways to *open* a file (double-clicking its icon, choosing its name from the Start→Documents command, and so on), but only a single way to *save* a new file.

UP TO SPEED

Playing Favorites

Most people think of Favorites as Internet Explorer's ver-sion of "bookmarks"—a list of Web sites that you've desig-nated as worth returning to. But Windows Me lets you des-ignate *anything* as a favorite: a folder you open often, a document you consult every day, a program, and so on.

You can designate a certain icon as a Favorite in any of several ways. For example, in the Save File or Open File dialog box, you can use the Add to Favorites command

described on page 122; in a desktop window, you can high-light an icon and then choose Favorites→Add to Favor-ites.

Later, when you want to open a Favorite, you can do so using an equally generous assortment of methods: Choose from the Start→Favorites menu, choose File→Open (from within a program) and click the Favorites folder, use the Favorites toolbar, and so on.

Moving Data Between Documents

You can't paste a picture into your Web browser, and you can't paste MIDI music information into your word processor. But you can put graphics into your word processor, paste movies into your database, insert text into Photoshop, and combine a surprising variety of seemingly dissimilar kinds of data. And you can transfer text from Web pages, email messages, and word processing documents to other email and word processing files; in fact, that's one of the most frequently performed tasks in all of computing.

Cut, Copy, and Paste

Most experienced PC users have learned to trigger the Cut, Copy, and Paste commands from the keyboard, quickly and without even thinking. Here's how the process works in slow motion:

1. **Highlight some material in the document before you (see Figure 6-6).**

   In most cases, this means highlighting some text (by dragging through it) in a word processor, layout program, email application, or even a Web page in your browser. You can also highlight graphics, music, movie, database, and spreadsheet information, depending on the program you're using.

2. **Use the Cut or Copy command.**

   You can trigger these commands in any of three ways. First, you can choose the Cut and Copy commands found in the Edit menu of your document window. Second, you can press the keyboard shortcuts Ctrl+X (for Cut—think of the X as representing a pair of scissors) or Ctrl+C (for Copy). Finally, you can right-click the highlighted material and choose Cut or Copy from the shortcut menu.

   When you do so, the PC memorizes the highlighted material, socking it away on an invisible storage pad called the Clipboard. If you chose Copy, nothing visible happens. If you chose Cut, the material disappears from the original document.

FREQUENTLY ASKED QUESTION

Invasion of the Temp-File People

Help! My desktop windows are overrun with little files called things like WordTemp 349293498. What are they?

Both Windows and your various programs create these *temp* (temporary) files. Word, for example, creates temporary files in case you decide to go on a spree of choosing Edit→Undo; the temp files help the program remember what your document *used* to be like.

When you exit the application, it's supposed to delete all of these .tmp files automatically so that you never have to

look at them; but if your system crashes or freezes, the temp files get left behind, orphaned.

Every now and then, you can recover some text that you hadn't yet saved; just double-click one of these .tmp files to see what's in it. Usually you find only gobbledygook, however, and there's nothing to be done except to throw it away.

Using Disk Cleanup, described in Chapter 15, is one quick way to get rid of them en masse.

At this point, most people take it on faith that the Cut or Copy command actually worked; but if you're in doubt, choose Start→Programs→Accessories→ System Tools→Clipboard Viewer. The Clipboard window appears, showing whatever you've copied. (If you don't find Clipboard Viewer, see page 387-388.)

3. **Click the cursor to indicate where you want the material to reappear.**

This may entail switching to a different program, a different document in the same program, or simply a different place in the same document. (Using the Cut and Paste commands within a single document may be these commands' most popular function; it lets you rearrange sentences or paragraphs in your word processor.)

4. **Choose the Paste command.**

Here again, you can do so either from a menu (choose Edit→Paste), by right-clicking and choosing Paste from the shortcut menu, or from the keyboard (press Ctrl+V). The copy of the material you had originally highlighted now appears at your cursor—that is, if you're pasting into a program that can accept that kind of information. (You won't have much luck pasting, say, a paragraph of text into Quicken.)

The most recently cut or copied material remains on your Clipboard even after you paste, making it possible to paste the same blob repeatedly. Such a trick can be useful when, for example, you've designed a business card in your drawing program and want to duplicate it enough times to fill a letter-sized printout. On the other hand, whenever you next copy or cut something, whatever was already on the Clipboard is lost forever.

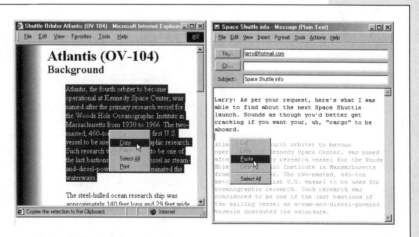

Figure 6-6:
Suppose you want to email some text you find on a Web page to a friend. Left: Start by dragging through it and then choosing Copy from the shortcut menu (or choosing Edit→ Copy). Now switch to your email program, and paste it into an outgoing message (right).

Drag-and-Drop

As useful and popular as it is, the Copy/Paste routine doesn't win any awards for speed; after all, it requires four steps. In many cases, you can replace that routine with the far more direct (and enjoyable) drag-and-drop method. As shown in Figure 6-7, you click in the middle of some highlighted text and drag; when you release the mouse button, the text jumps into the position of the insertion-point cursor.

Tip: To drag highlighted material to a spot that's off the screen, drag the cursor until it approaches the top or bottom edge of the window. The document will scroll automatically; as you approach the destination, jerk the mouse away from the edge of the window to stop the scrolling.

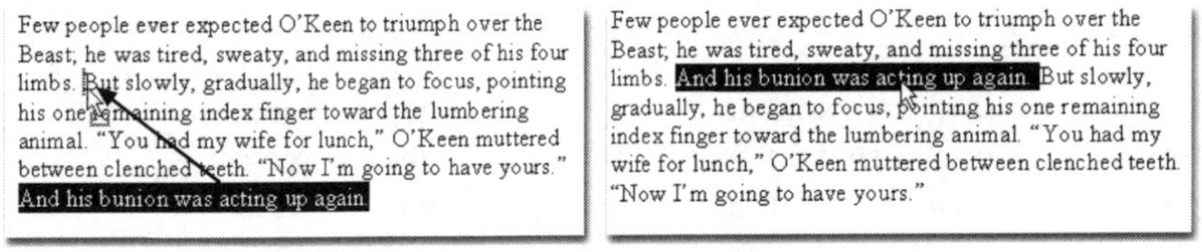

Few people ever expected O'Keen to triumph over the Beast; he was tired, sweaty, and missing three of his four limbs. But slowly, gradually, he began to focus, pointing his one remaining index finger toward the lumbering animal. "You had my wife for lunch," O'Keen muttered between clenched teeth. "Now I'm going to have yours." And his bunion was acting up again.

Few people ever expected O'Keen to triumph over the Beast; he was tired, sweaty, and missing three of his four limbs. And his bunion was acting up again. But slowly, gradually, he began to focus, pointing his one remaining index finger toward the lumbering animal. "You had my wife for lunch," O'Keen muttered between clenched teeth. "Now I'm going to have yours."

Figure 6-7:
You can drag highlighted material (left) into a new spot (right).

Several of the built-in Windows Me programs work with the drag-and-drop technique, including WordPad, America Online, and Outlook Express. Most popular commercial programs offer the drag-and-drop feature, too, including email programs and word processors, Microsoft Office programs, and so on.

As shown in Figure 6-7, drag-and-drop is ideal for transferring material between windows or between programs. It's especially useful when you've already copied something valuable to your Clipboard, because drag-and-drop doesn't involve (and doesn't erase) the Clipboard.

Its most popular use, however, is rearranging the text in a single document. In, say, Word or WordPad, you can rearrange entire sections, paragraphs, sentences, or even individual letters, just by dragging them—a terrific editing technique.

Tip: When you use drag-and-drop to move text within a document, you *move* the highlighted text, deleting the highlighted material from its original location. If you press Ctrl as you drag, however, you make a *copy* of the highlighted text.

Using drag-and-drop to the desktop

As shown in Figure 6-8, you can even drag text or graphics out of your document windows and directly onto the desktop. There your dragged material becomes an icon—a *Scrap file*.

When you drag a clipping from your desktop *back* into an application window, the material in that clipping reappears. Drag-and-drop, in other words, is a convenient and powerful feature; it lets you treat your desktop itself as a giant, computer-wide pasteboard, an area where you can temporarily stash pieces of text or graphics as you work.

Tip: You can drag a Scrap file onto a document's Taskbar button, too. Don't release the mouse button yet. In a moment, the corresponding document window appears, so that you can continue your dragging operation until the cursor points to where you want the Scrap file to appear. Now release the mouse; the Scrap material appears in the document.

In Microsoft Office applications, this works with entire document icons, too. You can drag one Word file into another's window to insert its contents there.

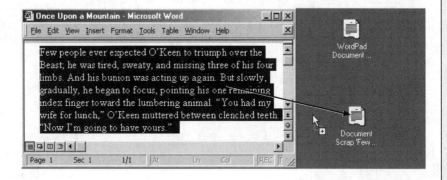

Figure 6-8:
When you drag material out of the document window and onto the desktop, you get a Scrap file. You can view a Scrap file just by double-clicking its icon.

Insert Object (OLE)

Here's yet another relative of the Copy and Paste duo: the Insert Object command, which is available in most Windows programs. (You may hear it referred to as Object Linking and Embedding technology, or OLE, or even "oh-LAY.")

Using this feature, you can actually borrow the menus and toolbars from one program, such as Paint or Excel, for use in another one, such as Word or WordPad. OLE is designed to give each program many more features than it has on its own—by sharing features with other programs.

As the name implies, you can either *link* another kind of document or *embed* it:

- **Linking** means that you're grabbing a certain kind of document (such as a painting you've made in Paint) and inserting it into another kind (such as a word processor document). In this scenario, your transferred material is "live": When you edit the original source material, any copies of it update themselves to reflect the changes. You might link your letterhead, for example, so that when you update it, all of your invoices and memo documents change automatically.

  The good news is that a linked file (the graphic) isn't actually *in* your document (the memo), so the memo document doesn't get huge. The bad news is that if you move or distribute your memo file, the graphic won't go along for the ride.

- **Embedding** puts the inserted file (such as the graphic) directly into the document (the memo). The memo document therefore becomes much larger, and changes you make to the "source" document aren't reflected in the embedded copies. But at least you can email it to somebody without losing the embedded letterhead.

Tip: Object Linking and Embedding has a reputation for behaving oddly from time to time. It works best on computers that have a lot of memory.

When Formatting Is Lost

How come pasted text doesn't always look the same as what I copied?

When you copy text from, for example, Word, and then paste it into another program, such as the Notepad, you may be alarmed to note that the formatting of that text (bold, italic, the choice of font, size, and color, and so on) doesn't reappear intact.

There are several reasons for this problem.

For example, not every program *offers* text formatting; Notepad, for example, doesn't. And the Copy command in some programs (such as Web browsers) doesn't pick up the formatting along with the text; when you paste something you've copied from Internet Explorer and paste it into Word or WordPad, you get plain, unformatted text.

Finally, a note on *text wrapping:* Thanks to limitations built into the architecture of the Internet, email messages aren't like word processor documents. The text doesn't flow continuously from one line of a paragraph to the next, such that it re-flows when you adjust the window size. Instead, email programs insert a press of the Enter key at the end of each line *within* a paragraph.

Most of the time, you don't even notice that your messages consist of dozens of one-line "paragraphs"; when you see them in the email program, you can't tell the difference. But if you paste an email message into a word processor, the difference becomes painfully apparent—especially if you then attempt to adjust the margins, as shown here.

To fix the text, you have to delete the invisible carriage return at the end of each line. Veteran PC users sometimes use the word processor's search-and-replace function for this purpose.

> With the addition of mission STS-106 to the International Space Station
> Assembly sequence, the assignments originally planned for STS-101 were
> split between the two missions. While at the International Space Station,
> the STS-106 astronauts will conduct at least one space walk to perform
> tasks linked to the presence of the service module. Also, they will
> transfer various supplies to outfit the station in preparation for the
> first resident crew, which is scheduled to launch Oct. 30.

Creating an OLE insertion

If the idea of self-updating inserted material intrigues you, here's an example of how it works:

1. **Create a document in a program that offers OLE features.**

   Some programs that do: Excel, Word, WordPad, PowerPoint, Paint.

2. **Click to indicate where you want the inserted object to appear. Choose Insert→Object.**

   The command may be in a different place, but that's the wording in Microsoft Office programs. Now an Object dialog box appears, as shown in Figure 6-9.

It offers two tabs: Create New, which lets you create a *new* graph, picture, spreadsheet, or other element; and Create from File, which lets you import a document you've *already* created (using, for example, Excel, Paint, Graph, or Imaging).

3. **To create new data, click Create New, choose the kind of data you want to create and click OK.**

You return to your document, where a special rectangle appears (see Figure 6-10). The menus and toolbars may change, too, also as shown in Figure 6-10.

4. **To insert an existing file into the middle of this one, click the Create from File tab. Click Browse, locate the existing document you want, click "Link to file" if appropriate, and click OK.**

As noted in Figure 6-9, this method depends on your already having a picture, spreadsheet, or other document that you want to insert. The "Link to file" option is especially important; it determines whether the inserted material will be *embedded* or (if you turn on the checkbox) *linked*.

If you turn on "Link to file," now the fun begins: you can make changes in the inserted document file and watch the revision appear automatically in any documents in which it's been linked.

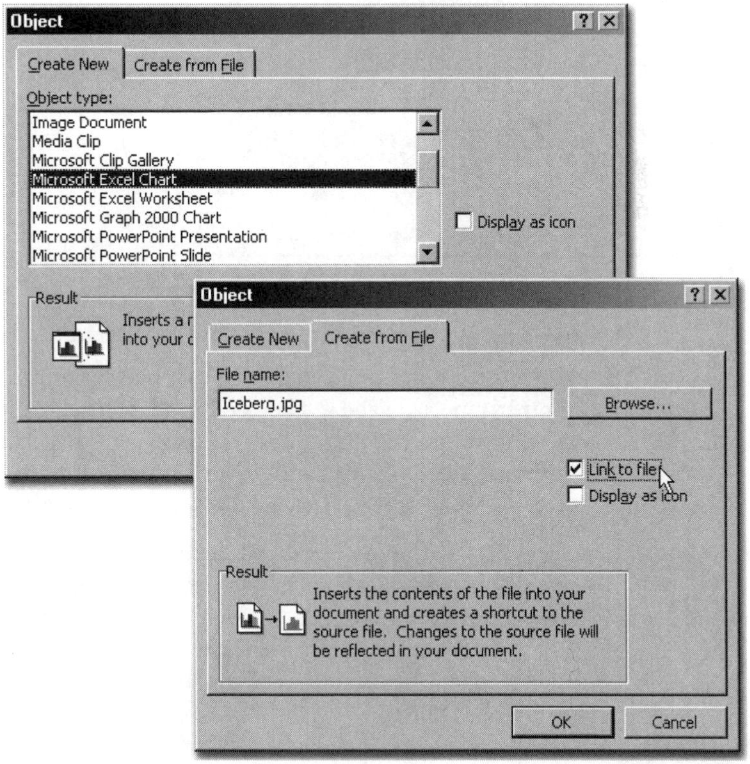

Figure 6-9:
Top: You can insert many different kinds of "objects" into a Microsoft Word or WordPad document: a Paint file ("Bitmap Image"), Image Document (something you've scanned), an Excel chart or spreadsheet ("Worksheet"), a sound or video clip, and so on.

Bottom: You may prefer to slap an entire existing document file into the middle of the one you're now editing. Do that using the Create from File tab. Remember to turn on "Link to file" if you want the data to update automatically when the source file is edited separately.

5. **When you're finished touching up the inserted data, click anywhere outside the box to make the handles and border disappear.**

You've successfully embedded or linked new information. When you want to edit it, just double-click it; the menus and palettes you need to modify this info reappear. (If you linked to a separate document, double-clicking the embedded object actually opens that other document.)

Figure 6-10:
If you insert an OLE object into Word or WordPad, you get eight tiny black handles around the embedded object; they let you reshape the box. For example, you can use the painting tools to create a graphic, right here in the word processor that otherwise has no such painting features. In the future, whenever you want to touch up this image, just double-click the embedded image to summon these menus and palettes again.

Export/Import

When it comes to transferring large chunks of information from one program to another, especially address books, spreadsheet cells, and database records, none of the data-transfer methods described so far in this chapter do the trick. For these purposes, use the Export and Import commands found in the File menu of almost every database, spreadsheet, email, and address-book program.

These Export/Import commands aren't part of Windows, so the manuals or help screens of the applications in question should be your source for instructions. For now, however, the power and convenience of this feature are worth noting; it means that your four years' worth of collected names and addresses in, say, an old address-book program can find its way into a newer program, such as Palm Desktop, in a matter of minutes.

Filename Extensions

Every operating system, including Windows, needs a mechanism to associate documents with the applications that created them. When you double-click a Microsoft Word document icon, for example, Word launches and opens the document.

In Windows, every document bears a filename suffix, a *filename extension:* a period followed by a suffix that's usually three letters long. Every time you install a new program, the installer lets Windows know about the file types (the filename extensions) the new application is capable of opening.

Here are some common examples:

When you double-click this icon...	this program opens it
Fishing trip**.doc**	Microsoft Word
Quarterly results**.xls**	Microsoft Excel
Home Page**.htm**	Internet Explorer
Agenda**.wpd**	Corel WordPerfect
A Home Movie**.avi**	Windows Media Player
Animation**.dir**	Macromedia Director

Tip: For an exhaustive list of every file extension on the planet, visit *www.whatis.com*; click the link for Every File Format in the World.

Figure 6-11:
Every software program you install must register the file types it uses. The link between the file type and the program is called an association. This dialog box displays the icon for each file type, and an explanation of the selected listing.

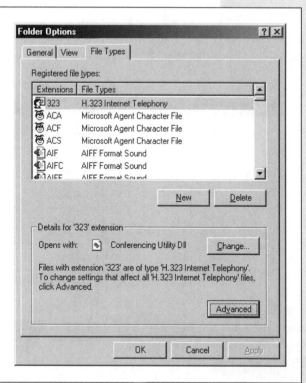

Behind the scenes, Windows maintains a massive table that lists every extension and the program that "owns" it. To see this list, choose Tools→Folder Options from the menu bar of any folder window. As shown in Figure 6-11, the Folder Options box appears; click the File Types tab.

Making File Extensions Show Up

It's possible to live a long and happy life without knowing much about these filename extensions; indeed, because they don't feel very user-friendly, Microsoft designed Windows to *hide* the suffixes on most icons. (See Figure 6-12.) If you're new to Windows, and haven't poked around inside the folders on your hard drive much, you may never even have seen them.

Note: Hiding file extensions also makes it harder for you to change one accidentally, which would confuse Windows and maybe even prevent you from opening open the icon to see what's in it.

Some people appreciate the way Windows hides the extensions, because the screen becomes less cluttered and less technical-looking. Others make a good argument for the Windows 3.1 days, however, when every icon appeared with its suffix.

For example, suppose a folder contains several icons with the same primary name; only the suffixes are different. You might have a program called PieThrower, whose folder contains three icons: a configuration file called PieThrower.ini, an Internet-based software updater called PieThrower.upd, and the actual PieThrower program, which is called PieThrower.exe. In this situation, Windows Me would show you three icons, all just called PieThrower. Sometimes the icons themselves provide a clue as to which is which, but usually you can't tell the players without the scorecard.

Figure 6-12:
Windows lets you see the filename extensions only when it doesn't recognize them. If Windows recognizes the filename extension on an icon, it hides the extension (left).

Right: You can ask Windows to display all extensions, all the time.

One way to make sense of such situations is simply to look at the window in Details view (right-click in the window and choose View→Details from the shortcut menu). But that's too easy. To breathe in Windows technology to the fullest, consider making Windows show the file suffixes on *all* icons. To do so, choose Tools→Folder Options from any folder window's menu bar. In the Folder Options dialog box, click the View tab. Turn off "Hide file extensions for known file types," and then click OK.

Now you can see filename extensions for all icons.

Hooking up a file extension to a different program

Windows Me comes with several programs (Notepad and WordPad, for example) that can open text files (whose file extension is *.txt*). Windows also comes with several programs (Paint, Imaging, Internet Explorer) that can open JPEG picture files (whose file extension is *.jpg*). So how does it decide *which* program to open when you double-click a .txt or .jpg file?

Windows comes with its own extension-to-application pairing list, as shown in Figure 6-11. But at any time, you can re-assign a particular file type (filename extension) to a different application.

To do so, right-click the file's icon and choose Open With from the shortcut menu. Windows Me presents the Open With dialog box shown in Figure 6-13. Just find, and double-click, the name of the program you want to open this kind of file from now on.

As you do so, be sure to check the status of the checkbox below the list; it says, "Always use this program to open these files." If that checkbox is on, then *all* files of

Figure 6-13:
Scroll through the list of installed programs to select the one that can handle the file you're trying to open. If you turn on "Always use this program to open these files," Windows will, henceforth, open every similarly suffixed file with the application you're choosing.

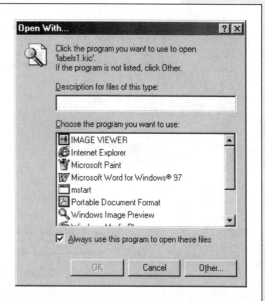

this type (.jpg, for example) will open in the newly selected application from now on. If the checkbox is off, then the new application will open only *this* .jpg file, only this once.

Tip: This right-click→Open With technique is a good cure when a new program you install performs a "power grab," claiming a particular file type for itself without asking you.

Creating your own file associations

Every now and then, the dialog box shown in Figure 6-13 appears unbidden. It comes up automatically whenever you try to open a file whose extension Windows doesn't recognize. Maybe you've tried to double-click a document created by an old DOS program that doesn't know about the Windows file-association feature, or maybe your company's programmers wrote a custom application that Windows doesn't yet know about.

In any case, there are two ways to teach Windows to use a particular application whenever you open similar documents in the future. First, you can open the Folder Options dialog box shown in Figure 6-11; the New button lets you associate the mystery document with an application of your choice.

Tip: It's sometimes useful to associate a particular document type with a program that *didn't* create it. For example, if you double-click a text file, and the Open With dialog box appears, you might decide that you want such documents to open automatically into WordPad. (It's fine to set up a single application to open documents of different types—text files, Word files, and RTF files, for example.)

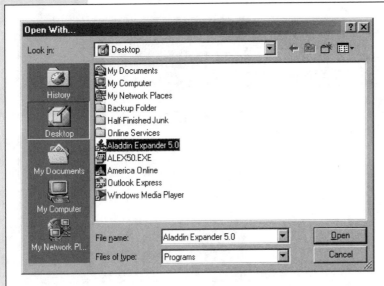

Figure 6-14:
Use this window (a cousin to the Open File dialog box described earlier in this chapter) to search your system and locate the application you want to associate with a specific file type. Double-click a folder to open it, or use the icons on the left side of the window to move instantly to a particular location. Here, a mysteriously compressed downloaded file is about to be opened by a decompression program called Aladdin Expander.

Second, you can use the Open With dialog box shown in Figure 6-13; this method is often simpler, because all you have to do to summon this dialog box is to double-click the mystery file.

If the program you want to take over the document-opening task doesn't show up in this list, click Other in the Open With dialog box. Windows Me opens the window shown in Figure 6-14. Double-click the name of the application you'll want to open this file type. Add a description of this file type, if you like.

Installing Software

Today, almost all new software comes to your PC from one of two sources: a CD or the Internet. The era of floppy-disk installers is over; you'd need a wheelbarrow to hold all the floppies required to install the average modern application.

In general, you can't use any of these programs without first *installing* them, using a special program provided by the software company. The installer program has been written expressly to take care of all the installation tasks. Besides the obvious chore of transferring the software files to your hard drive, the installer also adds the new program's name to the Start→Programs menu, tells Windows about the kinds of files (filename extensions) it can open, transfers certain required files to special locations on your drive, and makes certain changes to your *registry* (the behind-the-scenes Windows software-settings database).

Preparing for Software Installation

Before you begin the installation process for any software, take the following safeguards:

• Exit any open programs. (One quick way: Right-click the buttons on the Taskbar, one at a time, and choose Close from the shortcut menu.)

• Check the memory situation by right-clicking My Computer, choosing Properties, and clicking the Performance tab. If the System Resources are lower than 80%, restart the computer.

• Turn off your virus-scanning software, which may take the arrival of your new software the wrong way.

Installing Software from a CD

The CD you received from the software company is probably a self-starter; it offers the *AutoPlay* feature, which means that as soon as you put the CD into the CD-ROM drive, the installer launches.

Installing software with CD AutoPlay

If AutoPlay is working, a few seconds after you insert the CD into your drive, your cursor becomes an hourglass. A few seconds later, the welcome screen for your new software appears; its setup application has been launched automatically.

The installation process is usually a wizard, so you'll be asked to answer questions, choose options, and click Next at each window. Along the way, you may be asked to type in a serial number, which is usually printed on a sticker on the back of the plastic CD case, the paper CD envelope, or the registration card.

If the last installer window has a Finish button, click it. The installation program transfers the software files to your hard drive, and the program's name appears on your Start→Programs menu.

Installing software without AutoPlay

If the installation routine doesn't begin automatically when you insert the CD, then you'll have to take matters into your own hands. One of two factors is at play:

- **There's no AutoPlay file.** If the CD wasn't designed to launch an installer automatically when it's inserted, then you'll have to follow the instructions that came with the software.

- **You've got AutoPlay turned off.** If the instructions imply that the CD *should* have AutoPlay, you can manually launch the installation program. Open My Computer and double-click the icon for your CD-ROM drive. In the CD-ROM drive window, look for an icon called Setup.exe or Autorun.inf. Double-click the former; right-click the latter and choose Install from the shortcut menu.

  If you find both files, it doesn't matter which method you use. The installation now gets under way.

Installing CD-based games

Most computer games get their zip from sound effects, elaborate animation, big colorful graphics, and other bells and whistles. The files that produce all those special effects are enormous; even a few games can quickly fill your hard drive. Some manufacturers of large, complex games have established a clever method for avoiding the need for games to be hard-drive hogs: They don't transfer *all* those files to your drive.

Instead, these installers transfer only the game files needed to launch the software to your hard drive. Then, when you run the game, those startup files retrieve the fancy stuff from the CD-ROM itself, which must be actually in the CD drive when you're playing the game.

FREQUENTLY ASKED QUESTION

Microsoft InstallShield?

I'm a bit confused. I bought a program from Infinity Workware. But when I run its installer, the welcome screen says InstallShield. Who actually made my software?

Most of the time, the installer program isn't part of the software you bought or downloaded, and doesn't even

come from the same company. Most software companies pay a license to installer-software companies. That's why, when you're trying to install a new program called, say, JailhouseDoctor, the first screen you see says InstallShield. (InstallShield is the most popular installation software.)

If you're offered a choice between installing the entire game to your hard drive or playing the game from your CD-ROM, choose the latter option. Even if you have an enormous hard drive, it will quickly run out of space if you're a heavy gamer.

Installing Downloaded Software

The files you download from the Internet usually aren't ready-to-use, double-click-able applications. Instead, almost all of them arrive on your PC in the form of a *compressed* file, all the software pieces crammed together into a single, easily down-loaded icon. The first step in savoring your downloaded delights is restoring this compressed file to its natural state, using a utility like WinZip *(www.winzip.com)*.

After you've unzipped the software, you'll usually find, among the resulting pieces, an installer, just like the ones described in the previous section.

Tip: Windows Me comes with its own version of WinZip called WinPop, but you must install it manually, as described on pages 387–388.

Installing Pre-loaded Software

As you probably know, Microsoft doesn't actually sell computers (yet). You bought your machine, therefore, from a different company, who may have installed Windows on it before you took delivery.

Many PC companies sweeten the pot by preinstalling other programs, such as Quicken, Microsoft Works, Microsoft Office, more games, educational software, and so on. The great thing about pre-loaded programs is that you don't have to install - them. Just double-click their desktop icons, or choose their names from the Start→Programs menu, and you're off and working.

POWER USERS' CLINIC

Disabling AutoPlay

Many people disable the AutoPlay feature because they don't like to have their work interrupted the moment they put a CD into the CD-ROM drive. If you sympathize with that view, you can disable the AutoPlay feature on your PC like this:

1. Right-click My Computer; choose Properties from the shortcut menu.

2. Click the Device Manager tab.

3. Click the + button to the left of the CD-ROM device listing.

4. Right-click the CD-ROM drive icon; choose Properties from the shortcut menu.

5. Click the Settings tab.

6. Click "Auto insert notification" to remove the checkmark.

7. Click OK twice.

From now on, your PC won't try to auto-launch the installer that arrives aboard CD-ROMs. In the meantime, you've had a glimpse of the Device Manager screen, where you can find out the name and model number of each of your system's dozens of mechanical components.

Uninstalling Software

When you've had enough of a certain program, and you want to reclaim the disk space it occupies, don't just delete its folder. The typical application installer strews software components all over your hard drive; only some of it is actually in the program's folder.

Therefore, use one of these two methods of ditching software you no longer need:

- Look for an Uninstall command in the program's Start→Programs submenu. If you find it, such a command launches a reverse installer, which cleans out most of the software's pieces from your system.

- If there's no Uninstall command, use the Add/Remove Programs function shown in Figure 6-15.

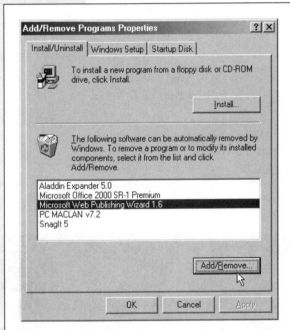

Figure 6-15:
To remove a program, choose Start→Settings→ Control Panel, and then open the Add/Remove Programs icon. Click the name of the program you want to vaporize and then click Add/Remove. If you click Yes in the confirmation box, the program is history.

Tip: Even after you uninstall a program, the folder that contained it usually still exists. In fact, the folder may still have some program files within it. It's safe to remove the folder, along with the files.

If the program you want to jettison isn't listed in the Add/Remove Programs dialog box, contact the manufacturer for removal instructions. If you get nowhere with that approach (a frequent occurrence), then just remove the folder and the software files it holds.

The Freebie Software

ven after a fresh installation of Windows Me, a glance at your Start→Programs menu reveals a rich array of applications that come preinstalled. As an infomercial might put it, they're your *free bonus gift*. This chapter offers a crash course in these programs, many of which could probably merit Missing Manuals of their own.

The Windows Me Accessories

Many of these built-in programs are what Microsoft calls *accessories*. They have two things in common. First, they're all smallish, single-purpose programs that you'll probably use from time to time, but not daily. Second, they're all listed in the Start→Programs→Accessories menu.

Note: Not all of these programs may appear in your Start→Programs menu. What you get depends on your selections during the installation process, as described in Appendix A. If you see something in this chapter that looks attractive but isn't in your Start menu, open the Start→Control Panels→Add/Remove Programs icon. Click Add/Remove, click the Windows Setup tab, and see if the missing component is listed there.

If not, you may have to click Have Disk, insert your Windows CD, click Browse, and select the software you want to install.

Accessibility Features

If you have trouble using your keyboard or making out small text on the screen, the programs in the Start→Programs→Accessories→Accessibility folder may be just what you need.

Accessibility Wizard

Windows Me is one of the most disability-friendly operating systems on Earth. It includes a long list of features that let you magnify the elements of the screen. The Accessibility wizard offers these features to you, one feature at the time, when you choose Start→Programs→Accessories→Accessibility→Accessibility Wizard.

Magnifier

Magnifier is a floating window that shows a horizontal slice of your screen displaying an enlarged version of whatever your cursor touches. Using its Settings control panel shown in Figure 7-1, you can specify how much magnification you get, which area of the screen gets magnified, and so on.

On-Screen Keyboard

If you're having trouble typing, keep the On-Screen Keyboard program in mind. It lets you type just by clicking the mouse (Figure 7-1), which you may find useful in a pinch.

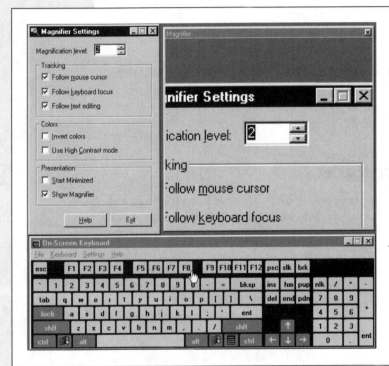

Figure 7-1:
Open Magnifier by choosing Start→Programs→ Accessories→Accessibility→ Magnifier. Don't forget that you can drag the large magnified window (top right) around to a more convenient spot on the screen, and even resize it by dragging the lower-right corner. Use the Magnifier Settings panel (top left) to choose more high-contrast colors, if you like. The On-Screen Keyboard (bottom), meanwhile, may be just the ticket if your keyboard's keys (or your hands) aren't fully functional.

Communications Folder

The Start→Programs→Accessories→Communications menu contains several shortcuts:

- **Dial-Up Networking.** A shortcut to the Dial-Up Networking window described in Chapter 10.

- **Home Networking Wizard.** Helps you set up the software for connecting PCs to each other. See Chapter 16 for details.

- **Internet Connection Wizard.** Helps you establish an Internet account, as described in Chapter 10.

- **MSN Messenger Service.** This wizard is your gateway to live Internet "chat" with your friends. It's described in Chapter 11.

- **NetMeeting.** Lets you collaborate with other people on the Internet or your local network by sending files, drawing on the shared "white board," chat, and so on. Also covered in Chapter 11.

- **Phone Dialer.** This little program is useful if you have your modem and your telephone plugged into the same phone jack. It lets the modem *dial* your phone, as shown in Figure 7-2.

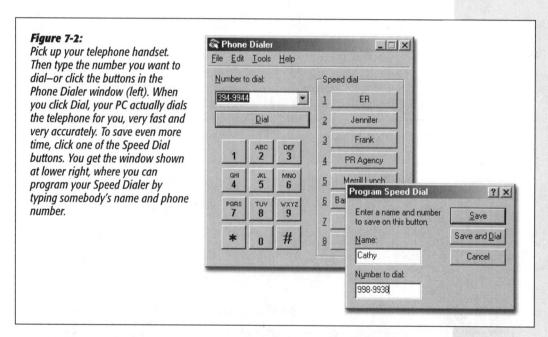

Figure 7-2:
Pick up your telephone handset. Then type the number you want to dial—or click the buttons in the Phone Dialer window (left). When you click Dial, your PC actually dials the telephone for you, very fast and very accurately. To save even more time, click one of the Speed Dial buttons. You get the window shown at lower right, where you can program your Speed Dialer by typing somebody's name and phone number.

Entertainment Folder

The truth is, you probably won't find the programs in the Entertainment folder particularly entertaining (unless there's *very* little going on in your life). A better name for this folder might be Multimedia, because all the programs in it relate to video and sound. They're described in Chapter 8, which is, by happy coincidence, called "Sound and Movies."

System Tools Folder

Many of the programs included in this folder are utilities designed to keep your PC in good health. Disk Cleanup, Disk Defragmenter, DriveSpace, Maintenance Wizard, ScanDisk, Scheduled Tasks, System Information, System Monitor, and System Restore are all described in Chapter 15.

That leaves only a handful of other utilities: Character Map (described next), Clipboard Viewer (see page 388), and Net Watcher (see page 364).

Character Map

Your computer is capable of creating hundreds of different typographical symbols—the currency symbols for the Yen and British pound, diacritical markings for French and Spanish, various scientific symbols, trademark and copyright signs, and so on. Obviously, these symbols don't appear on your keyboard; to provide enough keys for all of the symbols, your keyboard would have to be the width of Wyoming. Fortunately, you can indeed type the symbols—but they're hidden behind the keys you do see.

The treasure map that reveals their locations is Character Map. When you first open this program, use the upper-left drop-down menu to specify the font you want to use (because every font contains a different set of symbols). Now you see every single symbol in the font. As you hold your mouse down on each symbol, you see a magnified version of it to help you distinguish them. See Figure 7-3 for details on transferring a particular symbol into your document.

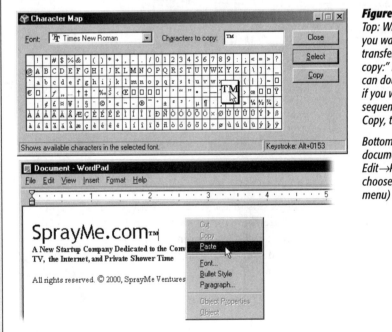

Figure 7-3:
Top: When you find the character you want, double-click it to transfer it into the "Characters to copy:" box, as shown here. (You can double-click several in a row, if you want to capture a sequence of symbols.) Click Copy, then Close.

Bottom: You return to your document, where you can choose Edit→Paste (or right-click and choose Paste from the shortcut menu) to insert the symbols.

Tip: In general, Internet email can't handle the fancy kinds of symbols revealed by Character Map. Don't be surprised if your copyright symbol turns into a gibberish character when received by your lucky correspondent.

FREQUENTLY ASKED QUESTION

When Alt+0169 is Faster

I use the copyright symbol quite a bit, so I figured I would just memorize the keystroke for it instead of having to open Character Map every time I need it. When I click the symbol in Character Map, the lower-right corner of the window says "Keystroke: Alt+0169." But when I try to enter that key sequence into my word processor, I don't get the copyright symbol!

That's absolutely right. You're leaving out two critical steps: First, you can't type those Alt+number codes unless you're in NumLock mode. If the NumLock light (usually at the top

of your keyboard) isn't illuminated, press the NumLock key first. Once you're in NumLock mode, *then* you can use the Alt-key combinations suggested by Character Map.

Second, you must type the numbers using the numeric keypad at the right side of your keyboard, not the numbers on the top row. (If you're on a laptop without a numeric keypad, God help you.)

You have to keep the Alt key pressed continuously as you type the suggested numbers.

Address Book

The Address Book is a central Windows directory for phone numbers, email addresses, and mailing addresses.

Once you've launched the program (see Figure 7-4), choose File→New Contact. You're shown a dialog box with seven tabbed panels for various categories of contact information. You're supposed to type the name, email address, phone number,

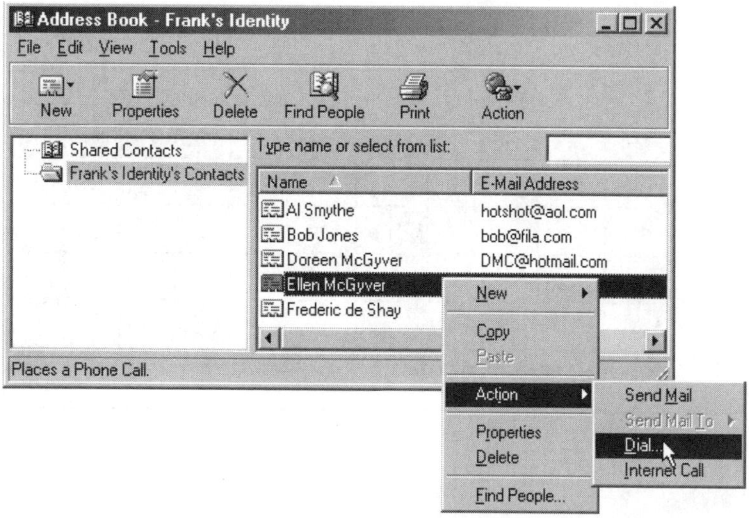

Figure 7-4:
At left: Each identity is actually a different address book (for different people sharing the same PC who want separate address books). Switch from one to the next by choosing File→Switch Identity. (Everyone sees the names in the Shared Contacts category.) Lower right: Right-click a name for a shortcut menu that offers such useful commands as Send Mail and Dial.

and other information for each person in your social or business circle. After you've gone to the trouble of typing in all of this information, Windows Me repays your efforts primarily in two places:

- **In Outlook or Outlook Express.** As Chapter 11 makes clear, a well-informed address book is extremely useful when you want to send an email message. You don't have to remember that your friend Harold Higgenbottom's email address is *hhiggenbottom@crawlsapce.ix.net.de;* instead, you have to type only *hhig.* The program fills in the email address for you automatically.

- **In the Search dialog box.** As noted in Chapter 2, you can quickly look up somebody's number by choosing Start→Search→People. This function searches your address book and pulls up the name and number you requested.

Tip: You can import address-book information from another program, too, by choosing File→Import. Windows can inhale the information from any of several popular address-book programs. (You'll see them listed at the right side of the dialog box that appears.)

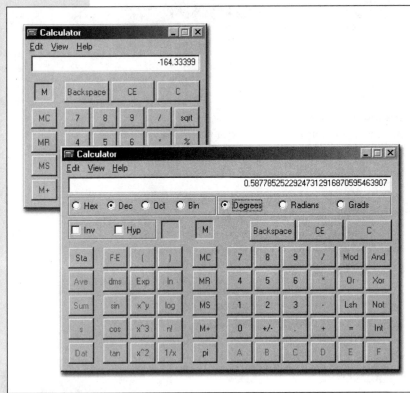

Figure 7-5:
After ducking into a phone booth, the humble Calculator (left) emerges as Scientific Calculator (right), which contains a hexadecimal/octal/ decimal/binary converter for programmers, mathematical functions for scientists, and enough other intimidating buttons to impress almost anyone. To find out what a particular button does, right-click it and choose What's This? from the shortcut menu. Don't miss the online help, by the way, which reveals that you can control even the scientific mode from the keyboard.

Calculator

This calculator looks at first like nothing more than a thinner version of every pocket calculator you've ever seen (Figure 7-5). You can operate it either by clicking the buttons with your mouse or by pressing the corresponding keys on your keyboard. Most of the buttons look just like the ones on the plastic calculator that's probably in your desk drawer at this very moment, but several require special explanation:

- /. This symbol, the slash, means "divided by" in Computer-ese.

- *. The asterisk is the multiplication symbol.

- **sqrt.** Click this button to find the square root of the currently displayed number.

- %. Type in one number, click this button, type a second number, and click this button again to find out what percentage the first number is of the second.

Tip: This calculator may appear to have almost every feature you could desire, but it lacks a paper-tape feature. It's easy to get lost in the middle of long calculations.

The solution is simple: Type your calculation, such as *34+(56/3)+5676+(34*2)=,* in a word processor. Highlight the calculation you've typed, choose Edit→Copy, switch to the Calculator, and then choose Edit→Paste. The previously typed numbers fly into the Calculator in sequence, finally producing the grand total on its screen. (You can then use the Edit→Copy command to copy the result back out of the Calculator, ready for pasting into another program.)

But by choosing View→Scientific, you turn this humble five-function calculator into a full-fledged scientific number cruncher, as shown in Figure 7-5.

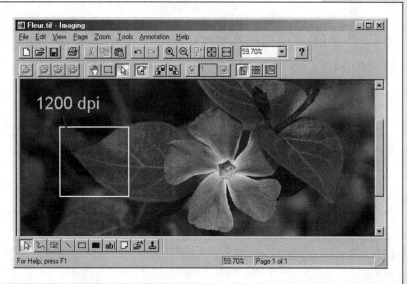

Figure 7-6:
A host of editing tools makes it easy to jazz up images and graphics. Use the tools on the toolbar to manipulate any part of an image, and use the annotation tools at the bottom of the window to add notes, comments, and arrows like the ones shown here.

Imaging

You can use Imaging (Figure 7-5) to view and edit photograph files from a scanner or digital camera; in fact, you can even operate your scanner using this little program. Although it can't actually retouch your photos, it can process scans and photographs in many other useful ways, such as flipping or rotating them, cropping them, marking them up with lines or text labels, changing their resolution, and so on.

Imaging is also handy for converting graphics from one file format to another, using the "Save as type:" control at the bottom of the File→Save As dialog box.

Imaging also works directly with your scanner (if it's a *TWAIN-compatible* scanner). Use the commands on the File menu (which vary depending upon the type of scanner you have) to preview or scan whatever you've put into your scanner. You can control the resolution, color, size, and cropping of a scanned image with the Tools menu and the icons on the toolbars.

MS-DOS Prompt

Double-click this icon to summon the MS-DOS window, the black, empty screen that's familiar to longtime PC users. At the C:> prompt, you can type any of hundreds of DOS commands; when you press Enter, the PC executes your typed instruction.

You may need to use this DOS mode to run certain older, Windows-incompatible programs; masters of DOS also extol its ability to manipulate (rename, for example)

GEM IN THE ROUGH

Notepad Log Files

As stripped-down as it is, Notepad offers one surprising feature that's not available in any other text or word processor: automated log files. When you use this feature, every time you open a certain file, Notepad automatically inserts the current date and time at the bottom of the file. Using this feature, when you type your text and save the file, you've got a tidy record of when you last worked on it—a nifty way to keep any type of a log, such as a record of expenditures or a traditional diary.

To set this up, create a new Notepad document (choose

File→New). Type *.LOG* at the top of the new document. (Put nothing, not even a space, before the period.)

Now save the document (File→Save). Give it a name. (Notepad adds the extension *.txt* automatically.)

When you next open the file, Notepad types out the date and time automatically and puts your cursor on the next line; now you're ready to type the day's entry.

To make your log file easier to read, press the Enter key to insert a blank line after each entry before saving the file.

---

many files at once, to poke and prod a network (using DOS utilities such as *ping.exe* and *netstat.exe),* and so on.

Tip: To learn a few of the hundreds of DOS commands at your disposal, consult the Internet, which teems with excellent lists and explanations. To find them, visit a search page such as *www.google.com* and search for *DOS command reference.* You'll find numerous ready-to-study Web sites that tell you what you can type at the MS-DOS prompt.

Notepad

Notepad (Figure 7-7) is a bargain-basement *text editor,* which means it lets you open, create, and edit files that contain plain, unformatted text, such as the Read Me files that often accompany new programs. You can also use Notepad to write short notes or to edit text that you intend to paste into your email program after editing.

Notepad basics

Notepad opens automatically when you double-click text files (those with the filename extension *.txt,* as described in the previous chapter). You can also open Notepad by choosing Start→Programs→Accessories→Notepad.

You'll quickly discover that Notepad is the world's most frill-free application; its list of limitations is almost longer than its list of features.

For example, Notepad can't open large files. If you double-click a text-file icon that contains more than about 50 KB of text, Windows Me automatically opens the file in WordPad, described on page 152, instead of Notepad. (Windows Me no longer asks your permission before doing so, as it did in previous versions.)

Many common word processing features are missing from Notepad. The Notepad window has no toolbar, lacks most standard keyboard shortcuts (such as Ctrl+S for

Figure 7-7:
Notepad is a text processor, not a word processor. That means that you can't use any formatting at all: no bold, italic, centered text, and so on. That's not necessarily bad news, however; the beauty of text files is that any word processor on any kind of computer—Windows, Mac, Unix, whatever—can open plain text files like the ones Notepad creates.

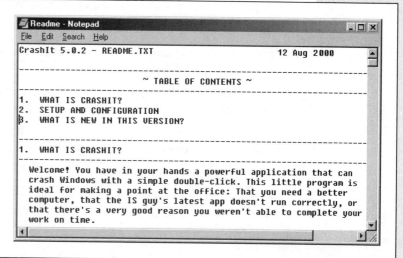

Save and Ctrl+O to open a file), and has few menu commands. Note, too, that Notepad can only work with one file at a time. If you choose File→New or File→Open, the current document closes (after you're given an opportunity to save your changes).

The Print command on the File menu doesn't even open the Print dialog box; instead, it sends the file directly to your printer. You can't specify which pages you want, for example.

About word wrap

As you may have noticed, Notepad doesn't automatically wrap lines of text to make everything fit in the software window. As a result, chunks of the text may get chopped off by the right side of the window.

The Edit→Word Wrap command is the solution. Choose it once to make your lines of text wrap around into standard paragraphs; choose it again to restore the lines-extend-beyond-the-window mode. (You can tell when Word Wrap is on by the presence of a checkmark next to the command in the Edit menu.)

Tip: When you print from Notepad, the text wraps to the paper size of the default paper for your printer, regardless of whether Word Wrap is on or off. Choose File→Page Setup from the Notepad menu bar to configure different margins for printing.

Paint

You can use Paint to "paint" simple artwork or to edit graphics files from other sources. Common tasks for this program include:

- Making quick sketches.
- Removing red-eye from digital photos.
- Fixing dust specks or tears on scanned photographs.
- Entertaining kids for hours on end.

The fundamentals are simple. Launch Paint by choosing Start→Programs→Accessories→Paint, and then:

1. **Choose Image→Attributes to specify the dimensions of the graphic you want to create. Click OK.**

   Later in your life, you may want to pursue the other commands in this menu, which let you stretch or flip your graphic.

2. **Click a tool on the palette at the left side.**

   If you need help identifying one of these tools, point to it without clicking. A tooltip identifies the icon by name, and a help message appears at the very bottom of the window.

3. If you've selected a painting tool, such as the paintbrush, pencil, or line tool, choose a "paint" color from the palette at the bottom of the window.

   You may also want to change the "brush" by choosing from the options below the tool palette, such as the size of your three spray-paint splatter (see Figure 7-8).

4. If you've selected one of the bottom four tools on the palette, *right*-click a swatch to specify the color you want to fill the *inside* of the shape.

   These tools all produce enclosed shapes, such as squares and circles. You can specify a different color for the border of these shapes and for the fill color inside.

5. Finally, drag your cursor in the image area (see Figure 7-8).

   As you work, don't forget the Edit→Undo command. Paint is especially forgiving; by choosing Undo three times, you can "take back" the last three painting maneuvers you made.

   For fine detail work, click the magnifying-glass icon and then click your painting. You've just enlarged it so that every dot becomes easily visible.

Paint can open and create several different file formats, including *.bmp, .jpg,* and *.gif.* In other words, it offers every file format you would need to save your masterpiece for use on your Web site.

Tip: Paint also offers a nifty way to create wallpaper (see page 189). After you create or edit a graphic, choose File→Set as Wallpaper (Tiled) or File→Set as Wallpaper (Centered) to transfer your masterpiece to your desktop immediately.

Figure 7-8:
The Paint tools include shapes, pens for special uses (straight lines and curves), and coloring tools (including an airbrush). The top two tools don't draw anything; instead, they select portions of the image for cutting, copying, or dragging to a new location.

Windows Explorer

See page 88 for details on this navigational tool.

Windows Movie Maker

Chapter 8 has the details.

WordPad

Think of WordPad, Windows Me's built-in word processor, as Microsoft Word Junior; it looks much the same as Word (see Figure 7-9) and creates files in exactly the same file format. That's a great feature if you don't *have* Microsoft Word, because WordPad lets you open (and edit) Word files sent to you by other people.

Note: One of the most important differences between WordPad and Word: WordPad can open only one document at a time.

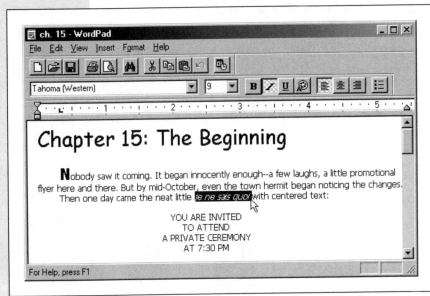

Figure 7-9:
WordPad has menu bars, toolbars, rulers, and plenty of other familiar Windows features. Unlike Notepad, WordPad lets you use bold and italic formatting to enhance the look of your text. You can even insert graphics, sounds, movies, and other OLE objects (see Chapter 6).

If Microsoft Word isn't on your PC, then any icon with the filename extension *.doc* opens into WordPad when double-clicked. (If you install Microsoft Word, however, it "takes over" the *.doc* extension, so that .doc files now open into Word.) WordPad can also open and create plain text files, Rich Text Format (RTF) documents, and Microsoft Write documents.

Using WordPad

When you first open WordPad, you're shown an empty sheet of electronic typing paper. Just above the ruler, you'll find drop-down menus and icons that affect the formatting of your text, as shown in Figure 7-9. As in any word processor, you can apply these formats (such as bold, italic, or color) to two kinds of text:

- Text you've highlighted by dragging the mouse across it, as shown in Figure 7-9.

- Text you're *about* to type. In other words, if you click the I button, the next words you type will be italicized. Click the I button a second time to "turn off" the italics.

The rightmost formatting icons affect entire paragraphs, as shown in Figure 7-10.

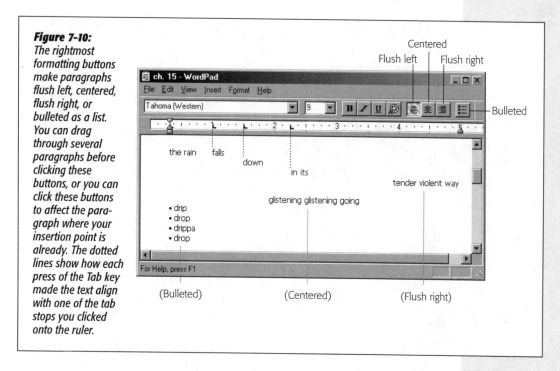

Figure 7-10:
The rightmost formatting buttons make paragraphs flush left, centered, flush right, or bulleted as a list. You can drag through several paragraphs before clicking these buttons, or you can click these buttons to affect the paragraph where your insertion point is already. The dotted lines show how each press of the Tab key made the text align with one of the tab stops you clicked onto the ruler.

WordPad doesn't offer such big-gun features as spell checking, style sheets, or tables. But it does offer a surprisingly long list of Microsoft Word-like core word processing features. For example:

- **Edit→Find, Edit→Replace.** Using the Find command, you can instantly locate a particular word or phrase, even a long document. The Replace command lets you go a step further, replacing that found phrase with another one (a great way to change the name of your main character all the way through the novel, for example).

- **Indents and Tab stops.** As shown in Figure 7-10, you can click to place Tab stops on the ruler. Each time you press the Tab key, your insertion point cursor jumps in line with the next Tab stop.

- **Object Linking and Embedding.** As described in the previous chapter, this Insert→Object feature lets you create or insert a picture, graph, chart, sound, movie, spreadsheet, or other kind of data into your WordPad document. Even though WordPad doesn't have the tools, menus, or toolbars for such data, the OLE feature borrows them from other programs on your machine.

- **Drag-and-drop editing.** Instead of using the three-step Copy and Paste routine for moving words and phrases around in your document, you can simply drag highlighted text from place to place on the screen. See page 127 for details.

UP TO SPEED

Text-Selection Fundamentals

Before you do almost anything to text in a word processor, such as making it bold, changing its typeface, or moving it to a new spot in your document, you have to *highlight* the text you want to affect. For millions of people, this entails dragging the cursor, perfectly horizontally, across the desired text. And if they want to capture an entire paragraph or section, they click at the beginning, drag very carefully diagonally, and release the mouse button when they reach the end of the passage.

That's all fine, but because selecting text is the cornerstone of every editing operation in a word processor, it's worth knowing about some of the faster and more precise ways of going about it. For example, double-clicking a word highlights it, instantly and neatly. In fact, if you keep the mouse button pressed on the second click, you can now drag horizontally to highlight text in crisp one-word chunks, which lets you highlight text both faster and more precisely. (These tricks work anywhere you can type.)

In most programs, including Microsoft applications, additional shortcuts await. For example, if you *triple*-click anywhere within a paragraph, you highlight the entire paragraph. (Once again, if you *keep* the button pressed at the end of this maneuver, you can then drag to highlight your document in one-paragraph increments.)

In many programs, including Word and WordPad, you can highlight exactly one sentence by clicking within it while pressing Ctrl.

Finally, here's a universal trick that lets you highlight a large blob of text, even one that's too big to fit on the current screen. Start by clicking to plant the insertion point cursor at the very beginning of the text you want to capture. Now scroll, if necessary, so that the ending point of the passage is visible. While pressing Shift, click there. Windows instantly highlights everything that was in between your click and your Shift-click.

Windows Me Games

If you upgraded to Windows Me from a previous version of Windows, you're in for a surprise: Microsoft has more than tripled the number of free games, for your procrastination pleasure.

More interesting still, several of them have been enhanced so that you can play them against other people on the Internet. At the Microsoft Game Center (*www.zone.com*), players from all over the world gather to find worthy opponents. When you choose one of the Internet-enabled games, your PC connects automatically with this Game Center. An automated matchmaker searches for someone else who wants to play the game you chose and puts the two of you together.

The game board that opens, like the one in Figure 7-5, provides more than just the tools to play; there's even a pseudo-chat feature. By choosing from the canned list of phrases, you can send little game exclamations to your opponent ("Good move," "King me!", "Bad luck," and so on).

Tip: The canned list of utterances deprives you of the chance to type out, for example, "That was uncalled for, you sniveling, ulcerated cockroach!" But it has a virtue of its own: You can exchange platitudes with players anywhere in the world. Your quips show up automatically in the language of your opponent's copy of Windows, be it Korean, German, or whatever.

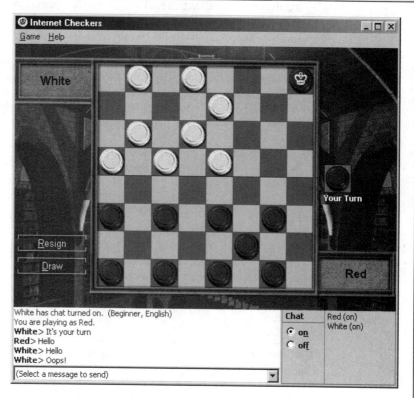

Figure 7-11:
It may look like a simple game of checkers to you, but you're actually witnessing one of the most spectacular developments of Windows Me: instantaneous anonymous Internet gaming. Two Inter-net visitors in search of recreation have made contact, a game board has appeared, and the game is under way. The Chat window sits below the game board. You can turn Chat off if you're planning to play a cutthroat game and don't want to fake having friendly feelings toward your opponent.

Here's the Windows Me complement of games, all of which are listed in the Start→Programs→Games submenu.

Tip: Complete instructions lurk within the Help menu of each game. That's fortunate, because the rules of some of these card games can seem elaborate and quirky, to say the least.

- **Classic Hearts, Internet Hearts.** The object of this card game is to get rid of all the Hearts you're holding by passing them off to other players. At the end of each round, everybody counts up her points: one point for each heart, and 13 points for the dreaded Queen of Spades. The winner is the person with the fewest points when the game ends (which is when somebody reaches 100).

What makes it tricky is that even while you're trying to ditch your hearts, somebody else may be secretly trying to collect them. If you can collect *all* of the hearts *and* the Queen of Spades, you win big-time; everybody else gets 26 big fat points, and you get off scot-free.

You can play Classic Hearts either against Windows, which makes up names and hands for three other fictional players to play against you, or against people on your network. And if you open Internet Hearts, you get to play against other similarly bored Windows PC owners all over the world.

- **Classic Solitaire.** Here it is: the program that started it all, the application that introduced millions of people to the joys of a graphic interface like Windows. (Ask the advanced-beginner Windows user what a good program-file code to type into the Start→Run dialog box might be, and he might not know *winword* or *msconfig*—but he'll probably know *sol.*)

In Solitaire, you try to build four piles of cards, one for each suit, in ascending order (starting with Aces). To help you do this, you maintain seven smaller stacks of cards in the second row. You can put cards onto these piles as long as you alternate red and black, and as long as the cards go in descending order; you can put a Four of Hearts on a Five of Spades, for example. Click a face-down card on one of these piles to turn it over, and remember that, if it helps you to continue the red/black/red/black sequence you've got going, you can drag stacks of face-up cards on these piles around. And when you can't find anymore moves to make, click the deck in the upper-left corner to reveal some more cards.

If you win, you get an animated simulation of what's euphemistically called "52 Pickup."

Tip: Unfortunately, you can't play Solitaire over the Internet. Even Microsoft hasn't figured out a way to turn Solitaire into a multiplayer game.

- **FreeCell.** You might think of this card game as Solitaire on steroids, a more challenging and complicated game. When you choose Game→New Game, the computer deals eight piles of cards before you. Your goal is to sort them into four piles of cards, one suit each, in sequence from Ace to King, in the spaces at the upper-right corner of the screen. (You move a card by clicking it and then clicking where you wanted to go.)

You can use the upper-left placeholders, the "free cells," as temporary resting places for your cards; from there, cards can go either onto one of the upper-right piles or to the bottom of one of the eight piles in the second row. But when you move cards to the eight piles, you must place them alternating red/black, and in descending sequence.

Tip: When you're stuck, move your cursor back and forth in front of the little King icon at top center. Watch his eyes follow your arrow as though hypnotized.

- **Internet Backgammon.** Here's classic Backgammon, with a twist: Now you are playing against people you've never met, via the MSN Gaming Zone.

- **Internet Checkers.** It's just checkers; once again, though, you can now play against some random player on the Internet (see Figure 7-11).

- **Internet Reversi.** Like Othello, you play this strategy game on a chess-type board against another player from the MSN Gaming Zone.

- **Internet Spades.** Here's yet another card game, again designed for Internet playing.

Figure 7-12:
Once the Pinball ball is in orbit around the screen, you twitch the flippers by pressing the Z and / keys. (Put your pinkies there—this feels much more logical than it reads. Even so, you can reassign these functions to other keys by choosing Options→ Player Controls.) You can even "bump the table" by pressing the X, period, or up-arrow key.

- **Minesweeper.** Under some of the cells of the grid are mines; under others, hints about nearby mines. Your goal: to find the mines without blowing yourself up.

When you click a random square, you might get blown up instantly. You lose; them's the breaks. But if you get lucky, you uncover little numbers around the square you clicked. Each number tells you how many mines are hidden in the

squares surrounding it. Using careful mathematical logic and the process of elimi-
nation, you can eventually figure out which squares have mines under them. (To
help yourself keep track, you can right-click the squares to plant little flags that
mean, "Don't step here.") You win if you mark all the mine squares with flags.

• **Pinball.** To start this noisy, animated, very realistic pinball machine (Figure 7-
12), choose Game→New Game. You get three balls; launch the first one by tap-
ping the Space bar. (Hold the Space bar down longer before releasing for a more
powerful ball launch.) See Figure 7-12 for details.

Tip: The game becomes a lot more fun when it fills the screen. Press F4 to make it so.

• **Spider Solitaire.** If your spirit needs a good game of solitaire, but you just don't
have the time or patience for Solitaire or FreeCell, this kinder, gentler, *easier* game
may be just what you need. Thanks to the built-in cheat mechanism, which suggests the next move with no penalty, you can blow through this game with all of
the satisfaction and none of the frustration of traditional solitaire games.

You play with 104 cards. You get ten stacks across the top of the screen, and the
rest in a pile in the lower-right corner of the screen. By dragging cards around, all
you have to do is create stacks of cards in descending order, from King down to
Ace; as soon as you create such a stack, the cards fly off the playing board. The
goal is to get *all* of the cards off the playing board.

In the easiest level, you don't even have to worry about color or suit, because the
game gives you *only* Spades. If you run out of imagination, you can press the
letter M key to make the program propose a move, accompanied by a heavenly
sounding harp ripple. And if even the game can't find a legal move, you can click
the deck in the lower-right corner to distribute another round of cards, which
opens up a new round of possibilities.

Sticking with the game to the very end gives you an animated confetti/fireworks
display—and a tiny, budding sense of achievement.

Everything Else

The remainder of the programs listed in the Start→Programs menu are covered
elsewhere in this book: Internet Explorer and Outlook Express are described in Chapter 11, and Windows Media Player is covered in Chapter 8.

Sound and Movies

Microsoft has a fancy word for sound and movies: *multimedia*. Whether you use the traditional phrase or the buzzword, Windows Me is the most advanced Windows version yet when it comes to playing and displaying these visual and audio treats. New features make it easier than ever for your PC to control your digital camera or scanner, play movies and sounds, and play radio stations from all over the world as you work, thanks to your Internet connection.

In this chapter, you'll find guides to all of these features.

Windows Media Player

You can use Windows Media Player—one of the most useful freebie features of Windows Me—to play sounds, play digital movies, or tune in to Internet radio stations. It's easy to see how excited Microsoft is about Version 7:

- Microsoft listed Media Player *twice* in the Start menu: once in the Programs menu and again in the Programs→Accessories→Entertainment menu.

- Microsoft gave Media Player a desktop shortcut icon.

- Media Player even appears in the Quick Launch toolbar.

Choosing any of those methods opens Windows Media Player.

Audio CDs

For its first trick, Media Player can simulate a $200 CD player, capable of playing your music CDs while you're working at your computer. To fire it up, just insert a CD into your computer's CD-ROM drive (see Figure 8-1).

Tip: As the music plays, you get to watch psychedelic screen-saver-like displays that bounce and shimmer to the music. Microsoft calls them *visualizations.* To try a different one, click the Next Visualization arrow (the tiny arrow button just below the shimmery display), or press Tab+Enter, or choose View→Visualizations. And if you tire of the 48 displays built into Windows, you can download more of them from the Internet by choosing Tools→Download Visualizations.

Get album information

If the Media Player window shows names like "Track 1" and "Track 2" instead of actual song names, and doesn't display the name of the performer, it's because that data wasn't encoded on the CD by the record company. In such cases, you have a choice:

- You can simply listen to the music without seeing such information on the PC screen. Read the back of the CD case if you're curious.

- You can let the Internet fill in the missing information for you, thanks to a useful Media Player feature that consults a massive Internet database of almost every CD in existence.

To get album information from the Net, click the CD Audio button at the left side of the Media Player window, and then click Get Names at the top of the window. If you're not already connected to the Internet, your PC dials now. Your browser opens to Microsoft's media site, where a wizard walks you through the steps needed to identify the album in your CD drive (Figure 8-2).

Figure 8-1:
Media Player automatically displays the album title and the titles of each track, if that information was encoded onto your music CD. The track that's currently playing is highlighted (along with its length) and the elapsed time appears below the scroll bar. Double-click a song name to listen to it. The controls at the bottom of the Media Player window are like the controls on a physical CD player (Pause, Play, Next Track, Volume, and so on).

If the artist or the album *isn't* on the list of known albums, the wizard lets you fill in the information yourself (see Figure 8-2). (Typing the names in manually isn't nearly as much fun as watching the Internet do the work for you—but that's what you get for buying an obscure recording.)

After you enter the CD and song names for a particular CD, Windows Me saves this information in your music library (see "Copying Music to Your Hard Drive," later in this chapter). The next time you insert this CD, the Media Player will recognize it and display the track names and album information automatically.

Tip: If the Media Player window is taking up too much screen space, making it harder for you to do other work, press Ctrl+2, or click the Compact Mode button in the lower-right corner of the window. Either way, the Media Player reappears in the lower-right corner of your screen as shown in Figure 8-3, a fraction of its former size, its useful controls still visible. Press Ctrl+1 to return the Media Player window to its full-size glory. (Of course, you can also just minimize Media Player, as you would any window.)

Figure 8-2:
Top: If your CD comes up with generic track names, start by typing in the name of the performer or musical group. (If it's a soundtrack or collection, click the corresponding checkbox.)

Middle: After a search of Internet-based information, the wizard shows you the names of all recordings it can find connected with that artist.

Bottom: If your album is included in the list, click its name; Windows Me fills in the missing informa-tion in the Media Player window.

Change the skin

In hopes of riding the world's craze for MP3 files (compact, downloadable, CD-quality sound files), Microsoft has helped itself to one of MP3-playing software's most interesting features: *skins*. A skin is a design scheme that completely changes the look of Windows Media Player (see Figure 8-4).

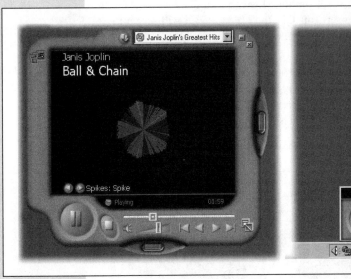

Figure 8-3:
The full-size Media Player window occupies a large chunk of your screen (Figure 8-1). Compact Mode (left) summons a small control window (right), which appears simultaneously in the lower-right corner of your desktop. Double-click the compact window to restore Media Player to full size, or click it for a shortcut menu of handy commands.

To choose a new skin, click the Skin Chooser button on the left side of the Media Player window. Then click each of the available skins to see a preview of its appearance (see Figure 8-4). When you click the Apply Skin button, your player takes on the look of the skin you chose *and* shrinks down into Compact mode, as described in the previous tip.

Copy the CD to your hard drive

You can copy an album, or selected tracks, to your hard drive in the form of stand-alone music files that play when double-clicked. Having CD songs on your hard drive affords you a number of benefits:

• You can listen to whatever songs you like, without having to hunt for the CDs they came from. Now you can listen even if you're using the CD-ROM drive for something else (such as a CD-based game).

• You can build your own *playlist* (set of favorite songs) consisting of cuts from different albums.

• You can compress the file in the process, so that each song takes up very little disk space. (Microsoft says that its compression system creates even smaller files than MP3 compression.)

Follow these steps to copy audio from a CD to your hard drive:

1. **Click the CD Audio button on the left side of the Media Player window. Turn off the checkbox of any track you *don't* want to copy.**

   Before you proceed, choose Tools→Options; on the CD Audio tab, make sure that Digital Copying is selected. Click OK.

2. **Click the Copy Music button on the toolbar.**

   The button changes its name to Stop Copy, which you can click to interrupt the process. Windows now copies the selected tracks onto your hard drive.

When you perform this copying procedure, Windows builds a *music library*—a set of nested folders in the My Documents→My Music folder on your desktop. Over time, your My Music folder will develop a structure that looks like Figure 8-5.

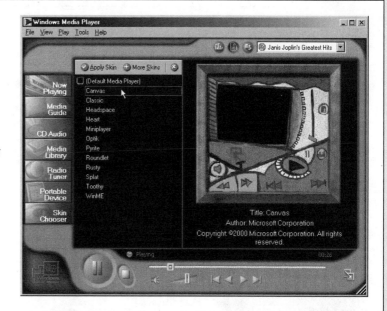

Figure 8-4:
When you find a skin you like, click Apply Skin. If you don't like any of the designs or just want to keep looking, click More Skins. This sends you to the Internet for a visit to Microsoft's Windows Media Skin Gallery. If you don't find something there that strikes your fancy, check back later, as Microsoft intends to expand the collection periodically.

Burning your own CDs

If your PC has a CD burner attached, you can create audio CDs that play in any standard CD player. Candidates for this treatment are MP3 files, WAV files, and Windows Media files (.asf, .wma, and .wmv).

1. **Copy the music you'll want to your hard drive.**

   If you're using MP3 or WAV files, they're probably already on your hard drive. If you're planning to use tracks from a CD, copy them as directed in "Copy the CD to your hard drive," above. Remember that the quality settings you use will affect the sound quality of the finished disc.

2. Create a playlist.

A playlist, in this case, is a list of the tracks you'll want on your homemade CD. To create a playlist, click the Media Library button, click New Playlist, type a name for the list. Then add tracks to the new playlist by highlighting their names (at the right side of the window) and then clicking "Add to playlist" on the toolbar; choose "Add to [your new playlist's name]" from the tiny menu. The maximum length for a CD is 74 minutes.

3. Choose File→Copy to CD; double-click the name of the playlist you want converted to a CD.

If the equipment gods are smiling, your CD burner now spins into action, and the messages on the screen keep you posted as the CD is created.

Tip: If you want to play the resulting CD in a standard stereo CD player, use a CD-R disc (which you can record only once); CD-RW (rewritable) discs play only in computers.

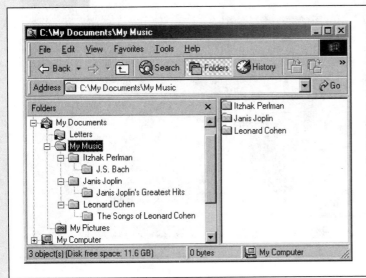

Figure 8-5:
Your music library has a hierarchy that makes it easy to find exactly the artist, album, and music track you want to hear. Within the My Music folder, you'll find a folder for each performer; within the performer folder, there's a folder for each CD; and within that folder, you'll find icons representing the tracks you copied. To play a song, just double-click its icon.

Copy the CD to a portable device

If you have a palmtop computer that's capable of playing music, such as a Diamond Rio or a Windows CE-based palmtop, you can copy your CD files there. To do so, connect the palmtop, and then click the Portable Device button on the left side of the Media Player window. Now Media Player displays a split window: the left side lists the tracks on the CD, and the right side lists the music currently installed on the palmtop. Turn on the checkboxes of the tracks you want, and then click Copy Music; Windows copies the music you selected to your portable player.Copy the CD to a portable device

Finding music on the Internet

Your CD collection isn't the only source of music worth listening to as you work. The Internet is crawling with Web sites that harbor music files you can download and make part of your music library (or download to your palmtop). To find them, click the Media Guide button on the Media Player window. You're shown a list of Microsoft media Web sites, where you'll find lists, search engines, and other methods for finding music.

Listen to the Radio

You can use your PC as a radio that can tune in to any of hundreds of stations from all over the world, each brought to you by the Internet.

To do so, open Windows Media Player. Click the Radio Tuner button to connect to the Internet, where you can select the stations you want to hear (see Figure 8-6).

To create your own list (to replace Microsoft's Featured List), choose My Presets from the drop-down menu at the top of the left pane. Then find the stations you want to add by using the search features in the right pane. When you find a radio station you like, select it and click Add. (To remove a station from your preset list, select it and click Delete.)

Tip: Once you've set up your list of favorite stations in this way, you don't have to summon Windows Media Player to "turn on" and "turn off" your PC radio. Instead, you can fiddle with your radio controls from any folder window, just by summoning the Radio toolbar as described on page 71.

Figure 8-6:
The left side of the Radio Tuner window lists your preset stations (Microsoft features several popular stations in a collection named Featured); the right side provides search features you can use to find stations you want to add to this canned list.

Watch Video

Media Player can also play movie files, such as those you've downloaded from the Internet, made yourself, or grabbed from a CD-ROM. The standard Windows movie-file format is *.avi,* but Media Player can also play files with the extensions *.wmv, .wvx, .avi, .mpeg, .mpg, .mpe, .m1v, .mp2, .mpa,* and *.ivf.*

If you don't happen to have any such files sitting around to play, choose Start→ Programs→Accessories→Entertainment→Windows Millennium Edition Preview. You'll get to enjoy an encore performance of the state-of-the-art filmmaking opus that greeted you when you ran Windows Me for the first time.

Tip: Media Player doesn't recognize two of the most popular video-file formats, QuickTime and RealVideo. To play these kinds of files, you'll need QuickTime Player (available free from *www.apple.com/quicktime)* or RealPlayer *(www.real.com),* respectively.

Movie Maker

You can use the Movie Maker program, new in Windows Me, to edit the boring parts out of your camcorder footage, add crossfades, and save the resulting production as a digital file that you can email to friends or save onto a disk. Movie Maker is not to be confused with such "real" video-editing programs as EditDV, Adobe Premiere, and so on. Movie Maker is extremely limited, offering only a single kind of transition between clips, no special effects, no way to add credits and titles, no way to edit audio, and relatively poor picture quality. But for just-for-fun, here's-what-the-new-baby-looks-like projects, it may be just the ticket.

Doing the actual editing is the easy part. The hard part is getting equipped to do so; the standard PC can't communicate at all with the standard camcorder. To use Movie Maker, you can proceed in any of three ways:

- **Use analog equipment.** In other words, use a standard camcorder or VCR, and play your footage into your PC from standard VHS, 8 mm, or Hi-8 tapes.

  Of course, a typical PC has no connector for a VCR. Therefore, you also need to buy a *video capture card* or one of those inexpensive USB capture boxes designed to let you pour video into your PC. The quality won't be very good; Movie Maker achieves its goal of creating emailable movie files by heavily compressing your video, which can make the finished product look grainy or stuttery.

- **Use digital equipment.** If you prefer better quality, you can use Movie Maker with a *digital* (DV) camcorder. A digital camcorder ($600 and up) uses special tapes called MiniDV cassettes. (The exception: Sony Digital8 models are also digital camcorders, but they save you money by recording onto ordinary Hi-8 tapes.)

  Next, you need a *FireWire card.* This kind of add-on circuit board, often called an *IEEE-1394* or *i.link card*, goes into your PC and lets it communicate with the digital camcorder.

On the side of almost every digital camcorder model is a special connector, called a FireWire or IEEE-1394 port, that connects to the PC with a special FireWire *cable*. This single cable communicates both sound and video, in both directions, between the PC and the camcorder.

- **Use existing pictures or movies.** You can use Movie Maker to edit existing movie files you've downloaded from the Internet or copied from CD-ROMs. It can even create a living photo album by splicing together still photos that you've scanned or captured from a digital camera.

Note: Regardless of what you intend to do with Movie Maker, the program requires a PC with a 300-MHz Pentium II (or equivalent) and 64 MB of memory at the very least. If you're working with a digital camcorder, you also need a *lot* of hard drive space. Digital video footage takes up 3.6 MB *per second* of video—enough to fill up a 10 GB hard drive in about 40 minutes.

See Chapter 13 for tips on installing cards. And be sure to ask about Movie Maker/Windows Me compatibility before you buy such a card.

Getting Started with Movie Maker

To open the program, choose Start→Programs→Accessories→Windows Movie Maker. The first time you run Movie Maker, you're shown an animated sales pitch/guided tour of the program. Behind the scenes, meanwhile, Windows Me creates a folder in your My Documents folder called My Videos. This is where you'll find icons representing the various video clips that you capture from your camcorder.

How you get footage into Movie Maker for editing depends on what kind of equipment you've got: analog, digital, or none.

Note: Getting the footage into Movie Maker is by far the most difficult aspect of desktop moviemaking. Movie Maker may not recognize your USB video-capture device or DV camcorder; copy-protected tapes may show garbage on the screen; and, as with any new Windows technology, you may run into driver conflicts and other headaches. Don't miss the Help→Help Topics command, whose lengthy list of Troubleshooting topics is a great place to start if you have problems.

Capturing analog footage

If you want to capture footage from a non-digital camcorder or a traditional VCR, make sure that your video capture card and software are properly installed, and that the VCR or camera is correctly hooked up to it.

Now proceed as follows:

1. **Choose File→Record.**

   The dialog box shown in Figure 8-7 appears. Check to make sure that the capture card or capture box is correctly identified where it says "Video device." If not, click Change Device to select the correct one.

2. **Start your camcorder or VCR playing. Click Record on the screen.**

   As Windows records, the word Recording blinks.

3. **When the recording is complete, click Stop.**

   Windows asks you to type a name for your new clip.

4. **Type a new name, and then click Save. Stop the VCR or camcorder.**

Repeat this process until you've captured all the pieces you need to create your motion-picture masterpiece.

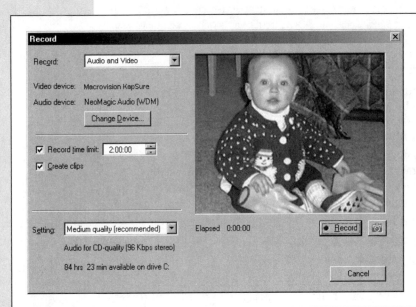

Figure 8-7:
Note the "Create clips" checkbox. It detects where new camera shots begin (that is, where you turned the camera off, then on again). At each such joint, Movie Maker creates a new independent clip, which often makes it much easier for you to arrange and organize them after the importing process is over. If you turn it off, Movie Maker imports your footage as one gigantic video stream.

Capturing from a DV camcorder

Once your FireWire card is correctly installed in the PC, make sure the camcorder is turned on and connected to the IEEE-1394 (FireWire) cable. Cue it up to the footage you want to capture.

When a digital camcorder is attached, you get some extra controls in Movie Maker. Start by turning on "Begin recording my video from the current position on my tape." Click OK.

Now you can click the Play and Stop buttons *on the screen* to control the camcorder sitting beside you on the desk. Click Record on the screen when the scene you want to grab appears. The word Recording blinks while the PC is capturing; unfortunately, you don't get to hear the audio while the tape plays. Once again, Movie Maker creates a new clip for each new scene you filmed (unless you choose View→Options and turn off "Automatically create clips").

Finally, click Stop. Now type a name for the new clip, and then click Save.

Tip: The files Movie Maker creates are Windows Media Files. Their filenames bear the extension *.wmv,* which play back in Media Player.

Importing pictures and movies

To use Movie Maker, you don't have to have fancy equipment hooked up. By choosing File→Import, you can choose any movie or picture file on your hard drive. Movie Maker turns it into a clip, which you can edit, chop up, or manipulate exactly as described in the following paragraphs.

For example, while you wait for your video-capture card to arrive, you can try your hand at editing an existing movie that comes with Windows. In your My Documents→My Videos folder, you'll find a sample video file (called Windows Movie Maker Sample File). Double-click its icon to watch a convincing home movie of a Microsoft employee's son romping in a playground. (This movie, like most Windows movies, plays back in Media Player, described at the beginning of this chapter.)

Tip: To the ancient question, "What is the sound of one hand clapping?", you can now add, "What is the duration of a still picture?" As far as Windows is concerned, the answer is: "Five seconds." When you drag a still-image clip into your Timeline, as described below, Windows gives it a five-second proposed duration. You can make a still image stay on the screen for longer or shorter interval, however, by dragging its right-hand triangle on the ruler, a shown in Figure 8-8.

Editing Video in Movie Maker

Once you've accumulated a few clips in this way, you can go about the business of organizing them: rearranging them, trimming off excess footage from the ends, and so on. You can also apply a *transition* effect between clips, better known as a cross-fade or dissolve.

Phase 1: Organize your clips

At the far left side of the screen, you'll see a folder hierarchy that looks something like Windows Explorer. These are *collections*—folders into which you can organize your clips. Just drag a clip's icon onto a folder to store it there. Movie Maker remembers your collection of collections even after you quit the program; the clips you store there will be waiting the next time you use the program.

Tip: You can create a new storage folder by right-clicking in the folder area and choosing New Collection from a shortcut menu. You can rename or delete a folder, too, by right-clicking it and choosing from the shortcut menu.

When you click a collection folder, the middle part of the window shows the icons of the clips inside it. To play one of these clips, click its icon and then press the Space bar. (If you want to stop playback before the end of the clip, press Space again.)

Phase 2: Drag them into the storyboard

At the bottom of the screen is what looks like a filmstrip; this is where you'll organize the scenes of your movie. As shown in Figure 8-8, you just drag the clips down into this area to place them in the order you want. You can rearrange them once they're there, too, just by dragging.

As you go, you can preview your film in progress by choosing Play→Play Entire Storyboard/Timeline. (Press the period key to interrupt playback.)

Tip: You can choose Play→Full Screen (or press Alt+Enter) to make the movie fill your monitor as it plays back. Unless you're working with digital video and a very fast PC, the blotchy, blurry enlargement will probably disappoint you. But this trick is useful when you're trying to show your finished movie to a group of people in a room. From a few feet away, the poor picture quality isn't as noticeable.

Figure 8-8:
The filmstrip at the bottom of the window offers two different views; switch between them by clicking the tiny View-switching icon, circled here. In Storyboard view (top), you get no indication of the relative lengths of your clips, but you get a good feel for the overall shape of your movie. In Timeline view (bottom), you see the relative timing of each clip.

In each case, you can trim unwanted material off the beginning or ending of each clip by dragging the triangles in the ruler, as shown by the cursor (and tooltip) in the lower example.

Phase 3: Chop up the clips

As you work, you may frequently find it useful to cut your clips into smaller pieces, thereby eliminating boring material and gaining even more editorial freedom. You can do this in either of two ways:

- **Split a clip.** When the scroll bar underneath the movie-screen window is correctly aligned with the spot where you want to chop up the clip, choose Clip→Split. Movie Maker turns the single clip into two different clips, adding a number to the name of the second one.

Tip: You can do the opposite, too. After you've arranged a few clips into a satisfying sequence, you may want to consider merging them into a single, new uni-clip for easier manipulation. To do that, click the first one, and then click successive clips while pressing Shift. Finally, choose Clip→Combine. Movie Maker joins the clips and names them according to the first one you selected.

- **Trim a clip.** Sometimes you just want to trim off unwanted footage from either end of a clip. Movie Maker lets you perform this task only after you've added a clip to the Timeline window at the bottom of the screen. The easiest way to go about it is to drag the triangle handles, as shown in Figure 8-8. You can also use the scroll bar under the movie-screen window, scroll to the new spot where you want the clip to begin, and choose Clip→Set Start Trim Point. Then scroll to the spot where you want the clip's new ending to be, and choose Clip→Set And Trim Points.

Phase 4: Add crossfades

To create a smooth transition between clips—a *cross dissolve* from one to another instead of just cutting—switch to the Timeline view shown at bottom in Figure 8-8. Then just drag a clip in the Timeline slightly to the left, making it overlap the preceding clip. The amount of overlap determines how long the crossfade lasts; you're welcome to adjust this amount by dragging the clip again. (If you drag it all the way to the right so that it no longer overlaps, you've just eliminated the crossfade altogether.)

Phase 5: Save the movie

When your flick looks good, you can save it as a stand-alone file on your hard drive, which you can then double-click to play or send to potential backers.

To do so, Choose File→Save Movie. In the Save Movie dialog box, you can specify the playback quality from the Setup drop-down menu. Low, Medium, and High actually mean Small file, Medium file, and Large file—something to think about if you plan to put the movie on a Web page or email it to somebody.

Tip: If you choose Other from the Setting drop-down menu, you can then use the Profile drop-down menu below it. This menu gives you much more specific choices for the quality/file size trade-off. Using it, you can specify how you imagine that this movie will be viewed as it appears on a Web page. That is, you might choose "Video for Web servers (56 Kbps)" if you think most people will be connecting to your Web site using 56 K modems, or "Video for broadband NTSC (256 Kbps)" if cable modem owners are your primary audience.

Name the file and click OK. In the Save As dialog box that appears now, name the file again and choose a folder for it. Click Save, and go have a few cups of coffee while Movie Maker processes your movie.

When it's all over, Movie Maker asks you if you'd like to watch the movie now. If you click Yes, Windows Media Player launches and plays back the video. (In the future, you can play the movie back yourself just by double-clicking its icon in the My Documents→My Videos folder, or wherever you saved it.)

WebTV

If you've equipped your PC with a *TV tuner card* (a special kind of video card), you can watch television that's sent to you via the Internet: the ultimate cable TV. The key is the WebTV software included with Windows Millennium. Although it's not part of the standard installation, you can add it by using the Add/Remove control panel described in Chapter 9. (You don't actually need a WebTV set-top box. That gadget is designed for people who don't have a PC.)

After installing the tuner card, begin your new career as a desk potato by choosing Start→Programs→Accessories→Entertainment→WebTV for Windows. Windows now connects you to the WebTV for Windows Web site, where you can select channels, programs, and other configuration options.

After the initial configuration, your WebTV window opens. Use the search tab to look for programs you want to schedule for viewing. Use the drop-down lists to

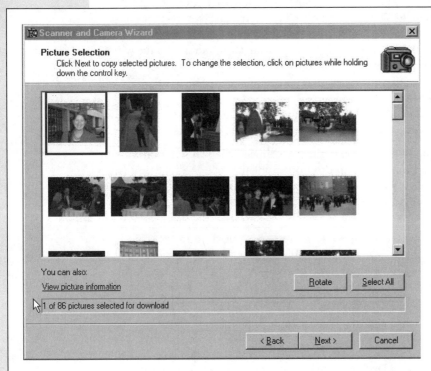

Figure 8-9:
The Picture Selection box shows you quickly downloaded thumbnail images of everything on your WIA-ready camera. Click and Ctrl+click the pictures you want to download from the camera at full size, and then click Next.

Other buttons let you see information about a picture, rotate one of the thumbnails, select all thumbnails at once, and so on.

change the Date, Time of Day, or the Channel Listing, so you can program your TV watching. WebTV obeys your instructions and displays programs at the times you choose.

Scanners and Cameras

Scanners and digital still cameras are wildly popular gadgets. A scanner converts the image of a page or photo into a graphic image file on your hard drive; a digital camera takes pictures without film, and then transfers them via cable to your PC. From there, you can view, edit, or email them.

Windows Image Acquisition

With Windows Me, Microsoft introduces Windows Image Acquisition (WIA), a new technology that makes it much easier to transfer images from scanners and cameras onto the PC. If you've bought a scanner or camera that's advertised as WIA-compatible, you can take advantage of two new features. First, the Start→Settings→Control Panel→Scanners and Cameras folder contains an Add Device wizard, which makes driver installation extremely easy. (If you have a USB camera, you won't even need it; Windows Me self-configures itself when you hook up such a camera.)

Second, when you choose the Start→Programs→Accessories→Scanner and Camera Wizard, a wizard walks you through getting images from your scanner or camera. The first two wizard screens are the most important:

- **Select Picture.** In the olden days, you'd have to download (transfer) the pictures from your digital camera. Because high-resolution images take up a lot of disk space and memory, this process took forever, especially if you only wanted one of the pictures.

  This screen, however, shows you thumbnails of all the pictures on the camera (and takes relatively little time to do so). As shown in Figure 8-9, it's simple to choose only shots you want.

- **Picture Destination.** Make up a name for this batch of downloaded pictures (such as "Disney Trip") and choose a folder location. Windows Me proposes storing them in the My Pictures folder, which is in your My Documents folder. That's a great place for them, because the My Pictures window contains buttons for zooming in or out, rotating, enlarging, or printing your pictures—even viewing them as a slide show.

Eventually, all scanner and camera manufacturers will sell WIA-compatible gadgets. However, for the moment, the number of manufacturers building WIA-based devices is limited, partly because WIA doesn't work in older versions of Windows; visit *www.microsoft.com/hwdev/wia* for a current list.

Tip: WIA-savvy programs, such as Word 2000 and Outlook, can import pictures directly from a WIA-friendly camera, thanks to the Insert→Picture→From Scanner or Camera command.

TWAIN

Before the invention of WIA, most scanners and cameras were built to support *TWAIN*, a different image-grabbing technology. If you have a TWAIN scanner or camera, here's what you can expect:

- If you upgraded to Windows Millennium from Windows 95/98, and you were already using a TWAIN device, the Windows Me installation procedure leaves everything as it was. Keep scanning or downloading camera pictures just as you did before the Windows Me upgrade.

- If you buy a new camera or scanner, install it using the software provided by the manufacturer. (Windows Me doesn't provide any automatic installation features, as it does for WIA equipment.)

- You use the software provided by the manufacturer to open and edit your image files. Or, if you prefer, you can use the Windows Me Imaging program—Start→ Programs→Accessories→Imaging (see page 150).

Note: In Windows Me, the Paint and WordPad accessory programs no longer work with TWAIN cameras and scanners, as they did in previous versions of Windows.

Installing Scanners and Cameras

After you physically connect your scanner or camera to your computer, restart the PC. If the scanner or camera connects to your USB port, it's probably a *Plug and Play-compatible* gadget (see Chapter 13), which means that Windows Me will "see" it and install its software driver automatically when it starts up. The installation is complete.

Installing WIA Scanners and Cameras

If your camera or scanner supports WIA, you can use the new Scanner and Camera Installation Wizard to install it. Use these steps, clicking Next to move from one wizard window to the next:

1. Choose Start→Settings→Control Panel.

   The Control Panel window opens.

2. Double-click the Scanners and Cameras icon.

   The Scanners and Cameras window opens.

3. Double-click the Add Device icon.

   The Scanners and Cameras Installation Wizard opens its introductory window.

4. Click Next. Choose the manufacturer's name in the left pane of the wizard window; choose your device's model name from the list in the right pane.

Note: If you have WIA drivers for your device from the manufacturer, but the device doesn't appear in the list of manufacturers, click Cancel. Start over with Steps 1–3, but when the list of manufacturers and models appears, click Have Disk. Then follow the on-screen instructions to complete the installation.

---

5. **Select the port to which you've connected your device.**

   You can also choose Automatic Port Selection to tell Windows Me to find the port.

6. **Give the device a name.**

   The name you specify here will appear on the device's icon in the My Computer window and in the Scanners and Cameras folder in the Control Panel window.

7. **Click Finish.**

   Windows transfers the required driver files to your hard drive. You may be asked to insert your Windows Me CD.

Installing TWAIN scanners and cameras

To install a TWAIN device, you need the manufacturer's software—not a driver, but the application that handles the installation and actually operates the scanner or camera.

Connect the device to your computer, following the manufacturer's instructions. Then put the CD from the manufacturer into the CD-ROM drive and install the software. (Instructions should be available in the documentation that came with your device.)

Making WAVs with Sound Recorder

Windows Me comes with a generous assortment of sound files that you can use as error beeps, as described in Chapter 12. But no error beep is as delightful as one that you've made yourself—of your two-year-old saying, "Nope!" for example, or your own voice saying, "Dang it!"

Using Sound Recorder (Figure 8-10) requires a healthy assortment of equipment: a sound card, speakers, and a microphone. If your PC has all that, and it's all working correctly, you can use this little program to record snippets of your life, which can serve as error beeps or any other purpose.

Recording a New Sound

Here's how to do it:

1. Choose Start→Programs→Accessories→Entertainment→Sound Recorder.

   The window shown in Figure 8-10 appears.

---

2. **Choose File→New.**

   You can take a detour at this point by choosing File→Properties. In the resulting Properties for Sound dialog box, you can click Convert Now to specify the sound quality of the recording you're about to make. The choices—Radio Quality, CD Quality, and so on—indicate not only how good the sound will sound, but also how much disk space the file will consume. (Better quality takes up more disk space.)

3. **Click Record, make the sound, and then click Stop as soon thereafter as possible.**

   If you see animated sound waves in the Sound Recorder window, great; that's your VU (sound level) meter. It tells you that the PC is hearing you. If you don't see these yellow lines, however, then the sound isn't getting through. The problem is most likely that your PC control panel isn't set to record the appropriate sound source. Choose Edit→Audio Properties, and then use the Sound Recording drop-down menu to choose your microphone's name.

   If it's impossible to get a clean sound, free of dead space—because you're recording babies or animals who refuse to perform on cue, for example—you're not out of luck. You can always edit out the dead space. Use the scroll bar to position the handle just before the dead space at the end of the sound, and then choose Edit→Delete After Current Position. (To get rid of dead space *before* the good part, position the handle and then choose Edit→Delete *Before* Current Position.)

   At this point, you can click the Play button to see what you've got. If it isn't quite what you had hoped, repeat Step 3; your first take is automatically obliterated.

Tip: Don't miss the good times that await you in the Effects menu. You can make your recording play faster or slower, add an echo effect, or even play it backward—great for finding subliminal messages in your own utterances.

When you've got something worth keeping, go on:

4. **Choose File→Save As. Type a name for your sound file, choose a folder for it, and click Save.**

   You've just created a *.wav* file—a standard Windows sound file.

Note: In previous versions of Windows, you could also record a song from a music CD using Sound Recorder. Doing so involved clicking the Record button in Sound Recorder, then *quickly* switching back to CD Player and clicking Play.

Fortunately, you don't have to do any of that in Windows Me; just use Windows Media Player to convert CD tracks into files on your hard drive automatically.

What to Do With Sounds

When you save a .wav file, you're actually creating a new icon on your desktop. When you double-click it, the file opens in Windows Media Player and plays back immediately. (Press Esc to interrupt playback.) Sound files are also great for emailing to other Windows users, posting on Web sites, transferring over the network, and so on. Many a Bart Simpson sound clip proliferates via the Internet in exactly this way.

Finally, if you put a .wav file into your my Computer→C: drive→Windows→Media folder, it joins the other sound files that Windows uses for its various error beeps. You can then use the instructions on page 211 to replace Windows Me's sound effects with ones you've created yourself.

Figure 8-10:
Sound Recorder (left) lets you capture the sounds of your world–digitally. Volume Control (right) offers left-to-right stereo balance controls and volume adjustments for every sound-related component of your PC.

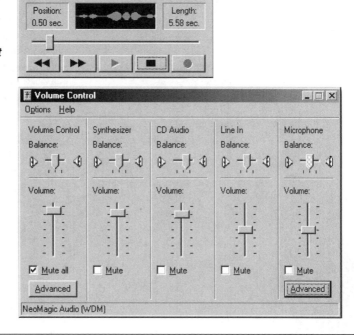

Volume Control

This program has perhaps the most understated name of all time. As you can see by Figure 8-10, this program looks more like a 747 cockpit than a simple volume knob.

In any case, the controls you see here govern the volume and balance levels of the speakers, microphones, and sound-card elements of your PC. Every PC's sound card and other features are different, so not all of the controls may be operational on your machine, but you get the idea.

Here are a few things you might want to do with Volume Control:

- **Shut your PC up.** By clicking "Mute all" at the lower-left corner of the window, you make your PC completely silent—a handy feature when you don't want some errant beep or squawk to let the world know that you're using your laptop in, for example, church.

- **Adjust the stereo balance of your PC speakers.** If one of the speakers is farther away from your head, you might want to drag the Balance sliders so that the distant speaker plays a little bit louder.

- **Fine-tune MIDI playback.** If your sound card can play back MIDI files (a compact file format for instrumental music), use the Synthesizer balance and volume controls to tweak its sound.

- **Adjust the bass and treble.** These knobs don't appear on the Volume Control screen; you have to choose Options→Advanced Controls, and then click Advanced, to see these sliders (Figure 8-10).

Tip: If you rarely use some of the Volume Control features, or if some of them don't apply to your system, or if your system has features (such as a microphone) that *don't* have corresponding controls, you can hide or show individual panels. To do that, choose Options→Properties. In the Properties dialog box, a scrolling list of checkboxes lets you hide or show each of the volume controls—Synthesizer, CD Audio, Line In, Microphone, and so on—independently.

The Control Panel

The Control Panel is filled with miniature applications, affectionately known as *applets*, that let you change the settings for every conceivable component of your computer. Sometimes these applets open automatically, such as when you install hardware (such as a modem or a printer). Others are so obscure, you'll probably never use them. This chapter covers them all.

Figure 9-1:
In an attempt to separate the useful control panels from the rarefied or technical ones, Windows Me starts out showing you only the commonly used control panels (top right). It hides the rest until you ask to see them by clicking "view all Control Panel options." Then the display changes so that you can see all the applets (lower left).

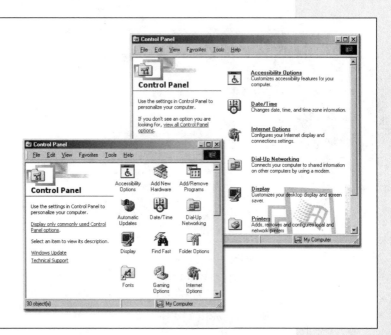

To see your PC's collection of control panels, open the Control Panel window by choosing Start→Settings→Control Panel (see Figure 9-1).

Tip: If your Control Panel window contains applets that aren't described in this chapter, it may be because one of your programs has installed its own applets there. Microsoft Office, for example, deposits two new control panels onto your PC: Fast Find and Mail.

Accessibility Options

Most of the options here are designed to make computing easier for people with disabilities, but some can be useful for almost anyone (Figure 9-2).

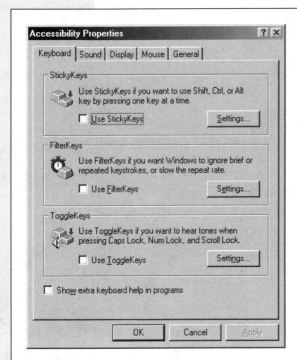

Figure 9-2:
Double-click the icon to open the Accessibility Options dialog box shown here. You start out looking at the Keyboard tab, which offers useful ways to adjust keyboard behavior. By clicking Settings, you can fine-tune many of these features, making it even easier to accommodate special computing needs.

Keyboard Tab

The Keyboard tab offers a set of helpful adjustments that make it easier to type without causing errors.

StickyKeys

StickyKeys is useful for people who have difficulty pressing two keys at once—such as triggering Ctrl, Alt, and Shift key combinations.

Once you've turned this feature on, you can press each key of such combinations

---

one at a time instead of simultaneously. To do so, press the first key (Ctrl, Alt, or Shift) *twice,* which makes it "stick." Then press the second key (usually a letter key). Windows responds exactly as though you had pressed the two keys simultaneously.

If you click Settings, you get a dialog box offering several useful options. One turns StickyKeys off automatically if two keys are pressed at the same time (useful if two people share a computer and only one of them requires StickyKeys); another makes Windows Me beep when a key is double-pressed and "stuck," as a confirmation that you're about to trigger a keyboard shortcut.

FilterKeys

In Windows, holding down a key for longer than a fraction of a second produces repeated keystrokes (such as TTTTTTT). When you turn this option on, Windows Me treats such a repeated key as a single keystroke, which can be useful if you have trouble pressing keys lightly and briefly.

The Settings button opens a dialog box that offers additional options, such as:

- **Use shortcut.** Requires that you also press the right-side Shift key for between 8 and 16 seconds as the on/off switch for the filtering mode.

- **Show FilterKey status on screen.** Puts a stopwatch-like icon on your Taskbar Tray when you're in FilterKeys mode.

ToggleKeys

When you turn on this option, the computer beeps whenever you press the CapsLock, NumLock, or ScrollLock key.

You don't have to be disabled to find this option attractive; the confirmation beep means that you're less likely to look up after five minutes of typing to find a page of text tHAT lOOKS lIKE tHIS.

Sound Tab

Turn on SoundSentry to tell Windows Me to make your screen flash or blink when a sound occurs—a useful feature if you're hearing impaired. Click the Settings button to specify the part of the screen you want to use as a warning: the title bar of the active window, the active window itself, or the desktop. If you're working with text that's running in full-screen mode, you can ask Windows Me to flash your text itself, the window border, or the entire screen.

Turn on ShowSounds if you'd like your applications to display an explanatory caption every time a sound is generated. (Not all programs do, although those specifically advertised as being Windows Millennium–compatible generally do.)

Display Tab

If your sight is going, you may find that Use High Contrast makes text easier to read. Use the Settings button to choose white lettering on black, black on white, or any color combination that works for you.

You can also use this dialog box to make your blinking insertion point (which appears when you're editing text) easier to see. You can change the blink rate, the width of the blinker, or both. (Making it fatter comes in especially handy on older laptops whose screens aren't the greatest.)

Tip: One of the simplest and most powerful aids to those with failing vision is the "Windows Standard (large)" and "Windows Standard (extra large)" *Desktop Themes.* You'll find these controls in the Display control panel, on the Appearance tab, as described later in this chapter. With a single click, you can make Windows enlarge the type used in all of its dialog boxes, menus, icon names, tooltips, and so on.

Don't miss the Mouse control panel (page 203), either, where you can select much larger arrow cursors.

Mouse Tab

If you find using the mouse difficult, or if you'd like more precision when using graphics programs, consider turning on the MouseKeys feature (by turning on the "Use MouseKeys" master switch on this tab, and then pressing the NumLock key to turn MouseKeys mode on and off). It lets you use the number keypad to control the arrow cursor. Pressing the 2, 4, 6, and 8 keys on this pad moves the mouse around your screen down, left, up, and right. (Check your keyboard—you'll see the corresponding directional arrows on these keys.)

In MouseKeys mode, the other numeric-keypad keys also have new assignments:

- Hold down the Ctrl key to make the cursor jump in larger increments, or Shift to move it in smaller, more precise increments.

- Use the 5 key to simulate a mouse click (left-click).

- Use the minus-sign key to simulate a right-click.

- Use the + key to simulate a double-click.

To fine-tune the MouseKeys behavior, click Settings. One useful such option: If you'd like to require that the left-side Alt and Shift keys be pressed in addition to NumLock (to prevent accidental MouseKeys triggering), turn on the "Use shortcut" checkbox.

MouseKeys also offers a way to drag, so you can select text or move objects on the screen without using the mouse:

POWER USERS' CLINIC

Keeping a Control Panel At Hand

If you find that you're opening a certain control panel frequently, you can give yourself one-click access to its icon.

Right-click the applet's icon in Control Panel window; choose Create Shortcut from the shortcut menu. Windows tells you that you can't create this shortcut in this folder, and asks if you want the shortcut placed on the desktop. Click Yes. Drag the resulting desktop shortcut icon onto the Quick Launch toolbar (see page 79) to give yourself one-click access to the applet.

---

1. Use the keypad arrows to position the cursor on the highlighted text, icon, or whatever you want to drag.

2. Press Ins (the zero key on your numeric keypad).

   To "right-drag," press the minus-sign key, *then* Ins.

3. Use the keypad arrows to drag to the target location.

4. Press Del on the keypad to "drop" the object.

General Tab

Using the settings on the General tab, you can set Windows Me to turn off accessibility options if it's been awhile since anyone used them. That's a useful setup if, for example, several people share a computer and only one of them requires these options. You can also ask Windows Me to notify you by playing a sound or a message when options are turned on or off.

The General tab also has an option to enable support for *SerialKey* devices: special equipment (usually keyboard and mouse replacements) for people with disabilities. If you select the option, Windows relies on a SerialKey device for input.

Add New Hardware

This icon isn't really a control panel at all; it's a wizard, and one that's described in Chapter 13.

Add/Remove Programs

This control panel offers three tabs that offer important (though unrelated) functions:

- **Install/Uninstall.** This tab displays a list of every program you've installed onto your PC. As described in Chapter 6, you can remove one from your system by clicking its name and then clicking Add/Remove. You can also launch the installer for a new piece of software by inserting its floppy or CD and then clicking Install.

- **Windows Setup.** You can think of this tab as a miniature version of the Windows Me installer described in Appendix A. It gives you the opportunity to install a new Windows software component without having to reinstall all of Windows.

  The list of checkboxes on this tab shows everything Microsoft offers: Accessories, Desktop Themes, Games, and other software categories (Figure 9-3, left). To see which software components are in one of these categories, click its name and then click Details (Figure 9-3, right). Now you can turn on the checkbox of something you want to install, click OK, and insert the Windows Me CD when you're asked for it. Windows grabs the component you requested and installs it onto your PC.

• **Startup Disk.** If you didn't make a Windows Me emergency floppy disk when you installed the operating system (Appendix A), do so right now. (Just click Create Disk and insert a floppy.)

Having this safety disk is a fast, cheap precaution. It means that you'll be able to start up your PC even when your copy of Windows, or your hard drive, has called in sick.

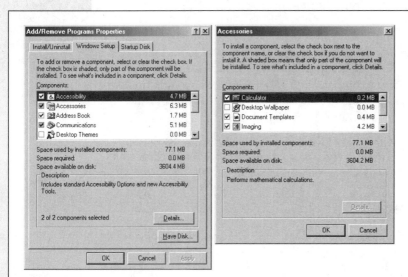

Figure 9-3:
Left: Checkmarks indicate software you've already installed; gray checkboxes mean that you've got only some of the software in this category; and empty checkboxes are Windows components that aren't on your PC. If you click Details, you get the box at right.

Right: If you're missing an element from your Windows installation, turn on its checkbox and then click OK.

Automatic Updates

Thanks to this new Windows Me feature, you no longer have to be a PC magazine subscriber to find out when Microsoft comes up with bug fixes or other Windows enhancements. If you go onto the Internet with any regularity, the Automatic Updates feature will *tell* you about these inevitable software patches (Figure 9-4). This control panel lets you control how (and whether) you're notified about such new features.

The first time Windows discovers an update, it puts an Automatic Update icon on your taskbar (Figure 9-5). Click the icon to find out what Microsoft has for you.

If Windows Me tells you that an update is ready to be installed, but you choose not to install it (by clicking the Don't Install button shown in Figure 9-5), Windows makes the updater invisible on your hard drive (if it has space). If, later in life, you decide that you really *would* like to have that particular update, you can click the Restore Hidden Items button. Then, the next time you install an update, those choices become available once again.

Tip: All of the software updates that Windows Me tells you about are also available for do-it-yourself download and installation at *http://windowsupdate.microsoft.com*.

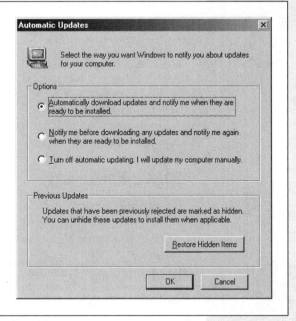

Figure 9-4:
You can turn off Windows Me's new auto-update-installation feature by choosing the bottom option ("Turn off automatic updating"). In that case, you can always get your updates directly from the Microsoft Web site by choosing Start→Windows Update. You can also ask to be notified before the software patch is downloaded (middle choice), or only after it's been downloaded and is ready to install (top choice).

Figure 9-5:
Top: When Windows finds an update, a Taskbar note lets you know. If you click the Taskbar icon, a wizard (bottom) walks you through the installation process. Click Details to read about the files that have been downloaded, or Install to proceed with the installation.

Date/Time

Your PC's conception of what time it is can be very important. Every file you create or save is stamped with this time; every email you send or receive is marked with this time; and when you drag a document into a folder that contains a different draft of the same thing, Windows warns you that you're about to replace an older or newer version—but only if your clock is set correctly. (Don't forget to set your time zone, too, using the bottom drop-down menu.)

To set the date, choose the month and year from the drop-down menus, and click the correct calendar square. To specify the current time, click one of the numbers in the time box. Then adjust the corresponding number either by typing the numbers, pressing your up or down arrow keys, or by clicking the tiny up or down arrow *buttons*. To jump to the next number for setting, press the Tab key.

Dial-Up Networking

This icon isn't a control panel at all; it's a folder that contains the Make New Connection Wizard and any Internet-account icons you've established. (Both are described in Chapter 10.)

Display

Ever admired the family photo or Space Shuttle photo plastered across a co-worker's monitor desktop? The Display applet is your ticket to such interior-decoration stunts, and many others. You get the window shown in Figure 9-6, whose controls are divided into six tabs: Background, Screen Saver, Appearance, Effects, Web, and Settings.

Tip: A quick way to open the Display control panel: right-click any blank spot on the desktop and choose Properties from the shortcut menu.

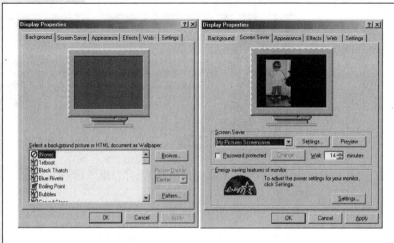

Figure 9-6:
Left: In addition to redecorating the desktop, Display Properties even lets you redo the design scheme used for the windows you open as you work. Right: Some screen savers are animated; they move, grow, or appear with TV-like effects such as fade-ins. The My Pictures Screensaver shown here, for example, offers an endless slide show.

Background Tab: Desktop Pictures and Patterns

The background surface of your desktop doesn't have to be "Windows Me blue"; you can decorate it with a picture, pattern, or solid color.

Applying wallpaper

Wallpaper, in Windows lingo, is a picture to "hang" on your screen backdrop. Click one of the names in the "Select a background" list to see how it looks on the miniature monitor in the dialog box. (Most of the graphics listed in the list are designed to be repeating patterns, not full-screen backdrops, which explains why they look so puny and lonely in the middle of the miniature monitor.)

If nothing in the list excites you, you can use one of your own graphic files to use as wallpaper, such as a scanned photo of your family, your dog, or your family dog. Click Browse to find the file you want. You can use as wallpaper any graphics file whose name ends with one of these extensions: *.bmp, .gif, .jpg, .jpeg, .png, .dib, .htm,* or *.html.* (A few of these require you to turn on the Active Desktop [page 194] before you can use them as wallpaper.)

If the graphic is a small picture, you can force it to fill your desktop by choosing one of these commands from the Picture Display drop-down menu:

- **Tile** multiples the image, repeating it over and over, until it fills the entire desktop.

- **Stretch** expands the single image to fill the desktop, sometimes with extremely coarse and grainy results.

When you've selected a backdrop you like, click OK to apply it and close the dialog box, or Apply to see what the wallpaper looks like, leaving the dialog box open so that you can make another choice if the first one looks hideous.

To remove wallpaper, return to the Display Properties dialog box and select None as the Wallpaper choice.

GEM IN THE ROUGH

Webby Wallpaper

If you find a graphic on the Web that strikes your fancy, you can install *it* as wallpaper—without even having to pay a visit to the Display control panel. To do so, right-click the image—right there in your Web browser—and choose Set as Wallpaper from the shortcut menu. The graphic moves immediately to the middle of your desktop. (You'll probably have to close or minimize your browser window to see it.)

Windows Me saves the file in your Windows folder, naming it *Internet Explorer Wallpaper.bmp* or *Netscape Wallpaper.bmp* (depending on your browser). If you find another Web graphic you like and want to repeat the steps to turn it into wallpaper, be aware that Windows Me will save the new file with the same name, *replacing* the original file. To have access to both files, change the filename of the previous wallpaper file before you grab a new image.

Repeating patterns

If the graphic you've selected to hang on your desktop isn't big enough to fill the monitor, you can choose a repeating pattern to fill in the gap around it as a frame. Click the Pattern button to see a list of patterns that Microsoft's artists have worked up for you. Click one in the list to view a preview; when you find one you like, click OK to return to the Display Properties dialog box.

Tip: Although the tools are extremely crude, you can even create two-toned patterns of your own. Click Edit Pattern to open the Pattern Editor, where you can click a blank dot to make it black, or a black one to make it blank.

Solid colors

To change the color of your backdrop without actually putting a picture there, click the Appearance tab, described on page 191.

Screen Saver Tab

Screen savers are animations that take over the monitor when a certain amount of time has elapsed without keyboard or mouse activity. They were originally designed to prevent motionless images from leaving permanent ghost images on your monitor after many hours. Today's far more sophisticated, long-life monitors aren't susceptible to the burn-in phenomenon. In other words, there are only two reasons for using a screen saver: to add password protection to your PC when you're away from your desk, or just to look cool.

If you leave your computer, whatever work you were doing is hidden behind the screen saver; passers-by can't see what's on the screen. To make the screen saver go away, move the mouse, click a mouse button, or press a key.

Tip: Moving the mouse is the best way to get rid of a screen saver. A mouse click or a key press could trigger an action you didn't intend—such as clicking some button in one of your programs or typing the letter whose key you pressed.

Choosing a screen saver

To choose a Windows Me screen saver, choose from the Screen Saver drop-down menu. A miniature preview appears in the preview monitor on the dialog box (see Figure 9-6, right).

Tip: If you've got some graphics files in the Start→Documents→My Pictures folder, select the My Pictures screen saver from the Screen Saver drop-down menu shown in Figure 9-6. Windows Me gives you a slide show that features your My Pictures images one at a time, bringing each to the screen with a special effect (flying in from the side, fading in, and so on).

To see a *full-screen* preview, click Preview. The screen saver display fills your screen and remains there until you move your mouse, click a mouse button, or press a key.

The Wait box determines how long the screen saver waits to kick in since your last activity. Click Settings to play with the chosen screensaver module's look and behavior. For example, you may be able to change the colors, texture, or animation style.

In the "Energy saving features" panel at the bottom of this tab, there's a Settings button. It opens the Power Options control panel described later in this chapter.

POWER USERS' CLINIC

Password-protecting screen savers

When you password-protect a screen saver, trying to "wake up" the PC by clicking the mouse or pressing a key produces a password dialog box. Until somebody types the correct password, the screen saver remains on the screen. This setup protects the data that's currently on your screen from prying eyes; it also prevents anyone from using your computer.

To turn on password protection, turn on the Password Pro-

tected checkbox (see Figure 9-6, right); click Change to produce the Change Password dialog box. When you click OK, a password-enhanced screen saver now protects your PC.

Note: A password-protected screen saver won't stop a determined ne'er-do-well. If he really wants to get into your computer and its files, he can just push the Power or Restart button on the computer to restart the PC and bypass the screen saver.

Appearance Tab: Choosing Fonts and Colors for Your World

Windows Me includes a number of *schemes*, pre-designed accent-color sets that affect the look of all the windows you open. These color-coordinated themes affect the colors of your window edges, title bars, window fonts, desktop background, and so on. They also control both the size of your desktop icons and the font used for their names, as shown in Figure 9-7 at right, and even the fonts used in your menus.

The factory setting is the theme called Windows Standard; you can examine it or change it on this tab of the Display Properties dialog box (see Figure 9-7).

You can proceed with your interior-decoration crusade in any of several ways:

• Use the Scheme drop-down menu to choose one of the canned themes that come with Windows. The top half of the dialog box gives you a preview of the effect.

• Change the elements of the scheme one at a time. Start by choosing from the Item drop-down menu (or by clicking a piece of the illustration, as shown in Figure 9-7). Then use the Size, Color, and Color 2 drop-down menus to tailor the chosen element—such as Desktop or Scrollbar—to suit your artistic urges.

• Some of the screen elements named in the Item drop-down menu have text associated with them: Icon, Inactive Title Bar, Menu, Message Box, ToolTip, and so on. When you choose one of these text items, the Font drop-down menu at the bottom of the dialog box comes to life. Using this menu, you can change the typeface (font, color, and size) used for any of these screen elements. If you have trouble reading the type used in tooltips, wish your icon names showed up a little bolder, or would prefer a more graceful font used in your menus, these controls offer the solution.

If you come up with an attractive combination of colors and type sizes, you can add them to the Scheme drop-down list by clicking Save As. You'll be asked to name your creation; thereafter, you'll see its name listed along with the "official" Microsoft schemes.

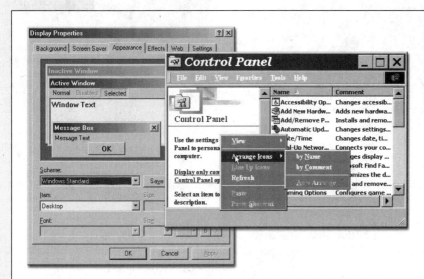

Figure 9-7:
As you click parts of the illustration (left), the Item drop-down menu identifies what you clicked (such as Desktop, Menu, Title Bar, and so on). After this click, you can use the Size and Color menus to choose colors and type sizes for that interface element. Right: These controls can radically change the look of your desktop and windows.

Effects Tab: Changing Your Icon Pictures

This tab of the Display Properties dialog box offers what Microsoft calls special effects. No science-fiction film producer is haranguing Microsoft to learn these effects secrets; they're so subtle as to be almost invisible. Nevertheless, they exist, and you can control them in this dialog box. Here's what you'll find:

Desktop icons

The top section of the dialog box lets you change the tiny pictures that Windows uses for the important desktop icons. If, say, you can't stand the look of the Recycle Bin icon, click it in this scrolling list and then click Change Icon. You'll be shown an assortment of potential replacement images; if you've created or downloaded additional miniature pictures, you can use one of those instead by clicking the Browse button and navigating to the folder that contains them.

Visual effects

Using these checkboxes, you can turn on a variety of effects (special and not-so-special):

- **Use transition effects for menus and tooltips.** When this box is checked, a menu doesn't just pop open when clicked; instead, it gracefully *slides* open—an attractive, but time-wasting, effect. (Try it on your Start menu.)

- **Smooth edges on screen fonts.** When fonts are enlarged, they get ragged on the curves. But when you turn on this option, Windows Me smoothes and softens the jagged edges, using a process called *anti-aliasing*. This setting works only when you've set your monitor to 16-bit color or more, as described next.

- **Use large icons.** This checkbox refers to desktop icons. If you're having trouble seeing your desktop icons, turn on this option to get jumbo icons. (If you have a slower, older PC, this feature may sap some of its memory and speed.)

- **Show icons using all possible colors.** When you turn this item on, Windows displays your icons using as much color as is available in the color setting for your system (on the Settings tab, described later in this chapter). If you disable this option, Windows Me displays icons using a palette of only 16 colors, which may result in a tiny speedup as your folder windows open. (You may not even notice the difference in either speed or color, however.)

- **Show window contents while dragging.** If the option is off (the factory setting), when you drag a window, you see a faint outline of its border; you don't see all the items *in* the window coming along for the ride. As soon as you stop dragging, the contents reappear. If you enable this feature, however, as you drag a window across your screen, you see all the contents, too—which often slows the dragging process.

Figure 9-8:
Active Desktop puts a live Web page (or picture) on your screen backdrop; the sports-scores ticker shown here is a typical example. Sometimes, Active Desktop can drive you crazy, especially if the Web site you choose has blinking animations; selecting more than one of these Web-page tidbits can make your desktop look like Times Square at midnight.

Web Tab (Active Desktop)

You use the Web tab to turn on *Active Desktop,* a feature that lets you see information from the Web directly on your desktop, live and self-updating. If you want to keep an eye on an approaching tornado, the stock market, or some live Webcast, this is the feature for you. Of course, getting live, continuous Internet information works only while you're actually connected to the Internet; it's great if you have a cable modem or DSL line, for example, but less practical if you dial the Internet using a modem.

To turn on Active Desktop, you can visit this tab in the Display control panel. (As a shortcut, you can also right-click a blank spot on the desktop and choose Active Desktop→Show Web Content from the shortcut menu.)

GEM IN THE ROUGH

Active Desktop for Modem Fans

While Active Desktop works best if you have a full-time Internet connection, using it with a dial-up modem isn't impossible. You can set up your PC to connect at a certain time of day (just before you arrive at your desk, for example), update the Web page on your desktop, and then hang up. That way, a recent (but detached-from-the-Internet) Web page greets you each morning. (To ensure that the PC is on at its designated connection moment, see "Power Options" on page 207.)

To set up this arrangement, open the Web tab of the Display control panel. Click the name of the Web page you want to self-update, and then click Properties.

As shown here, a special dialog box appears. Turn on "Make this page available offline," and then click the Schedule tab. Turn on "Using the following schedule"; click Add; use the controls to indicate which time of day you want your desktop updated; name the schedule, if you like; and turn on the "automatically connect for me" checkbox at the bottom of the window.

But before you click OK, consider this. At the specified time, your PC will dial the Internet and update the Web page on your desktop. But what then? You can read what's on the page, but you can't very well click one of the links on it. The Web page is frozen onto your desktop, disconnected from the Internet. If you click one of the links on it, you'll get only an error message.

That's the virtue of the final tab, the Download tab. The "Download pages __ links deep" option makes your PC download not just the specified Web page, but also all Web pages *connected* to it. If you change the number here to 2, then you'll also be able to click links on *those* pages; you'll have the freedom to explore the links on your Active Desktop Web page to the extent of pages-from-pages you specify. (All of these additional downloaded Web pages take up disk space, however, which is why there's a "Limit hard-disk usage" checkbox, too.)

When you're finished setting up your automatic download, click OK.

Turning on Active Desktop

Once you've got the Web tab in front of you, turn on Active Desktop like this:

1. **Turn on "Show Web content on my Active Desktop."**

2. **Turn on a checkbox in the list (such as "My Current Home Page").**

   These checkboxes represent the various Web pages you'd like to see plastered across your desktop. To add to this list, click the New button, type the URL (Web address), and click OK.

   You can add any kind of Web information to your Active Desktop. Frequently updated pages like stock tickers are popular, but you can also use Web pages that don't change much.

   By clicking New and then Visit Gallery, in fact, you can check out the Microsoft Web site, which offers an array of newsy, constantly updating Active Desktop elements, such as sports, weather, or travel news. These aren't actually Web pages, but blurbs that appear in their own little boxes on your living desktop.

   And if you click Browse, you can choose a graphics file or HTML (Web-page) document on your hard drive for displaying on the desktop. (Using the Background tab of the Display control panel, described earlier, is a more direct way of placing a picture on your desktop. But choice, Microsoft always says, is good.)

3. **Click Apply (to preview the Web page on your desktop) or OK (to apply it to your desktop *and* close the dialog box).**

Now a strange thing happens: Your entire desktop becomes a Web browser. You can click links, move to other Web pages, and so on. (Clicking a link opens a standard browser window, however.) If you push your cursor to the top of the Web-page area, you can even make a little menu bar appear, complete with commands (in a tiny, upper-left drop-down menu) that pertain to the desktop-as-Web-page feature. If you drag the lower-right corner of one of these Web areas, you can make it larger or smaller.

Tip: When your desktop is your browser, the usual Internet Explorer menu bar doesn't appear. You won't find standard IE commands like Back, Forward, Add to Favorites, and so on.

But if you right-click the desktop, a shortcut menu appears that contains all of these important Web-browsing commands.

If you right-click *outside* the Web-page portion of your desktop (in the unaffected desktop to either side), you get a shortcut menu bearing an Active Desktop command. Its submenu offers several useful commands:

- **Customize My Desktop.** Returns you to the Web tab of the Display control panel.

- **New Desktop Item.** Lets you choose a new Web item to add to your desktop.

- **Show Web Content.** The on/off switch for putting a Web page on your desktop.

(Other Active Desktop items, such as pictures or patterns, still appear.)

- **Show Desktop Icons.** Displays the desktop icons, which you may find distracting if you're using your desktop as a full-blown Web browser.

- **Lock Desktop Items.** Freezes the size and position of Active Desktop items.

- **Synchronize.** Updates the Web page on your desktop by connecting to the Internet. (This feature is useful if your PC doesn't have a full-time Internet connection.)

- **[Web page names].** At the bottom of this submenu are the names of any Web pages you've selected. Use these commands to switch your desktop from one Web page to another, like a glorified Favorites command.

Turning off Active Desktop

To turn off the Active Desktop, right-click a blank spot on the desktop and choose Active Desktop→Show Web Content from the shortcut menu.

Settings Tab: Colors and Resolution

The Settings tab (Figure 9-9) is the place to make sure Windows Me is getting the most out of your video hardware.

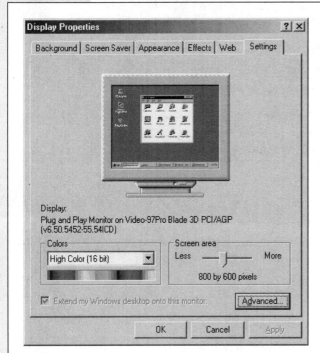

Figure 9-9:
All desktop screens today, and even some laptop screens, can make the screen picture larger or smaller, thus accommodating different kinds of work. You do this magnification or reduction by switching among different resolutions (the number of dots that compose the screen).

Adjusting your resolution

The "Screen area" slider snaps to the various possible *resolution* settings (see Figure 9-9) your monitor's software driver makes available: 640 x 480, 800 x 600, and so on.

When you use a low resolution setting, such as 640 x 480, the pixels (dots) that make up your screen image get larger, thus enlarging the picture—but showing a smaller slice of the page. Use this setting when, for example, playing a small movie so that it fills more of the screen. At higher resolutions (such as 800 x 600 or 1024 x 768), the pixels get smaller, making your windows and icons smaller, but showing more overall area. Use this kind of setting when you want to see as much screen area as possible: when working on two-page spreads in a page-layout program, for example.

Color settings

Today's monitors offer different *color depth* settings, each of which permits the screen to display a different number of colors simultaneously. This drop-down menu varies by video driver, but generally offers three settings: 256 Colors, High Color (16 bit), and True Color (24 bit).

In the early days of computing, higher color settings required a sacrifice in speed. Today, however, there's very little downside to leaving your screen at its maximum bit depth setting ("True Color"). Photos, in particular, look best when your monitor is set to higher bit depth settings. The 256 Colors option, on the other hand, makes photos look blotchy; it's useful only for certain computer games that, having been designed to run on ancient PCs, require the lower color setting.

Using multiple monitors

If you've installed two graphics cards, or one graphics card with two connections, you can hook up two different monitors to your PC. (With more video cards, you can hook up even more than two.) You can use this feature to create a gigantic virtual desktop. As you work, you can move icons or toolbars from one monitor to another, or stretch windows across multiple screens. You can keep an eye on Web activity on one monitor while you edit data on another.

FREQUENTLY ASKED QUESTION

Video Levels Reset Themselves

I tried to set my resolution and color palette for the highest settings, but Windows Me changes the settings before I can click OK. What's going on?

It takes a lot of graphics card memory and processor resources to display a lot of colors *and* high resolution. To protect you from establishing settings that will bring your PC to its knees, Windows Me checks your processor speed and memory level when you change video settings, and adjusts them automatically to keep your system from slowing to a crawl.

For instance, if you choose a high resolution and then select True Color, Windows Me automatically lowers your resolution.

You configure multiple monitors using the Settings tab of the Display Properties dialog box; the tab changes its contents when you've got multiple monitors attached. Icons appear for both monitors. You can arrange the icons in this dialog box to reflect the way Windows "thinks" of them: beside one another, or stacked vertically, for example. That is, you can indicate which edge of your primary monitor permits your cursor to travel beyond the glass and onto the next monitor.

Tip: To avoid insanity, position the monitor icons so they represent the way your physical monitors are arranged. If you have icon #2 on the right side of the dialog box, but monitor #2 is on the left side of your desk, you'll drive yourself crazy. If you set up the icons for top-to-bottom dragging, build a little two-shelf bookcase and stack the monitors on your desk.

One monitor is considered the *primary* monitor. This is the screen that will display your opening Windows Me screen, the Logon dialog box (if you use one), and so on. When you configure the monitor settings, be sure to assign your primary monitor to monitor icon #1.

Advanced settings

If you click the Advanced button on the Settings tab, you're offered a collection of technical settings for your particular monitor model. Depending on your video driver, you may find controls here that adjust the *refresh rate* to eliminate flicker, install an updated adapter or monitor driver, and so on. In general, you'll rarely need to adjust these controls except on the advice of a consultant or help-line technician.

Folder Options

This applet offers three tabs, all of which are described elsewhere in this book: General (see page 66), View (page 72), and File Types (page 134).

Fonts

This icon is a shortcut to a folder; it's not a control panel. It opens into a window that reveals all of the typefaces installed on your machine, as described at the end of Chapter 12.

Gaming Options

If you're a serious gamer, the Gaming control panel may interest you. You use it to configure and control the joysticks, steering wheels, game pads, flight yokes, and other controllers you've attached to your PC.

Controllers Tab

If your joysticks and controllers aren't installed and configured properly, you can't pulverize aliens to your full capacity. On this tab, you can install the driver software for your game controller.

Click Add to view the list of controller models for which Windows already has the driver software; if yours isn't listed, click Add Other to grab the driver software from the CD or floppy that came with your gadget.

Controller IDs Tab

Some game controllers work by controlling the port they're assigned to, using special drivers supplied by the manufacturer. You can assign such drivers on this tab.

Voice Chat Tab

The Voice Chat tab of the Gaming applet lets you turn on *voice chat* for certain kinds of games. That is, you can speak into your PC's microphone (if you have one), and hear your opponent's replies from your PC's speakers (if you have them)—even across the Internet.

None of this works unless you meet a long list of conditions, however. For example, you won't see any games listed on this tab unless:

- They lack *built-in* voice-chat features; the Voice Chat tab adds voice chat functions only to games that don't already have it.

- They use DirectPlay technology.

Furthermore, you can turn on voice chat only if:

- The player hosting a game being played across the Internet has turned on voice chat in *her* copy of the Gaming applet.

- The Web site that's hosting the game (if you're playing via Internet) is designed to permit voice chat for games.

- You choose "Internet TCP/IP connection for DirectPlay" on the game's configuration screen (if it's an option).

- You don't mind that voice chat slows the game way down, especially if you're playing via Internet using a standard modem.

Internet Options

A better name for this control panel would have been "Web Browser Options," because all of its settings apply to Web browsing—and, specifically, to Internet Explorer. Its six tabs break down like this:

- **General, Security, Content.** Controls your home page, cache files, and history list, and lets you define certain Web pages as off-limits to your kids. Details on these options are in Chapter 11.

- **Connections.** Controls when your PC modem dials; see page 229 for details.

- **Programs.** Use these drop-down menus to indicate which Internet programs you generally prefer for email, creating Web pages, and so on. For example, the email program you specify here is the one that will open automatically whenever you click an "email me!" link on a Web page. The checkbox at the bottom of the dialog box tells Windows to watch out for the day when you install a browser other than Internet Explorer; at that time, you'll be asked which program—IE or the new one—you want to use as your everyday browser.

- **Advanced.** On this tab, you'll find dozens of checkboxes, most of which are useful only in rare circumstances or affect your Web experience only in minor ways. For example, "Enable Personalized Favorites Menu" shortens your list of bookmarks over time, as Internet Explorer hides the names of Web sites you haven't visited in a while. (A click on the arrow at the bottom of the Favorites menu makes them reappear.) "Show Go button in Address bar" lets you hide the Go button at the right of the Address bar; after you've typed a Web address (URL), you have to press Enter to open the corresponding Web page instead of clicking the actual Go button on the screen. And so on.

You can get a relatively coherent description of each one by clicking the question-mark button in the upper-right corner of the window and then clicking the checkbox in question.

Keyboard

You can gain more control over your keyboard's behavior with the Keyboard control panel. It has two tabs: Speed and Language.

Speed Tab

You're probably too young to remember the antique known as a *typewriter*. On some electric versions of this machine, you could hold down the letter X key to type a series of XXXXXXXs—ideal for crossing something out in a contract, for example.

On a PC, *every* key behaves this way. Hold down any key long enough, and it starts spitting out repetitions, making it easy to type, for example, "No WAAAAAY!" or "You go, girrrrrl!"

FREQUENTLY ASKED QUESTION

The Usefulness of Repeating Keys

I can't think of any time I would need to type a repeating line of the letter "m." Why would I bother with keyboard repeat settings?

Do you use the arrow keys or the PageUp/PageDown keys to move through a text document or a spreadsheet? Have you ever overshot the mark? Slow down the repeat rate.

Do you ever repeat a special character, such as the equals

sign or underline, to create a separator line between paragraphs or sections? If so, how many times have you had to use the Backspace key to eliminate characters that wrapped to the next line?

In short, it's true that you might not need to repeat a letter of the alphabet very often—but being able to make the *other* keys repeat comes in surprisingly handy.

Character repeat

The two sliders in the "Character repeat" box govern this behavior. The Repeat Delay slider determines how long you must hold down the key before it starts repeating (to prevent triggering repetitions accidentally). The Repeat Rate slider governs how fast each key spits out letters once the spitting has begun.

Your keyboard model and typing habits have a great deal of influence on these settings. Some keyboards offer more resistance than others. Touch typists usually have a much lighter touch than hunt-and-peck typists, who use the index fingers a lot (and therefore press the keys fairly hard).

After making these adjustments, click in the test area at the bottom of the dialog box to try out the new settings.

Cursor blink rate

The "Cursor blink rate" slider governs the blinking rate of the *insertion point* (the cursor that shows where typing will begin when you're word processing). A blink rate that's too slow makes it more difficult to find your insertion point in a window filled with data. A blink rate that's too rapid can be distracting.

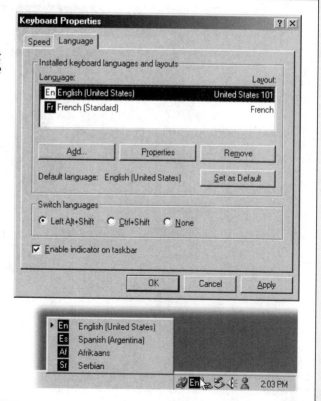

Figure 9-10:
After you've added a couple of layouts to the Language tab (top), specify which one you want by clicking its name and then click Set as Default. A special icon—a blue square bearing a two-letter country code—appears on your Taskbar Tray (bottom), which is a useful reminder as to why your typing is producing unexpected symbols. (To see what your new keyboard arrangement looks like, use the Character Map program described on page 146.)

Language Tab

The symbols you use when you're typing Swedish aren't the same as when you're typing English. Microsoft solved this problem by creating different *keyboard layouts,* one for each language. Each keyboard layout rearranges the letters that appear when you press the keys. For example, when you use the Swedish layout and press the semicolon key, you don't get a semicolon (;)—you get an ö.

To get a choice of keyboard layouts, you use this control panel to install the appropriate driver by clicking Add, and, in the resulting window, choosing the languages you want (see Figure 9-10).

Tip: Instead of using the Keyboard control panel, you can switch from one keyboard layout to the next by pressing the left-side Alt and Shift keys, or by right-clicking the Language indicator on your Tray and choosing a language from the shortcut menu.

Modems

For details on this modem-configuration control panel, see page 292.

FREQUENTLY ASKED QUESTION

Not Your Father's Keyboard

I know that the Alt and Ctrl keys are used to trigger menu functions without the mouse. But my latest keyboard has even more keys that I don't recognize. What are they?

If you have a keyboard built especially for using Windows, you have three extra keys:

- A key with the Windows logo. Press it to open the Start menu without having to use the mouse. (This key is usually on the bottom row of desktop PCs; it may be at the top of a laptop keyboard.)

- On the right may be a duplicate Windows key and a key with an icon representing a menu, complete with a tiny cursor pointing to a command. Press this key to simulate a right-click at the current location of your pointer.

Even better, the Windows logo key has a number of useful functions when it's pressed in conjunction with other keys. For example:

[Windows]+**D** hides or shows all application windows (great for jumping to the desktop for a bit of housekeeping).

[Windows]+**E** opens Windows Explorer (see page 88).

[Windows]+**F** opens the Search for Files and Folders window (see page 28).

[Windows]+**Ctrl+F** opens the Search for Computers window (see page 36).

[Windows]+**M** minimizes all open windows, revealing the desktop.

[Windows]+**Shift+M** restores all minimized windows.

[Windows]+**R** opens the Run command (see page 24).

[Windows]+**V** turns your speaker on and off.

[Windows]+**Tab** switches through all the application buttons on the Taskbar.

[Windows]+**Break** opens the System Properties dialog box.

Mouse

All of the icons, buttons, and menus in Windows make the mouse a very important tool; the Mouse control panel is its configuration headquarters (Figure 9-11).

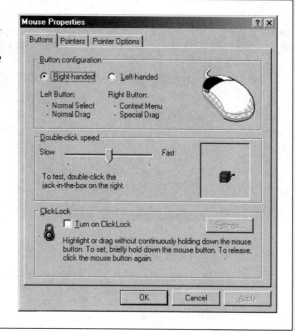

Figure 9-11:
If you're a southpaw, you've probably realized by now that the advantages of being left-handed when you play tennis or baseball were lost on the folks who designed the computer mouse. Most mice are even shaped wrong for lefties, but at least you can correct the way the buttons work.

Buttons Tab

This tab offers three useful controls: button configuration, double-click speed, and ClickLock.

Button configuration

If you're left handed (and keep your mouse on the left side of the keyboard), this tab lets you switch the functions of the right and left mouse buttons, so that your index finger naturally rests on the primary button (the one that selects and drags).

Double-click speed

Double-clicking isn't a very natural maneuver. If you double-click too slowly, the icon you're trying to open remains stubbornly closed. Or worse: If you accidentally double-click an icon's name instead of its picture, Windows sees your double-click as two single clicks, which makes Windows think you're trying to rename the icon.

The difference in time between a double-click and two single clicks is usually well under a second. That's an extremely narrow window, so let Windows Me know what you consider a double-click by adjusting this slider. The left end of the slider bar represents 0.9 seconds, and the right end represents 0.1 seconds. If you think you need more time between clicks, move the slider to the left; if your reflexes are highly tuned (or you drink a lot of coffee), try sliding the slider to the right.

Each time you adjust the slider, you can test your adjustment by double-clicking the jack-in-the-box in the Test area. If the creature pops out, you've successfully double-clicked. If not, adjust the slider again.

TROUBLESHOOTING MOMENT

Sharing a Computer Between a Lefty and a Righty

If a right- and left-hander share a computer, confusion and marital discord may result. If the mouse is set for the righty, nothing works for the lefty, who may assume that the PC is broken or cranky.

If you use the multiple-users feature (see Chapter 14), Windows Me solves the problem by switching the left- and right-button modes automatically when each person logs on.

But if you're not using the multiple-users feature, you can provide a quick way to switch the mouse buttons between lefties and righties. The easiest way to do this is to create a shortcut of the Mouse control panel. Put it on the desktop or the Quick Launch toolbar on the Taskbar, as described on page 79.

ClickLock

ClickLock is for people blessed with large monitors or laptop trackpads who, when dragging icons on screen, get tired of keeping the mouse button pressed continually. You can, instead, make Windows Me "hold down" the button automatically, avoiding years of unpleasant finger cramps and messy litigation.

When ClickLock is turned on, you can drag something using this technique:

1. **Point to the item you want to drag, such as an icon. Press the left mouse or trackpad button for the ClickLock interval.**

   You specify this interval by clicking Settings in this tab.

2. **Release the mouse button.**

   The button acts as though it's still pressed.

3. **Drag the icon across the screen by moving the mouse (or stroking the trackpad) without holding any button down.**

   To release the button, hold it down again for the time interval you specified.

Pointers Tab

If your fondness for the standard Windows arrow cursor begins to wane, you can assert your individuality by choosing a different pointer shape.

Selecting a pointer scheme

Windows has many more cursors than the arrow pointer. At various times, you may also see the hourglass cursor (which means, "wait; I'm thinking" or "wait; I've crashed"), the I-beam cursor (which appears when you're editing text), the little pointing-finger hand made famous by Microsoft's advertising (which appears when you point to a Web-page link), and so on.

All of these cursors come prepackaged into design-coordinated sets called *schemes*. To look over the cursor shapes in a different scheme, use the Scheme drop-down list; the corresponding pointer collection appears in the scrolling list. (Some, the ones whose names include "large," offer jumbo, magnified cursors that are ideal for very large screens or failing eyesight.) When you find one that looks like an improvement over the "(None)" set, click OK.

Note: If you only see one or two schemes in the drop-down list, you probably didn't install all the available schemes when you installed Windows Me. You can add more collections of mouse pointers by using the Add/Remove components feature (see page 185).

Select individual pointers

You don't have to change to a completely different scheme; you can also replace just one cursor. To do so, click the pointer you want to change, and then click Browse. You're shown the vast array of cursor-replacement icons (which are in the C: drive→Windows→Cursors folder). Click one to see what it looks like; double-click to select it.

Create your own pointer scheme

Once you've replaced a cursor shape, you've changed the scheme to which it belongs. At this point, you can either click OK to make your change take effect and get back to work, or you can save the new, improved scheme under its own name, so that you'll be able to switch back to the original when nostalgia calls. To do so, click Save As, name the scheme, and then click OK.

Pointer Options Tab

This tab offers a few more random cursor-related functions.

Pointer speed

It may surprise you that the cursor doesn't move five inches when you move the mouse five inches on the desk. Instead, you can set things up so that moving the mouse one millimeter moves the pointer one full inch—or vice versa—using the Pointer speed slider.

It may come as even more surprise that the cursor doesn't generally move *proportionally* to the mouse's movement, regardless of your "Pointer speed" setting. Instead, the cursor moves farther when you move the mouse faster. How *much* farther depends on how you set the slider that appears when you click Accelerate.

The Fast setting is nice if you have an enormous monitor, because it means that you don't need an equally large mouse pad to get from one corner to another. The Slow setting, on the other hand, can be frustrating, because it forces you to pick up and put down the mouse frequently as you scoot across the screen. (You can also turn off the "Pointer acceleration" completely using the checkbox.)

SnapTo

A hefty percentage of the times you reach for your mouse, it's to click a button in a dialog box. If you, like millions of people before you, usually click the *default* (outlined) button, such as OK, Next, or Yes, the SnapTo feature can save you the effort of positioning the cursor before clicking.

When you turn on SnapTo, every time a dialog box appears, your mouse pointer jumps automatically to the default button, so that all you have to do is click. (And if you want to click a different button, such as Cancel, you have to move the mouse only slightly to reach it.)

Visibility

The options available for enhancing pointer visibility (or invisibility) are mildly useful under certain circumstances, but mostly, they're just for show.

- **Show pointer trails.** *Pointer trails* are ghost images of your mouse pointer that trail behind the pointer like a bunch of little ducklings following a mother duck. In general, this stuttering-cursor effect is irritating; on rare occasions, however, you may find that it helps you locate the cursor if you're making a presentation on a low-contrast LCD projector.

- **Hide pointer while typing.** Hiding the insertion point while you're typing is useful if you find that it sometimes gets in the way of the words on your screen. As soon as you start using the keyboard, the pointer disappears; just move the mouse to make the cursor reappear.

- **Show location of pointer when you press the CTRL key.** If you've managed to lose the cursor on an LCD projector or a laptop with an inferior screen, this feature helps you gain your bearings. When you press and release the Ctrl key after turning on this checkbox, Windows displays animated concentric rings that pinpoint the cursor's location.

Network

For details on this headquarters for your network settings, see Chapter 16.

Passwords

If you're using the multiple-users feature of Windows Me (Chapter 14), this control panel lets you change the password you use to sign into the PC. The User Profiles tab is described in Chapter 14, too.

If you connect to other machines on the network, you can change that password, too; click Change Other Passwords. (If this button is dimmed, it's because you don't have access to any other networked, password-protected equipment.)

PC Card (PCMCIA)

If you have this control panel at all, you're probably using a laptop. The Socket Status tab lists the PC-card slots you've got available, and what (if anything) is in each.

The Global Settings tab is for very technical people; it lets you specify which area of your laptop's memory your PC cards use. (Great idea: Leave "Automatic selection" turned on.)

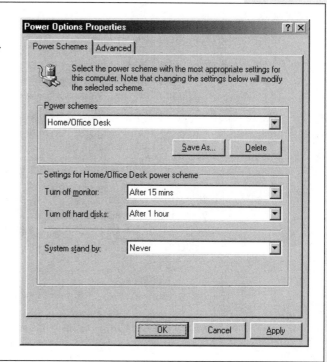

Figure 9-12:
The hardware configuration of this computer produces two tabs on the Power Options dialog box. Your desktop computer may also have a third tab named Hibernate. The Power Options for laptops usually include two additional tabs: Alarms and Power Meter.

Power Options

The Power Options control panel lets you manage the power consumption of your computer. Power savings is important when you're operating a laptop on battery power, but it's also important if you'd like to save money (and the environment) by cutting down on the amount of electricity your desktop PC uses.

The options you see in this control panel depend on your PC's particular features. Figure 9-12 shows the Power Options Properties dialog box for a typical desktop computer.

Power Schemes Tab

The Power Schemes tab lets you select, change, or create *power schemes.* A power scheme defines which components of your PC shut down (to save power) a certain amount of time since you last used your keyboard, mouse, or processor. Power schemes can save power using three different tricks:

- **Turn off monitor.** Your monitor goes dark, and the power light on it changes from green to yellow.

- **Turn off hard disks.** The hard drives stop spinning.

- **System standby.** The computer goes into *standby mode*, which is something like being asleep. All of its components go into reduced-power mode.

You can use the "Power schemes" drop-down menu to choose from Windows Me's three built-in power schemes:

- **Home/Office Desk** is designed for desktop computers. The factory settings put the monitor into low-power mode first, then the hard drive, then the computer itself (that is, it goes into standby mode).

- **Always on** puts your monitor and hard drive to sleep after 10 minutes or an hour, but never invokes standby for the PC itself.

- **Portable/Laptop** puts the monitor, hard drive, and computer to sleep sooner than the desktop schemes in order to save battery power.

You're welcome to change the settings for any of these schemes. Once you've done so, you can click Save As to preserve your new settings under their own new scheme name. Finally, click OK to close the Power Options Properties dialog box and put the selected power scheme into effect.

Waking up your PC

To bring your computer out of any power-saving mode, just move the mouse or press a key. The PC can wake itself up, too, when you've programmed something to happen (such as setting up your email program to check for new messages) or when a fax call comes in (if you've set up your PC to receive faxes).

When the task or the phone connection ends, the computer goes back into standby automatically.

Alarms and Power Meter Tabs: For Laptops

Notebook computers have additional power options, which help them conserve power when running on battery power.

Alarms tab

When your battery starts running out of juice, your laptop shows a warning message. When it's only got a few seconds of power left, you get a second, more urgently worded message. Both messages are designed to clue you in that *now* is a good time to save whatever document you've been working on; the laptop is about to go to sleep until you've plugged the power cord into the wall.

The controls on this tab let you specify when (or whether) these messages appear, what kind of notification you want (a message, a sound, or both), and what the laptop does as a result (such as going into standby mode).

Power Meter tab

This tab is your laptop battery's fuel gauge. If your computer has two batteries, turn on "Show details for each battery"; you'll see an icon for each battery, which slowly "empties" as your power runs down.

Advanced Tab

The "Always show icon on the taskbar" option puts a tiny power-plug icon (or battery icon, if you're using a laptop that's unplugged) on your Taskbar Tray. You can click this icon to produce a menu listing the power *schemes* you've established (see page 207), making it easy for you to switch among them. And if you right-click this icon, you're offered commands that take you directly to the Power Options control panel or its Power Meter tab.

If you select "Prompt for password," you're asked to enter a password. Thereafter, the PC won't wake up from sleep until the password has been entered—a weak security measure, to be sure, but better than nothing.

Finally, on some PCs, this tab contains a third option, which lets you specify what happens when you press the power button on your computer. Instead of turning the computer off, you may prefer that it put your computer into Standby mode or Hibernate mode. This feature comes in handy on those occasions when the computer is in Standby mode but, upon seeing that your monitor is dark, you assume that it's turned off. You hit the power button to turn it *on*—but actually cut the power, which obliterates any unsaved documents and may cause other file damage.

Hibernate Options

If you have a Hibernate tab—which is likely if you bought your computer with Windows Me already installed—you can use it to enable the *hibernation* feature (see page 22). When you turn on "Enable hibernate support," these things happen:

• The Power Schemes tab displays a new power scheme named System Hibernates. It lets you specify a period of idle time before your PC hibernates automatically.

• Your Shut Down dialog box (see page 22) includes a Hibernate option in addition to Shut Down, Restart, and Stand by.

In other words, to make your PC hibernate manually, choose Start→Shut Down, choose Hibernate in the Shut Down dialog box (or press H), and click OK (or press Enter).

Because the hibernate feature saves everything in memory as a file, it consumes a lot of free disk space. The more RAM you have, the more disk space you need. The Hibernate tab displays the amount of free disk space, along with the amount of disk space that's required for the PC to hibernate.

Troubleshooting Standby and Hibernation

Both standby and hibernation modes can cause glitches. For example:

The feature's not there

The most common power-management "problem" arises when your computer simply lacks the necessary circuitry for these power features. That's why the Hibernate tab might not appear on the Power Options Properties dialog box, the Stand by command might not be listed in the Shut Down dialog box, and so on.

Standby doesn't save data

When your computer is in standby mode, any unsaved documents on the screen remain unsaved. In fact, your computer is in the same state it would be if you walked away without using standby. The only difference is that the PC is consuming less power. Contrast with hibernation, in which the current state of the computer is saved to a file on your hard drive.

If you shut off the computer, or if power fails, any documents you forgot to save are gone forever. Therefore, use the File→Save command for any documents you're working on before putting the computer into standby mode or leaving your computer unattended (which will make it go into standby mode automatically).

Your disks don't work right away

Because standby mode affects all the hardware devices in your system, moving your mouse to wake up your computer doesn't make every device available to you in a nanosecond. Some add-on gear, notably removable-disk drives like Jaz, Zip, and CD-ROM drives, require several seconds to "warm up" after your PC awakens.

Computer fails to enter hibernate or standby mode

Standby and hibernate modes work only with the cooperation of all the gear attached to your system. Behind the scenes, Windows notifies the device drivers that power is being reduced. Those drivers are supposed to respond with a message indicating they're capable of *awakening* from standby or hibernate mode. If a device driver doesn't indicate that it can be awakened, the PC stays on.

In such cases, an error message appears telling you that your system cannot go to standby/hibernate mode because "*<name of device driver>* failed the request." The exact wording of the message depends on whether you're trying to enter standby or hibernate mode, and on the specific hardware problem. The most common culprits are video-controller drivers and sound-card drivers.

Until you update the hardware driver (or replace the component with one that has a standby-capable driver), you won't be able to put the PC into standby or hibernate mode.

Printers

This one isn't a control panel at all; it's a shortcut to your Printers folder, described in Chapter 12.

Regional Settings

If you think that 7/4 means July 4 and that 1.000 is the number of heads you have, skip this section.

But in some countries, 7/4 means April 7, and 1.000 means one thousand. If your PC isn't showing numbers, times, currency symbols, or dates your way, use these tabs to rearrange the sequence of date elements. The Time tab, for example, lets you tell Windows whether you prefer a 12-hour clock ("3:05 PM") or a military or European-style, 24-hour clock ("1505").

You'll see the changes you make here reflected in the date and time stamps on your files in list-view folder windows, and (in the case of your Currency-tab choices) in Microsoft Excel.

Scanners and Cameras

This icon isn't a control panel at all; it's a shortcut to the Scanners and Cameras folder, which is described on page 175.

Scheduled Tasks

Here's another folder-masquerading-as-a-control-panel. For more on scheduled tasks, see Chapter 15.

Sounds and Multimedia

Multimedia devices are hardware components, such as your CD-ROM drive and sound card, which produce sound, pictures, and movies.

Assigning Sounds

Windows plays little sound effects, such as beeps, musical ripples, and chords, all the time: when you turn on the PC, trigger an error message, empty the Recycle Bin, and so on. And if you like, you can hear them on many other occasions, such as when you open or exit a program, open a menu, restore a window, and so on. Using the Sounds and Multimedia Properties control panel (see Figure 9-13), you can specify which sound effect plays for each of these situations.

Sound events

A speaker icon denotes the occasions when a sound will play. If you click an occasion's name, you can:

• Remove a sound from the event by choosing (None) from the Name drop-down
list.

• Change an assigned sound, or add a sound to an event that doesn't have one, by
clicking Browse and choosing a new sound file from the list that appears in the
Open dialog box.

When you select a sound, its filename appears in the Name box. Click the triangular
Play button to the right of the box to hear the sound.

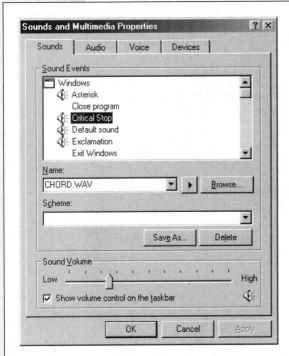

Figure 9-13:
*The Sound Events list shows every conceivable
computer event that generally plays a sound,
organized into categories: Windows, sound
recording, NetMeeting, and so on. (Your
applications' installers may have added categories of their own.)*

Tip: When you click the Browse button, Windows Me opens the C:→Windows→Media folder, which
contains the *.wav* files that provide sounds. If you drag *.wav* files into this Media folder, they become
available for use as Windows sound effects. Many people download *.wav* files from the Internet and stash
them in the Media folder to make their computing experience quirky, more fun, and richer in "Austin
Powers" sound snippets.

Scheme

Each set of sounds is called a sound *scheme;* sometimes the sound effects in a scheme
are even sonically related (perhaps the collection is totally hip-hop, classical, or performed on a kazoo). To switch schemes, use the Scheme drop-down list.

> **Note:** If you don't see more than two schemes, your Windows Me installation process didn't install all the possible schemes. See Appendix A to learn how to add components to Windows Me.

You can also define a new scheme of your own. Start by assigning individual sounds to events. Once you've got your scheme constructed, click Save As to save your collection and make up a name for it.

Sound volume

The Sounds dialog box has a volume slider, but it's inconvenient to open the Control Panel and this applet every time you want to adjust your PC's speakers. Fortunately, the "Show volume control on the taskbar" checkbox puts a speaker icon on your Taskbar Tray, near the time display. Click that icon to open a much more convenient volume slider.

Audio, Voice, and Devices Tabs

The other three tabs on the Sounds and Multimedia Properties dialog box let you change the settings for your various multimedia gadgets.

• Use the Audio tab to select and configure your microphones and speakers. (Most people have only one gadget for each purpose, so there's no real difficulty making a choice.)

• Use the Voice tab for selecting and configuring your microphone.

• The Devices tab offers a subset of the System control panel's Device Manager tab, which is introduced in the next section; it shows you a list of the sound, video, and movie-related hardware components on your PC, and identifies them by brand and model.

System

This advanced control panel is the same one that appears when you right-click your My Computer icon and choose Properties from the shortcut menu. It has four tabs that identify the equipment inside, or attached to, your PC: General, Device Manager, Hardware Profiles, and Performance.

General Tab

You can't change anything on this screen, but that doesn't mean it's not useful. Here you can find out, if you've forgotten, exactly which version of Windows Me you have (don't be surprised if the version number contains far more decimal points than you were taught is legal), the model name of your PC's processor chip (such as Pentium III), and how much memory your PC has—a very helpful number to know, particularly when it comes time to sell your old computer.

Device Manager Tab

This powerful dialog box (see Figure 9-14) lists every component of your PC: CD-ROM, Modem, Mouse, and so on. If you double-click a component's name (or click the + symbol), you get to see the brand and model of that component. Many of these items are *controllers,* the behind-the-scenes chunks of electronics that control the various parts of your computer, with technical-looking names to match. For much more on the Device Manager, see page 304.

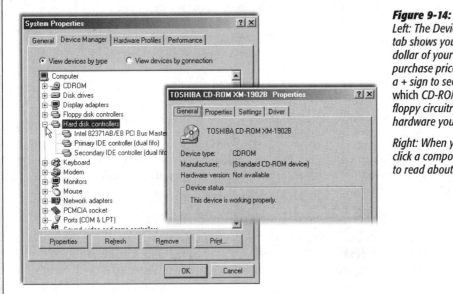

Figure 9-14:
Left: The Device Manager tab shows you where every dollar of your PC's purchase price went. Click a + sign to see exactly which CD-ROM drive, floppy circuitry, or other hardware you've got.

Right: When you double-click a component, you get to read about its specs.

Hardware Profiles

You can configure your laptop to turn off certain features when you're on the plane, but to turn them back on when you're at the office; see page 308 for details.

Performance

This tab reveals several technical specs about your computer, such as how much memory (RAM) it's got, how many *system resources* (see page 298) are free, and so on. This information, along with the three buttons at the bottom of the screen, are primarily valuable when you're on the phone with a help-desk technician who's trying to help you troubleshoot.

Taskbar and Start Menu

This control panel controls every conceivable behavior of the Taskbar and Start menu. You can read all about these options in Chapters 2 and 3.

Telephony

These options establish your local area code, numbers your modem needs to dial (such as 9) for an outside line, calling-card numbers, and so on. All of these come into play primarily when you're dialing the Internet, especially from a laptop that you transport from city to city. See page 234 for more detail.

Users

This control panel is the master switch for the multiple-users feature described in Chapter 14. If you're the only one who uses your PC, you can (and should) ignore it.

Part Three:
Windows Online

Chapter 10: Hooking Up to the Internet

Chapter 11: What to Do on the Internet

3

Hooking Up to the Internet

Plenty of people get a PC to crunch numbers, scan photos, or cultivate their kids' hand-eye coordination. But for millions of people, Reason One for getting a PC is to use the Internet. Few computer features have the potential to change your life as profoundly as the World Wide Web and email.

To join the Internet party already in progress, you need three components: a *connection*, such as a modem, cable modem, DSL, or corporate network; an Internet *account*; and Internet *software*, such as the Web browsers and email programs described in the next chapter.

How to Get Online

Most people connect to the Internet using a *modem,* a piece of circuitry that connects your PC to a phone line. Almost every modern computer comes with a built-in, pre-installed modem. If your PC has been preconfigured in this way, smile; you've been spared the least enjoyable part of the Internet experience.

Installing a Modem

If not, you can choose between an internal modem (a small circuit board that you push into a slot inside the PC, saving you some desktop clutter, a power socket, and a few dollars) or an external one (easier to transfer from machine to machine.) An external modem attaches to a serial port on the back of your computer via a modem cable. After you complete the physical installation of your modem, you have to install the modem's software—its *drivers*. Once again, the instructions that accompany the modem should guide you through the process.

Cable Modems and DSL

Although most people connect to the Internet via modem and telephone line, a growing minority connects with much faster gear called *cable modems* and *DSL*. These contraptions offer several gigantic advantages over traditional dial-up modems. For example:

- **Speed.** These modems operate at 5 to 50 times the speed of a traditional dial-up modem. For example, if you download a 2 MB file with a standard modem, you have to wait at least five minutes for the transfer. A cable modem, on the other hand, transfers the same file in about ten *seconds*. Complex Web pages that take almost a minute to load into your browser with a standard modem pop up almost immediately when you use a cable modem or DSL.

- **No dialing.** These fancier connection methods hook you up you to the Internet permanently, full-time, so that you never waste time connecting or disconnecting. You're *always* online.

- **No weekend lost to setting it up.** Best of all, you don't have to do any of the setup yourself. A representative from the phone company or cable company comes to your home or office to install the modem itself and set up your Windows Me software. If you sign up for a cable modem, the cable TV company pays you a visit, supplies the modem, installs a network card into your PC, and sets up the software for you.

- **Possible savings.** At this writing, cable modems and DSL services cost about $40 a month. That includes the Internet account for which you'd ordinarily pay $20 if you signed up for a traditional ISP. And since you're connecting to the Internet via cable-TV wires or unused signal capacity on your telephone lines, you may be able to save even more money by canceling your second phone line.

UP TO SPEED

What "Modem" Means

Telephone lines use *analog* technology, which means that signals of varying frequency carry voice or data messages. The word "analog" is a shortened form of the word "analogous," because if you watch the process of an analog transmission on a device that measures the waves, the sound wave goes up and down in a way that's analogous to the human voice.

A computer, on the other hand, communicates using *digital* data—millions of tiny on/off pulses. On is represented by the number 1, and Off is represented by the number 0. To a computer, every kind of data from photos to word-processing files looks like a massive string of 1's and 0's.

When your modem sends information across a phone wire, it must first translate the digital data into analog form, a conversion process called *modulating*. At the other end, the receiving modem converts the analog data back into digital form, so that the receiving computer can handle it. That process is called *demodulating*.

In other words, the gizmo that dials the Internet is a modulator/demodulator. But that's nine syllables; life's too short. That's why the *modulator/demodulator*, these days, is called a *modem*.

Not all cable TV companies offer cable-modem service, but the list is quickly growing. (If you don't have cable TV service, you generally can't have a cable modem.) And you can't get DSL unless the phone company has a central office within 18,000 feet of your home—about three miles.

It's also worth noting that cable modems and DSL modems aren't always blazing fast. The speed of your cable modem goes down slightly when lots of people in your area are using their cable modems simultaneously. And DSL modems are slower the farther you are away from the telephone company. Even so, the speed is always better than that of a dial-up modem.

Tip: Actually, neither cable modems nor DSL modems are *modems.* They don't modulate or demodulate anything, as described on page 220. Still, we have to call them *something,* so most people call them modems anyway.

ISP vs. Online Service

Once you've chosen a method of connecting to the Net, you need an Internet *account.* You can get one in either of two ways: by signing up for an *online service,* such as America Online or MSN; or by getting a direct Internet account with an Internet Service Provider (or *ISP,* as insiders and magazines inevitably call them).

National ISPs like EarthLink, IDT, AT&T, and MCI WorldCom have local telephone numbers in every U.S. state (and many other countries). If you don't travel much, you may not need such broad coverage; you may be able to save money by signing up for a local or regional ISP. Either way, dialing the Internet is a local call for most people.

Tip: The Internet is filled with Web sites that list, describe, and recommend ISPs. To find such directories, visit a search page like *www.google.com* and search for *ISP listings.* One of the best such Web-based listings, for example, is at *www.boardwatch.com.* (Of course, until you've actually got your Internet account working, you'll have to do such research on a PC that *is* online, such as the free terminals available at most public libraries.)

Each route (online services or ISP) has significant pros and cons.

• Most ISPs cost $20 a month for unlimited Internet use; America Online (an online service) costs $22 per month.

Tip: You can also get *free* Internet access if you're willing to tolerate an ad window that sits on your desktop. It's also worth noting that some stores offer a gigantic discount on a new computer if you commit to paying for several years of service with one online service or another.

• Online services strike many people as easier to use, because you use a single program for all Internet functions, including email and Web surfing. When you sign up for an ISP, you use a different application for each function: Internet Explorer for surfing the Web, Outlook Express for email, and so on.

- Some online services, notably America Online, disconnect automatically if you haven't clicked or typed for several minutes. ISPs don't hang up on you nearly as quickly, if at all.

- Online services are screened to block out pornography. The Internet itself, of course, isn't sanitized in this way. (However, you can get *to* the Internet from any online service, which makes this point less relevant.)

- Because online services are slightly easier to use than ISP accounts, you'll run into people who look down on MSN and America Online numbers.

Configuring Online Services

If you'd rather use an online service than a "pure" Internet account, you're in luck. Windows Me offers built-in access to every popular online service: America Online, AT&T Worldnet, and Prodigy. You can create a new account on any of these services during the configuration process, or use an account you already have.

To install MSN (an ISP designed to feel like an online service), double-click the Setup MSN Internet Access shortcut on your desktop to get started.

Tip: If you have no intention of signing up for an MSN account, feel free to delete the MSN Internet Access icon that came pre-installed on your desktop. Just drag it onto the Recycle Bin, thus freeing your life from another bit of commercial clutter.

To install any of the other online services, open the Online Services folder on your desktop to see the icons shown in Figure 10-1.

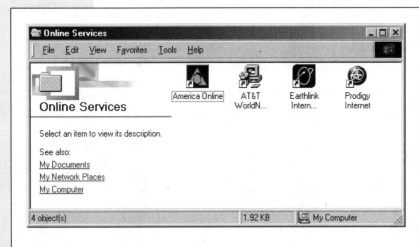

Figure 10-1:
Double-click the service you want to install. Each of the setup programs runs completely on autopilot, guiding you through installing the necessary software and then dialing out with your modem and connecting to its own server. (You may be asked to select a local telephone number from a list, or the software may use an 800 number.)

Once connected, you'll be guided through the process of setting up an account (or logging in with an existing account). For example, when creating a new account, you'll be asked to type in your credit card information and to choose a local telephone number. When it's all over, you'll be ready to go online. The Internet service creates a desktop icon for you; double-click it to open the software and dial out automatically. When you exit the program, the modem disconnects automatically.

The rest of this chapter is dedicated to signing up for a "real" Internet account—an ISP account.

The Internet Connection Wizard

If your PC came with a modem already installed, or if you have a cable modem or DSL system that has been set up for you, you're ready to get your ISP account going. Windows walks you through the process using one of its ubiquitous wizards.

Actually, the Internet Connection Wizard is three wizards in one. On the very first screen, you're asked to specify which category you fall into (see Figure 10-2):

• You want to sign up for a new Internet account.

• You already have an Internet account that you've been happily using on another computer.

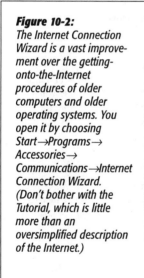

Figure 10-2:
The Internet Connection Wizard is a vast improvement over the getting-onto-the-Internet procedures of older computers and older operating systems. You open it by choosing Start→Programs→ Accessories→ Communications→Internet Connection Wizard. (Don't bother with the Tutorial, which is little more than an oversimplified description of the Internet.)

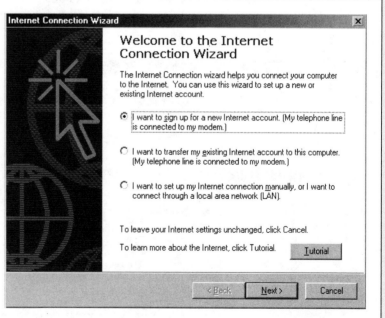

Tip: If you already have an Internet account that you've been happily using on *this* computer, and you've just upgraded from Windows 95 or 98, you don't even have to bother with the Connection Wizard. The installation process described in Appendix A is smart enough to preserve the settings you already had in place. You can skip to Chapter 10.

- Your PC is connected to an office network (via your Ethernet card, for example—see Chapter 16). The Internet account is provided by the corporation.

The following discussion takes these three projects one at a time.

Signing up for a New Internet Account

Maybe you've never had an Internet account, or maybe you'd like to switch to a new ISP (having decided to drop, for example, America Online). In either case, you sign up for a fresh Internet account like this:

1. **Open the Internet Connection Wizard.**

   You can do so by choosing Start→Programs→Accessories→Communications→ Internet Connection Wizard. Make sure that your computer's modem is plugged into a phone jack.

2. **Click the top button on the Internet Connection Wizard (see Figure 10-1), and then click Next, then Next again.**

   Your computer now dials the toll-free number. Your modem performs the shrieking and hissing that's become a familiar sound to millions of Internet fans.

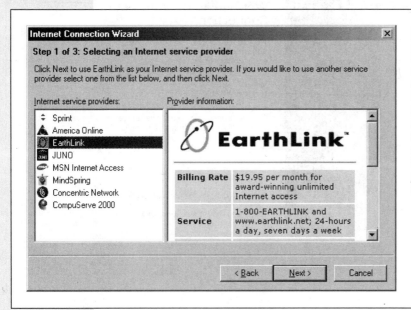

Figure 10-3:
The Internet Connection Wizard shows you a list of national Internet access companies that have worked out deals with Microsoft. Click each logo on the left side of the screen to read about the terms of the service (usually $20 per month for unlimited service).

The wizard is now consulting Microsoft's database of ISPs to find those with service in your area (in general, this means "in your country"). As shown in Figure 10-3, a list eventually appears.

3. **Click the service that appeals you, and then click Next. In the following screens, type in your name, address, phone number, credit card information, and so on.**

   Now the wizard dials a second time; this time, it's contacting the Internet company you've selected. The details of the service plan now appear on your screen.

4. **If you agree with the ISP's rules, click Accept, and then click Next.**

   Now you're asked to invent an email address for yourself. The ending part of it is determined by your choice of ISP—*@earthlink.net* or *@juno.com,* for example. The first part is up to you, but keep in mind that names like *Bob* and *Seinfeld* were snapped up long ago. If the name you type in isn't original, you'll be asked to try again with a different email name.

   If you get lucky, however, you're shown a list of local phone numbers. From this drop-down menu, choose a phone number that's local. If there are no local numbers listed here, and you'd rather not pay long distance charges every time you connect to the Internet, consider canceling this entire signup operation and spending some time researching smaller, regional ISPs.

5. **Finish up with the wizard.**

   This may entail clicking your way through a few final welcome screens.

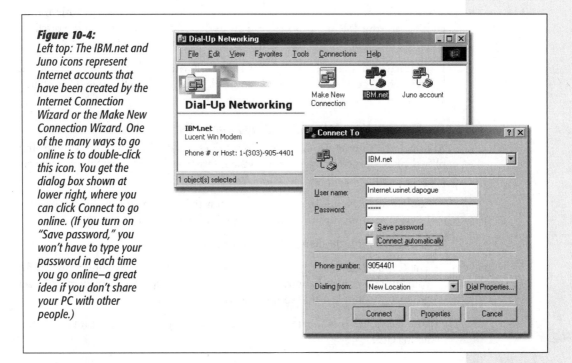

Figure 10-4:
Left top: The IBM.net and Juno icons represent Internet accounts that have been created by the Internet Connection Wizard or the Make New Connection Wizard. One of the many ways to go online is to double-click this icon. You get the dialog box shown at lower right, where you can click Connect to go online. (If you turn on "Save password," you won't have to type your password in each time you go online—a great idea if you don't share your PC with other people.)

Windows Me stores the information about your ISP, your name, password, and so on, into a single icon called a *connection icon.* You can see the one you've just created by choosing Start→Settings→Dial-Up Networking, as shown in Figure 10-4. There are dozens of ways to get online, but one way is to double-click this special icon.

Doing so produces the dialog box shown in Figure 10-4 at right—a box that will soon become extremely familiar. You encounter it every time you connect to the Internet for any reason.

Having setup your connection, you can skip ahead to "Connecting to the Internet." You're ready to explore the Net.

Transferring an Existing Internet Account

If you already have an Internet account (that you use on another computer, for example), you may be able to save yourself some headaches by using the second option of the Internet Connection Wizard. It's designed to consult the actual membership database of your ISP, and then to fill your PC's settings automatically.

Once again, you open the wizard by choosing Start→Programs→Accessories→ Communications→Internet Connection Wizard. When you click "I want to transfer my existing Internet account to this computer" and then click Next, your PC dials the Internet and shows you a list of ISPs that work with Microsoft's "fill in my settings for me" feature. If you see your ISP in the list, click it; you'll be asked to provide your account name (email address), password, and other information to prove that you're you.

Then, if all goes well, the wizard automatically extracts the necessary configuration codes from your ISP and proceeds exactly as described from Step 4 in the previous section. The result is a connection icon like the ones shown in Figure 10-4.

Unfortunately, at this writing, very few ISPs work with this feature. You lose nothing by trying, but the wizard may simply conclude its efforts by telling you to configure your Internet settings manually, as described next.

Configuring Your Internet Settings Manually

Although the Internet Connection Wizard does an admirable job of trying to simplify the hairy process of getting onto the Internet, it doesn't always work. Here are a few cases when you'll have to setup your settings manually:

• You already have an Internet account, but the "I want to transfer my existing Internet account" option of the Connection Wizard didn't work.

• You have a cable modem or DSL connection.

• The Connection Wizard didn't find any ISPs that had local phone numbers for you, but you've heard about a very local service—offered by your local PC user group, for example—that sounds just right.

• Your computer is connected to an office network; your company provides Internet service.

In each of these cases, you can still use the Internet Connection Wizard, but you'll have to do a good deal more typing.

Connecting via dial-up modem

If you connect to the Internet via telephone jack like most of the world, choose Start→Programs→Communications→Accessories→Internet Connection Wizard. Make sure that your computer is plugged into a phone jack.

Click "I want to setup my Internet connection manually," and then click Next. Now click "I connect through a phone line and a modem," and then click Next.

On the next several screens, you'll be asked to type in several pieces of information that only your ISP can provide. They include:

- The local phone number that connects your PC to the Internet

- Your user name and password

- Your incoming mail server address (which usually contains the terms *pop3* or *IMAP)* and outgoing mail server address (which usually contains the term *SMTP).*

You can call your ISP for this information, or you can consult the literature that came by postal mail when you signed up for an ISP account.

When it's all over, you'll be shown the Connect To screen shown at right in Figure 10-4. You'll also find a connection icon on your hard drive, as shown at left in Figure 10-4. If you typed in all of the necessary code correctly, you should be ready to surf.

Tip: If you have a laptop that you carry from city to city, each requiring a different local Internet number, you might want to create more than one connection icon. Instead of using the Internet Connection Wizard over and over again, you can save a little bit of time by using the Make New Connection Wizard.

Choose Start→Settings→Dial-Up Networking. Double-click the Make New Connection icon, and click your way through the settings screens the wizard offers you. This wizard has a lot in common with the Internet Connection Wizard, but saves you a couple of clicks.

Connecting via cable modem, network, or DSL

As noted earlier in this chapter, you're generally spared the hassle of setting up these kinds of accounts; the installation person generally handles this for you. But if you're handy with proxy servers, configuration scripts, and so on, you can use the bottom option in the Connection Wizard shown in Figure 10-2.

You may find it much simpler, however, to configure your cable modem, DSL, or network connection directly, in the Network control panel, exactly as the installer or administrator would have done. This entails rooting around in some of Windows's most technical-looking settings, but all you have to do is type in a few codes that have been specified by the cable modem, DSL, or network administrator. Here's the procedure:

---

1. **Choose Start→Settings→Control Panel. In the control panel window, double-click Network.**

   The Network control panel window appears (see Figure 10-5).

   You can't connect to a cable modem, DSL modem, or network Internet account without an Ethernet card (see Chapter 16). In the scrolling list that appears on the Configuration tab, you should see the name of your Ethernet card, identified by brand and model.

2. **Click the listing that says "TCP/IP→[your Ethernet card model]," and then click Properties.**

   As shown in Figure 10-5, an even more intimidating dialog box now appears, containing seven different tabs that pertain to configuring your Internet account.

3. **With your cable company, DSL company, or network administrator on the phone, type in the information for your account.**

   These differ depending on the company with whom you're working, but the Gateway, IP Address, and DNS Configuration are among the tabs you may be asked to visit for the purpose of typing in settings.

4. **Click OK.**

   You'll probably be told that you need to restart the computer for the changes to take effect.

When you complete this task, you won't wind up with a connection icon, as you would if you intended to connect to the Internet using a dial-up modem. Instead, you're online 24 hours a day—or at least whenever your cable/DSL/network is working correctly.

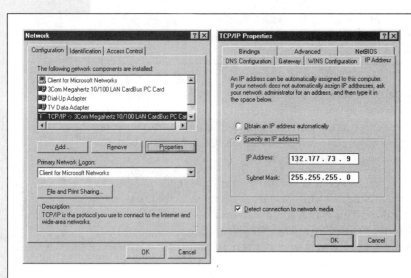

Figure 10-5:
Left: Click the TCP/IP item that corresponds to your Ethernet card and then click Properties. Right: The Internet access company generally configures these settings for you. But if a freak solar eclipse wipes out all of your settings, you can re-enter them here. When you click OK, you'll be asked to reboot, and then you should be back online.

Connecting to the Internet

If you have a full-time Internet connection such as a cable modem or DSL, you don't have to do anything special to connect to the Internet; you're connected constantly (although you may be required to enter a password each time you go online). Skip to the next chapter.

If you have a dial-up modem, however, you should now have a connection icon in your Start→Settings→Dial-Up Networking folder.

Connecting Manually

Double-click your Connection's icon in the Dial-Up Networking window (Figure 10-4, left). The Connect To dialog box appears, as shown in Figure 10-4, right. Just press Enter, or click Connect, to go online.

But that's just the beginning. Here are a few other ways of opening the connection:

- Right-click your connection icon and choose Connect from the shortcut menu.

- Create a desktop shortcut of your connection icon (the icon in the Dial-Up Networking window) by right-dragging the icon out of the window and onto the desktop. When you release the mouse button, choose Create Shortcut(s) Here from the shortcut menu. Now you can double-click the shortcut to connect to your ISP.

- Drag a shortcut of your connection icon onto the Quick Launch toolbar (page 79), which means one click gets you to the Internet.

Using automatic connections

It's important to understand that when your PC dials, it simply opens up a connection to the Internet. But aside from tying up the phone line, your PC doesn't actually *do* anything until you then launch an Internet program, such as an email program or a Web browser. By itself, making your PC dial the Internet is no more useful than dialing a phone number but then not saying anything.

Therefore, using the Internet is generally a two-step procedure: first, open the connection; second, open a program.

Fortunately, Windows offers a method of combining these two steps. Using the automatic dialing option, you can make the dialing/connecting process begin automatically whenever you launch an Internet program. You're saved the trouble of fussing with your connection icon every time you want to go online.

To set this up this convenient arrangement, proceed as follows:

1. **Choose Start→Settings→Dial-Up Networking.**

    The Dial-Up Networking window appears.

2. **Right-click your connection icon. Choose Properties from the shortcut menu.**

   The Properties dialog box for your connection appears.

3. **Click the Dialing tab (Figure 10-6). Select "Always dial my default connection," and then click OK.**

   Alternatively, you can just turn on the "Connect automatically" checkbox in the Connect To dialog box (Figure 10-4) as you're about to go online manually.

From now on, whenever you use a feature that requires an Internet connection, your PC dials automatically. (Examples: specifying a Web address in a window's Address bar, clicking the Send and Receive button in your email program, clicking a link in the Windows Help system, and so on.)

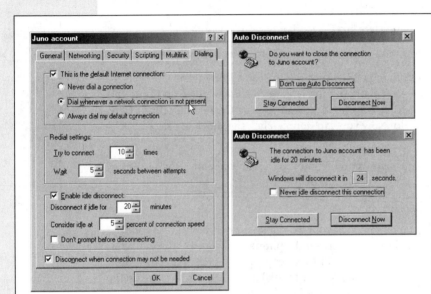

Figure 10-6:
Left: If you turn on "Disconnect when connection may not be needed," your PC will hang up the phone when you quit the program that you launched first (after showing the warning at upper right). If you turn on "Don't prompt before disconnecting," your PC will hang up after the specified idle period without showing you the warning box (lower right).

Disconnecting

While you're connected to your ISP, Windows Me puts an icon on the Taskbar next to the clock (Figure 10-7). It indicates that you're online. You can watch it light up as data is transmitted across the connection.

Disconnecting automatically

When you quit the program that originally made your PC dial, Windows Me shows the message shown at upper right in Figure 10-6. It offers to hang up your phone line for you. If you're finished with your surfing for the moment, click Disconnect Now (or press Enter).

Disconnecting manually

Sometimes, however, you're not finished with your Internet connection. Yes, you may be done with your email program, but perhaps now you intend to do a little Web surfing. In such cases, you can simply click Stay Connected in the dialog box (see Figure 10-6).

If you find that Auto Disconnect dialog box popping up more often than you'd like, however, you can get rid of it. In other words, you can tell Windows Me: "Look, when I want my Internet connection to hang up, I'll tell you. Don't try to disconnect me yourself."

One way to do so is to turn on the "Don't use Auto Disconnect" checkbox (Figure 10-6). Another way is to right-click your connection icon (Figure 10-4), choose Properties, click the Dialing tab, and turn off "Disconnect when connection may not be needed."

If Windows no longer auto-disconnects you, however, you run the risk of forgetting that your modem is tying up the phone line, much to the frustration of the national sweepstakes-winner notification committee that may be trying to call you. When you're finished using the Internet, therefore, you can end the phone call by doing one of the following:

- Right-click the little connection icon on your Taskbar. Choose Disconnect from the shortcut menu (Figure 10-7, lower right).

- Double-click the little connection icon on the Taskbar. Click Disconnect in the information box that appears (Figure 10-7, top) or press Alt+C.

- Right-click the connection icon in your Dial-Up Networking window. Choose Disconnect from the shortcut menu.

- Wait. After about 20 minutes of not doing anything online, your PC shows a small box that lets you know that it's about to hang up. You can adjust the timing of this "idle disconnect" period, or turn off the idle disconnect feature altogether, using the Dialing tab shown (see Figure 10-6).

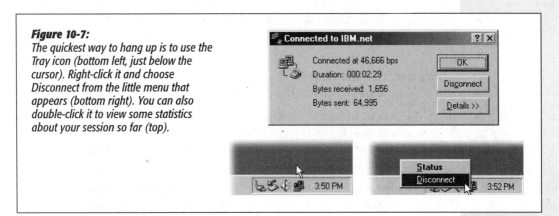

Figure 10-7:
The quickest way to hang up is to use the Tray icon (bottom left, just below the cursor). Right-click it and choose Disconnect from the little menu that appears (bottom right). You can also double-click it to view some statistics about your session so far (top).

Advanced Modem and Internet Settings

Because so many people consider the Internet such an important PC feature, Windows Me lets you fine-tune its dialing, modem, and Internet settings to within an inch of their lives. You should consider the rest of this chapter optional—or power-user—reading.

The Modem Control Panel

To adjust the settings on your modem, choose Start→Settings→Control Panels. Double-click the Modem icon in the resulting window. (See Chapter 9 for more on the Control Panel window.)

In the dialog box shown in Figure 10-8 at left, click Properties to summon the settings for your specific modem (Figure 10-8 at right). The number of tabs that appear here depends on your modem model, but everyone sees tabs called General and Connection. (The other tabs, if you have them, refer to special features of your modem and telephone service, such as Distinctive Ring and Call Forwarding.)

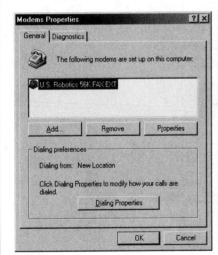

Figure 10-8:
Left: If you click the name of your modem and then click Properties, you see the dialog box at right, which lets you adjust the speaker volume and other settings. The Distinctive Ring feature (available only on some modem models) is designed to differentiate between incoming voice, fax, and modem calls.

Properties: the General tab

The General tab has basic settings for the modem. You can specify, for example:

- **The port to which the modem is connected.** There's no reason to change this setting unless (a) you've physically moved the cable of an external modem from one serial port to another *and* (b) Windows doesn't recognize that fact the next time you start the computer.

- **The volume of the modem speaker.** To turn the speaker off, so that you no longer hear the shrieks and squeals of two modems connecting every time you dial, drag the slider bar all the way to the left; to blast the speaker, drag the slider bar all the way to the right.

Tip: The slider affects the speaker volume only while it's dialing and making a connection to another computer. After the connection is established, the speaker *always* goes silent, so you don't have to listen to all the squawking noises that indicate data transmission.

- **The maximum speed for the modem.** Many people, perhaps thinking wishfully, set a speed higher than the modem's rated speed, but the speed doesn't actually improve as a result.

Properties: the Connection tab

The Connection tab holds the settings for computer-to-computer communication protocols, most of which never need adjusting. Some are occasionally useful in special circumstances:

- **Wait for dial tone before dialing.** This checkbox is normally turned on. If you travel abroad with your laptop, however, you may have trouble connecting if the foreign country's dial tone doesn't sound the same as it does back home. Turning off this checkbox sometimes solves this problem.

- **Cancel the call if not connected within __ seconds.** The factory setting is 60 seconds. If your ISP's modem generally takes a long time to answer the modem call, increase the number.

- **Disconnect a call if idle for more than __ mins.** It's a good idea to select this option if you connect to the Net using your household phone line. If you *don't* use this option, then your PC may continue to tie up the line, with its open connection to the Internet. (See page 230 for more on automatic disconnection settings.) This setting makes the PC release the line, "hanging up" your modem, after an amount of idle time you specify. (*Idle* means time during which no data is coming in or going out.)

UP TO SPEED

Laptop Computers May Need Multiple Dialing Locations

Laptop computers frequently need *multiple* dialing setups. For example, you may take your laptop on the road and dial out from hotels, where it's common to dial 8 or 9 to reach a long distance line. You'd name that location "hotels." Furthermore, if you charge long distance calls to a credit card, you can pre-load the credit card number and PIN into the credit-card information fields. Sometimes your laptop may travel with you to a client site, where dialing out requires a 9, and you may or may not charge the call to a credit card. You can name that location "Amalgamated Doodads" (or whatever your client's name is).

You can create as many locations as you need. Click New, give the location a name, and use the guidelines presented here to configure each location.

Dialing properties

Click Dialing Options in the Modems Properties dialog box (see Figure 10-8) to configure the modem's dialing behavior. The Dialing Properties dialog box, shown in Figure 10-9, may seem to be more comprehensive, and more complicated, than necessary.

Fortunately, unless you're setting up a laptop, you have to visit this dialog box only once, to establish the options required to dial your telephone line (such as "9" for an outside line).

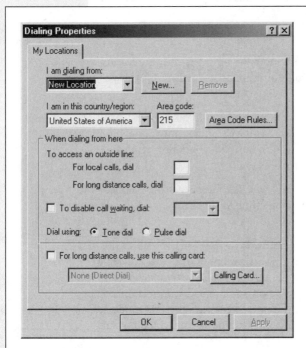

Figure 10-9:
This dialog box has two priorities: to let you set rules for dialing out; and to let you define as many different sets of rules for dialing as you need. This feature can be handy for laptop users who have to dial from hotels, homes, or client offices. But if you're setting up dialing properties for a regular desktop computer, you won't need to change these settings after the first successful call.

Here are the guidelines for filling out this dialog box:

- **Country, Area code.** These boxes tell Windows where you are now. When your modem dials another city or country, Windows Me will know when to dial a 1 (and a country or area code, when necessary) before dialing.

- **To access an outside line.** In many offices, the tone you hear when you pick up the handset is the dial tone for the inter-office phone system. You have to dial a number (usually 9) to get an outside line. Some office phone systems require a separate number (usually 8) if you need a long-distance line. If your computer is in an office with such a system, enter the appropriate digits here. Windows will henceforth dial them automatically before dialing the regularly scheduled Internet access number.

- **To disable call waiting.** If you've signed up for call-waiting service, your Internet connection can get scrambled by the little beep that announces another call coming in. Fortunately, it's easy to turn off call waiting when you use the modem. Turn on this checkbox; from the drop-down list to its right, choose from the list of the common call-waiting disabling key sequences (*70, 70#, and 1170). (If you don't know which sequence works for your local telephone company, check the front of your telephone book.)

  When the modem disconnects from the Internet after your online session, call waiting returns to the phone line automatically.

- **Tone or Pulse dialing.** Specify whether your telephone service is touch-tone (push-button) or pulse (as on old-fashioned rotary-dial phones).

Setting area code rules

It used to be easy to dial the telephone in America. For local calls, you dialed a seven-digit number; for calls to other area codes, you started with 1 and the area code.

Not any more. *Ten-digit dialing* has arrived in many metropolitan areas. It's an insidious system that requires you to dial the full area code even for your next-door neighbor. Worse, some cities have several *different* area codes, and not all of them require a 1+area code dialing pattern; you sometimes dial *only* the area code plus seven-digit number.

To clue your modem in on the vagaries of your own region's area-code practices, click the Area Code Rules button to open the Area Code Rules dialog box shown in Figure 10-10.

- If you have 10-digit dialing (if you must dial your own area code for local calls), turn on "Always dial the area code (10-digit dialing)."

Figure 10-10:
This dialog box can handle any weird and convoluted area code rule in your town. If you don't need special rules, it's only a matter of time. When your local phone company changes the rules, don't forget to open this dialog box and explain the changes to your modem.

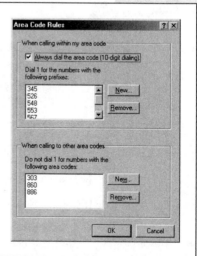

- If you must dial 1 before dialing certain exchanges within your own area code, tell Windows about each one. Click New and enter the exchange. (Your own area code already appears in the dialog box.)

- If there are area codes in your city that *don't* require you to dial 1 first, you must tell Windows about each of those, too. Area codes within the town are not long distance calls and may not require you to dial 1. Click New to enter an area code that fits this category.

Click OK when you finish configuring area code rules; you return to the Dialing Properties dialog box.

Setting up a calling card

If you want to charge calls to a calling card, click Calling Card (Figure 10-9) to open the dialog box shown in Figure 10-11.

Tip: Creating a calling-card profile doesn't lock you into using it every time you use your modem. Each time you dial out, you can choose whether or not to use the calling card.

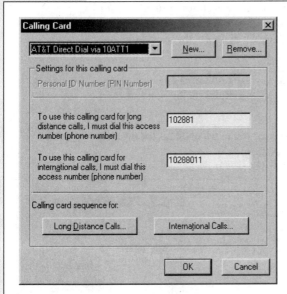

Figure 10-11:
Windows Me already knows about the dialing requirements for most major calling cards. When you choose one from the drop-down list at top left, Windows Me automatically populates the fields with the correct information. On the remote chance you can't find your own card, you can type in the necessary dialing codes manually.

If your calling card isn't listed, you can create a setup for it yourself, which Windows then adds to the list. Using the instructions from your calling card company, take these steps to create a profile:

1. **Choose New, enter a name for this calling card, and click OK.**

   Windows Me displays a message telling you that you must enter the rules for using this card. Click OK.

2. **Enter the access number required by your calling card company.**

   It's usually an 800 number (or other toll-free number).

3. **Click Long Distance Calls to open a new dialog box, where you can specify the steps needed to use the card for long distance.**

   For instance, you may have to dial a number and then wait for a tone that confirms that your number has been accepted. In this dialog box, you can specify the number of seconds you want Windows to wait. You can enter even more elaborate dialing steps if your calling card requires it.

4. **Click International Calls; enter the data required to make calling-card calls to other countries.**

   When you've finished configuring the calling card, click OK to return to the Dialing Properties dialog box.

From now on, you can bill your modem calls to the calling card whenever necessary, like this:

1. **Open the icon for your connection.**

   For more on using connection icons, see page 229.

2. **Click Dial Properties.**

   The dialog box in Figure 10-9 appears.

3. **Turn the credit card option on or off, and then click OK to return to the Connect window. Now click Connect to start your call.**

Tip: You can even create additional Dial-Up Networking connections, each configured for a specific credit card. For example, you can name one connection Regular, another AT&T, another Sprint, and so on. Then all you have to do is double-click the connection icon that matches your credit card need at the moment, and click Connect. You save the slog through several dialog boxes each time you switch.

Connection Settings

Creating a connection icon (see page 229) is usually enough to get you into the Net. But if you right-click the icon and choose Properties from the shortcut menu, you're offered a wealth of additional connection settings (Figure 10-12, left). The connection's dialog box appears (Figure 10-12, right). It offers six tabs: General, Networking, Security, Scripting, Multilink, and Dialing.

Networking tab

If you haven't experienced problems connecting to the Internet, you won't have to adjust any of the settings in this dialog box. If you are having trouble, however, the cheerful tech-support representative on the other end of the phone may ask you to check, or change, some of the options here on the Networking tab.

Here are the guidelines for entering information in the Networking Tab:

- **Type of Dial-Up Server.** The factory setting (PPP) is what you want if you're running Windows Me. (The other choices are for connecting to networks that use other operating systems.)

- **Enable software compression.** This feature compresses data as it travels through telephone lines, making delivery faster. It only works if the computers at both ends of the connection are using the feature. Most ISPs support software compression, which is why this checkbox is usually turned on. (If in doubt, contact your ISP.)

- **Record a log file for this connection.** If you select this checkbox, Windows keeps a log—a text file on your hard drive—detailing everything that happens when you use this connection: what your computer dialed, what the other computer "answered," and so on. (The log file can become enormous, taking up a lot of disk space.) The only reason to keep a log is for troubleshooting purposes; for example, your ISP may ask you to send them the log file if you're having difficulty connecting.

- **Allowed network protocols.** This section of the dialog box lists three network protocols. The only protocol you need for Internet connections is *TCP/IP*.

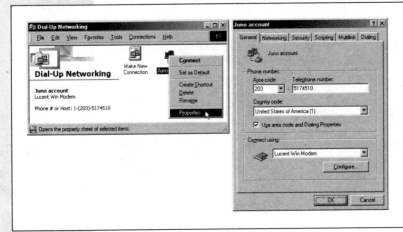

Figure 10-12:
Left: To adjust the settings for a particular Internet connection, right-click its icon. Right: This dialog box appears, rife with tabs and blank text boxes. Most of the information you need is provided by your ISP. In fact, the General Tab is already filled in for you, thanks to the wizard you've presumably already encountered.

Tip 1: To avoid embarrassment in public places, pronounce TCP/IP without the slash: "TCP Eye Pee."

Tip 2: *NetBEUI* (pronounced "NET boo-ee") is used for Windows networks (as is TCP/IP); IPX/SPX (pronounced without the slash) is used for Netware networks.

At the bottom of the dialog box, there's a TCP/IP Settings button. If your ISP so instructs you, you can use the resulting dialog box to specify the way IP addresses are assigned.

Click OK to return to the connection's dialog box.

Security tab

The Security tab stores the data Windows needs to transmit to your ISP each time it connects, such as:

- **User name.** Some ISPs require you to enter your complete email address here, such as *yourname@earthlink.com*. Other ISPs expect only the first part, omitting the ISP address; just *yourname*.

- **Password.** Enter your password carefully, because you can't see the characters you're typing. Windows Me substitutes an asterisk (*) for each character you type, to prevent password theft by somebody peeking over your shoulder.

  Your ISP may have assigned you a password, and then provided instructions for changing it to something you prefer the first time you log on. Other ISPs ask you to establish a permanent password when you sign up for your account.

Tip: If you believe that somebody has figured out your password, you can change it. Some ISPs give you a special URL (Web address) where you can make password changes. Other ISPs require you to call the help line to make a such a change. Either way, you'll be asked for your current password.

If you *forget* your password, on the other hand, you have to contact your ISP and work your way through a fair amount of red tape. Most ISPs make the process fairly difficult (to prevent some unscrupulous stranger from calling the ISP and impersonating you).

Therefore, write down your password, and store it in a safe place. (An example of a *bad* place: a Post-it note stuck to your monitor.)

- **Domain.** This field is used for dialing in to an office network, not the Internet. If you're such a telecommuter, your network administrator will provide all the information you need to set up the connection.

- **Connect automatically.** Select this option if you'd like your PC to dial the Internet instantly when you open your connection icon, bypassing the Connect To dialog box shown in Figure 10-4. (The Connect To box gives you an opportunity to make configuration changes, such as selecting a calling card, before clicking the Connect button.)

- **Log on to network.** This option is another one designed for connecting to your office network, not the Internet.

- **Require encrypted password.** If your ISP requires encrypted passwords for additional security, select this option; but few, if any, ISPs require this feature.

  In the unlikely event that you *are* required to encrypt your password, you don't have to do anything beyond turning on this checkbox; Windows Me will encrypt your password automatically before transmitting it.

- **Require data encryption.** Here's another extremely rare setting, generally reserved for communication with a highly secured host computer. If you work for a top-secret government agency, you'd probably select this option on a Dial-Up Networking connection you create to dial into work. (Then again, if you work for a top-secret government agency, you've probably got a highly paid computer geek on hand to set up all this stuff for you.)

Scripting tab; Multilink tab

You'd use the Scripting tab to create *logon scripts,* which are unnecessary for standard Internet connections.

The Multilink tab configures connections that use two modems simultaneously as a trick to double the bandwidth and speed. However, very few (if any) ISPs permit their members to use this feature.

Dialing tab

The Dialing tab offers options for dialing in and hanging up automatically. For example:

- **Never dial a connection.** When you've selected this option, Internet software (like email programs and Web browsers) won't automatically dial out. Instead, you must manually start the connection by double-clicking the connection's icon.

- **Dial whenever a network connection is not present.** The modem will dial out as soon as the computer starts up; if you get disconnected, it will dial again automatically. Doing so ties up both your phone line and the ISP's modem all day. Put another way, using this feature is a sure way to get your account canceled, because this greedy behavior is against the rules of most ISPs.

- **Always dial my default connection.** If you're not online when you open your browser or email software, your PC will dial automatically.

- **Redial settings.** If so many customers have dialed into your ISP that it has run out of available modems, you get a busy signal. Fortunately, this is a rare event these days. Still, when it happens, you'll be ready: Using the "Redial settings" options on this tab, you can instruct Windows to redial as many times as you specify, saving you from having to typing your password with each attempt.

- **Enable idle disconnect.** You can tell Windows to hang up the line automatically if you haven't done anything online (or used the mouse or keyboard) for a specified period, as described on page 231. Use these controls to specify the amount of idle time—or to turn off the auto-disconnect feature entirely.

In either case, these auto-hang up options are useful indeed. If you don't take advantage of them, your modem keeps the phone call going—even after you've finished surfing the Web or sending email. As a result, your phone line is tied up until you remember to disconnect (or somebody in the family yells at you for tying up the line for hours).

What to Do
on the Internet

Microsoft has gone to great lengths to integrate the Internet into every nook and cranny of Windows Millennium. Links and buttons that spur your modem into a dialing frenzy are everywhere: on the Help screens, in the Search window, and even on the Favorites toolbar that's available at the top of every folder window. Once you've got your Internet connection working (Chapter 10), you may find that it's easier to go online than it is *not* to.

The Internet offers dozens of different features, most of them graced with such unhelpful, invented-by-government-scientists-in-the-Sixties names as FTP, Telnet, Gopher, and so on. But a few of the most popular Internet services are both easy to understand and easy to use: the World Wide Web, email, online chatting, and virtual meetings.

You can use whichever software you prefer for these functions. To connect to the Web, for example, you can use Netscape Navigator, Opera, or any of several less famous Web browsers. For email, you can use Eudora, Lotus Notes, and so on.

But most Windows Me users wind up using the Internet programs that come built right into the operating system: Internet Explorer for Web browsing, Outlook Express for email, MSN Messenger Service for chatting (and free long-distance "phone" calls), and NetMeeting for meetings and remote control of other people's PCs. This chapter covers all four of these programs.

Internet Explorer

Internet Explorer (or IE, as it's often abbreviated) is the most famous Web browser on earth, thanks to several years of Justice-department scrutiny and newspaper headlines. The initial release of Windows Me comes with IE version 5.5; you can launch it in a number of ways:

- Double-clicking its desktop icon

- Clicking its shortcut on the Quick Launch toolbar

- Choosing a Web site's name from your Start→Favorites menu

- Typing a Web address—sometimes called its *URL* (*Uniform Resource Locator*) into the Address bar of a window. A Web-page URL usually begins with the prefix *http://*, but you can leave that part off when typing into the Address bar.

- Clicking a blue, underlined link on a Windows help screen

…and so on.

As you can see in Figure 11-1, the Internet Explorer window is filled with tools that are designed to facilitate a smooth trip around the World Wide Web.

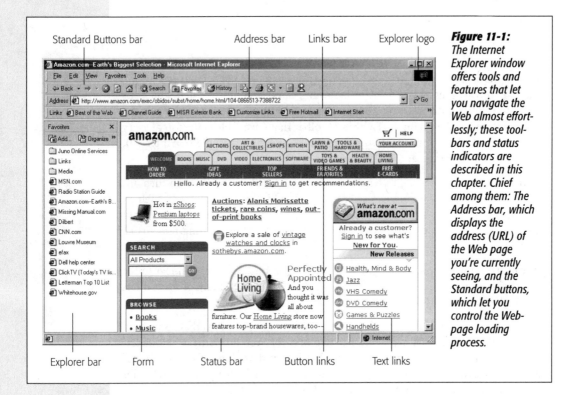

Figure 11-1:
The Internet Explorer window offers tools and features that let you navigate the Web almost effortlessly; these toolbars and status indicators are described in this chapter. Chief among them: The Address bar, which displays the address (URL) of the Web page you're currently seeing, and the Standard buttons, which let you control the Web-page loading process.

Browsing Basics and Toolbars

Navigating the Web requires little more than clicking buttons and links, as shown in Figure 11-1.

When you click an underlined phrase, called a *link* (or *hyperlink*), you're automatically transported from one "page" (screen) to another. One page may be the home page of General Motors; another may contain critical information about a bill in Congress; another might have baby pictures posted by a parent in Omaha. Several hundred *million* Web pages await your visit.

Around the edges of any Web page, as well as within it, you'll encounter standard Internet controls. For example:

- **Explorer logo.** When this globe is spinning, your PC is still downloading (receiving) the information and graphics on the Web page. In other words, you're not seeing everything yet.

- **Button and picture links.** Clicking a picture or a button generally takes you to a new Web page.

- **Text links.** Clicking a link takes you to a different Web page (or a different place on the same Web page).

Tip: Text links aren't always blue and underlined. Modern Web designers sometimes make it very difficult to tell which text is clickable, and which is just text. You can get a hint by moving your cursor over some text. If the arrow changes to a pointing-finger cursor, you've found yourself a link.

Actually, you can choose to hide *all* underlines, a trick that makes Web pages look cleaner and more attractive. Underlines appear only when you point to a link (and wait a moment). If that arrangement appeals to you, choose Tools→Internet Options, click Advanced, scroll down to "Underline links," click Hover, then click OK.

- **Graphics worth saving.** When you see a picture you'd like to keep, right-click it and choose Save Picture As from the shortcut menu. After you click the Save button, the result is a new graphics file on your hard drive containing the picture you saved. (You can also choose Set as Wallpaper, which makes the picture part of your desktop image itself.)

- **Scroll bars.** Use the scroll bar to move up and down the page—or to save mousing, press the Space bar each time you want to see more. Press Shift+Space to scroll *up*. (The Space bar has its traditional, space-making function only when your insertion point is blinking in a text box or the Address bar.)

  You can also press your up and down arrow keys to scroll. Page Up and Page Down scroll in full-screen increments; and Home and End take you to the top or bottom of the current Web page.

Tip: If you have an IntelliMouse mouse from Microsoft, you can use your roller wheel (and other IntelliMouse scrolling tricks) to scroll Web pages, too.

Internet Explorer Toolbars

Many of Internet Explorer's most useful controls come parked on toolbars exactly like those described in Chapter 3. You summon or hide them the same way, too: by choosing their names from the View→Toolbars submenu. Here's what you'll find on each:

Tip: You can drag the tiny "grab bar" at the left end of a toolbar up or down to rearrange the bars' vertical stacking order. You can even drop this grab bar halfway across *another* toolbar, thus placing two toolbars side-by-side on the same horizontal strip.

The Standard Buttons toolbar

This toolbar, identified in Figure 11-1, contains the buttons that most people use for browsing most of the time. Some of them lack text labels, but all offer tooltip labels:

- **Back button, Forward button.** Click the Back button to revisit the page you were just on. *(Keyboard shortcut:* Backspace, or Alt+left arrow.)

  Once you've clicked Back, you can then click the Forward button (or press Alt+right arrow) to return to the page you were on *before* you clicked the Back button. Click the tiny black triangle for a drop-down menu of *all* the Web pages you've visited during this online session.

- **Stop button.** Click to interrupt the downloading of a Web page you've just requested (by mistake, for example). *(Keyboard shortcut:* Esc.)

- **Refresh.** Click if a page doesn't look or work quite right, or if you want to see the updated version of a Web page (such as a stock ticker) that changes constantly. This button forces Internet Explorer to re-download the Web page and re-interpret its text and graphics.

- **Home button.** Brings up the Web page you've designated as your home page (see page 252).

Tip: You can rearrange these buttons, delete some, or add additional function buttons, by choosing View→Toolbars→Customize. For details on operating Microsoft's toolbar-rearrangement window, see page 69.

The Address bar

When you type a new Web page address (URL) into this strip and press Enter, the corresponding Web site appears. (If only an error message results, then you may have mistyped the address, or the Web page may have been moved or dismantled—a relatively frequent occurrence.)

Because typing out Internet addresses is so central to the Internet experience and such a typo-prone hassle, the Address bar is rich with features that minimize keystrokes. For example:

- You don't have to click in the Address bar before typing; just press Alt+D.

- You don't have to type out the whole Internet address. You can omit the *http:// www.* and *.com* portions; by pressing Ctrl+Enter, you make Internet Explorer fill in those standard address bits for you. To visit Amazon.com, for example, a speed freak might press Alt+D to highlight Address bar, type *amazon,* and then press Ctrl+Enter.

- Even without the Ctrl+Enter trick, you can still omit the *http://* from any Web address; Internet Explorer adds it automatically. (Most of the time, you can omit the *www,* too.) To jump to today's Dilbert cartoon, type *dilbert.com* and then press Enter.

- You can press F4 (or use the drop-down menu at the right end of the Address bar) to view a list of URLs you've visited during this browsing session. Then you can press the up or down arrow keys to highlight them, and the Enter key to select one.

- When you begin to type into the Address bar, the AutoComplete feature compares what you're typing against a list of Web sites you've recently visited. IE displays a pop-up list of Web addresses that seem to match what you're typing. So that you're spared the tedium of typing out the whole thing, you can click the correct complete address with your mouse, or use the down arrow key to reach the desired listing and then press Enter. The complete address you selected pops into the Address bar.

  (To make Windows *forget* the Web sites you've visited recently, choose Tools→Internet Options, click the General tab, and then click Clear History.)

Tip: IE can also remember user names, passwords, and other information you type into text boxes *(forms)* you encounter on Web pages. You can turn on this feature by choosing Tools→Internet Options, clicking the Content tab, clicking AutoComplete and turning on the appropriate checkboxes. Or you can just wait for Internet Explorer to *invite* you to turn it on, via a little dialog box that appears when you first type something into such a form. Having your browser remember the names and passwords for your various Web sites is a great time and memory saver, even though it doesn't work on all Web sites.

When you want Internet Explorer to "forget" your passwords—for security reasons, for example—choose Tools→Internet Options, click the Content tab, click AutoComplete, and then click Clear Forms and Clear Passwords.

You can also type a plain English phrase into the Address bar. When you press Enter, IE does a Web search for that term and opens up the first Web page that seems to contain what you're looking for. At the same time, the Search pane appears at the left side of the browser window, offering a list of other Web sites that seem to match your query.

The Links toolbar

The Favorites menu described on page 250 is one way to maintain a list of Web sites you visit frequently. But opening a Web page listed in that menu requires *two mouse clicks*—an exorbitant expenditure of energy. The Links toolbar offers enough room for a few Web-page icons. They let you summon a few, very select, *very* favorite Web pages with only *one* click.

Figure 11-2 shows how you add buttons to this toolbar; you remove one by right-clicking it and choosing Delete from the shortcut menu. It's also worth noting that you can rearrange these buttons simply by dragging them horizontally.

Tip: As shown in Figure 11-2, you can drag a link from a Web page onto your Links toolbar. But you can also drag it directly to the desktop, where it turns into a special Internet shortcut icon. You can double-click this icon whenever you like to launch your browser and visit the associated Web page. Better yet, stash a few of these icons in your Start menu or Quick Launch toolbar for even easier access. (If you open your My Computer→C: drive→Windows→Favorites folder, moreover, you'll see these shortcut icons for *all* your Favorites. You can drag them to the desktop, Quick Launch toolbar, Links toolbar, or wherever you like.)

Figure 11-2:
Add a Web page to the Links bar by directly dragging its tiny page icon, as shown here. (You can also drag any link, such as a blue under-lined phrase, from a Web page onto the toolbar.)

Status Bar

The Status bar at the bottom of the window tells you what Internet Explorer is do-ing (such as "Opening page..." or "Done"); when you point to a link without click-ing, the Status bar also tells you what URL will open *if* you click.

If you consult this information only rarely, you may prefer to hide this bar, thus increasing the amount of space actually devoted to showing you Web pages. To do so, choose View→Status Bar.

Explorer Bar

From time to time, the *Explorer bar* appears at the left side of your browser window. Helpful lists appear here when you choose commands from the View→Explorer Bar menu:

- **Search.** Offers a compact search feature, like the one described on page 28.

- **Favorites.** A duplicate of the bookmarked pages listed in the Favorites menu.

- **History.** A list of Web sites you've visited recently; see page 254 for details.

- **Folders.** Shows you the contents of your hard drive. (This function isn't particularly relevant to Web browsing, but it keeps the Explorer bar consistent with the one described on page 57.)

- **Tip of the Day.** This command takes away a *second* chunk of screen space from your Web-browsing activities, the better to display a daily hint or tip about Internet Explorer.

- **Discuss.** Opens a special toolbar at the bottom of the browser that lets you control and participate in Web-based chat rooms. The Add or Edit Discussion Servers dialog box appears, where you can specify the Web page's *server address* and your online nickname.

Ways to Find Something on the Web

There's no tidy card catalog of every Web page. Because Web pages appear and disappear hourly by the hundreds of thousands, such an exercise would be futile.

The best you can do is to use a *search engine:* a Web site that searches *other* Web sites. The best of them, such as *www.google.com,* consist of little more than a text box where you can type in what you're looking for. When you click Search (or press Enter), you're shown a list of links to Web sites that contain the information you're seeking.

Other popular search-engine pages include *yahoo.com, altavista.com, infoseek.com,* and *hotbot.com.* Using the Search panel of the Explorer bar, you can even search several of these simultaneously (as described on page 38). That's handy, because no single search engine "knows about" every Web page out there.

More Web Pages Worth Knowing

The Web can be an overwhelming, life-changing marketplace of ideas and commerce. Here are some examples of Web pages that have saved people money, changed their ways of thinking, and made history.

- *www.louvre.com*—The Louvre museum home page, where you can look at hundreds of famous paintings.

- *www.amazon.com*—The electronic bookstore that changed the way the world buys books (and CDs, videos, kitchenware, electronics, farm equipment, and so on). Amazon's catalog includes several *million* books, most of which are sold at a 20 percent discount. The fact that readers are invited to post their own reviews make it much less likely that you'll buy a lousy book.

- *www.dilbert.com*—A month's worth of recent Dilbert cartoons.

- *www.clicktv.com* or *tvguide.com*—Free TV listings for your exact area or cable company.

- *www.shopper.com, www.dealtime.com, www.mysimon.com*—These are special comparison-shopping sites that produce a list of Web sites that sell the particular book, computer gadget, PalmPilot, or other consumer good you're looking for—

and shows you their prices. You can save a *lot* of money by doing this quick, simple research before buying something.

- *www.efax.com*—A free service that gives you a private fax number. When anybody sends a fax to your number, it's automatically sent to you by *email*. You read it on your screen with a free fax viewer program. You're saved the costs of a fax machine, phone line, paper, and ink cartridges, and you can get your faxes no matter where you are in the world.

- *http://terraserver.microsoft.com*—Satellite photographs of everywhere (your tax dollars at work). Find your house!

- *http://rr-vs.informatik.uni-ulm.de/rr/gui2*—An interactive model railroad.

- *www.yourdictionary.com*—A web of online dictionaries.

- *www.homefair.com/homefair/cmr/salcalc.html*—The International Salary Calculator. Find out the cost-of-living hit you'll take *before* you move to a new city.

- *www.dpsinfo.com/index.shtml*—The Dead People Server, where you can find out who's dead and who's not.

- *http://digital.library.upenn.edu/books*—The Online Books Page, where you can find downloadable versions of 11,000 free, complete, electronic books, from almost every author whose copyright has expired.

- *http://us.imdb.com*—The Internet Movie Database: an astoundingly complete database of almost every movie ever made, including cast lists, awards, and reviews by the citizens of the Internet.

- *www.____.com*—Fill in the blank with your favorite major company: Microsoft, Apple, Honda, Sony, CBS, Palm, Symantec, NYTimes, Disney, MissingManual, and so on. If it's a big company, you can probably guess its Internet address.

Tips for Better Surfing

Internet Explorer is filled with shortcuts and tricks for better speed and pleasant surfing. For example:

Full-screen browsing

All of the toolbars and other screen doodads give you plenty of surfing control, but also occupy huge chunks of your screen space. The Web is supposed to be a *visual* experience; this encroachment of your monitor's real estate isn't necessarily a good thing.

But if you press F11 (or choose View→Full Screen), all is forgiven. The browser window explodes to the very borders of your monitor, hiding the Explorer bar, status bar, stacked toolbars, and all. The Web page you're viewing fills your screen, edge to edge—a glorious, liberating experience. Whatever toolbars you had open collapse into a single strip at the very top edge of the screen, their text labels hidden to save space.

You can return to the usual, crowded, toolbar-mad arrangement by pressing F11 again—but you'll be tempted never to do so.

Bigger text, smaller text

You can adjust the point size of a Web page's text using the View→Text Size commands (and then pressing F5 to refresh the screen). When your eyes are tired, you might like to make the text bigger; when you visit a Web site designed for Macintosh computers (whose text tends to look too large on PC screens), you might want a smaller size.

Of course, a Web page is usually composed of both text *and* graphics; the Text Size command doesn't affect the images. If you'd like to enlarge those, too, consider changing your monitor's resolution, as described on page 197.

Figure 11-3:
When you're looking at a Web page that might be worth returning to, choose Favorites→Add to Favorites (top). Later, you can return to that Web site simply by choosing its name from the Favorites menu. To edit the menu, choose Favorites→Open Favorites. When the Open Favorites window opens (bottom), you can drag names up or down to rearrange the list, as shown, or click one and then use the buttons at left to rename, delete, or file it in a folder.

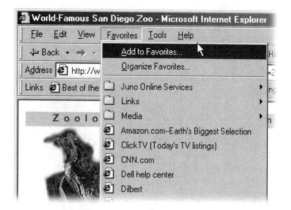

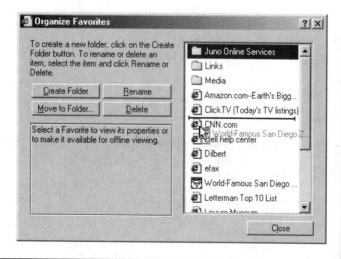

Faster browsing without graphics

If you're frustrated by how long it takes Web pages to appear on your screen, you can try out a drastic but very effective trick: turning off the pictures.

Of course, graphics are part of what makes the Web so compelling. But they're also responsible for making Web pages take so long to arrive on the screen. Without them, Web pages appear almost instantaneously. You still get fully laid-out Web pages; you still see all the text and headlines. But wherever a picture would normally be, you see an empty rectangle containing a generic "graphic goes here" logo, usually with a caption that tells you what that graphic would have been.

To turn off graphics, choose Tools→Internet Options, which opens the Internet Options control panel applet. Click Advanced, scroll down halfway into the list of checkboxes, and turn off "Show pictures" (in the Multimedia category of checkboxes). Now try visiting a few Web pages; you'll feel a substantial speed boost.

And if you wind up on a Web page that's nothing without its pictures, you can choose to summon an individual picture. Just right-click its box and choose Show Picture from the shortcut menu.

"Bookmarking" Web sites (making Favorites)

When you find a Web page you might like to visit again, choose Favorites→Add to Favorites (or press Ctrl+D). The Web page's name appears instantly at the bottom of your Favorites menu. The next time you want to visit that page, just choose its name from your menu to go there.

You can edit, rename, or delete the commands in your Favorites menu easily enough, as shown in Figure 11-3.

Viewing Web pages offline

You don't necessarily have to be connected to the Net to read a favorite Web page. Using the Offline feature, you can make Internet Explorer *store* a certain Web page on your hard drive so that you can peruse it later—on your laptop during your commute, for example.

The short way is to choose File→Save As, name the file, and click Save. Doing so preserves the Web page as a file on your hard drive, which you can open later by choosing File→Open.

UP TO SPEED

What You Need to Know About Plug-ins

Most Web pages contain text and pictures. A few, however, offer sound, movies, or animation. By itself, Internet Explorer doesn't know how to play this kind of onscreen show. It needs assistance from a software add-on called a *plug-in.* Once installed on your PC, a plug-in teaches Ex-plorer how to play a specific kind of sound, movie, or animation. Plug-ins are free; most are available at *www.plugins.com.* (The ones you'll need most often are Flash, Shockwave, and RealPlayer.)

That sweet, simple technique isn't quite what Microsoft has in mind when it refers to Offline Browsing, however. This more elaborate feature adds more options, such as automatic *updating* of the page you've saved and the ability to click *links* on the page you've saved.

To store a Web page in this way, follow these steps:

1. **Add the Web page to your Favorites menu or Links toolbar, as described earlier in this chapter.**

   You can't save a Web page for offline viewing unless you first designate that it's a Link or Favorite.

2. **Right-click the Web page's name in the Favorites menu or on the Links toolbar; from the shortcut menu, choose "Make available offline."**

   The Offline Favorite Wizard appears.

3. **Answer the questions posed by the wizard, clicking Next after each answer.**

   You'll be asked, for example, whether or not you want IE to store pages that are *linked* to the page you're saving—and how many "levels deep" you want this page-to-linked-page storage to proceed. In other words, if you're storing a World News page, you'll probably find nothing but headlines on its home page; when you're sitting on the train to work with your laptop, you'll appreciate the ability to click one of the headlines to open the article pages attached to them, one link "deep."

   On the other hand, be careful; links to links exponentially increase the amount of disk space IE uses. If you increase the "Download pages _ deep" number too high, you could fill your hard drive with hundreds of Web pages and thousands of graphics you never intended to download.

   The wizard also asks you how often you want this stored page *updated* when you *are* connected to the Internet. (If you decline to specify a schedule, you can always update the stored page manually by choosing Tools→Synchronize.)

4. **When you want to look at the pages you've stored offline, choose File→Work Offline. Then use the Favorites menu or Links toolbar to choose the name of the Web page you want.**

   It springs instantly to the screen—no Internet connection required.

Setting Basic IE Options

By spending a few minutes adjusting Internet Explorer's settings, you can make it more fun to use (or less annoying). To see the most important options, choose Tools→Internet Options, and then click General (see Figure 11-4).

Set your home page
The first Web site you see when IE connects to the Internet is a Microsoft Web site. Windows Me comes pre-configured to use this site as your *home page*. Unless you

actually work for Microsoft, however, you'll probably find Web browsing more fun if you specify your *own* favorite Web page as your home page.

In the Home Page section of the General tab (Figure 11-4, right), enter the Internet address of a favorite Web site. You might consider one of the Web sites described in the previous section, for example, or a search engine like google.com.

Tip: Instead of typing in a URL into the Address box to specify a new home page, you may prefer to click Use Current. Clicking this button means: "Use the Web page I'm looking at *right now* as my home page in the future."

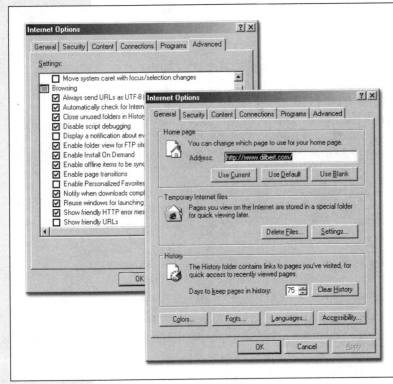

Figure 11-4:
Peculiar though it may seem, choosing Tools→ Internet Options takes you out of Internet Explorer. It opens the Internet Options control panel; two of its tabs are shown here. (See Chapter 9 for more detail on this control panel.) Except for designating a new home page, you may want to let the default settings stand.

If you can't decide on a home page, or your mood changes from day to day, click Use Blank. Some people prefer this setup, which makes IE load very quickly when you first launch it, and doesn't waste any time loading some home page you've specified; only an empty window appears. Once this window opens, *then* you can tell the browser where you want to go today.

Set storage options for temporary files

Most Web pages take a long time to show up in your browser window because they're crammed with *pictures*, which, on the great scale of computer files, are complicated and large. If you use a modem, moving from one Web page to the next can be an agonizing test of patience.

Every now and then, you might decide to go back to a Web page you've already visited, perhaps during a recent Internet session. To help speed the process of loading pages you've already seen, Internet Explorer saves the contents of *every* page you visit onto your hard drive. When you revisit a site, the saved file is opened—fast— thus eliminating the time-consuming process of downloading the contents again.

You can test this mechanism for yourself. Direct IE to a page you've never seen before; let's call it Page A. Click a link on it to visit Page B. When you click the Back button at the top of your browser, you return to Page A *very* quickly. IE doesn't have to download all those graphics a second time; having stored them on your hard drive during Page A's first appearance, it whips them onto your screen almost instantaneously.

These saved-up Web-page files are called *cache* files. (Cache, pronounced "cash," is French for "hide."). IE stashes its cache in the C:→Windows→Temporary Internet Files folder. This folder has a limited capacity, which you can adjust (see Figure 11-5); Windows Me deletes older files automatically to make room for new files.

Figure 11-5:
To change the size of your cache folder, click Settings (Figure 11-4), and then adjust the number shown here. Enlarging it makes it possible to store more files, enhancing the odds that when you revisit a Web site you've seen before, it will pop up onto the screen quickly. To see the temporary files (if you can even think of a reason to do so), click View Files. To see a list of programs you've downloaded, click View Objects.

Set options to check for changes

The cache-file scheme is great when it comes to speeding up the reappearance of Web pages you've seen before. Unfortunately, it has one significant drawback: If you decide to visit a Web page you've seen before, and IE blasts it onto your screen from its saved temporary-files folder, you're seeing *an old version* of that page—as it was the last time you visited. If that Web page has been updated in the meantime, you're looking at old news, which is a particular hazard if it's a news Web site.

Fortunately, the dialog box shown in Figure 11-5 offers a great deal of control over when IE checks to see if a particular Web page has changed since your last visit:

- **Every visit to the page.** This option forces IE to check *every* Web page to see if its contents have changed since you last visited. If so, IE loads the updated page from the Internet. Unfortunately, this option slows the process of re-opening Web pages, because IE must download all of those pages' contents anew. Select this option only if you consistently visit Web sites with rapidly changing contents (such as a stock ticker or news page).

- **Every time you start Internet Explorer.** This option divides your Web browsing into two categories: sites you've visited during *this session* of using IE, and sites you visited in previous sessions.

    When you select this option, IE checks for new contents only on pages you visited in previous sessions. Revisiting any pages you viewed in the *current* session (which, of course, are less likely to have changed) produces the stored file. If you think the contents of the Web page may have changed, click the Refresh button on the toolbar to reload the page from the Internet.

- **Automatically.** This option, the factory setting, is similar to the previous one, but it's smarter. It makes IE keep an eye on your Web activity, trying to determine a pattern for the type of pages you visit. Most of the time, IE reloads pages from the Internet exactly as described in the previous paragraph—that is, only when you visit a site you've visited in a previous session. But this time, IE pays attention to individual Web sites: When reloading them from the Internet, what percentage of the time have they actually changed? Eventually, IE stops checking for updates on sites that change infrequently.

- **Never.** This option instructs IE to load the stored, hard drive–based, cache files for any Web site you're revisiting. The site's contents are never checked to see whether they've changed. You can click the Refresh button to check for changed contents manually.

Configure and view the History folder

This *history* is a list of the Web sites you've visited. It's the heart of three IE features: AutoComplete, described at the beginning of this chapter, the drop-down menu at the right side of the Address Bar, and the History list in the Explorer bar. All of these are great features if you can't remember the URL for a Web site you visited, for example, yesterday.

You can configure the number of days for which you want to track your Web visits. To do so, choose Edit→Internet Options, and click the General tab (Figure 11-4). The more days IE tracks, the easier it is for you to refer to those addresses quickly. On the other hand, the more days you keep, the longer the list becomes, which may make it harder to use the list easily and efficiently.

Tip: Some people find it creepy that Internet Explorer maintains a complete list of every Web site they've seen recently, right there in plain view of any family member or co-worker who wanders by. If you're in that category, you can turn the history feature off completely. Just click the Clear History button. Then set the "Days to keep pages" to 0. (After all, you might be nominated to the Supreme Court some day.)

To delete a site from the list, right-click its name and choose Delete from the short-cut menu.

Figure 11-6:
The History panel (left) offers more details than the history list you see in the Address Bar. Click one of the time-period icons to see the Web sites you visited during that era. Click the name of a Web site to see a list of each visited page within that site—information you don't get from the pop-up list on the Address Bar). You can sort the sites by clicking View on the left pane and choosing one of these sorting schemes: Date, Site, Most Visited, Order Visited Today.

Turn off animations

If blinking ads make it tough to concentrate as you read a Web-based article, choose Edit→Internet Options, click the Advanced tab, and then scroll down to the Multimedia heading. Turn off "Play animations" to stifle animated ads.

Configure the Content Advisor

The IE Content Advisor is designed to give parents a way to control what their children view on the Web—an especially important feature for home computers. You can specify sites you approve, and sites you want to block, using both your own knowledge and the ratings systems prepared by organizations dedicated to this purpose. If somebody tries to visit a Web site that you have declared off-limits using this feature, he'll see a message saying that the site isn't available.

To turn on the Content Advisor, choose Tools→Internet Options; click the Content tab; and then click the Enable button. The Content Advisor dialog box, shown in Figure 11-7, presents four tabs, called Ratings, Approved Sites, General, and Advanced.

Ratings tab

On the Ratings tab, select a content category (such as Language, Nudity, or Sex) and move the slider bar to the right to loosen the restrictions. The more you move the slider, the fewer restrictions you're establishing.

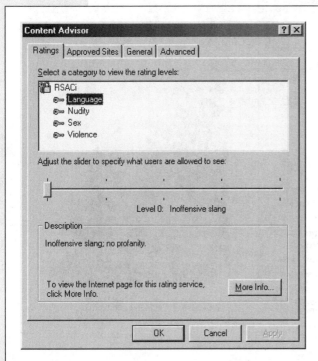

Figure 11-7:
The Internet represents ultimate freedom of expression for everybody, and some parents think of it as a wild frontier town where anything goes. To protect young eyes, you can use the options in the Content Advisor to control what's available to your copy of IE. You can also password protect these settings so nobody else can make changes to them.

The Internet Content Rating Association defines the ratings. You can visit its site by clicking More Info (or by entering *www.icra.org/ratingv01.html* in the Address Bar). It's important to note, however, that the Content Rating Association doesn't actually rate Web sites. Web sites are supposed to rate *themselves*. As you can well imagine, the Ratings feature is, therefore, far from foolproof.

Approved Sites tab

Use the Approved Sites tab to enter the addresses of sites you either want to permit or block. (It's normal for this list to show up empty; it's designed to list Web pages *you* specify.) After you enter a URL, select Always to make the site available, or Never to make it unavailable, to your Web browser.

The listings in the Approved Sites tab take precedence over the Ratings tab. If you type in a Web address and then click Always, your kids will be able to see that site regardless of where it falls in the Ratings scheme.

General tab

It wouldn't do you much good to declare certain Web sites off-limits to your 12 - year-old if, after you've gone to bed, she could simply open the dialog box in Figure 11-7 and declare those Web sites available again. Fortunately, you can use the Change Password button to assign yourself a supervisor's password. Once that's accomplished, nobody can change the settings or visit a forbidden Web site without knowing the password.

Caution: Be very careful not to lose this password. There's no way to recover it, and no way to change your security settings without it.

Two of the options on the General tab let you make your controls more flexible:

• **Users can see sites that have no rating.** Some sites aren't rated; if you turn on this option, you make unrated sites available to Internet Explorer.

The lack of a rating usually means the site owner didn't use the rating system, either because she didn't know about it or because the site is so bland and non-threatening that a rating request seemed unnecessary. On the other hand, the lack of a rating could mean it's a pornographic site whose owner is hoping to circumvent the ratings systems of Web browsers like yours. Use your judgement, and remember you can always change this setting.

• **Supervisor can type a password to allow users to view restricted content.** Select this option to make every restricted site available—if you type in the correct password. For example, you can share the password with the adults in your household. You may also want to use it so that your children will have to explain to you why they need access to a restricted site. If you buy their explanation, you can type the supervisor's password to permit one-time access to the site.

Also on the General tab is a Find Rating Systems button. Click it to travel to the Internet to find more rating systems you can use to help IE withhold or permit access to sites.

Advanced tab

The Advanced tab is the place to add new rating systems and rating rules as Internet citizens invent them.

Note: Such programs as Symantec's Norton Internet Security and McAfee's Internet Guard Dog give you finer control over what your browser can see on the Web. These products don't rely on Content Ratings, and they let you define different standards for different users on the computer.

Using Outlook Express for Email

Email is a fast, cheap, convenient communication medium; it's almost embarrassing these days to admit that you don't have an email address. To spare you that humiliation, Windows Me includes Outlook Express, a program that lets you get and send email messages and read *newsgroups* (Internet bulletin boards).

Note: Outlook Express won't work if you're using an online service, such as America Online or Prodigy. Instead, you're supposed to check and send your email using the like-named programs (America Online or Prodigy, for example) that came with Windows Me.

To use Outlook Express, you need several technical pieces of information: an email address, an email server address, and an Internet address for sending email. Your ISP (see Chapter 10) provides all of these ingredients.

Setting Up Outlook Express

The first time you use Outlook Express, the Internet Connection Wizard shows up to walk you through the process. The wizard collects the information about your Internet connection and your email account, and uses that information to set up Outlook Express.

Note: If you provided information about your account name and password when you set up a Dial-Up Networking connection, the Internet Connection Wizard may not appear when you use Outlook Express for the first time. In that case, skip to the next section.

Click Next on each wizard window to step through the process, providing the following information:

- **Display Name.** The name that will appear in the "From:" field of the email you send.

- **Email Address.** The email address you chose when you signed up for Internet services, such as *bill@microsoft.com*.

- **Mail Servers.** Enter the information your ISP provided about its mail servers: the type of server, the name of the incoming mail server, and the name of the outgoing mail server. Most of the time, the incoming server is a *POP3 server* and its name is connected to the name of your ISP, such as *popmail.mindspring.com*. The outgoing mail server (also called the *SMTP server*) usually looks something like *mail.mindspring.com*.

- **Logon Name and Password.** Enter the name and password provided by your ISP.

  If you wish, turn on "Remember password," so that you won't have to enter it each time you want to collect mail. (But turn on Secure Password Authentication only if your ISP gives you instructions to do so.)

Click Finish to close the wizard and open Outlook Express. (If Outlook Express doesn't open automatically, double-click its icon on the desktop, or click its icon on the Quick Launch toolbar.)

Tip: *If you want to add a second email account (for someone else who uses this PC), choose Tools→Accounts. In the resulting dialog box, click Add→Mail; the account-setup wizard will reappear.*

Sending and Receiving Mail in Outlook Express

When Outlook Express opens for the first time, it contains a message for you; you've got mail. The message is a welcome from Microsoft, but it wasn't actually transmitted over the Internet; it's a starter message built into Outlook Express just to tease you. Fortunately, all your future mail will come via the Internet.

The message from Microsoft is in your *Inbox,* one of the elements of your Outlook Express window (see Figure 11-8).

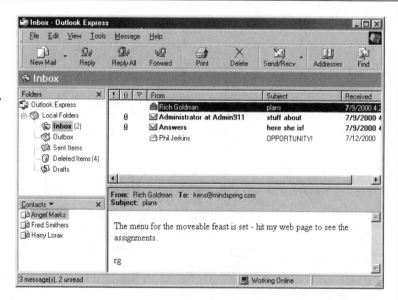

Figure 11-8:
The four panes of Outlook Express. Click a folder in the upper-left pane to see its contents in the upper-right pane. When you click the name of a message (upper-right pane), you see the message itself in the lower-right pane. At lower left: your list of MSN Messenger Service "buddies," as described later in this chapter.

Mail folders in Outlook Express

Outlook Express organizes your email into *folders* at the left side of the screen. To see what's in a folder, click it once:

- **Inbox** holds mail you've received.

- **Outbox** holds mail you've written but haven't yet sent.

- **Sent Items** holds copies of messages you've sent.

• **Deleted Items** holds mail you've deleted. It works a lot like the Recycle Bin, in that messages you put there don't actually disappear. They remain in the Deleted Items folder, awaiting rescue on the day you decide that you'd like to retrieve them. To empty this folder, right-click it and choose "Empty 'Deleted Items' Folder" from the shortcut menu.

Tip: To make the folder empty itself every time you exit Outlook Express, choose Tools→Options, click the Maintenance tab, and turn on "Empty messages from the 'Deleted Items' folder on exit."

• **Drafts** holds messages you've started but haven't yet finished, and don't want to send just yet.

Composing and sending messages

To send email to a recipient, click the New Mail icon on the toolbar. The New Message form, shown in Figure 11-9, opens so you can begin creating the message.

Composing the message requires several steps:

1. **Type the email address of the recipient into the "To:" field.**

   If you want to send this message to more than one person, separate their email addresses using semicolons, like this: *bob@earthlink.net; billg@microsoft.com; steve@apple.com.*

   You don't have to remember and type out all those complicated email addresses, either. You may find it much easier just to double-click a plain-English name (such as *Bob Smith)* from your address book, as described in the next section.

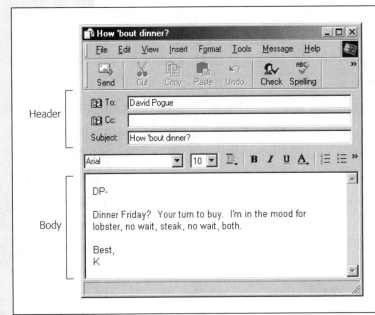

Figure 11-9:
A message has two sections: the header, *which holds information about the message; and the* body, *which contains the message itself. In addition, the Outlook Express window has a menu bar and a toolbar, which you can use to access other features for composing and sending messages.*

As in most Windows dialog boxes, you can jump from blank to blank in this window by pressing the Tab key (to proceed from the "To:" field to the "CC:" field, for example).

2. **To send a copy of the message to other recipients, enter the email address(es) in the CC: field.**

   CC stands for *carbon copy.* There's very little difference between putting all your addressees on the "To:" line (separated by semicolons) and putting them on the "CC:" line; the only difference is that the CC people will know that they've been CC'ed. When your name is in the "CC:" line, the person who sent it is implying: "I sent you a copy because I thought you'd want to know about this correspondence, but I'm not expecting you to reply."

   Once again, you can use the address book to speed up typing in these names, and you can separate email addresses with semicolons. Press Tab when you're finished.

3. **Type the topic of the message in the "Subject:" field.**

   Some people, especially those in the business world, get bombarded with email. That's why it's courteous to put some thought into the Subject line (use "Change in plans for next week" instead of "Hi," for example).

   Press the Tab key to make your cursor jump into the large message-body area.

4. **Enter the message in the message box (the bottom half of the message window).**

   You can use all the standard editing techniques, including using the Cut, Copy, and Paste commands to rearrange the text as you write it.

5. **Click Send.**

   Your modem dials, squeals, connects to the Internet, and sends the message.

If you'd rather have Outlook Express place each message you write in the Outbox folder instead of connecting to the Net each time you click Send, see "Send tab" on page 367. There you'll find out how to make Outlook Express quietly collect your outgoing mail until you click the Send & Receive icon on the toolbar.

Using the Address Book

You can accumulate names in an address book—the same one described on page 147—which saves you the work of entering complete email addresses whenever you want to send a message. Click the Address Book button on the toolbar; then, to begin adding names and email addresses, click New.

Tip: Outlook Express offers a convenient time-saving feature: The Tools→Add Sender to Address Book command. Whenever you choose it, Outlook Express automatically stores the email address of the person whose message is on the screen. (Alternatively, you can right-click an email address in the message and choose "Add to Address Book" from the shortcut menu.)

Attaching files to messages

Sending little text messages is fine, but it's not much help when you want to send somebody a photograph, a sound recording, a Word or Excel document, and so on. Fortunately, attaching such files to email messages is one of the world's most popular email features.

To attach a file to a message, click the Attach tool on the message toolbar. When the Insert Attachment dialog box opens, navigate through the folders on your drive (see page 124) to locate the file and select it. The name of the attached file appears in the message in the Attach field. (In fact, you can repeat this process to send several attached files with the same message.) When you send the message, the file tags along.

If you have a high-speed connection like a cable modem, by the way, have pity on your recipient. A big picture or movie file might take you only seconds to send, but tie up your correspondent's modem for hours.

Tip: If you can see the icon of the file you want to attach—if you can see it in its folder window behind the Outlook Express window—you can also attach it by *dragging* the icon directly into the message window.

Reading email

Outlook Express puts all the email you get into your Inbox; the bold number in parentheses after the word "Inbox" lets you know how many of its messages you haven't yet read. (In the upper-right part of the Outlook Express window, where the names of the messages appear, bold type also means "You haven't opened this one yet.")

Click the Inbox folder to see a list of received messages in the upper-right pane of the Outlook Express window (see Figure 11-8). Click the name of a message once

---

UP TO SPEED

Blind Carbon Copies

A *blind carbon copy* is a secret copy. This feature lets you send a copy of a message to somebody secretly, without any of the other recipients knowing that you did so. The names in the "To:" and "CC:" fields appear at the top of the message for all recipients to see, but nobody can see the names you typed into the BCC: box. To view this box, choose View→All Headers.

You can use the "BCC:" field to quietly signal a third party that a message has been sent. For example, if you send your co-worker a message that says, "Chris, it bothers me that you've been cheating the customers," you could BCC your boss or supervisor to clue her in without getting into

trouble with Chris.

The BCC box is useful in other ways, too. Many people send email messages (containing jokes, for example) to a long list of recipients. You, the recipient, have to scroll through a very long list of names the sender placed in the "To:" or "CC:" field.

But if the sender used the "BCC:" field to hold all the recipients' email addresses, you, the recipient, won't see any names but your own at the top of the email. (Unfortunately, spammers, those awful people who send you junk mail, have also learned this trick.)

(select it) to read it in the lower-right pane of the window, or double-click a message to open it into a separate window of its own.

Opening attachments

Just as you can attach files to a message, so people often send files to you. Sometimes they don't even bother to type a message; you wind up receiving an empty email message that has a file attached. You know when a message has an attachment because a paper-clip icon appears next to its name in the Inbox.

Outlook Express doesn't store downloaded files as individual icons on your hard drive. Instead, it stores all your messages *and* all the attached files as one big, encoded file on your hard drive. To extract an attached file from this mass of software, you have to detach it from its message.

If you're reading a message in the Preview pane, click the paper-clip icon in the upper-right corner of the message. From the list that appears, select the attachment you want to open, or select Save Attachments to save the files to your hard drive.

But if you double-click a message's name in the list, so that it opens into its own window, you have more flexibility:

- Right-click the attachment icon, select Save As from the shortcut menu, and then specify the folder in which you want to save the file.

- Drag its icon clear out of the message window and onto your Windows desktop, as shown in Figure 11-10.

Figure 11-10:
Dragging a file attachment's icon onto your desktop takes the file out of the Outlook Express world and onto any visible portion of your Windows desktop, where you can file it, trash it, open it, or manipulate it as you would any file.

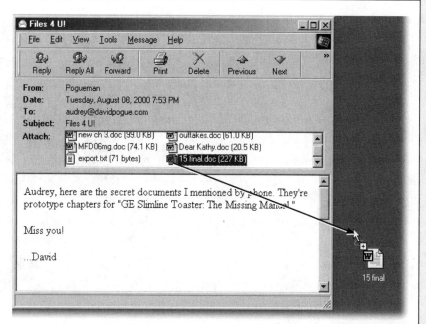

- Double-click the attachment's icon in the message. If you were sent an application, it now runs (but be wary of viruses). If the attachment is a document (such as a photo, Word file, Excel file, and so on), it now opens in the corresponding program (Photoshop, Word, Excel, or whatever). After the attachment is open, use the File→*Save As* (not Save) command to save the file into a folder of your choice; otherwise, you won't be able to open the file again except from within Outlook Express.

Replying to a message

To reply to a message, click the Reply button on the message window toolbar. If the message was originally addressed to multiple recipients, you can send your reply to everyone simultaneously by clicking the Reply All button instead.

A new message window opens, already addressed. As a courtesy to your correspondent, Outlook Express places the original message at the bottom of the window, denoted by brackets, as shown in Figure 11-11.

Your cursor appears at the top of the message box; you can begin typing your reply. You can also:

- Add recipients to the message by adding names in any of the recipient fields (To:, CC:, or BCC:).

- Remove one or more recipients from the header (by dragging through their names and then pressing Delete).

- Edit the Subject line or the original message.

FREQUENTLY ASKED QUESTION

Everybody Doesn't Have the Same Software

People send me documents in Microsoft Word, but I use WordPerfect. I write back and tell them to paste the text into the email message itself, but they don't like to do that. Do I have to buy tons of software I don't want just to open attachments?

No; there's often a way to open attachments even if you don't own the program used to create them. Microsoft Word documents, for instance, automatically open in Word-Pad (see page 154) if you don't have Microsoft Word on your system.

Word processors and spreadsheet programs can usually *import* documents created by other applications, complete

with formatting. To try this approach, open the email message that contains the attachment. Then right-click the icon for the attachment. From the shortcut menu, choose Save As and save the file in a folder (the My Documents folder is a good choice).

Finally, launch your own equivalent application (word processor, spreadsheet program, or whatever), and then choose File→Open or File→Import. Locate the file you moved into your My Documents folder. You'll be pleased at how often this trick works to open a document created by the program that you don't have using a program that you do.

- Use the Enter key to create blank lines within the original message in order to place your own text within it. Using this method, you can splice your own comments into the paragraphs of the original message, replying point by point. The brackets preceding each line of the original message help your correspondent keep straight what's yours and what's hers.

- Attach a file.

Note: If the original message came with an attached file, Outlook Express doesn't fasten the attachment to the reply.

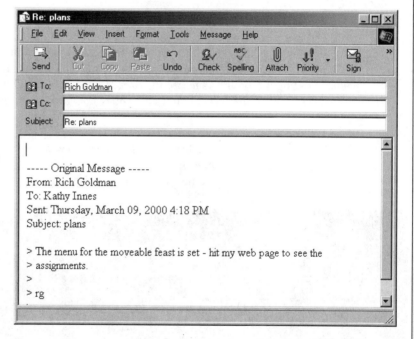

Figure 11-11:
A reply includes the original message, marked with special > characters to differentiate it from the text of your reply. The original sender's name is automatically placed in the "To:" field. The subject is the same as the original subject with the addition of "Re:" (shorthand for regarding). You're ready to type your response.

Forwarding messages

Instead of replying to the person who sent you a message, you may sometimes want to *forward* the message—pass it on—to a third person.

To do so, click the Forward button on the toolbar of the original message. A new message opens, looking a lot like the one that appears when you reply. Once again, before forwarding the message, you can edit the subject line or the message itself. (For example, you may wish to precede the original message with a comment of your own, along the lines of: "Frank: I thought you'd be interested in this joke about Congress.")

All that remains for you to do is to specify who gets the forwarded message. Just address it as you would any outgoing piece of mail.

Note: If the original message contained an attachment, this time, Outlook Express *does* keep the attachment attached (unless you delete it from the Attach field).

Configuring Outlook Express

Outlook Express has enough features and configuration options to fill an entire, and very thick, book. You can see them for yourself by choosing Tools→Options from the Outlook Express window (see Figure 11-12). Here's an overview of some of the features you'll find here.

General tab

Most of the General tab options govern what Outlook Express does when you first launch it. Take note of the options for configuring automatic connection to your ISP; you can select the option to check for messages every few minutes (the factory setting is 10), and then use the drop-down list to tell Outlook Express how, and whether, to connect at that time if you're not already online.

Read tab

Use the options in the Read tab to establish how the program handles messages in the Inbox. One of these options marks a message as having been read—changing its typeface from bold to non-bold—if you leave it highlighted in the list for five sec-

---

UP TO SPEED

A Word About Viruses

Newspaper reporters periodically get breathless and wide-eyed about new Windows *viruses* (programs that have been deliberately written to gum up your PC), such as the Melissa and I Love You viruses. These little programs often come attached to, or masquerade as, ordinary files that get sent to you—sometimes inadvertently by people you know.

Avoiding virus trouble is fairly easy if you use some common sense. First of all, most viruses are transmitted as file *attachments;* you can't get your PC infected just by reading an email *message.* If a stranger sends you a message with a file attachment you didn't ask for, just delete the message. You've just destroyed the virus, if there was one.

If you get a file attachment that's an application (file extension *.exe),* don't double-click the attachment unless you know what it is.

Viruses may also come embedded in Microsoft Word and Excel attachments. Be especially careful with these; among virus writers, one popular trend is to embed macro viruses in these documents that propagate by reading your address book and sending themselves to everyone listed there.

Fortunately, detecting macro viruses is extremely easy: When you open such an attachment, a huge, important-looking warning appears on your screen. It tells you that the file contains *macros,* which may harbor viruses. Just click the Open Without Macros button to open the file without any potentially dangerous virus programming.

Finally, if you're especially worried about viruses, use an anti-virus program like Norton Antivirus to check attachments before opening them.

---

onds or more, even without opening it. That's one option you may want to consider turning off.

Receipts tab

You can add a *return receipt* to messages you send. When the recipient reads your message, a notification message (receipt) is emailed back to you, *if* the recipient's email program offers a similar feature. (Outlook Express, Outlook, and Eudora all do.)

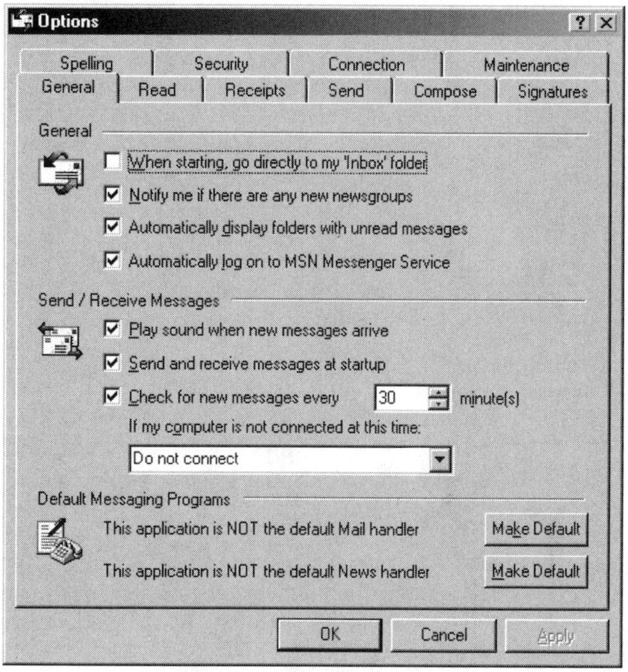

Figure 11-12:
The Options dialog box has ten tabs. Each tab is loaded with options. Most tabs have buttons that open additional dialog boxes. Coming in 2006: Outlook Express Options: The Missing Manual.

Send tab

The options on the Send tab govern outgoing messages. One option to consider turning *off* here is the default option, "Send messages immediately": As soon as you click the Send button, Outlook Express tries to send the message, even if that means triggering your modem to dial. All of this dialing—and *waiting* for the dialing—drives some people crazy, especially in households with only one phone line.

If you turn this option off, then clicking the Send button simply places a newly written message into the Outbox. As you reply to messages and compose new ones, the Outbox collects them. They don't get sent until you choose Tools→Send and Receive (or click Send/Recv on the toolbar, or press Ctrl+M). Only then does Outlook Express command your modem to dial the Internet. It then sends all the outgoing mail at once.

Tip: To see the messages waiting in your Outbox, click the Outbox icon at the left side of the screen. At this point, you can click a message's name (in the upper-right pane of the screen) to view the message itself in the *lower*-right pane, exactly as with messages in your Inbox.

Don't bother trying to *edit* an outgoing message in this way, however; Outlook Express won't let you do so. Only if you double-click a message's name (in the upper-right pane), thus opening it into a separate window, can you make changes to a piece of outgoing mail.

The Send tab also includes features for configuring replies. For example, you can disable the function that puts the original message at the bottom of a reply.

Compose tab

Here's the place to jazz up the look of your messages. You can select fonts, backgrounds, and other fancy formatting effects. Design your own stationery (a custom-designed template you can use for all your outgoing email). You can also send email in *HTML format* instead of plain text, which lets you load up your message with graphics, links to Web sites, or even links to other parts of the message.

Not all email programs can show these fancy effects, however; your recipient may be deprived of your formatting efforts.

Signatures tab

Use this tab to design a *signature* for your messages. A signature is a canned line of text (or multiple lines) that Outlook Express stamps automatically at the end of your outgoing messages. Some people include contact (or commercial) information in their signatures: name, title, mailing address, phone number, and so on, on separate lines.

Other people take the signature opportunity to propagate pithy sayings, a philosophical thought, a one-line joke, or some other message. (In fact, some signatures are longer than the messages they accompany.)

To create a signature, click New on this tab. Enter your signature text in the box at the bottom of the dialog box. Click OK to save the signature. By repeating this process, you can create several *different* signatures: one for business messages, one for your buddies, and so on. (Outlook Express calls them Signature #1, Signature #2, and so on. You can rename one by clicking its name and then clicking the Rename button.)

If you'd like to tack your signature onto *every* outgoing message, turn on "Add signatures to all outgoing messages" at the top of the Signatures tab. If you'd prefer to insert signatures on a message-by-message basis, leave that checkbox turned off. Instead, whenever you're composing a message to which you'd like the signature appended, plant the insertion point where you want the signature to appear (usually at the bottom of the message). Choose Insert→Signature from the top of the message window.

Spelling tab

The Spelling tab offers configuration options for the Outlook Express spell-checking feature. You can even force the spell checker to correct errors in the *original* message when you send a reply (although your correspondent may not appreciate it).

Security tab

This tab contains options for sending secure mail, using digital IDs and encryption. If you're using Outlook Express in a business that requires secure email, the system administrator will provide instructions. Otherwise, you'll find that these settings have no effect.

Connection tab

You change the options for making and sustaining the connection with your ISP in the Connection tab. For example, you can tell Outlook Express to hang up automatically after sending and receiving messages (and reconnect the next time you want to perform the same tasks).

Maintenance tab

This tab is your housekeeping center. These options let you clear out old deleted messages, clean up downloads, and so on.

FREQUENTLY ASKED QUESTION

The Case of the Vanishing Software

Hey, where are Web Hosting Wizard, Front Page Express, and Personal Web Server? They're there on my Windows 98 machine, but I can't find 'em in Windows Me.

They're gone. In an effort to distinguish Windows Me, a *simple* operating system for *home* users, from its "professional" offerings, Microsoft removed software that it can't

imagine novice PC users using. Apparently, creating your own Web pages (in Front Page Express), putting them on the Web (Web Hosting wizard), and turning your PC into a Web site (Personal Web Server) aren't things you'd want to do at home. You'd do that kind of thing at work, where you're presumably running Windows 2000.

MSN Messenger Service

You might argue that, what with all of the games and programs included with Windows Me, you'll have plenty to do at your desk. But if you've got even more time to kill, Microsoft invites you to "chat" with other people on the Internet by typing live comments into a little window.

Better yet, you don't have to *type* all of these witty comments: If your PC has a microphone and speakers, you can also *speak* to your friends, using the Internet as a free long-distance service. It's not quite as handy as a phone—you and your conversation partner must arrange to be online at a specified time—but the price is delightful.

The software you need is MSN Messenger Service. You open it by choosing Start→Programs→Accessories→Communications→MSN Messenger Service. (Depending on your version of the program, it may be in Start→Programs instead.)

Setting Up the Service

Before you can type-chat or use your PC as a free long-distance phone, you must sign up for a Microsoft Hotmail email account (which is free). To do so, launch MSN Messenger Service as described above. When the wizard appears, click Next, and then click "Get a passport." At this point, you visit a special Web page, where you're asked to make up a name and password.

Once you're enrolled, you should see the MSN Messenger Service window (see Figure 11-13).

Figure 11-13:
If you don't see this window after you've signed up for a Hotmail account, bring it to the screen by choosing Start→Programs→ Accessories→Communications→MSN Messenger Service.

The setup isn't over yet; now you must go about the process of building a list of people you know who have also signed up for Hotmail accounts. To do that, click the Add button; click "By email address" if you know your friend's Hotmail or Microsoft Network address, or "Search for a contact" if your friend's email address is already listed in your address-book program.

Either way, don't even bother unless you're sure this person has a Hotmail or MSN account; Windows Me's chat feature works only if they do.

Beginning a Chat

To start a conversation, connect to the Internet. Then double-click somebody's name in your "Contacts Currently Online" list, also as shown in Figure 11-13. (You can't carry on a very meaningful conversation with somebody who *isn't* online.)

On his end, a special alert box appears at the lower-right corner of the screen, as shown at left in Figure 11-14. If he's interested in accepting your invitation to chat, he can click the words in that little box. Suddenly you're chatting: Anything you type is transmitted to his MSN Messenger window as soon as you press Enter, and vice versa. Figure 11-14 shows the effect.

Figure 11-14:
Left: You're being invited to chat. If you click the words in the little square invitation box, you open MSN Messenger Service, where you can type away (right).

Using your PC as a Telephone

If both you and your friend have PCs with fast Internet connections, microphones, and speakers, the two of you can switch into live, spoken conversation, exactly as though you're using a low-quality telephone. Your friend hears everything you say into the microphone, and you hear everything she says into hers.

To bring this about, begin a chat as described above. But once the window is open, click the Talk icon at the top of the window. (The very first time you do this, Windows will ask you to test the quality of your microphone and speakers.)

Your friend will see a typed invitation to join you in spoken voice conversation, as shown in Figure 11-14. If she clicks Accept, the two of you are in business: You can simply begin talking, even if you're in San Francisco and she's in Turkey. Clearly, the phone-company executives aren't thrilled with the development of this technology—until they go home at night and fire up MSN Messenger Service themselves.

Tip: If somebody is chat-harassing you, click Block. Your software will block his attempts to contact you. (To block lots of people at once, choose Tools→Options→Privacy; click a name, or several, and then click Block.)

The Rest of MSN Messenger Service

If you poke around, you'll find a few other useful features in MSN Messenger Service. For example:

- You can send a file from your hard drive to your conversation partner (choose File→Send a File)—a great way to turn this time-wasting feature into a useful collaboration tool. (Your partner will find the transmitted file in her My Documents→Messenger Received Files folder.)

- You can send a message to somebody's pager; just choose Tools→Send a Message to a Mobile Device. (If it's a text pager, you can even type up a little message to send.)

- You can include another person in your chat by choosing File→Invite→To Join This Conversation→[the name or address of the person you're inviting]. (Up to five people can participate in a chat.)

- During your chat, you can invite your partner to start a NetMeeting, the more elaborate online conferencing software described next, by clicking the Invite toolbar icon and choosing To Start NetMeeting from the menu that appears.

To read much more detail about privacy, sending files and invitations, troubleshooting, and the MSN Messenger Taskbar Tray icon, choose Help→Help Topics from the main MSN Messenger Service window menu bar.

Microsoft NetMeeting

You can think of NetMeeting as a genetically enhanced MSN Messenger Service. This program, too, lets you use the Internet to collaborate and communicate with other people inexpensively—but instead of just typing and speaking, you can also send video images back and forth, draw on a virtual "white board," and even use each other's software. All of this works best if you have a fast Internet connection and a bit of technical setup; most people use this program under the guidance of a tech expert at work.

Setting up NetMeeting

Start NetMeeting by choosing Start→Programs→Accessories→Communications→ NetMeeting. The wizard appears; it walks you through the process of filling in your name and email address, specifying the directory that will list you, specifying your connection speed (such as modem or cable modem), adjusting your microphone and speaker levels, and so on.

But after you've set up NetMeeting, you must also set up your Net *meeting*. That is, you must schedule a time with your collaborators, just as you might schedule a conference call. Everybody has to be on the Internet (or intranet, if you have an in-office private network) at the same time, and running the NetMeeting program.

To place a call, open NetMeeting. In the text box at the top of the window, specify the email address or IP (network) address of the first person you want to add to the party, and then press Enter. If all goes well, the lucky recipient of your attentions will see a small pop-up window at the lower-right corner of her screen that indicates your invitation. If she clicks Accept, you're in business: the title bar of your NetMeeting screen will say "1 Connection," and the Status bar at the bottom says "In a call." Repeat this connection process for anyone else you want to invite to the meeting.

Figure 11-15:
The four buttons on the NetMeeting window don't have labels—not even tooltips. Let the labels shown here be your guide; a click on each of these buttons opens a different kind of collaboration window.

If you're lucky enough to have video equipment hooked up, you can even perform a crude kind of videoconferencing.

Conducting the NetMeeting

Once your meeting is under way, you can perform four remarkable stunts, which correspond to the four icons at the bottom of the NetMeeting window (Figure 11-15). Once you figure out how they work, you'll be very impressed; the amount of travel time and plane fares you can save using NetMeeting adds up quickly. Here's what they do:

Sharing a Program

Amazingly enough, other people in your meeting can use your programs—editing one of your Word documents, typing numbers into your Excel spreadsheet, and so on—even if they don't have Word or Excel on their machines.

It works like this:

1. **Launch the program you want everyone to be able to use. Then click the Sharing button (the first one on the left) on the NetMeeting screen (Figure 11-15).**

The Sharing window appears, as shown in Figure 11-16.

2. **Click the name of the program you want to share, and then click Share.**

Note, in particular, the desktop, which is always listed in the Share Programs window. If you share it, then everybody else in the meeting can see what you see as you work in Windows. As far as NetMeeting is concerned, the desktop is simply another program that you can share.

Under most circumstances, the other people in the meeting can just *look* at the program you're using. But if you'd like others in your meeting to be able to *control* the application—to edit the documents, use the menus, and so on—go on:

3. **Click Allow Control.**

Instantly, a new window appears on the screens of the other participants, showing exactly what you see in *your* copy of the program. When you move your cursor, it moves on their screens; when you open a dialog box, they see it, too. Because your microphone is working during a NetMeeting meeting, you can use this feature to collaborate on documents, to teach somebody a new program, to help somebody troubleshoot a PC, and so on.

And if you've shared your Desktop, giving away control means that other people can even manipulate your computer files and folders! They can open folders, rename files, make backup copies, delete files, and so on, from wherever on the Internet to happen to be.

Just clicking Allow Control, however, is not enough to transfer control of a program to one of your collaborators. He must also choose Control→Request Control from his shared-program window; only then can he edit your documents, manipulate your desktop, and so on.

It's worth noting, by the way, that all of this controlling and sharing requires an enormous amount of data to be shuttled over the wires. As a result, the cursor may seem jerky, and everything will feel very slow; that's normal, especially if you're connecting via standard dial-up modem.

Chat

If you click the second icon at the bottom of the NetMeeting window, you open a chat window very much like the one shown in Figure 11-14. Once again, you can type comments to your colleagues, as though you're conducting a typewritten conference call.

Whiteboard

Clicking the third icon opens up a graphics window that closely resembles the Paint program described in Chapter 7. The difference: Anything anybody paints (or pastes) into this window appears instantly on everybody else's screen. Using the various graphics tools and colors, you can draw maps for each other, propose design changes, or just play tic-tac-toe.

Tip: One of the most useful tools here isn't one you'll find in the regular Paint program—it's the little pointing-hand icon. As you move this hand around the screen, everybody else in the meeting sees exactly what you're pointing to. Because they can also hear what you're saying, thanks to your microphone, this makes a great way to comment on something—say, a photo you've pasted into this window.

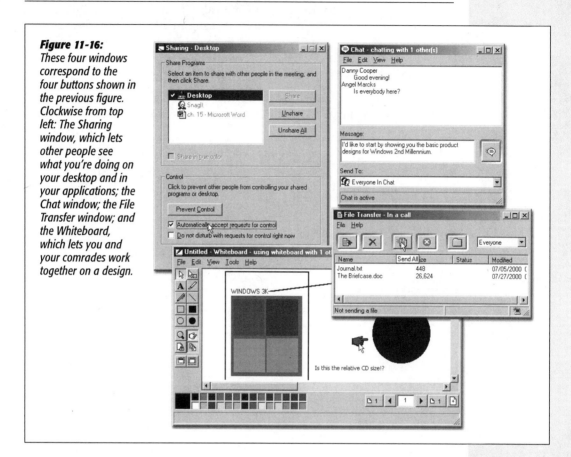

Figure 11-16:
These four windows correspond to the four buttons shown in the previous figure. Clockwise from top left: The Sharing window, which lets other people see what you're doing on your desktop and in your applications; the Chat window; the File Transfer window; and the Whiteboard, which lets you and your comrades work together on a design.

Exchange files

As the meeting proceeds, you may also want to distribute some documents to the meeting participants. To do so, click the rightmost icon at the bottom of the Net-Meeting screen. When the window shown in Figure 11-16 appears, click the first icon, choose a file that you want to send, repeat if necessary, and then click the Send All button shown in the illustration.

Audio and video

If your PC has a microphone and speakers that are correctly configured, audio is automatically turned on during a NetMeeting, so that everybody else can hear whatever you say. Note, however, that you may not be able to hear anybody else *while* you're speaking. Some sound cards don't offer this *full-duplex* audio feature; in that case, you'll get more of a CB radio effect, where only one person can speak at a time. (In that case, you may want to say, "Over!" after each comment.)

The videoconferencing feature is even more limited. It requires that you and the other participants each have a camera and video-capture card installed. You can send video to only one other person in the meeting. And "video" is a generous term: You may find that the picture is extremely jerky and grainy, more like a series of still images than a TV broadcast. (Click the Start Video button to begin transmitting; click Stop Video when you've had enough.)

Still, it's an interesting feature that, in the era of super-high-speed Internet connections that's sure to arrive within the next couple of decades, will put Dick Tracy to shame.

Part Four:
Plugging Into Windows Me

4

Printing and Fonts

Technologists got pretty excited about "the paperless office" in the Eighties, but the PC explosion had exactly the opposite effect: Thanks to the proliferation of inexpensive, high-quality PC printers, we generate far more printouts than ever before. There's not much to printing from Windows Me—*if* you can get the printer hooked up to begin with.

Installing a Printer

Most printers "connect" to your PC using one of three technologies:

- **A printer cable or parallel cable.** Most printers require this kind of cable, although it isn't generally included with the printer. The cable connects to your PC's parallel port, which Microsoft's help screens call the LPT1 port; it's a 25-pin, D-shaped jack. (On many PCs, this connector is marked with a printer icon.)

- **A serial cable.** Some printers can use a cable connected to one of your computer's *serial* (or *COM*) ports (which usually accommodate an external modem). The primary advantage of a serial connection is the cable length: Parallel cables should be no more than nine feet long, while serial cables up to 50 feet long work fine.

Tip: To protect its innards, turn off the PC before connecting or disconnecting a parallel or serial cable.

- **A USB cable.** More and more printers are designed to connect to the *USB* (Universal Serial Bus) jack on most modern PCs. USB cables have lots of advantages: They're easy to connect and disconnect, are very fast, conserve space, can be plugged and unplugged while the PC is running, and so on.

- **Ethernet.** If you work in an office that's equipped with a laser printer shared by several people on the network, the printer usually isn't connected directly to your computer. Instead, it's elsewhere on the network; the Ethernet cable coming out of your PC connects you to it indirectly.

- **Infrared.** Many printers from HP, Canon, Citizen, and other companies can print using infrared technology—that is, there's no cable at all. Instead, if your PC has an infrared lens (as many laptops do), it can communicate with the printer's similar lens wirelessly, as long as the printer and PC are within line of sight of, and relatively close to, each other.

After the printer is connected to the computer and turned on, you can begin installing the drivers.

Printer Drivers

A printer is designed to follow computer instructions called *printer codes* from your PC. These codes tell the printer what fonts to use, how to set margins, which paper tray to use, and so on.

But the codes aren't identical for every printer. Therefore, every printer requires a piece of software that tells it how to interpret what it "hears" from your computer. This software is called the *printer driver*, and it's written by either Microsoft or the printer manufacturer.

Windows Me comes with a large number of printer drivers built right in; your printer also came with a set of drivers on a CD or floppy. You can often find more recent drivers for your printer on the manufacturer's Web site, such as *www.epson.com* or *www.lexmark.com*. (You might also check *www.windrivers.com*—a great clearinghouse for drivers of all kinds.)

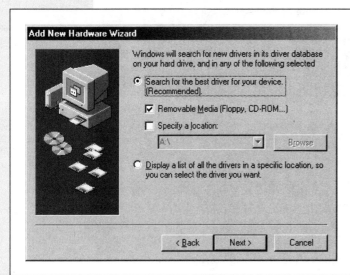

Figure 12-1:
In this window, you're asked to help the wizard search for the files you received from the manufacturer. The choices at the top of the dialog box are a way to tell the wizard "go find what you need." But you have to give Windows a hint about the location of the driver files.

Installing the software for Plug-and-Play printers

If your printer is connected directly to the PC, and it's Plug-and-Play-compatible (a feature probably advertised on its box), there's not much to the driver-installation process. As soon as your PC starts up and "sees" the printer attached to it, Windows Me reaches down into its bag of software and automatically installs the printer's drivers into itself. You'll see a message telling you that Windows has "found new hardware:" a printer. (This glorious moment is what Plug and Play is all about, as described in Chapter 13.)

Tip: Plug and Play usually detects the appearance of a new gadget—such as a printer—as the computer is starting up. But if you've just hooked up a new printer, you can force Windows to "notice" it and trigger the Plug-and-Play driver-installation process automatically, without having to restart the machine.

To do so, choose Start→Settings→Control Panel. When the Control Panel window opens, right-click the System icon and choose Properties from the shortcut menu. In the System Properties dialog box, click the Device Manager tab; click the Refresh button. The Plug and Play feature now checks all of your PC's various connectors, lists any newly attached devices, and offers to install their drivers.

The Add New Hardware Wizard

If Windows Me doesn't "know about" the printer model you're hooking up, it can't install its drivers automatically. In that case, the Add New Hardware Wizard appears. As in any Windows wizard, this one asks you one question per screen; you click Next to walk through the questions until you've correctly identified, and installed the software for, your printer.

The opening window explains that the wizard is going to search for drivers for the printer. Click Next (see Figure 12-1).

Here are the guidelines for using the next screen:

- If your driver files are on a CD or a floppy disk, click Removable Media and then click Next.

- If the driver files are on your hard drive, choose "Specify a location" and then click Next.

  Use this option if you've downloaded the drivers from the Web. Enter the location of the files—for example, *c:\downloads\drivers*. If you can't remember the exact name of the folder, click Browse to navigate your folders in search of the one that contains the driver files.

- If the wizard can't find the driver on the disk (or in the folder) you've specified, it tells you so. In that case, click the Back button to return to the window shown in Figure 12-1. Now click "Display a list of all the drivers." When you click Next, you'll be offered a list of drivers for specific printer models; if you don't see the one you want, see the sidebar on the bottom of page 282.

The Add Printer Wizard

But suppose the Add New Hardware Wizard doesn't quite do it for you. Maybe:

- The wizard had no luck finding driver software for your printer model, or

- You're feeling particularly efficient, and don't have the patience for the wizard's somewhat laborious method of installing your drivers. (In that case, click the Cancel button as soon as it appears, and proceed as described here.)

In these cases, you may find the Add Printer Wizard a more direct method for installing printer software, one that sometimes works when the Add New Hardware Wizard doesn't.

Start by putting the printer's software disk into your machine. (Or, to install a generic Windows driver, put the Windows Me CD into the drive.) Then follow these steps:

1. **Choose Start→Settings→Printers.**

   The Printers window opens. If this is the first printer driver you're installing, only the Add Printer icon appears in the window.

2. **Double-click the Add Printer icon.**

   The Add Printer Wizard opens with a welcoming message.

3. **Click Next. On the following screen, select "Local printer" to indicate that the printer is attached directly to your computer.**

   Use the other option—Network printer—if you're planning to use a printer that's available to your entire office network (see Chapter 17 for details).

4. **Click Next. On the following screen, click Have Disk. In the Install From Disk dialog box (Figure 12-2), indicate where the drivers are.**

   If you'd rather use the Windows-provided driver for your printer, click the name of your printer and its manufacturer instead (see Figure 12-2).

TROUBLESHOOTING MOMENT

If Your Printer Model Isn't Listed

If your printer model isn't in the list of printers (Figure 12-2), then Windows Me doesn't have a driver for it. Your printer model may be very new (more recent than Windows Me, that is) or very old. You have two choices for end-running this roadblock:

First, you can contact the manufacturer (or its Web site) to get the drivers. Then install the driver software as described in the previous section.

Second, you can use the *printer emulation* feature. As it turns out, many printers work with one of several standard drivers that come from other companies. For example, many laser printers work fine with the HP LaserJet driver; these laser printers are not, in fact, HP LaserJets, but they *emulate* one.

The instructions that came with your printer should have a section on emulation; the manufacturer's help line can also tell you which popular printer yours can impersonate.

---

5. Click Next. Specify how the printer is attached to your PC.

Most printers are connected to LPT1; some connect via serial, USB, or infrared ports.

6. Click Next, and specify a new name for the printer, if you like. Click Next, indicate whether or not you want to print a test page, and then click Finish.

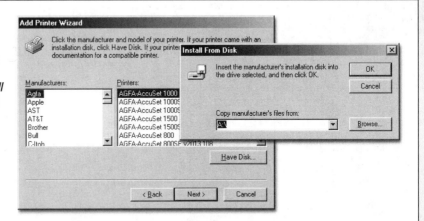

Figure 12-2:
Select your printer's manufacturer in the left-side pane. Doing so produces, in the right pane, a list of all the models from that manufacturer. The Have Disk button is for installing drivers supplied by the manufacturer, and summons the dialog box at right.

Installing Fake Printers

If your printer has two paper trays, switching to the secondary one is something of a hassle—you have to spend time making the changes in the Print dialog box, as described later in this chapter. Similarly, switching the printout resolution from, say, 300 dpi to 600 dpi when printing important graphics documents is a several-step procedure.

That's why you may find it useful to create several different icons for *the same printer.* The beauty of this stunt is that you can set up different settings for each of these icons. One might store canned settings for 600 dpi printouts from the top paper tray; another might represent 300 dpi printouts from the bottom one; and so on. When it comes time to print, you can switch between these "virtual printers" quickly and easily.

Start by installing the printer software to create the printer icon, as described in the first part of this chapter. At the

point in the installation where you name the printer, invent a name that describes this printer's settings, such as *HP6-600 dpi* or *Lexmark-Legal Size.*

When the installation process is complete, choose Start→Settings→Printers; you'll see your new printer icon in the Printers window. Right-click the new "printer's" icon and change the settings to match its role.

To specify which one you want to be your *default* printer—the one you use most of the time—choose Start→Settings→Printers, double-click the icon for your preferred printer, and choose Printer→Set As Default.

But when you need better graphics, a different paper tray, or other special options for a document, just select the appropriate printer from the drop-down menu in the Print dialog box (see Figure 12-5). You've just saved yourself a half-dozen additional clicks and settings changes.

Windows Me copies the driver files from the disk or folder you specified. If you requested a test page, your PC prints it now; check it to make sure it didn't print garbled characters.

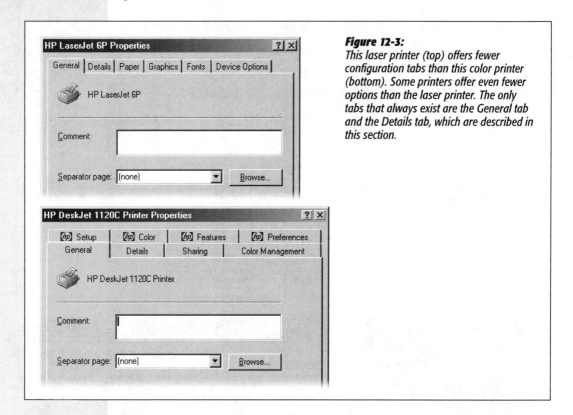

Figure 12-3:
This laser printer (top) offers fewer configuration tabs than this color printer (bottom). Some printers offer even fewer options than the laser printer. The only tabs that always exist are the General tab and the Details tab, which are described in this section.

As the test page prints, Windows Me displays a message asking if the test print came out OK. If so, click Yes. If not, click No, which makes Windows Me launch its printer *troubleshooter*: a specialized wizard that offers you one troubleshooting suggestion after another until either you or Windows gives up in frustration.

The Printer Icon

If your driver-installation efforts were ultimately successful, you're rewarded by the appearance of an *icon* that represents your printer. To see it, choose Start→Settings→ Printers. The window that appears now contains an icon bearing the name you gave it during the installation. This printer icon can come in handy in several different situations, as the rest of this chapter makes clear.

Adjusting Printer Settings

Every printer model is blessed with a different list of features. Some can print on both sides of a page, some can hold different types of paper in different trays, and some can print in color. The printer driver knows all about your model's particular talents; that's why the Print dialog box that appears when *you* choose File→Print in one of your programs may not look like the Print box on your friend's computer.

To have a look at your printer's special features—those that you can control via software—choose Start→Settings→Printers. When the Printers window opens, right-click the printer icon; choose Properties from the shortcut menu. Figure 12-3 shows the Properties of two typical printers.

The tabs you see in this dialog box depend on the specific printer model, but most run along these lines:

General Tab

The General tab is the same for every printer. It offers little more than a Comments box and a Separator page option, both of which are primarily useful for network printing (Chapter 17).

Details Options

The Details tab (Figure 12-4) offers several technical printer-related options, most of which you'll probably never need to adjust.

Here's what it contains:

- **Port settings.** The only time you'll ever have to change the options involving ports is when your printer is on a network and somebody's moved it.

Figure 12-4:
Most of the items on this tab never need changing. However, a couple of the options can help you tweak the speed of your printer.

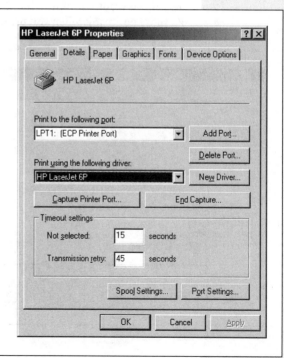

- **New Driver.** This button lets you update the driver for the printer, using a new, presumably improved version from the manufacturer.

- **Timeout settings.** These numbers specify how much time elapses before Windows reports an error when trying to communicate with the printer.

"Not selected" means the printer is not online (probably because someone is changing paper or a cartridge).

"Transmission retry" error messages occur only on rare occasions: when there's a broken or disconnected cable, or when the printer (almost always a serial printer) has become hopelessly confused. In theory, increasing the number of seconds here gives the printer more time before bothering you with an error. In practice, this setting is irrelevant for modern printers.

Paper Tab

If your printer has multiple trays, or it can handle a variety of paper sizes, this tab lets you specify the paper tray you'll use most of the time. (You can override this selection on a case-by-case basis when you actually print.)

Graphics Tab

On this tab, you can specify the maximum *resolution* you want from your printouts of drawings and photos. This resolution is measured in dots per inch (dpi), which indicates how many tiny dots of ink the printer places within a one inch area. The higher the resolution, the sharper the printed image. (The dpi setting you make here also affects printouts of *text*, but the difference between high and low resolution is far more noticeable when you print graphics.)

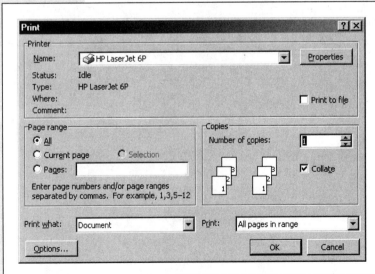

Figure 12-5:
The options in the Print dialog box are different on each printer model and each application, so your Print dialog box may look slightly different. Most of the time, the factory settings shown here are what you want (one copy, print all pages); just click OK (or press Enter) to close this dialog box and send the document to the printer.

Most printers offer dpi settings ranging from 150 to 1200 dpi. Graphics printed below 300 dpi may look jagged. But don't go wild; higher-resolution printouts use more ink or toner, take longer to print, and increase the likelihood that your printer will run out of memory on complex pages. Most people set the printer to either 300 or 600 dpi.

Sharing Tab

You'll see this tab only if your printer is on a network. See Chapter 17 for more about sharing printers on a network.

Printing

Fortunately, the setup described so far in this chapter is a one-time-only task. Once it's over, printing is little more than a one-click operation.

Printing from Applications

After you've created a document that you want to see on paper, choose File→Print. The Print dialog box appears, as shown in Figure 12-5.

Here's what you can change in the Print dialog box:

- **Name.** If your PC is connected to several printers, or if you've created several differently configured icons for the same printer, use the drop-down list to choose the one you want.

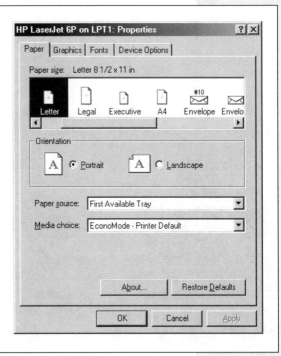

Figure 12-6:
When you choose Properties from the Print dialog box, you can specify the paper size you're using, whether you want to print sideways on the page ("Landscape" orientation), and so on. Making these changes for a particular printout doesn't affect the overall options for the printer.

- **Properties.** By clicking this button, you open a version of the printer's Properties dialog box, as shown in Figure 12-6.

- **Page range.** These controls specify which pages of the document you want to print. If you want to print only some of the pages, click Pages and type in the page numbers you want (with a hyphen, such as *3-6* to print pages 3 through 6).

Tip: You can also type in individual page numbers with commas, such as *2, 4, 9* to print only those three pages—or even add hyphens to the mix, like this: *1-3, 5-6, 13-18.*

Click Current Page to print only the page that contains the blinking insertion-point cursor. Click Selection to print only the text you selected (highlighted) before opening the Print dialog box. (If this button is dimmed, it's because you didn't highlight any text—or because you're using a program, such as Netscape Navigator, that doesn't offer this feature.)

- **Number of copies.** You can print out several copies of the same thing; use this box to specify how many copies. You'll get several copies of page 1, then several copies of page 2, and so on—*unless* you also turn on Collate, which gives you complete sets of pages, in order.

- **Print.** The Print drop-down list in the lower-right section of the dialog box offers three options: "All pages in range," "Odd pages," and "Even pages."

Use the Odd and Even pages option when you have to print on both sides of the paper, but your printer has no special feature for this purpose. You'll have to print all the odd pages, turn the stack of printouts over, and run the pages through the printer again to print even page sides.

- **Application-specific options.** The particular program you're using may add a few extra options of its own to this dialog box. Figure 12-7 shows a few examples from Internet Explorer's Print dialog box, for example.

When you've finished making any changes to the print job, click OK, or press Enter. You can go back to work in your software; thanks to the miracle of *background printing,* you don't have to wait for the document to emerge from the printer before you can keep working on your PC. In fact, you may even be able to exit the application while the printout is still under way.

POWER USERS' CLINIC

Printing from a DOS Program

Windows programs don't need any special setup steps to print. But if you want to print from a DOS application, you must first tell it which port your printer is connected to.

To do so, find the printing options menu. There you'll be able to tell the software the name of the port to which your printer is connected (usually LPT1).

Unfortunately, the commands required to print are unique to each DOS program; finding them is up to you.

Printing from the Desktop

You don't necessarily have to print a document while it's open in front of you. You can, if you wish, print it directly from the desktop. Just right-click the document icon, and then choose Print from the shortcut menu.

Now Windows launches the program that created it—Word or Excel, for example—and the Print dialog box appears, so that you can specify how many copies you want and how many of the pages you want printed. When you click Print, your printer springs into action, and then the program quits automatically (if it hadn't already been open).

Tip: *If you've opened your Start→Settings→Printers window, you can also drag a document's icon directly onto a printer icon—another easy way to specify which printer (or printer configuration) you want to use.*

Printing from the Internet

If you use Internet Explorer 5.5 or later to browse the Web (see Chapter 11), the Print dialog box offers a few special features for printing Web pages. Figure 12-7 shows a few of them; the new Print Preview command is another. (Other browsers don't offer nearly as much flexibility in printing Web pages.)

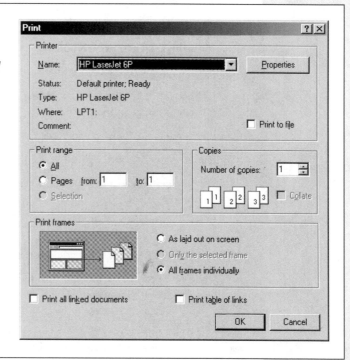

Figure 12-7:
The Web page about to be printed uses frames (individual, independent, rectangular sections). The Print dialog box in Internet Explorer recognizes frames, and lets you specify exactly which frame or frames you want to print. If the page contains links to other Web pages (and these days, what Web page doesn't?), you can print those Web pages, too, or just print a table of the links (a list of the URL addresses).

Printing to a File

Most of the time, when you think of printing, you probably think of printing onto paper. In certain circumstances, however, you may not actually want a printout—instead, you might want to create an electronic printer file on your hard drive, which you can print later. You might want to do so, for example, when:

- You're working on a document at home, where you've got only a cheesy $49 inkjet printer. By creating a printer file, you can hold off printing until tomorrow, when you can use the office's $6,000 color laser printer.

- You want to give a document to someone who doesn't have the program you used to create it, but has the same printer. If you email the *printer file* to her, she'll get to see your glorious design work slide out of her printer nonetheless.

To create such a printer file, choose File→Print, just as you would to print any document. The Print dialog box appears; turn on the "Print to file" option. When you then click OK, the Print to File dialog box opens. It resembles the standard Save dialog box; you can choose a drive, a folder, and a filename. The file type for a document printing to a file is Printer File, which has the file extension *.prn*.

To print a printer file, choose Start→Programs→MS-DOS Prompt. You've just started an MS-DOS command session; your cursor is blinking on the command line. To print the file, you'll have to type a DOS command, as people once did daily before Windows existed:

copy *c:\foldername\filename*.prn lpt1: /b

Here's how this instruction breaks down:

- **Copy** is the name of the command—notice that it's followed by a space.

- **C:** is the letter of the drive that contains your printer file. You can omit this part if the printer file is on the current drive (usually C:).

- **\foldername** is the name of the folder into which you saved the printer file.

- **\filename** is the name you gave the file.

- **.prn** is the filename extension (which Windows gave the file automatically when you saved the printer file).

- **lpt1:** is the port to which the printer is connected. Note the colon following the name, and also note there's a space *before* this part of the command. If the printer is attached to LPT2, substitute that port name.

- **/b** tells the Copy command that the file is binary (containing formatting and other codes), not simply text.

Note: You can print a printer file (a *.prn* file) only on the same printer model that was selected in the Print dialog box when the file was generated. If you want to create a printer file for that color printer at work, in other words, be sure to install its driver on your computer first.

Controlling Printouts

Between the moment when you click OK in the Print dialog box and the arrival of the first page in the printer's tray, there's a delay; if you're printing a complex document with lots of graphics, the delay can be considerable.

Fortunately, the waiting doesn't necessarily make you less productive, because you can go right back to work on your PC, or even quit the application and leave the room. A program called the *print spooler* supervises this background printing process. The spooler collects the document that's being sent to the printer, along with all the codes the printer expects to receive and then sends this information, little by little, to the printer.

Note: The spooler program creates huge printer files; a nearly full hard drive can wreak havoc with background printing.

To see the list of documents waiting to be printed—the ones that have been stored by the spooler—choose Start→Settings→Printers. In the Printers window, double-click your printer's icon to open its window.

Tip: While the printer is printing, a printer icon appears on the Taskbar Tray. As a shortcut to opening the printer's window, just double-click that icon.

The printer's window lists the documents currently printing and waiting. This list is called the *print queue* (see Figure 12-8); documents in the list print in top-to-bottom order. You can manipulate them in any of several ways:

- **Put one on hold.** To pause a document, right-click its name and choose Pause from the shortcut menu. Every document in line below it now jumps up to print ahead of it. When you're ready to let the paused document continue to print, right-click its listing and select Pause again to turn off the checkmark.

- **Put them all on hold.** To pause the printer, choose Printer→Pause Printing from the printer window menu bar. You'd do that when, for example, you need to

Figure 12-8:
The first document, called "user data management," has begun printing; two other documents are waiting. Using this dialog box, you can pause or cancel any document in the queue—or all of them at once.

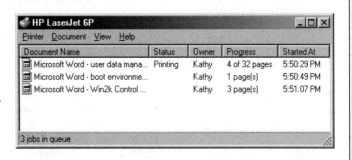

change the paper in the printer's tray. (Choose Printer→Pause Printing again when you want the printing to pick up from where it left off.)

- **Cancel one.** To cancel a printout, right-click the document's name and choose Cancel from the shortcut menu. The document disappears from the queue; it'll never print out.

- **Cancel all of them.** To cancel printing of all the documents in the queue, choose Printer→Purge Print Documents.

Note: Your printer has its own memory (the *buffer*) which stores the printout as it's sent from your PC. If you pause or cancel printing, you're only stopping the spooler from sending *more* data to the printer. That's why a page or two may still print after you've paused or canceled a printout.

- **Rearrange them.** To change the order of printing, drag the name of a printout up or down in the list. (You can't move a document ahead of the document that's printing, however.)

Printer Troubleshooting

If you're having a problem printing, the first diagnosis you must make is whether the problem is related to software or hardware. A software problem means the driver files have become damaged. A hardware problem means there's something wrong with the printer, the port, or the cable.

Test the printer by sending it a generic text file from the command line. (Printing a regular printer disk file isn't a good test, because if there's a problem with the driver, the codes in the file are likely to contain the problem.) To perform such a test, locate a text file, or create one in the Start→Programs→Accessories→Notepad program. Then choose Start→Programs→MS-DOS Prompt; send the file to the printer by typing *copy filename.txt prn* and then pressing Enter. (Of course, type the file's actual name and three-letter extension instead of *filename.txt.*)

If the file prints, the printing problem is software-related. If it doesn't work, the problem is hardware-related.

For software problems, use one of the following methods to reinstall the printer driver:

- Open the Printers window, right-click the printer's icon, and choose Delete from the shortcut menu. Then reinstall the printer as described at the beginning of this chapter.

- Open the Start→Settings→Printers window, right-click the printer's icon, and choose Properties from the shortcut menu. Click the Details tab, then click New Driver.

If the problem is hardware, try these steps in sequence:

1. Check the lights or the LED panel readout on the printer. If you see anything besides the normal "Ready" indicator, check the printer's manual to diagnose the problem.

2. Turn the printer off and on to clear any memory problems.

3. Check the printer's manual to learn how to print a *diagnostic* (printer self-test) page.

4. Check the cable to make sure both ends are firmly plugged—and into the correct ports.

5. Test the cable. Use another cable or take your cable to another computer/printer combination.

If none of these steps leads to an accurate diagnosis, you may have a problem with the port, which is more complicated, or—even worse—the problem may originate from your PC's motherboard (main circuit board). In that case, your printer needs professional attention.

Fonts

Some extremely sophisticated programming has gone into the typefaces that are listed in the Fonts dialog boxes of your word processor and other programs. They use *TrueType* technology, meaning that no matter what point size you select for these fonts, they look smooth and professional, both on the screen and when you print.

GEM IN THE ROUGH

The Secret Screen-Capture Keystrokes

If you're reading a chapter about printing, you may someday be interested in creating *screenshots*—printable illustrations of the Windows screen. Screenshots are a staple of articles, tutorials, and books about computers (including this one).

Windows offers two different techniques for creating screenshots. If you press the Print Scrn key on your keyboard, Windows silently creates a snapshot of the entire screen and places it onto your invisible Windows Clipboard. (If you press Alt+Print Scrn instead, you capture only the frontmost window or dialog box, saving you the trouble of cropping out unnecessary background details in your graphics program.)

To see, manipulate, or save your captured image, switch to a graphics program (such as Start→Programs→ Accessories→Paint), and paste (press Ctrl+V, for example). The captured image appears in the graphics program; you can now choose File→Save to preserve it as a file on your hard drive.

Of course, if you're really serious about capturing screenshots, opt instead for a more powerful add-on shareware program like SnagIt *(www.techsmith.com),* which gives you far more control over what portion of the screen you capture, what file format it's in, and what happens to it after you take the shot.

Managing Your Fonts

Windows Me comes with about 20 great-looking TrueType fonts: Arial, Book Antiqua, Times Roman, and so on. But the world is filled with additional fonts. You may find them on the CD-ROMs that come with PC magazines, on Windows software Web sites, or in the catalogs of commercial typeface companies. Sometimes you'll find new fonts on your system after installing a new program, courtesy of its installer.

To have a look at the files that represent your typefaces, choose Start→Settings→ Control Panel. In the Control Panel window, you'll find a Fonts folder. (If you don't see it, click "View all Control Panel options.")

Tip: The Fonts folder in your Control Panel window is only a shortcut to the *real* folder, which is in your My Computer→C: drive→Windows folder.

When you open the Fonts folder, you'll see that every font that appears in the Font menus of your various programs is represented on your hard drive by an icon—or several. As shown in Figure 12-9, it's easy and enlightening to explore this folder.

Figure 12-9:
All of your fonts sit in the Fonts folder (top); as you'll soon notice, you'll frequently find an independent font file for each style of a font: bold, italic, bold italic, and so on. You can tell a TrueType font by its TT icon; other font files (those bearing an A logo) aren't TrueType-format fonts. Some may be PostScript fonts, which are accompanied by a phalanx of printer font files that they require; others may look fine on the screen, but may not print out smoothly. You can double-click a font's icon to see what the font looks like (bottom).

To remove a font from your system, simply drag its file icon out of this window (or highlight it and then choose File→Delete). To install a new font, drag its file icon into this window (or choose File→Install New Font, and then navigate to, and select, the font files you want to install).

Either way, you'll see the changes reflected in the Font dialog boxes of your programs immediately.

Tip: Don't delete the font called MS Sans Serif. That's the one Windows uses in its menus, windows, and dialog boxes. If it's missing from your system, Windows will substitute something that doesn't look right.

Plug and Play

A Windows PC contains an amazing amount of hardware: dozens of chips, wires, slots, cards, and other assorted parts. Fortunately, you don't have to worry about installing, configuring, and troubleshooting these various elements; the PC maker did that part for you. (Unless you built the machine yourself, that is. In that case, best of luck.)

However, adding *new* gear to your computer is another story. You have to hook it up and install its *driver*, the software that lets a new gadget talk to the rest of the PC.

Fortunately, Microsoft has taken much of the headache out of such installation rituals by its invention of Plug and Play. This chapter guides you through using this much improved Windows Me feature—and counsels you on what to do when Plug and Play doesn't work. (You'll find additional details on installing a new printer in Chapter 12; a new modem, Chapter 10.)

What Can Go Wrong

Part of the installation process for a new piece of hardware is making sure that it doesn't interfere with any of your *other* components. To get a feeling for the kinds of snafus that may arise, it helps to know a little bit about drivers and hardware conflicts.

About Drivers

Windows is the mediator when a software program wants to communicate with your gear. For example, when your word processor needs the printer, it says, "Hey printer! Please print this document." Windows intercepts the message and gives the printer very specific instructions about printing, ejecting pages, making text bold, and so on. It speaks to the printer in Printer-ese, a language it learns by consulting the printer's driver software.

Other hardware components work similarly, including sound cards, Network Interface Cards (NICs), modems, scanners, and so on. All of them require specifically formatted instructions; all of them require driver software.

Message Pathways

You're already familiar with one common routing system for messages: area codes and telephone numbers. Together, they pinpoint a unique location in the nation's telephone system.

To send instructional codes to your hardware, Windows needs a similar communication channel for each device. During installation, the operating system learns the location (phone number) of the hardware and the path (area code) its messages must take to get there.

But instead of area codes and phone numbers, PC components have unique channels called *IRQs* (Interrupt Request Levels), reserved areas of memory called *I/O addresses,* and other technical assignments that claim their places in your system. These technical settings are generically called *resources.*

If your sound card occupies IRQ 11 and has an I/O address that starts at 6100, then Windows knows how to contact the card when, for example, your email software wants to play a "You've got mail" sound. If your printer also occupied those addresses, the operating system would send a sound code, the printer would become confused ("What am I supposed to do with this instruction? It has nothing to do with printing!"), and the sound card might not receive the "Wake up and make the music" command. And it's not enough to set just a hardware component to the right channels; their software drivers must be independently tuned to the same channels if they're to communicate.

Tip: If you're ever curious to see a list of your PC's components and how they've been assigned various communications channels, right-click your My Computer icon and choose Properties from the shortcut menu. Click the Device Manager tab, and then double-click the very first icon: Computer. You're shown the little-known, but fascinating, Computer Properties dialog box, which reveals all of the channel resources in question.

Clearly, Windows needs a traffic cop to ensure that each hardware gadget gets the correct messages.

About Plug and Play

Years ago, you had to set IRQs and I/O addresses physically, using a series of jumper switches or specialized configuration programs before installing new equipment. Today, Windows can take care of the address settings automatically, assigning unique resources to avoid conflicts.

Microsoft calls this miraculous installation-simplifying process *Plug and Play*. (At least it's miraculous to anyone who's ever had to perform this kind of configuration manually.)

After you install a Plug-and-Play device and start your computer, the new component tells Windows: "Hi, I'm new here. Here's my species, here's my name, here are the resources I'd like to use if they're free. If they're not free, please assign resources, and let me know what they are so I'll be listening for my orders on the right channel."

These days, almost every computer add-on you can buy is Plug-and-Play compatible. Chances are good that you'll live a long and happy life with Windows Me without ever having to lose a Saturday to manually configuring new gizmos you buy for it.

But gadgets that were designed before the invention of Plug and Play are another story. These so-called *legacy* devices often require manual configuration. Fortunately, Windows Me comes with wizards to walk you through this process, making it slightly less difficult.

Hardware Connections

When you install a new piece of hardware, you either insert it into an expansion slot on the *motherboard* (the computer's main circuit board) or connect it to a *port* (a connector usually on the back of your computer).

Installing Cards in Expansion Slots

Some add-on devices are circuit boards, or *cards*, that you install by inserting into an expansion slot (sometimes called a *bus*) inside your PC's case. Among the commonly installed cards are modems and adapter cards for video, sound, network cabling, disk drives, and tape drives.

The two common (and mutually incompatible) kinds of slots are called *ISA* and *PCI*. Most computers offer both kinds of slots; you'll have to open your PC's case to see which type of slot is empty:

• The plastic wall around an ISA slot is usually black. It has metal pins or teeth in the center and a small crossbar about two-thirds of the way down the slot.

• The plastic wall around a PCI slot is usually white, and it's shorter than an ISA slot. A PCI slot has a metal center and a crossbar about three-quarters of the way along its length.

Installing a card usually involves removing a narrow plate (the *slot cover)* from the back panel of your PC, which allows the card's connector to peek through to the outside world. After unplugging the PC and touching something metal to discharge static, unwrap the card and carefully push it into its slot until it's fully seated.

Back-Panel Attachments

When you buy a printer, scanner, digital camera, or something else that plugs into the back of the PC, you're buying a *peripheral,* in the lingo of PC magazines and clubs everywhere. A peripheral may plug into any one of the connectors on your PC's back panel, which may include:

- **Video (VGA) port.** A narrow female port with 15 holes along three rows. Your monitor plugs in here.

- **Parallel (DB-25) port.** A wide female port with two rows of holes. It's usually connected to a printer (which is why it's sometimes called the printer port). You can plug some other kinds of equipment in here, including Zip or Jaz drives, tape drives, and other drives.

- **Serial port.** A male connector with 9 or 25 pins. It connects to a *serial device,* such as a mouse, modem, camera, scanner, and some printers; it can also accommodate PC-to-PC communications. Most computers have two serial ports, which are also called *COM* ports.

- **PS/2.** A small round female connector (known in PC circles as a *6-pin mini-DIN* connector). Not all PCs have PS/2 ports; but if yours does, it probably has two, one for the keyboard and the other for the mouse.

- **Keyboard Port.** Into this small, round, 5-pin (DIN connector), female port, you can plug keyboards that don't use a PS/2 connection.

- **Wireless Port.** You'll find this kind of port most often on laptops. It lets your computer talk to similarly equipped gadgets (such as infrared-equipped printers, PalmPilots, and so on) through the air, via infrared or RF communication. An infrared port is a small, translucent plastic lens; RF ports look like little antennas.

- **USB (Universal Serial Bus) Port.** This compact, thin, rectangular connector accommodates a huge variety of USB gadgets: scanners, mice, printers, palmtop cradles, digital cameras, Zip drives, and so on. Most modern PCs come with two USB ports; if that's not enough to handle all your USB devices, you can attach a USB *hub* (with, for example, four or eight additional USB ports), so that you can attach multiple USB devices simultaneously. USB is the most modern type of connector; all USB devices are Plug-and-Play compatible.

- **Game Port.** This connector, which is usually part of a sound card, is a wide female port that accepts such gaming devices as joysticks or steering wheels.

Using Plug and Play

Installing new hardware is a two-part chore: first, you must perform the physical installation; next, you have to install the driver software. To complete the physical installation, read the instructions that accompanied the hardware.

If your new hardware device is Plug-and-Play compatible (a fact announced on the box and in the manual), installation is a breeze.

After you finish hooking up the new gadget, just turn on your computer. Windows Me now examines every connector, port, and slot on your machine, checking to see whether or not it's now occupied by a piece of equipment it hasn't seen before.

If it finds that you have indeed installed something new, Windows notes its make and model, and then installs the driver software for it *automatically.*

Windows Me comes with the driver software from hundreds of different companies for thousands of different pieces of gear. It keeps many of these on your hard drive, but not all of them; just after starting up the PC, you may be asked to put your Windows Me CD into the CD-ROM drive, so that Windows can grab a driver from its supplementary collection on the CD.

After a moment, you see a message that Windows has found a new piece of equipment, and that it's now all set to go.

Tip: If you didn't turn off the computer when you attached a peripheral to the back of your PC, you can initiate the Windows Me Plug-and-Play search manually. Right-click My Computer and choose Properties from the shortcut menu. Click the Device Manager tab, then click the Refresh button. The Plug-and-Play search begins. (Don't panic if your screen goes black for a moment: that's normal.)

When Plug and Play Doesn't Work

If Windows Me doesn't display a message telling you it's installing new hardware during startup, it probably can't "see" your new device. Here's what to check:

- If you've installed an internal card, make sure that it's seated in the slot firmly.

- If you've attached a peripheral, make sure that it has power and is correctly connected to the PC.

If nothing seems to be wrong with the hardware, contact the manufacturers to make sure that both your computer and the new gear support Plug and Play.

If you're still stuck, your device may be so new that it's not part of the Windows Me driver database. If one of these is the case, you can install the hardware using the Add New Hardware Wizard, described next.

Using the Add New Hardware Wizard

For non-Plug-and-Play devices, or Plug-and-Play devices that Windows doesn't install automatically, Windows comes with a wizard that walks you through the steps needed to get your new hardware running.

Start by making sure you have the software drivers handy, which you can get from one of these sources:

- The Windows Me CD.

- The disk that came with the hardware.

- The manufacturer's Web site, which generally offers the latest drivers for downloading.

To start the Add New Hardware Wizard, follow these steps:

1. **Choose Start→Settings→Control Panel.**

   The Control Panel window opens, as described in Chapter 9. If the Add New Hardware listing isn't visible, click "view all Control Panel options."

2. **Double-click the Add New Hardware icon.**

   The Add New Hardware Wizard appears.

3. **Click Next to move past the introduction page and start the wizard.**

The search for Plug and Play

The first thing the wizard wants to do is search for a Plug-and-Play device. You already know that it's not going to find one, because if the hardware you're trying to install were Plug-and-Play compatible, Windows Me would have found it and installed it when you restarted your computer.

Unfortunately, you can't stop the Hardware Wizard juggernaut. The only choices at your disposal are Next, which begins this fruitless search, or Cancel, which abandons the process. You have no choice but to click Next and proceed as in the next section.

Add Hardware Wizard searches for non-Plug-and-Play devices

If the search for Plug-and-Play hardware fails, a new wizard window opens and offers two choices:

- Let the wizard search for devices that are not Plug and Play.

- Have the wizard display list of device types from which you can select your new hardware.

It does no harm to let the wizard see if it can find your non-Plug-and-Play hardware. If the search succeeds, you've saved a couple of keystrokes; if the search fails, you move on to the second option (the list of all devices) anyway.

If the wizard does find a new device, a window opens to proclaim the achievement. You can install drivers from the Windows Me CD, or tell the wizard you want to use drivers from the manufacturer (see "Using Manufacturer Drivers" on page 304).

FREQUENTLY ASKED QUESTION

Using Manufacturer's Drivers for Plug-and-Play Devices

Windows Me finds my new Plug-and-Play device, but I don't want to use the Windows Me drivers. I have newer, better drivers from the manufacturer. How can I stop the automated installation so I can use the better drivers?

You can't stop Plug-and-Play detection, but you *can* update the drivers after Windows Me has installed your new hardware. You do that in the Device Manager, described on page 304.

Add Hardware Wizard performs manual installation

If the wizard finds no new hardware, or if you opted to see a list of devices, the wizard displays a list of device types. Select from that list the type of hardware you want to install (for example, Imaging for a digital camera or a scanner, or Port if you're installing another printer port). Then click Next to begin installing drivers.

Some kinds of hardware are made by a wide range of manufacturers, and many of those manufacturers offer several different models. Now Windows Me opens a two-paned window like the one shown in Figure 13-1.

Figure 13-1:
Scroll down the left pane to find the name of the manufacturer of your hardware (in this case, a monitor). The right pane of the window changes to display all the models that manufacturer offers (that Windows Me knows about). If you can't find your model number, check the hardware's instructions to see if selecting one of the listed models would work just as well.

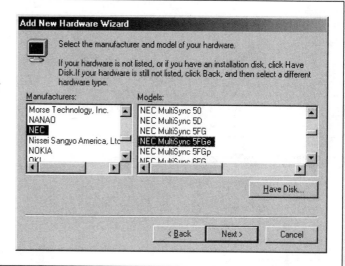

To complete the installation, click Next and go through the rest of the wizard windows. You may be asked to select a port or configure other settings. When you click Finish on the last screen, Windows transfers the drivers to your hard drive. (Along the way, you may be instructed to insert the Windows Me CD.) As a final step, you may be asked to restart the PC.

Figure 13-2:
You must specify the location of the drivers. If the files are on a floppy drive or CD-ROM, insert it now. If you downloaded the files, enter the path to the folder in which the files are located, such as \downloads. (Alternatively, enter the drive letter, and then click Browse to select the appropriate folder using the mouse.)

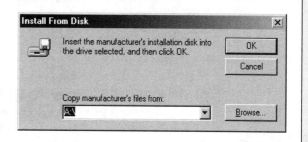

Using manufacturer's drivers

Even if your hardware appears in the list of devices that Windows shows you, it's a good idea to use the drivers that came from your gadget's manufacturer if you have them, especially if you got them from the manufacturer's Web site. They're likely to be newer versions of the drivers than the ones that came with Windows Me.

To do so, click Have Disk when the wizard offers that option. The Install From Disk dialog opens, as shown in Figure 13-2.

The Device Manager

The Device Manager is an extremely powerful tool that lets you troubleshoot and update drivers for gear you've already installed.

To use the Device Manager, right-click My Computer and choose Properties from the shortcut menu. (Alternatively, choose Start→Settings→Control Panel, and open the System icon.) In the Systems Properties dialog box, click the Device Manager tab to see a list of your PC's components, as shown in Figure 13-3.

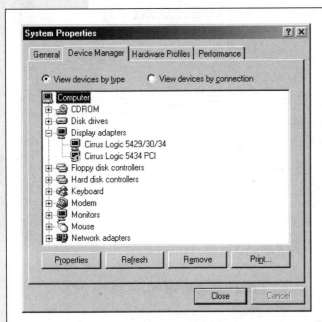

Figure 13-3:
The Device Manager lists device types; you must expand each type by clicking the + symbol to see the actual model(s) in each category. A device that's configured incorrectly is easy to spot, because the device category is automatically "expanded" to show the device model when you open this window. A yellow exclamation point—like the one here on the "Cirrus Logic 5434 PCI" component—indicates a problem.

Resolving Conflicts Using the Device Manager

The Device Manager for a healthy computer displays a list of every component: Floppy drive, CD-ROM drive, keyboard, modem, and so on. Each has a + sign to the left—click the + button to see the actual model names of your PC's components.

A yellow exclamation point next to the name indicates a problem with the device's driver. It could mean that you or Windows Me installed the wrong driver, or that the device is fighting for resources being used by another component. It could also mean that a driver can't find the equipment it's supposed to control. That's what happens to your Zip-drive driver, for example, if you've detached the Zip drive.

A red X next to a component's name, meanwhile, indicates that it just isn't working. Most of the time, this situation is the result of a serious incompatibility problem between the device and your computer, or the device and Windows Me. Unless you find a simple cause, such as a problem with the way you connected the cable, a call to the manufacturer's help line is almost certainly in your future.

Duplicate devices

If the Device Manager displays icons for duplicate devices (for example, two modems), remove *both* of them. (Click each and then click Remove.) If you remove only one of them, Windows Me will find it again the next time the PC starts up, and the Device Manager will show duplicate devices again.

If Windows Me asks if you want to restart your computer after you remove the first icon, click No, and then delete the second one. Windows Me won't ask again after you remove the second incarnation; you have to restart your computer manually.

When the PC starts up again, Windows finds the hardware device and installs it (only once this time). Open the Device Manager and make sure that there's only one of everything. If not, contact the manufacturer's help line.

Figure 13-4:
The Resources tab should have all the information you need to resolve a problem. Any resource with a conflict is marked with a red "not working" icon. Selecting a resource with a problem displays information about the conflict.

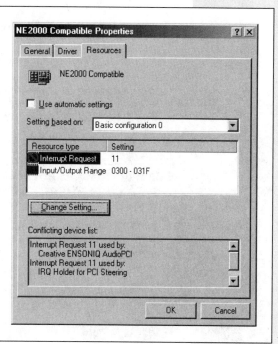

Resolving resource conflicts

If the "red-X" problem isn't caused by a duplicate component, click the component's name and then click Properties. The Device Status section of the Properties dialog box explains the problem, which is almost always a conflict in resources. Click the Resources tab (see Figure 13-4) to continue your investigation.

Click the name of the resource that's having the conflict and then click Change Setting. (If the Change Setting button is grayed out, turn off the "Use automatic settings" checkbox, which makes the Change Setting button available.)

Click the up and down control arrows next to the resource value, keeping an eye on the message in the Conflict Information box. When you select a value that has no conflict (as indicated by the Conflict Information box), move on to the next resource that indicates a conflict, and then click OK.

Turning Components Off

If you click a component's name and then click Properties, you may find an option to disable the device. You most often use this feature when you're creating *hardware profiles* (see page 308), but you can also use this function to test device conflicts. For example, if a red X indicates that you've got a resource conflict on your hands, you can disable one of the two gadgets, which may clear up a problem with its competitor.

When you disable a component, a red X appears next to its listing in the Device Manager. To undo your action, click the device's name and click Properties; in the resulting dialog box is the Enable Device button.

Updating Drivers with the Device Manager

If you get your hands on a new, more powerful (or more reliable) driver for a device, you can use the Device Manager to install it. Newer isn't *always* better, however; in

---

TROUBLESHOOTING MOMENT

Changing Resource Settings: Like Walking on Quicksand

You have to use antiquated hardware switches called *jumpers* or *DIP switches* to change the resource assignments of certain aged hardware devices (primarily internal cards). For this kind of gadget, changing the resources in the Device Manager window only solves half the problem you've been having; it can change the channel assignments only of *drivers*. You must follow up such a change by setting up the hardware to use the same settings, using those DIP switches or jumpers (or a special setup program, if one came with your card).

The point is that if you've got one of those old cards, and

it's conflicting with a more modern, easier to configure gadget, you may find it easier to change the resource numbers of the latter.

And through it all, remember that resource conflicts can be nerve-wracking, but you stand the best chance of remaining sane by following three guidelines: First, when you're having resource-conflict problems, read the instructions that came with the troublesome gadget. Second, make (and test) one change at a time. Finally, take notes about each step you take and its results—a tip that will pay off when you give up and call for technical support.

---

the world of Windows, the rule "If it ain't broke, don't fix it" contains a grain of truth the size of Texas.

In the Device Manager, click the + button for the appropriate type of equipment, select the name of the gadget, and click Properties. Move to the Driver tab and click Update Driver. The Update Device Driver Wizard walks you through the process.

Along the way, the wizard will offer to search for a better driver, or display a list of drivers in a certain folder so you can make your own selection. Ignore the fact that the wizard says the first choice is recommended; you *know* where the driver is, and it's faster to find it yourself. Select "Display a list of drivers," click Next, click Have Disk (if you have a driver disk) or Browse (if you downloaded the driver to your hard drive), and follow the wizard's prompts. You may have to restart the PC to put the newly installed driver into service.

Printing a System Report

When troubleshooting, it can be useful to print out a list of your PC's components and the resources they use. Such a list can make it easier to identify any IRQs (see page 298) or other resources that are still available for use by a new piece of gear you're trying to install or set up.

To print out such a list, click the Print button to open the Print dialog shown in Figure 13-5.

- The **System summary** report summarizes all the hardware in your system by resource type, listing each resource, then the specific value used by each device.

- The **Selected class or device** report lists all the resources and drivers for the se-lected device.

- The **All devices and system summary** report lists everything there is to know about every hardware device—probably more than you need to know. Put plenty of paper into your printer's tray; this report is extremely long.

If you select Print to File, the file that's saved on your drive is a printer file, not a text file. The only way to read the information is to print the resulting file, as described on page 290.

Figure 13-5:
You can generate a printed report of your system through the Device Manager. If you haven't clicked a device type or a specific device before clicking Print, the option to print a report about a selected device is grayed out. Use the Setup button to select a printer (if you have multiple printers) or to set printer options.

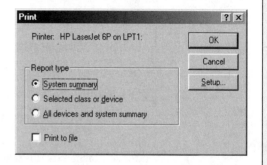

Hardware Profiles

Hardware profiles are canned sets of settings for particular equipment configurations. By switching from one profile to another, you can quickly inform your computer that you've got a different assortment of gear connected, which is primarily useful if you have a laptop.

If your laptop has a bay that can hold either a CD-ROM drive or a floppy drive, for example, you might create two hardware profiles, one for each of the drives. If you connect your laptop to a docking station at work, you can create one hardware profile for the devices available on the docking station (such as a monitor), and another hardware profile for use when you're undocked.

To create a hardware profile, open the System Properties box by right-clicking the My Computer icon and choosing Properties from the shortcut menu. Then click the Hardware Profiles tab (see Figure 13-6).

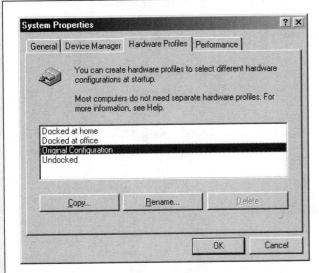

Figure 13-6:
Every computer comes with a hardware profile named Original Configuration. Creating a new profile is simply a matter of copying the existing profile, naming the copy, and then making changes to it.

Follow these steps to create another hardware profile for your computer:

1. **Click Copy, name the new profile, and click OK.**

   The new profile appears in the list shown in Figure 13-6.

2. **Click to select the new profile.**

   The following steps will apply to this profile.

3. **Click the Device Manager tab.**

   The window shows you a list of all the various hardware gadgets you've installed into, or attached to, this machine.

4. Click the + symbol, and then the name, of the component you want to turn on or off in this profile; click Properties.

The Properties dialog box appears.

5. Turn on "Disable in this hardware profile."

If the device is disabled in the profile you're copying, the selection changes to "Enable in this hardware profile."

6. Repeat steps 4 and 5 for any other devices you'd like to enable or disable for this profile, and then click OK.

Hereafter, whenever you start your computer, a dialog box appears asking you to select a hardware profile. Only after you choose one and click OK does Windows Me finish its startup process. Windows loads only the drivers for the hardware you've turned on in the selected profile.

The Multiple-Users Feature

For years, teachers, parents, and computer-lab instructors have struggled to answer a difficult question: How do you rig one PC so that several different people can use it throughout the day, without interfering with each other's files and settings? And how do you protect a PC from getting fouled up by mischievous (or bumbling) students and employees?

Some schools, labs, families, and businesses just muddled through as best they could. Fortunately, Windows Me offers a reliable, built-in solution to this traditional problem: a feature called User Profiles.

User Profiles

This feature lets you create an *account* for each student, family member, or employee. When you turn on the PC, it doesn't start up as usual; instead, it asks you to *log in,* as shown in Figure 14-1. If you like, it may even ask for a password.

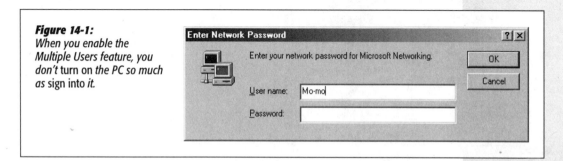

Figure 14-1:
When you enable the Multiple Users feature, you don't turn on the PC so much as sign into it.

When you identify yourself, you arrive at the Windows desktop in your own customized world: *your* desktop picture fills the screen, the Web browser lists *your* bookmarks (Favorites), My Documents folder lists *your* files, and so on. To be precise, Windows Me remembers how you left your:

- **Desktop.** Each person sees a different set of shortcut icons, folder icons, and other stuff left out on the desktop.

- **My Documents folder.** Each person sees only her own stuff in the My Documents folder (see Chapter 2).

- **Documents menu.** The Documents listed in the Start→Documents menu are the ones that *this* person used most recently.

- **Start menu.** If you reorganize the Start menu, as described in Chapter 2, you won't foul up anybody else when they try to use this machine; they won't even see the changes you make.

- **Favorites folder.** Any Web sites, folders, or other icons you've designated as Favorites (see page 125) appear in *your* Start→Favorites menu, nobody else's.

- **Internet cache.** You can read about *cached* Web pages in Chapter 11; this folder stores a copy of the Web pages you've visited recently for faster reappearance.

- **History and cookies.** Windows maintains a list of recently visited Web sites independently for each person; likewise the collection of *cookies* (Web-site preference files).

- **Control Panel settings.** Windows memorizes the settings each person establishes using the Control Panel (see Chapter 9), including keyboard and mouse settings.

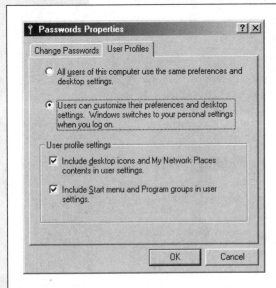

Figure 14-2:
After you enable the option to let people customize their settings, you can also specify which settings are saved in their profiles. Turning on both of the "User profile settings" checkboxes means that each person can maintain his settings for the desktop and for the Start menu.

This feature makes sharing the PC much more convenient, because you don't have to look at everybody else's files (and endure their desktop design schemes). It also adds a layer of security, albeit a thin one; a marauding six-year-old is less likely to throw away your files. (A determined Windows vandal, however, will have no trouble finding the folder where Windows actually stores each person's files and settings.)

Turning on User Profiles

To turn on the User Profiles feature, follow these steps:

1. Choose Start→Settings→Control Panel. Double-click the Passwords icon.

   Now the Passwords Properties dialog box appears.

2. Click the User Profiles tab. Turn on "Users can customize their preferences…" (see Figure 14-2). Click OK.

   You'll be prompted to restart the PC; do so. When it "comes to," you'll be offered the chance to create the first profile: your own.

Windows Me creates a *default* profile that inherits the current configuration of the PC at the moment. When each person signs in, he'll see the desktop, Start menu,

---

TROUBLESHOOTING MOMENT

The Trouble with Profiles: New Programs

When you turn on the multiple-user feature, the current desktop, Start menu, and other settings serve as a common starting point for all profiles. Thereafter, if you install some new software while logged in, you'll be the only person whose Start menu lists the newly installed software. The software's on the computer; it's just not on anyone else's Start menu, nor is there a shortcut on anyone else's desktop. (Some programs store important settings as part of a profile, too.)

That's a problem worth considering. It means that each person who installs software is the only one sees it in the Start menu. It may mean that some people won't be able to use the program at all, even if they know that it's been installed, because their profile accounts lack important settings files. Worse, it means that somebody else, not seeing the program's name on the Start menu, won't realize that you've already installed it—and is likely to install it *again*.

You can solve this problem in one of three ways. First, you can try to install all the software you'll ever need *before*

turning on the profiles feature. Another sure-fire solution is to log on using each profile, one at a time, and reinstall the program each time. If you always install it into the same folder, you don't actually get multiple copies of the program, but you ensure that the settings and Start menu will be correctly configured for everybody.

But if you've installed some new software after the profiles feature is already on, you can also use a sneaky trick. As it turns out, the My Computer→C: drive→Windows→ Profiles folder contains a folder for each profile. The profile folders contain subfolders for each element of the profile, such as desktop items, Start menu items, My Documents, and so on.

With this knowledge, you can copy, move, and delete items among user profile subfolders. To copy a Start menu item from one person's profile to another, for example, just copy its icon in the first person's Start-menu folder, and paste it into another.

Favorites menu, and other elements the way they are right now. But if he changes this setup, the modifications become part of his own profile, and will reappear each time he logs on.

Creating Profiles at Startup Time

Once you've turned on the profiles feature, it's time to start creating *profiles* (accounts) for the people who'll be using this machine. It's very easy to do: When the computer finishes starting up, it shows you a dialog box containing two boxes—User Name and Password (Figure 14-1).

To set up a profile for yourself, just type in a name for yourself, such as your first name. If you'd like to require a password, too, type one into the Password blank. (Windows substitutes asterisks for each character you type, so that evil over-the-shoulder lookers behind you won't be able to spy on your password.)

Tip: It's perfectly OK to skip the password field and click OK. When your computer starts up, you won't have to type in a password to gain access.

When Windows asks, "Would you like this computer to retain your individual settings?", click Yes. After Windows spends a minute shuffling and copying files, it creates your profile. From now on, any changes you make to the Windows setup (for example, by deleting, adding, or modifying shortcuts, program items, or software settings) become part of your profile. You'll see it all every time you log on.

This method makes it easy for each person to create his own profile, right at startup time. You can also set up profiles en masse, however, as described next.

Creating Profiles En Masse

If you'd like to set up several profiles at once, you'll probably find it inconvenient to use the one-at-a-time, type-your-name-at-startup method described above. Fortu-

---

FREQUENTLY ASKED QUESTION

The Original Windows Logon Box Doesn't Mean Much

The very first time I started Windows Me, I saw a logon dialog box with my name in it. So I entered a password. Now I have to fill in the password every time I start my computer. Am I using the User Profiles feature?

No. If the Logon box appears the first time you turn on a Windows Me PC, simply click OK without typing anything; you'll never see the Logon box again. But if it's too late for that, and you entered a password, you'll see the Logon box every time you start your computer. You haven't turned

on User Profiles; you've just committed yourself to logging on, for no particular reason or advantage, each time the computer starts up.

Unfortunately, there's no way out of this problem except to delete your password file, as described at the end of this chapter. (And doing so also deletes all of your other passwords, including those needed to connect to the Internet.)

---

nately, you can use the Users control panel applet to set up a group of accounts all at once.

Click Start→Settings→Control Panel to open the Control Panel window. Then double-click the Users icon. You can create a new profile in either of two ways:

- By copying a profile that's already listed (by clicking the Make a Copy button shown in Figure 14-3), or

- From scratch (using the New User button shown in Figure 14-3).

It takes a few seconds for Windows Me to create the new settings, folders, and files. When it's finished, you see the User Settings dialog box; the profile you've just created is now named in the list.

Figure 14-3:
Top: To create a new profile, click New User, or save time by copying someone else's. To do so, click a profile name, click Make a Copy, and answer the wizard's questions (regarding name, password, and so on).

Bottom: Along the way, you'll be asked which elements you want kept separate in this profile. If you copy items that contain files, such as the My Documents folder, you'll generally want to select "Create new items to save disk space" so you don't copy all the contents of the default My Documents folder. Instead, Windows Me creates blank folders for the new profile.

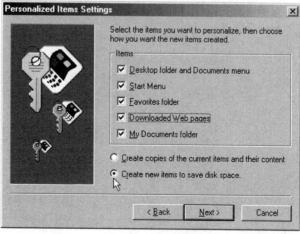

Changing profiles

To change the settings for a particular profile, click its name in the User Settings dialog box and then click Change Settings (Figure 14-3, top). The dialog box at bottom in Figure 14-3 re-opens, so that you can make your changes.

Deleting profiles

When somebody's no longer part of your classroom, workplace, or relationship, you can get his name off the list of profiles. Just click his name and then click the Delete button shown in Figure 14-3. Windows deletes his profile, along with all of the folders associated it; you reclaim the space they were using on your hard drive.

Signing In, Logging Off

After you've set up some profiles, you're ready to begin using them in the day-to-day process of logging on and logging off.

Logon name is already filled in

When the Logon dialog box appears at the end of the Windows startup process, the name of the last person who logged on appears in the User name field. The cursor is waiting in the Password field.

- If *you* were the last person who logged on, enter your password (if any) and click OK (or press Enter).

- If you don't see your own name in the Logon dialog box, press Shift+Tab to highlight the User name box. As you begin typing your logon name, it replaces the name that was there before.

In either case, you now arrive at the Windows desktop, where your own folders, desktop icons, and Start menu greet you.

If you make a typo

If you mistype your logon name, Windows thinks that you're trying to create a new profile. This kind of mistake could wind up creating a set of redundant, duplicate profiles for yourself, each bearing a name that includes your typo.

That's why, when you type a name that Windows doesn't recognize, it asks you if you're sure you want to create a new profile. Click No; you'll be given another chance to type your name correctly.

If you can't remember your logon name, click Cancel (or press the Esc key) to skip the logon process and go right to the desktop. Windows loads the default profile. You won't see your customized Start menu, desktop shortcut icons, and so on, but at least you can use the computer.

Tip: To find out what your logon name was, open the My Computer→C: drive→Windows→Profiles folder, where you'll find a folder named for each profile. Once you've been reminded, choose Start→Log Off, click Yes, and log in again.

If you continue to forget your logon name, consider the Family Logon feature described below, which offers a *list* of account names when you sign in.

If you can't remember your *password*, that's a different problem. See page 319 for advice and troubleshooting.

Logging off

When you shut down or restart the PC, you're offered the Logon dialog box again, so that the next person can sign in. But you don't have to restart the machine just to let somebody new sign in; instead, you can choose the Start→Log Off command.

Tip: If there *isn't* a Log Off command, right-click any blank spot on the Taskbar. Choose Properties from the shortcut menu. In the Taskbar and Start Menu Properties dialog box, click the Advanced tab. Turn on the Display Logoff checkbox, and then click OK.

Now you can choose Start→Log Off [your name] when you're finished working as an officially logged-on profile holder. When you log off, Windows closes any open programs and displays the Logon dialog box again. Your name is in the User name field (because you're the last person who logged on), but the next person who wants to use the computer can replace it by typing in her own logon name and password.

Note: Logging off isn't the same as restarting the computer; it won't suffice when, for example, you've just changed your network settings and a message tells you that you'll have to restart the PC to make the changes kick in.

Family Logon

If you'd rather not have to type your name every time you sign in, you can ask Windows Me to offer you a *list* of all accounts each time the PC turns on (see Figure

Figure 14-4:
When you use the Family Logon feature, you don't have to remember your logon name, and you don't have to worry about typing errors—just click your logon name in the list that Windows presents.

14-4). You can then sign in just by clicking your name (and typing in the password, if you've set one up).

You'll note that the Family Logon dialog box doesn't include a place to *type* your name; therefore, you can't very well create new accounts just by typing in a name and password, as you ordinarily can. Therefore, you have to create the profiles ahead of time. For example, you can set up all the accounts using the type-in-your-name technique described in the first part of this chapter—and *then* turn on Family Logon. Or you can set up all the profiles en masse, as described on page 314.

Turning on the Family Logon Feature

Even after you've carefully set up profiles for your PC, you still have to throw the Family Logon master switch. You do it like this:

1. **Right-click the My Network Places desktop icon. Choose Properties from the shortcut menu.**

   The Network dialog box opens, as shown in Figure 14-5.

2. **Click Add to see a list of network components. Select Client and click Add.**

   After a moment, the Select Network Client dialog box appears.

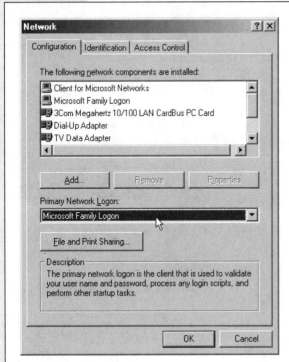

Figure 14-5:
The item of interest here is the field named Primary Network logon. If you see Microsoft Family Logon listed in the drop-down menu, choose it; if not, follow the instructions in this section to install the Family Logon network logon client.

3. Click Microsoft in the left pane.

   It's probably the only option.

4. In the right pane, click Microsoft Family Logon. Click OK.

   You return to the Network dialog box.

5. In the **Primary Network Logon** drop-down menu, choose **Microsoft Family Logon**, and then click OK.

   Windows Me moves some files around, then shows you a message announcing that you must restart your computer to put the new settings into effect.

6. Click Yes.

   When Windows starts up again, the Family Logon dialog box appears, listing every profile. To sign on and use your own personalized desktop, click your name (and enter your password, if you're using one), and then click OK.

UP TO SPEED

The Security of a Sieve

Windows Me has no computer-wide security whatsoever. Even if you've set up a password for your profile, a passing evildoer can easily bypass the entire logon/password process simply by clicking the Cancel button when the Logon dialog box appears. Voilà—she's in. She won't find your files in the My Documents folder on the desktop, but she won't have to dig very far into the folders on your C: drive to unearth them.

If security is a real issue in your office, Windows Millennium is the wrong operating system. Consider installing the much more secure Windows 2000.

Changing Your Password

You can change your password whenever you like. To do so, choose Start→Settings→Control Panel; double-click the Passwords icon. In the Passwords Properties dialog box, enter your old (current) password and the new one (twice, to guard against typos), and then click OK.

Tip: You can use the Passwords control panel to change the passwords you use for connecting to other servers on the network, too. To do so, click Change Other Passwords.

Troubleshooting Passwords

Two circumstances can interfere with your ability to use your password:

• You forget your password.

• Your password file becomes corrupted (damaged).

Both problems have the same solution: replace your password file. This means you'll have to start all over, creating the passwords you need to log on and perform password-protected activities. Unfortunately, even if the password you forgot is your logon password, all the other passwords you use that Windows stores are lost, too. Here's how to replace your password file:

1. **Choose Start→Search→For Files or Folders.**

   The Search window appears, as described on page 28.

2. **Enter *.pwl in the "Search for files or folders named" box, and then click Search Now.**

   Windows Me searches your hard drive for password files, and displays a list of any files it finds (see Figure 14-6). There's a separate password file for each profile.

3. **Find your own password file in the Search Results pane (Figure 14-6) and select it. Then press the Delete key to remove the file.**

   Doing so also deletes the passwords you've entered for connecting to your Internet account, to other PCs on the network, and so on.

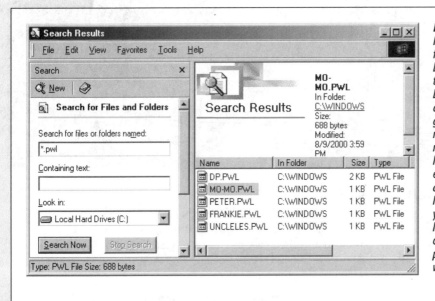

Figure 14-6:
It's a good idea to find password files by searching for the extension .pwl because Windows doesn't always give the file a name that exactly matches your logon name. For example, if there's a space in your logon name, or your logon name is longer than eight characters, the password filename won't match.

Unfortunately, a damaged password file isn't an especially rare event. Here are some clues that this headache has befallen you:

- You know you're entering the password correctly, but Windows doesn't let you in.

- When you select the option to store the password, an error message says Windows Me can't save the password.

- When you try to use a password, you see an error message "MPREXE not responding."

- When you start Internet Explorer or Outlook Express, you see an error message that contains the phrase "caused an invalid page fault in module Kernel32.dll."

After you delete your password file, Windows Me waits until the next time you log on to re-create the file for you—but now, of course, it has no passwords stored for you. That means the Logon dialog box you see when you next log on won't accept *any* password.

In that event, here's how to click your way out:

- If you use the standard Windows Logon dialog box, enter your name, then click OK to skip the Password field.

- If you use the Family Logon, select your name. The password field is inaccessible, so click OK.

Then use the Password or Users control panel applet to create a password.

TROUBLESHOOTING MOMENT

Linking the Password File to the Right Person

If several peoples' profile names begin with the same eight characters, you won't be able to figure out whose password file is whose in the Search dialog box (Figure 14-6).

For instance, suppose there are three Jennifers in your classroom. Their profile names are Jennifer1, Jennifer2, and Jennifer3. In such a case, Windows Me automatically truncates the password files to *Jennifer.pwl, Jenni000.pwl,* and *Jenni001.pwl.* They don't even correspond to the alpha-

betical sequence of the original Jennifers—instead, they represent the *order* in which each Jennifer created a logon name.

Unless you know for sure which Jennifer password file is which, it's dangerous to delete a password file. The solution: Create profile names composed of first initial/last name, such as BGates and SBallmer.

WINDOWS ME: THE MISSING MANUAL

PC Health and Troubleshooting

L ike you, your computer requires periodic checkups and preventive maintenance in order to stay healthy and productive. Fortunately, many of the new
features in Windows Millennium are heavily centered around "PC Health" (as
Microsoft calls it). Here's a crash course in the Windows Me tools that are designed
to keep your PC humming.

System Restore

There may well come a day when you prize this new Windows Me feature above all
others. Sure, Movie Maker has its charms, and the new Help system is fine, but when
something goes dramatically wrong with your PC, System Restore can be worth
hours of your time and hundreds of dollars in consultant fees.

As any grizzled PC veteran can tell you, the pattern of things going wrong in Windows is usually this: The PC works fine for a while, and then suddenly—for no
apparent reason, but often because of a recent installation or configuration change—
it goes on the fritz. At that point, wouldn't it be pleasant to be able to tell the computer: "Go back to the way you were yesterday, please"?

The System Restore does exactly that: It rewinds time, taking your PC back to the
condition it was in before your attempt to install or change something, before it got
infected by a virus, before you accidentally deleted a critical application. Better yet,
System Restore takes only your operating system back to its previous condition. It
doesn't touch anything in your My Documents folder, any documents with common filename extensions (such as *.doc* or *.xls)*, your email, your Internet Explorer
History or Favorites lists, and so on.

And if you don't like your PC after restoring it, you can always restore it to the way it was *before* you restored it!

About System Checkpoints

System Restore works by taking quiet snapshots of your operating system. In fact, your copy of Windows Me has been creating these memorized snapshots, called System checkpoints, ever since you began running it. When the worst comes to pass, and your PC starts acting up, you can use the System Restore calendar (see Figure 15-1) to "rewind" your machine to its configuration the last time you remember it working well—even if you accidentally deleted an application in the meantime.

As you can see by the calendar in Figure 15-1, Windows Me automatically creates landing points for your little PC time machine:

- The first time you boot up Windows Me.

- After every 10 hours of operation.

- After every 24 hours of real-world time (unless your PC is turned off all day; then you get a checkpoint the next time it's turned on).

- Every time you install a new program (whose installer uses InstallShield 6.1 Pro or higher, or the Windows Install program).

- Every time the Windows Automatic Update feature (see page 116) updates a component of your operating system.

- Every time you decide to create one of these snapshots because you feel like it— such as just before you install something new. (To create one of these manual checkpoints, choose Start→Programs→Accessories→System Tools→System Restore. Click "Create a restore point," and then click Next; name your new checkpoint and click OK.)

As you can well imagine, storing all of these copies of your Windows configuration consumes quite a bit of disk space: a minimum of 200 MB, and more if you have it available. That's why Windows Me automatically begins deleting system checkpoints after a couple of weeks, and along with them any chance you have of rewinding your system back that far. That's also why the System Restore feature stops working if your hard drive is very full. And that's *also* why you should run the System Restore feature promptly when you notice that your PC is acting strangely.

Tip: To specify how much disk space System Restore is allowed to use (and therefore how many weeks' worth of "rolling back" opportunities you have), choose Start→Settings→Control Panel; then double-click System. In the System Properties window, click the Performance tab, click File System, and drag the upper slider to change the amount of disk space you're willing to give up for this feature. Click Apply, and then OK.

Performing a System Restore

If something goes wrong with your PC, here's how to roll it back to the happy, by-gone days of late last week:

1. **Choose Start→Programs→Accessories→System Tools→System Restore.**

   The System Restore Wizard appears.

2. **Confirm that "Restore my computer to an earlier time" is selected, and then click Next.**

   Now you see the System Restore calendar (Figure 15-1). The calendar squares containing boldface numbers indicate the days on which Windows memorized your operating system condition.

3. **Click the calendar square closest to the last day you remember your PC working correctly; click one of the checkpoints listed on the right side, and then click Next.**

   You're now warned to close all your documents and programs (except, of course, System Restore itself).

4. **Click OK, exit any running programs, and then click Next.**

   Now Windows goes to town, reinstating your operating system to reflect its condition on the date you specified. Leave your PC alone while this goes on.

   When the process is complete, the computer restarts automatically. After it's up and running, the System Restore program greets you with a Restoration Complete message. Click OK; welcome back to the past.

Figure 15-1:
To change the month, click the < or > button at either end of the month banner. When you click a calendar square containing a bold number, the window on the right shows the restoration points available for that date. You may find System Checkpoints, for example, which Windows creates automatically; Installation checkpoints, which correspond to times you install new software; and Manual Checkpoints, which you created yourself.

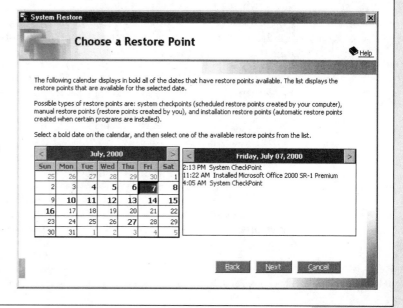

Tip: If rewinding your system to the golden days actually makes matters worse, you can fast forward back to the future, undoing this entire Restore process. To do so, choose Start→Programs→Accessories→System Tools→System Restore. Click "Undo my last Restoration," click Next, click OK, click Next, and wait for the process to reverse itself.

GEM IN THE ROUGH

Automatic System-File Replacement

One of Windows Me's best new features has no control panel, no window, or icon of its own. It's a behind-the-scenes, automatic feature that may have already saved your PC's hide a time or two without your knowledge. It's called System File Protection.

Ordinarily, you can't even see the icons of important Windows system files. Years of calls to Microsoft's help center have taught the company to keep these files hidden from the inexperienced, the curious, and the mischievous.

But if you make these files visible again (see page 73) *and* drag one of the vital files in the C:→Windows folder to the

Recycle Bin, you won't even get the satisfaction of seeing your machine crash. Instead, in the time it takes you close and open the Windows folder again, the operating system replaces the deleted system file with a perfect, fresh copy. Windows Me can take care of itself, thank you.

This feature also solves the age-old "My-application's-installer-replaced-an-important-system-file-with-an-older-version,-and-now-nothing-works!" snafu; Windows Me, simply put, won't allow an application to replace a Windows Me file with an older version. True, this means that the odd program won't run, but better it than your PC.

ScanDisk

When you use the Start→Shut Down command, Windows tidies up, making sure all files are saved properly on the drive, and also making sure that the FAT index knows where each piece of each file resides (as described in the sidebar on the next page). When all is well, Windows Me displays a message on your screen telling you it's OK to shut off your computer; modern PCs even turn off at this point. (The time that elapses between your Shut Down command and the actual power-down moment is the "tidying up" period.)

But sometimes, thanks to a system crash, power outage, or marauding toddler playing with your surge suppressor, your computer gets turned off without warning—and without the usual Shut Down checks. Whenever you turn on the PC after such a *dirty shutdown,* a program called ScanDisk runs automatically. ScanDisk is a utility designed to detect and, when possible, repair drive damage that may have occurred as a result of an improper shutdown.

But every few months, it's a good idea to run ScanDisk manually, so that it can check your hard drive for any nascent problems. To do so, choose Start→Programs→Accessories→System Tools→ScanDisk. The ScanDisk window opens, as shown in Figure 15-3.

Click Start to begin the scan, which checks the file structure, folders, files, and other elements on your drive. It pays particular attention to three kinds of problems:

- **Damaged sections of the drive.** When ScanDisk finds a damaged section of a drive, it moves any files located there elsewhere on the drive. Then the program surrounds that hard-disk area with the digital equivalent of a yellow "Police Line—Do Not Cross" tape, so that Windows Me won't use that damaged area for storing files in the future.

- **Orphaned file fragments.** Sometimes the FAT index described below becomes muddled, and loses track of which fragmented files are part of which files.

When ScanDisk finds such "floating" file fragments, it copies their contents into text files (called *File0000.chk, File00001.chk,* and so on) in your C: drive window.

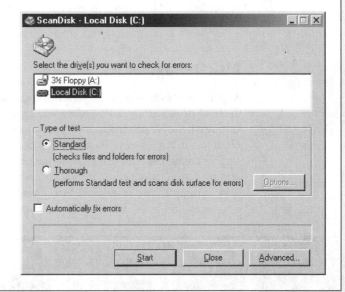

Figure 15-2:
When you run ScanDisk manually, the settings are the same as those applied when the program runs automatically after a "dirty" shutdown. You can change the settings to enlarge the scope of the software's activities, as explained in the next section.

All About FAT

Every file on your hard drive lies in data parking spaces known as *clusters*. Windows Me keeps track of each file's clusters in an index called the File Allocation Table, called *FAT* by people who make their living doing this kind of thing.

When you save a file or install a new program, the FAT notes which clusters it occupies. Then, when you open a file, Windows Me consults the FAT index to see where it is on the hard drive. If the file is fragmented, the FAT tells Windows which locations on the drive to visit, and in what order.

On an unfragmented drive, a file's clusters lie next to each other, like kernels in one row of an ear of corn. But if the drive is fragmented, the clusters may be scattered. As you can imagine, fetching the individual pieces for a fragmented file therefore takes your hard drive's data-reading heads much more time than if the clusters were consecutive. That's why a fragmented drive means slower computer speed.

Although you can open these rescued files using a word processor or Notepad, you probably won't find anything in them except computer-symbol gobbledygook; you may as well simply delete them.

- **Cross-linked files.** The FAT index file can get confused in another way, too: It occasionally lists a certain file fragment as belonging to *more* than one file.

If ScanDisk finds one of these *cross-linked* files, it offers you several choices. You can delete the cross-linked file, copy the file fragment onto *all* of the files to which the FAT index thinks it belongs, or choose *one* of the "parent" files to receive the fragment's material. (In that case, ScanDisk no longer lists the file fragment as belonging to multiple files.)

When ScanDisk completes its tasks, it reports its findings in a ScanDisk Results dialog box.

Disk Defragmenter

As you create files using your various programs, Windows lays them end-to-end on the hard drive surface. Later, when you type more data into a document (thus enlarging it), the file no longer fits in the same space. Windows Me puts as much of the file as fits in the original location, but may have to store a piece of it in the next empty spot on the hard drive. Ordinarily, you'll never even notice the fact that your files are getting chopped up in this way; when you double-click a particular icon, it opens promptly and seamlessly. Windows keeps track of where it's stored the various pieces, and reconstitutes them when necessary.

FREQUENTLY ASKED QUESTION

When Good Drives Go Bad

I was surprised when ScanDisk found some problems with my hard drive. I don't understand what could have gone wrong: I treat my PC with respect, talk to it often, and never take it swimming. Why did my hard drive get flaky?

All kinds of things can cause problems with your hard drive, but the most common are low voltage, power outages, voltage spikes, and mechanical problems with the drive itself or the drive controller.

An inexpensive gadget called a *line conditioner* (sold at computer stores) can solve the low-voltage problem. The more expensive gizmo known as an *Uninterruptible Power Supply* (UPS) maintains enough backup battery power to keep your computer going even when the power goes out completely; the more expensive models have line condi-

tioning built in. A UPS is also the answer to power outages, if they're common in your area.

Voltage spikes are the most dangerous to your PC. They frequently occur during the first seconds when the power comes back on after a power failure. A surge suppressor is the logical defense here. But remember that less expensive surge protectors are designed to sacrifice themselves in battle; after a spike, you often have to replace them.

If you're especially concerned about the quality of electricity in your office, and you want to go to extreme lengths, assemble your little defense squad like this: Power outlet→Surge suppressor→Line conditioner→UPS→ Computer.

Eventually, as your drive fills up, even new files may not fit in a single "parking place" on the hard drive surface, because there are no free spaces left that can hold it. In fact, Windows may have to store a file in five, six, or even more pieces. If your hard drive remains mostly full for a long time, this *file fragmentation* may result in noticeable slowdowns when you open or save files.

The solution: Disk Defragmenter, a program that puts together pieces of files that have become *fragmented* (split into pieces) on your drive. Although this program takes some time to do its work, a freshly "defragged" PC feels faster and more responsive than a heavily fragmented one.

Tip: Fragmentation doesn't become noticeable except on hard drives that have been very full for quite a while. Don't bother defragmenting your drive unless you've actually noticed it slowing down; the time you'll spend waiting for Disk Defragmenter to do its job is much longer than the fractions of seconds caused by a little bit of file fragmentation.

Defragmenting a Drive

Before you run Disk Defragmenter, exit all programs, close all files, disable any antivirus software, and cancel your appointments; defragging is time-consuming. It also temporarily puts your hard drive into a delicate condition; don't defragment if your hard drive is ailing, if there's a thunderstorm, when your laptop is running on battery, or when you've set up the Task Scheduler (see page 332) to trigger automatic tasks.

Then:

1. **Choose Start→Programs→Accessories→System Tools→Disk Defragmenter.**

   The Select Drive dialog box opens.

2. **Click the drive you want to work on.**

   Unless you have multiple hard drives, the C: drive is already selected.

3. **Click Settings to configure Disk Defragmenter.**

   The default settings don't just randomly re-join file fragments—in restoring them, Disk Defragmenter ordinarily tries to organize the files logically on the hard drive surface so that applications open up as quickly as possible. These proposed settings also make Disk Defragmenter check the drive for problems before defragmenting; in general, these settings are best left unchanged.

4. **Click OK to open Disk Defragmenter and begin defragmenting your drive.**

   A small window opens; the program begins checking your drive for errors. If the program finds any problems with your disk, the program tells you so and repairs the problem. Then Disk Defragmenter begins its work, displaying a progress bar to indicate how far along it is.

Disk Defragmenter works by juggling file segments, lifting some into memory and depositing them elsewhere on the drive, then moving other (smaller) files into the newly created free space. This shuffling process goes on for some time, as file fragments and whole files are moved around until every file lies on the drive in one piece.

To see a visual representation of the work Disk Defragmenter is doing, click Show Details. A window appears showing the storage slots (*clusters*) on your drive, along with their states. Click the Legend button to view a guide to the colors, as shown in Figure 15-2.

Tip: For best results, leave your PC alone while the defragmenting process is going on. If you absolutely must perform a task at your computer during the defragging process, click Pause.

If you save a file while the drive is being defragmented (whether you pause the program or not), Disk Defragmenter starts the process over from the beginning.

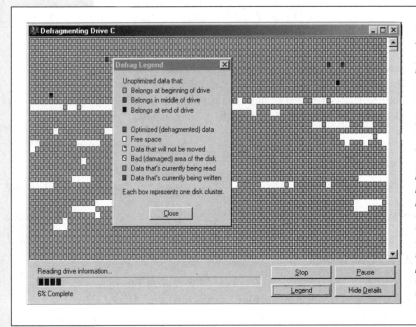

Figure 15-3:
A detailed view of the defragmentation process helps you understand what Disk Defragmenter is doing. The color of each little square is meaningful, as the program juggles software files, system files, and data files to put each file in the best possible place. At that point of perfection, Disk Defragmenter announces victory over fragmentation and asks if you want to close the program. Say Yes unless you have another hard drive you want to defrag.

Disk Cleanup

As you use your computer, Windows places a lot of temporary files on your hard drive. Application programs, utilities, and Web sites litter your hard drive with disposable files. Trouble is, Windows doesn't always clean them up when they're no longer needed.

Choose Start→Programs→Accessories→System Tools→Disk Cleanup to open a built-in housekeeper program. It's designed to inspect your drive and report on files you can safely remove.

Start by selecting the drive you want to clean, then wait while Disk Cleanup examines files. The Disk Cleanup dialog box shown in Figure 15-4 appears when the inspection is over.

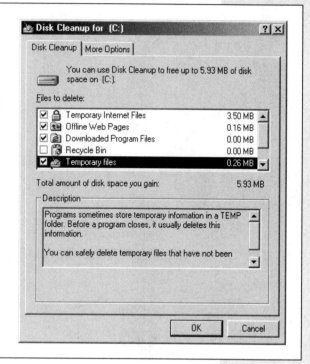

Figure 15-4:
Disk Cleanup shows you all the types of files that you can safely remove from your drive, and even announces how much free space you'll gain. Click each category to see an explanation of that file type. Click View Files to open the folder in which the files are located so you can see the individual file icons (so that you can delete files selectively). Click OK to let Disk Cleanup remove the file types you selected.

Maintenance Wizard

For the lazy and forgetful, Windows Me offers the Maintenance Wizard. This marvel of efficiency runs three of the system tools discussed in this chapter automatically: Disk Defragmenter, ScanDisk, and Disk Cleanup. You decide which programs are used, and when, then relax in the knowledge that your computer will never miss an important health checkup.

Choose Start→Programs→Accessories→System Tools→Maintenance Wizard to start. Choose **Express** if you want the wizard to run all three tools on a standard schedule (Disk Defragmenter and ScanDisk once a week, Disk Cleanup once a month), or **Customize** if you'd like to schedule these tools individually.

In either case, you decide what time of day or night the wizard runs; specify a time when you won't be at your PC (such as the middle of the night). When you finish configuring Maintenance Wizard, you have the option of running each selected maintenance tool immediately, or waiting until the first scheduled occurrence.

Tip: Don't shut down the PC at the end of the day if a midnight maintenance session is scheduled.

Task Scheduler

Task Scheduler is the calendar Windows Me keeps to trigger any application to launch itself according to a schedule that you specify. For example, you can program the Maintenance Wizard (described above) to "go off" on cue, an antivirus or backup program to run, ScanDisk or Disk Defragmenter to whirl into action, and so on.

To open the Task Scheduler (see Figure 15-5), click its icon on your Taskbar, or choose Start→Programs→Accessories→System Tools→Scheduled Tasks.

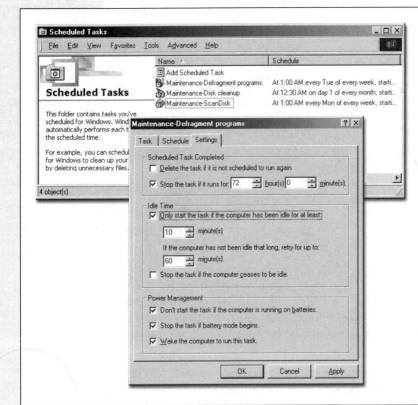

Figure 15-5:
Top: The Task Scheduler keeps a calendar for Windows Me. You can use the Task Scheduler window to add, modify, or remove tasks. (Make sure your computer is turned on during the time any task is supposed to run.)

Bottom: Some of the default settings are a bit ridiculous. For example, it's probably a good idea to stop a task if it runs longer than 4 or 5 hours, not 72 hours. In fact, except for defragmenting disks, most scheduled tasks take less than an hour. The bottom section of the dialog box applies to laptop computers.

Adding a Task to the Scheduler

To add a task to the schedule, double-click the Add Scheduled Task listing in the Task Scheduler window. A wizard appears; on the first screen, it shows a list of programs on your PC. If the one you want to schedule is listed, click it; if not, click Browse, find and open its folder, and double-click its icon.

Name the scheduled task, if you like, and then specify how often you want it to run: every day, every week, and so on. Finally, follow the wizard's prompts to schedule your task; for example, if you chose Monthly, you can tell the wizard which *day* of the month, and at which time.

Changing Scheduled Tasks

If you double-click a task's listing in the Task Scheduler window, you open its Properties dialog box, where you can make several kinds of changes.

- **Cancel a scheduled task.** You can stop a certain scheduled task from running in two ways: by deleting the task entirely (right-click its name and choose Delete from the shortcut menu) or by turning off its Enabled dialog box (on the Task tab of the Properties dialog box). The second method leaves the task in the Task Scheduler window, so that you can turn it back on at a later date.

Tip: Deleted tasks are sent to the Recycle Bin. If you change your mind about deleting it (and you haven't yet emptied the Recycle Bin), you can restore it by right-clicking its icon in the Recycle Bin window and choosing Restore from the shortcut menu.

- **Change the schedule for a task.** Click the Schedule tab of the Properties dialog box to change the schedule for a task.

- **Change the settings for a scheduled task.** Using the Settings tab of a task's Properties dialog box, you can design certain automated tasks to run, or not, according to certain conditions (see Figure 15-5, bottom). To manipulate the settings for a task, click the Settings tab of its Properties dialog box.

Start a Task Immediately

To trigger one of the listed programs right now, right-click its listing and choose Run from the shortcut menu. (The task will still run at its next scheduled time.)

Pause All Scheduled Tasks

To stop all scheduled events from happening, right-click the Task Scheduler's icon on the Taskbar and choose Pause Task Scheduler from the shortcut menu. A red X appears over the icon, and no further self-triggering events will take place (until you un-pause the Scheduler by right-clicking its Taskbar icon and choosing Continue Task Scheduler).

Stop Using Task Scheduler

If you don't use the Task Scheduler, you can get rid of its icon on your Taskbar. Double-click the icon to open the software window and choose Advanced→Stop Using Task Scheduler. The icon disappears. It's gone forever—or at least until you choose Start→Programs→Accessories→System Tools→Scheduled Tasks to start using it again.

Microsoft Backup

There's no point in creating documents if you don't back them up (make safety copies), because a day will come when you can't open them. Sooner or later, almost every hard drive or PC calls in sick.

You can back up your files by copying them to a backup disk (a floppy disk, another computer, or a removable disk such as a Zip or Jaz disk, for example). You can do this either manually or by using an automatic backup program like Microsoft Backup.

Running Backup

Windows Me comes with free backup software called Backup, but you'd never know it. Backup isn't installed by the Windows Me installer; nor does the program appear as a component you can add with the Add/Remove Programs control panel. Instead, you must install it manually from the Windows Me CD, like this:

1. **Insert your Windows Me CD-ROM. When the welcome window appears, click Cancel.**

   You arrive at the Windows Millennium CD-ROM screen.

2. **Click Browse This CD.**

   A folder window appears, listing the contents of the Windows Me CD-ROM.

3. **Open the "add-ons" folder, then the "MSBackup" folder. Double-click the "msbexp.exe" icon.**

   An installer whirls into action.

When the installation is complete, you'll have to restart your computer. When your computer is running again, choose Start→Programs→Accessories→System Tools→Backup to launch the Backup program.

The first time you run it, Backup tries to find a tape-backup drive attached to your PC. If it can't find one, it says it can't find any "backup devices," and offers to run the Add Hardware Wizard to locate your tape device; click No to proceed with opening the program.

Once Backup is up and running, you can build a list of folders and files to back up, choose an existing set, or restore a backup to your drive.

The first time you run Backup, you must specify which folders and files you want backed up. A wizard walks you through the creation of this list, which Microsoft calls a *backup job*. Here's a summary of the stops you'll make on your guided wizard tour:

Create a backup job

The first wizard window asks whether you want this backup job to include *all* the folders and files on your drive(s), or only selected folders and files. Backing up your entire hard drive (including several hundred megabytes of Windows itself) is generally unnecessary.

The wizard presents a Windows Explorer-like display (see Figure 15-6) so you can choose the folders and files you want to back up.

Specify file characteristics

The next wizard window asks whether or not you want to back up *every* folder and file you selected, or only "New and changed files" (since the last time you backed up). Backing up only the changed files is called an *incremental backup* (see "Configure the backup job," below).

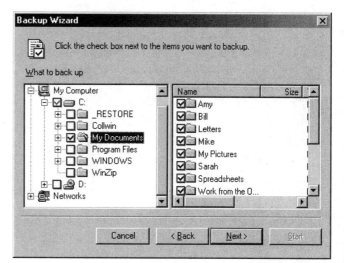

Figure 15-6:
Expand the listing of drives and folders by clicking the + buttons. Turn on the checkbox next to any folder that you want backed up. All folders and files inside it are automatically selected, too, although you can click the checkbox of any subfolder to remove its checkmark. To deselect a file, omitting it from the scheduled backup, click its folder in the left pane and turn off its checkbox in the right pane.

Select the disks

The next wizard window asks you to specify the backup disk. If you don't have a tape drive, the wizard suggests backing up your hard drive *onto* your hard drive—the world's worst choice for a backup disk. Instead, click the folder icon next to the selection and choose a different disk. (Backup can't back up onto floppy disks; a removable-disk system like a Zip drive is a much better idea. If you're on a network, you can also save your backup file onto another PC.)

Configure advanced backup options

The wizard next offers to *verify* each file that's backed up (to take a few extra seconds after copying it to confirm that the copy perfectly matches the original), and also to compress the data in the backup file to save space. Both are good ideas.

Name the backup job

In the last wizard window, name this backup job (for example *All Docs* or *Standard*) and click Start to make your first backup.

Depending on the number of files you're backing up, the backup can take anywhere from a few moments to an hour or more. When the job is complete, a window shows how many files and bytes were backed up. If you see a message indicating an error, click Report to see a written record of what went on during the backup.

Tip: Most backup errors arise when Backup tries to back up a file that's open. To avoid this problem, exit all your programs before backing up.

Configure the backup job

After creating your backup job, click OK to close the Report window and return to the Microsoft Backup window. Click the Options button at the bottom of the window to open the Options dialog box (see Figure 15-7).

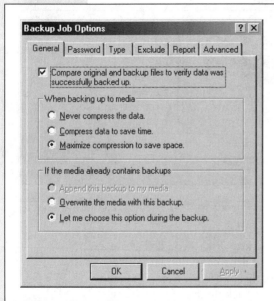

Figure 15-7:
The Password tab lets you add a layer of security to your backed-up information. The Advanced tab has an option to back up the Registry, along with the files you've selected for backup. This option backs up your Registry (see the end of this chapter)—a crucial step if you'll ever want to perform a complete restoration of your hard drive.

The Type tab in this dialog box offers an advanced function: a choice between *incremental* or *differential* backups.

- **Incremental backup.** If you choose this option, Backup copies only files that are new or changed since the last *full* backup. Incremental backups go much faster (and use fewer disks) than full backups, since Windows has to copy only a few files each time. But they're less convenient if the worst should happen, and you need to restore all your files from the backup disks; you'll have to restore each backup file in chronological order, beginning with the full-backup disks. (You may want to consider doing a full backup once a week or once a month, and incremental backups in between.)

- **Differential backup.** The first *differential* backup copies the files that have changed since the last full backup; so far, it's the same as an incremental backup. But the second differential backup *also* backs up all changed files since the full backup, and so does the third. In other words, if you perform a full backup on Monday, the differential backups on Tuesday, Wednesday, and Thursday each back up *all* the files that have changed since Monday.

  Of course, this system requires more backup disks, because you're actually making duplicate and triplicate copies of certain files. But the payoff comes when your hard drive dies and you have to restore the entire system. Instead of having to restore each day's backup job (as you would with an incremental backup), you have to restore only one full backup and *one* differential backup set (the most recent one)—a relatively fast and simple procedure.

This technical tradeoff between convenience at backup time and convenience in case of disaster should sound familiar to anyone who's ever had to choose between two insurance policies, one of which costs less but has a high deductible.

Restoring with Microsoft Backup

If the worst comes to pass, and you're forced to replace your hard drive (or your entire computer), you can restore all your data from the backup disks. Here's the agenda:

1. **Install Windows Me onto the new machine.**

   See Appendix A.

2. **Insert the tape or disk you used to make your backup.**

   If you backed up to another computer on a network, install and configure your Network Interface Card (see Chapter 16).

3. **Install Backup.**

   You'll find instructions at the beginning of this section.

4. **Be sure the tape or disk that holds your last backup is in its drive.**

   If you're restoring from a network drive, connect to it (Chapter 17).

5. **Open Backup. Choose Restore Backed Up Files.**

   The Restore Wizard opens to walk you through the process of restoring your files.

Choose the files to restore

You'll be asked to specify the location of your backup files and the backup file you want to restore. Backup displays the date and time each backup file was made, making it easy to select the right file.

The wizard opens an Explorer-like interface that shows the folders and files included in the backup. Click to select the items you want to restore, exactly as you did when selecting files to back up.

> **Tip:** By clicking the + button, you can expand a folder so that you can select an individual file inside it. This is what you'd do if you're restoring, from your backup file, a document that you've accidentally deleted from the hard drive.

Choose the location for the restored files

You can restore the files either to their original folder locations on the hard drive, or to new folders. If your hard drive at the moment contains exactly the same folder structure it did when you made the backup, the "original location" option works well.

Otherwise, select New Location and type in the path to the new folder (such as *c:\rescued)*. If there's no such folder, Backup will create it for you.

Specify file replacement rules

Backup's file-restoring feature isn't only useful when you've had to wipe out your hard drive completely; it can also be handy when something less drastic went wrong, such as when you threw out a folder accidentally. All the rest of your files and folders are OK.

But suppose you've indicated that you want your My Documents folder restored from the backup disks. What should Backup do when it encounters files that are *still in* your My Documents folder, perfectly OK? You can choose one of three options:

- **Do not replace a file on my computer.** Backup won't restore any file that's already on the hard drive.

- **Replace the file on my computer only if the file is older.** Backup will replace a file on your hard drive if it's an older version than the backed-up copy.

- **Always replace the file on my computer.** Backup will restore every file, replacing its equivalent on the hard drive, regardless of which is newer.

Click Start to begin restoring. A report appears after the procedure is complete; if there were any problems, you can click Report to see detailed information.

Backing up onto Floppies

If you create a lot of files, a removable drive, such as a Zip drive, Jaz drive, or record-able CD-ROM drive, is a good investment. Just drag the folders you want to back up onto one of your disks.

But if such a drive isn't in your budget or your future, you can back up your data files onto floppy disks—a very inexpensive, but time-consuming process.

The easiest way to back up to floppy disks is to open Windows Explorer (see page 88) and highlight a folder in the left pane. Then select the files you want to back up like this:

- To select all the files in a folder, press Ctrl+A.

- To select multiple files, hold down the Ctrl key while you click each file.

- To select multiple files that are listed consecutively, select the first file, then hold down the Shift key and select the last file.

When all the files are highlighted, right-click any one of the selected files and choose Send To→3½ Floppy from the shortcut menu. When the first floppy disk is filled to capacity, a message tells you to insert a new disk. Put a new blank disk in the drive, and then click Retry. Continue this process until all the files are backed up.

Tip: Don't use the Copy and Paste commands to back up files from your hard drive onto a floppy disk. That's slow and cumbersome, and it doesn't automatically instruct you to insert another disk when necessary.

You can also use a disk compression program such as WinZip to back up to floppy disks. WinZip, which is available at *www.winzip.com,* is the most popular compression software for Windows. This software provides two advantages over the Send To command: First, it compresses the files as it backs them up, so that more files fit on each floppy disk; second, it can handle files too big for a single floppy (by breaking them up into multiple-disk chunks).

Tip: Because floppy disks are considered less reliable than other kinds of disks, consider creating several sets of backup floppies.

The Briefcase

When you first encountered Windows, you may have discovered a My Briefcase icon on your desktop. In its way, the Briefcase is a form of backup program, but for a very specific purpose: It's designed to help you keep your files straight when you transport them from desktop to laptop, or from home to work. If you learn to use the

Briefcase, you'll be less likely to lose track of which copies of your documents are the most current.

To use the Briefcase, start by finding the icons of the documents you'll want to work on when away from your main PC. (Use the My Computer or My Documents window, for example.) Drag them onto the My Briefcase icon.

Now connect your laptop to the desktop PC, if it isn't already. (See Chapter 16 for more on connecting machines.) Or, if you plan to take your files with you on a disk (such as a floppy or Zip disk), insert the disk. Drag the My Briefcase icon onto the laptop or the disk.

You're ready to leave your office. When you get wherever you're going, feel free to open and edit the documents in the copied Briefcase "folder" icon; just be sure to leave them there.

When you return to your main PC, re-connect the laptop or re-insert the travel disk. Now all of your careful step-following is about to pay off. Open the disk or laptop window, and double-click its My Briefcase icon. In the Briefcase window, click Update All. Windows copies the edited files back to their original folders on your desktop-PC hard drive, automatically replacing the older, original copies. (If you highlight only some of the icons in the Briefcase window, you can instead click Update Selection; Windows copies only the highlighted icons back to the main PC.)

Troubleshooting Basics

Troubleshooting PC problems is among the most difficult propositions on earth, in part because your machine has so many cooks: Microsoft made the operating system, another company made the computer, and dozens of others contributed the various programs you use every day. The number of conflicts that can arise, and the number of problems you may encounter, are nearly infinite. That's why, if you were smart, you bought your PC from a company that offers a toll-free, 24-hour help line for life. You'll need it.

Windows Me is the least troublesome version of the Windows 95 family, thanks to the improved problem solvers (and problem preventers) described in this chapter. But here are a few fundamental troubleshooting techniques that may spare you that help-line call.

The Startup Menu

If the problems you're having are caused by drivers that load just as the computer is starting up, it would be helpful to be able to turn them all off, at least so that you can get into your machine to begin your troubleshooting pursuit. Thanks to the secret Startup menu, you can do exactly that.

To see the Startup menu, hold down the Ctrl key while the computer is starting up; eventually, you'll see the Startup menu. Against a black DOS screen, in crude lettering, you get a list that includes these options: Normal, Logged, Safe Mode, and Step-by-Step Confirmation. (You may see additional choices.)

To select a choice, type its number (or arrow-key down to it) and press Enter. Here's what the Startup menu commands do:

Normal

Choose Normal to start the operating system in its usual fashion, exactly as though you never summoned the Startup menu to begin with. The Normal option means, "Sorry to have interrupted you… go ahead."

Logged (\Bootlog.txt)

Choose Logged to record every step of the operating system's startup process. This startup method is the same as choosing Normal, except that every technical event is recorded in a log file named *Bootlog.txt* that appears on the startup (usually C:) drive.

Most of the time, you'll use the Logged option only at the request of a support technician you've phoned for help. After the operating system boots, the technician may ask you to open Bootlog.txt in your Notepad program and search for particular words or phrases—usually the word "fail."

Safe Mode

Safe Mode starts up Windows Me in a special, stripped-down, generic startup mode; only the most basic Windows and PC functions are operational. Starting up in Safe Mode, in other words, is a tactic to take if your PC won't start up normally, thanks to some recalcitrant driver.

Tip: To go right into a Safe Mode startup without having to bring up the Startup menu first, hold down the F5 key instead of the Ctrl key during startup.

Safe Mode lets you undo a damaging configuration error you may have made in your previous Windows session. For example, you may have installed hardware or drivers that aren't compatible with some other hardware/driver combination—or that just don't work in Windows Me. Just use the Shut Down→Restart option, then boot into Safe Mode.

Once in Safe Mode, Windows Me opens the *Safe Mode Troubleshooter*, a wizard that walks you through the process of figuring out why your operating system won't boot normally. If the PC took you into Safe Mode without your requesting it—a sure sign of a problem—the Safe Mode Troubleshooter can also help you figure out why you're *in* Safe Mode.

If you know that a change you made caused the problem, select the option to use the System Restore feature described at the beginning of this chapter, or choose Next to go through the wizard's suggestions. If this procedure doesn't solve the problem, you'll have to contact a support technician.

Tip: If you're on a network, the option to start Windows Me in "Safe Mode with network support" is also available on the Startup menu. Use this option if you installed Windows Me from a network server instead of a CD. The files and drivers necessary to connect to the network will be loaded, so that you can get to any drivers or other system files you might need.

FREQUENTLY ASKED QUESTION

Generic Video Drivers

I booted successfully into Safe Mode, but my screen image looks like it was designed by drunken cave men. Why do all the graphics and text look some jagged and awful?

When you boot into Safe Mode, Windows doesn't load the driver for your video card. (It avoids that driver, on the assumption that it may be causing the very problem you're trying to troubleshoot.) Instead, Windows Me loads a generic driver that works with *any* video controller.

The generic driver asks for very little from your video controller, taking no advantage of the power of the hardware. Its job is to provide just enough graphics to let you get work done as you go about your repairs. As a result, your desktop looks fuzzy, enlarged, and pale—awful.

Don't panic. This is not the new look of your desktop; it's not punishment for whatever configuration change you made that caused problems. The next time you boot Windows Me normally, your full-sized desktop will return.

Step-by-Step Confirmation

Use this startup mode to confirm each step of the operating boot process as it occurs—yet another troubleshooting technique. A normal startup ensues, but Windows asks your permission before performing each stage of the startup process. Along the way, you may be able to isolate troublesome drivers and commands.

Tip: To bypass the Startup menu and automatically launch Windows Me in the Step-by-Step Confirmation mode, hold down Shift+F8 instead of the Ctrl key during the startup.

As each command appears, you must tell your PC whether or not to carry it out, using the Enter key for Yes and the Esc key for No. The first few commands you see are usually for memory management, the loading of important low-level drivers, and the loading of the Registry. (Say Yes to all of those.) Eventually, you'll be asked if you want to load all Windows drivers. Say Yes (by pressing Enter), and then confirm or deny the loading of each driver.

At this point, you have two methods for trying to ascertain the problem:

- Press the Esc key to stop the loading of the driver you (or a tech-support person) believe to be causing the problem. If this solves the problem, you can replace the bad driver with the previous version (if you just updated it) or obtain a new, good driver from the manufacturer.

- Load all drivers and see if any of them generate an error message. During the confirmation startup process, you'll be notified of the success or failure of each step.

Tip: If your PC won't start up at all, remember that you can always get into it using your emergency disk—the special floppy disk created by the Add/Remove Programs control panel applet (see page 186). If this disk is in the drive when you start up or restart the machine, Windows boots from it. You won't be offered the full-color, wonderful world of Windows, but you'll be able to run the Windows ScanDisk and Uninstall programs, as well as edit text files, manage disk partitions, and reformat your drives.

FREQUENTLY ASKED QUESTION

"Invalid system disk" Message

OK, I'll bite. I started up my PC, but it won't finish starting up; instead, I get a message that says, "Invalid system disk (or Non-system disk); Replace and strike any key when ready." What gives?

You probably left a floppy disk in your floppy drive. Remove the floppy disk, and then press any key, to proceed with the startup. (It's evidently too much trouble for Microsoft to just *tell* you that.)

When the PC Locks Up

Sometimes your computer *freezes*—it doesn't respond to keystrokes or mouse clicks. The windows on the screen won't close, and running programs seem to come to a screeching halt. You're experiencing a *hang, freeze, lockup,* or *bad day.*

There's only one way out of a freeze (other than just cutting the machine's power): Press Ctrl+Alt+Delete. The famous window shown in Figure 15-8 appears.

Figure 15-8:
This window lists every program and Windows function that's currently running. In addition, the window has three buttons: End Task, Shut Down, and Cancel. When the PC is locked up, this box and these buttons are your ticket to freedom.

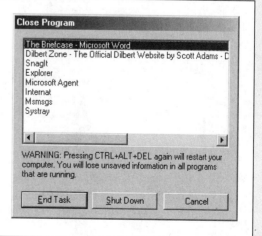

Look for a listing that displays "(not responding)." If you see it, you've found your problem. Click the name of the "not responding" program to select it, then click End Task. Then wait. If nothing seems to happen, don't click End Task again—just wait some more. Eventually, one of two things will occur:

The Registry

Here and there, in books, articles, and conversations, you'll hear hushed references to something called the Windows *Registry*—usually with either knowing or bewildered glances.

Microsoft would just as soon you not even know about the Registry. There's not a word about it in the basic user guides, and only three Help index items even mention it. If you're curious, however, read on.

The Registry is your PC's master database of preference settings, most of which are extremely technical. It keeps track of every program you install, every Plug-and-Play device you add, every multiple-user profile you create (Chapter 13), your networking configuration, and much more. If you've noticed that shortcut menus and Properties dialog boxes look different depending on what you're clicking, you have the Registry to thank; it knows what you're clicking and what options should appear as a result.

As you can well imagine, therefore, the Registry is an extremely important cog in the Windows machine. That's why Windows marks your Registry files as invisible and nondeletable, and why it makes a Registry backup every single day. If the Registry gets damaged or randomly edited, a grisly plague of problems may descend on your machine. Fortunately, Windows Me's System Restore feature (described in this chapter) can get you out of such a mess; but at least you now know why the Registry is rarely even mentioned to novices.

Still, the Registry is worth knowing about. You shouldn't edit it arbitrarily, but if you get a step-by-step "recipe" from a book, magazine, Web site, or technical-help agent, you shouldn't fear opening the Registry to make a few changes. You can do so using a program called RegEdit, which appears when you choose Start→Run, type *regedit,* and press Enter. (There are dozens of other Registry-editing, Registry-fixing, and Registry-maintenance programs, too, from Norton and other companies.)

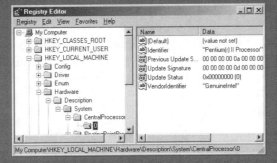

You'll discover that the Registry uses cryptic abbreviations to describe the operating system's various components and settings. (You're generally shielded from all of this geekiness by friendlier "front ends." For example, most of the applets in the Control Panel are nothing more than dialog boxes that modify settings in the Registry.)

These settings are organized hierarchically; RegEdit looks a lot like Windows Explorer. But there's no way to figure out which part of the Registry holds a particular setting or performs a particular function; it's like flying a plane that has no windows.

If you think you're ready to dip into the programmery netherworld of Registry editing, a world of "recipes" awaits you on the Web. You might start with *www.regedit.com* and *www.winreg.com,* which provide dozens of useful tips and tricks for making your PC world a better place via Registry adjustments.

- The recalcitrant window closes, and your system unfreezes.

- A message appears telling you that the program isn't responding to the request to end. Click the option to end the task immediately.

Then shut down your computer using the Start→Shut Down→Restart option. (When the PC starts up next, it runs ScanDisk automatically to nip any nascent hard drive problems in the bud.)

If no program is noted as "not responding," click the Shut Down button. If nothing happens right away, wait at least three minutes before giving up. If the Shut Down button doesn't work, shut off the computer manually by pressing its Power button. Windows Me may not like it, but it didn't exactly give you much choice.

A Gaggle of Monitors

Deep in your Start→Programs→Accessories→System Tools menu lurks a handful of diagnostic programs that most Windows users have probably never even seen: DriveSpace, Resource Meter, System Information, and System Monitor. Someday, however, some help-line technician, on a mission to talk you out of some computer glitch, may ask you to run one of them. Here's what they're for:

- **DriveSpace.** Windows versions before Windows Me offered a program called DriveSpace. It was designed to compress your files so that they occupied less space on your disks. The advantage was that, back in the days when a 500 MB hard drive was considered a luxury for the wealthy, your hard drive could hold more files; the disadvantage was a slight speed penalty.

  As far as Windows is concerned, DriveSpace compression is a thing of the past. This version of DriveSpace can't compress anything. It simply lets you, a Windows Me person, use disks that were compressed using earlier Windows versions.

- **Resource Meter.** If you're wondering why nothing seems to happen when you open this program, it's because you're not looking in the right place. When you choose Resource Meter from your System Tools submenu, the welcome message fails to mention that the meter takes the form of an icon on your Taskbar Tray (see page 75), which indicates how much of your memory and other PC resources are being used by the programs you're running. You can dismiss this Tray icon by right-clicking it and choosing Exit from the shortcut menu.

- **System Information.** This command summons an extremely technical, extremely informative page of the Help and Support window described in Chapter 5. In the place of the left-side list of help topics, you'll find a Windows Explorer-like display of technical information categories. The Hardware Resources and Components categories closely resemble the Device Manager (see page 304); the Software Environment and Internet Explorer categories offer technical specs about the drivers, network settings, cache, and other parameters of your software.

• **System Monitor.** This program shows a simple, real-time graph of your computer's power and how it's being used. As you go about your work, you'll see spikes shoot upward to illustrate the moments when the PC is straining to keep up with its workload.

Getting Help from Microsoft

If you run into trouble with the installation—or with any Windows Me feature—the world of Microsoft is filled with sources of technical help. For example, you can consult:

• **The Microsoft Support Web pages.** Direct your Web browser (if, indeed, your computer even works) to *www.microsoft.com/support.* There you'll find a long list of automated help resources that handle many of the most common questions.

• **Free phone help.** If you bought Windows Me (that is, it didn't come on your computer), you can call Microsoft for free phone help during business hours—twice. You'll be asked to provide your 20-digit product ID number, which you can look up by right-clicking My Computer in your desktop and clicking the Properties tab. The number is (425) 635-3311.

(If Windows Me came preinstalled in your machine, on the other hand, you're supposed to call the computer company with your Windows questions.)

• **Expensive phone help.** Once you've used up your two free calls, you can still call Microsoft with your questions—but they'll charge you $35 per incident. (They say "per incident" to make it clear that if it takes several phone calls to solve a particular problem, it's still just one problem.) This service is available 24 hours a day. The U.S. number is (800) 936-5700.

Tip: If you're not in United States, direct your help calls to the local Microsoft office in your country. You'll find a list of these subsidiaries in the document called Support.txt on the Windows Me CD-ROM—or you can look them up at *www.microsoft.com/support.*

Part Five:
Building a Small Network

5

Chapter 16: Setting Up a Network

Chapter 17: Using Your Network

Setting Up a Network

Whenever you connect computers so that they can access each other's files and share equipment (including printers), you create a *network*. As PC fans buy second and third computers for their homes and offices, networks are becoming increasingly common.

Networking isn't a simple task; it involves buying some equipment, running some wiring, and configuring software. Fortunately, Windows Me's new Home Networking Wizard makes the software-setup part as painless as possible. And the payoff is considerable: Once you've created a network, you can copy files from one machine to another just as you'd drag files between folders on your own PC. Everyone on the network can consult the same database or calendar. You can play games over the network. You can share a single laser printer, cable modem, fax modem, or phone line among all the PCs in the house.

Four Kinds of Networks

As with almost any PC feature, networking requires both hardware and software. The hardware requirements begin with a *network interface card,* or NIC ("nick"), a circuit board that goes into a slot in your PC, as described in Chapter 13. You need a networking card for each PC that you'll want to be part of the network.

Tip: If all the computers in your network have the same kind of expansion slot available, you can save money by buying a networking *kit,* which contains everything you need to create a network for a certain number of computers.

You can buy these cards in any of several different types. Most office networks are wired using *Ethernet cable,* but all kinds of possibilities await, including networking systems that rely on the phone or power lines already in your walls, and even wireless systems that don't need cables at all. Here's an overview of the four most popular networking systems.

Ethernet

Ethernet is today's standard networking technology. It gives you fast, reliable, trouble-free communication that costs very little and imposes no limitations on where you can place the PCs. The downside: You have to connect the PCs by installing Ethernet cable, which often entails snaking the cabling through the walls of your house or office.

This kind of network requires three components:

- **Ethernet cables.** The wiring looks like telephone wire, but isn't the same; both the wire (called *10BaseT, 100BaseT cable* or *Cat 5* cable) and the little clip at each end (called a *RJ-45* connector) are slightly fatter than those on a phone cable.

- **Networking cards.** The network cards you'll need (one per computer) are called Ethernet cards, and they're inexpensive.

- **A hub.** An Ethernet network also requires an Ethernet *hub.* Hubs come in different sizes, according to the number of PCs and printers you intend to hook up; five- and eight-port hubs are very popular. (Buy more ports than you need; the day may come when you want to attach more computers to your network.)

Tip: Ethernet gear can be shockingly inexpensive; a search at, for example, *www.buy.com* reveals Ethernet cards for $11 and five-port Ethernet hubs for $30. Prices this low confirm, however, that you're buying off-brand gear. If you're willing to pay slightly more—$40 for the card, $70 for the hub, for example—you can get brand-name gear (such as 3Com or Intel) whose installation, phone help, and driver-updating through the years may reward you many times over.

Figure 16-1:
Each Ethernet cable is connected to a computer at one end, and the hub (shown here) at the other end. The computers communicate through the hub; there's no direct connection between any two computers. The opposite side of the hub has little lights for each connector port; lights appear only on the ports that are in use. You can watch the lights flash as the computers communicate with each other.

On paper, setting up the network itself is simple: Just connect each computer or printer, using an Ethernet cable, directly to the hub (Figure 16-1). In practice, it's the "using an Ethernet cable" part that gets sticky; depending on where your PCs are, this wiring process may involve drilling holes in floors or walls, stapling cables to baseboard trim, or just calling in an electrician to do the job.

Tip: If your network has modest ambitions—that is, if you have only two computers you want to connect—you can skip buying the Ethernet hub. Instead, you just need an Ethernet *crossover cable*—about $8 from a computer store or online mail-order supplier. Run it directly between the Ethernet jacks of the two computers.

UP TO SPEED

Network Devices Have Speed Limits

Ethernet cards and hubs are sold with different speed specifications; the most common are *10BaseT* (10 megabits/second) and *100BaseT* (100 megabits/second, sometimes called *fast Ethernet*).

If you bought a *dual-speed* hub, each networking card will run at its own maximum speed. If your hub operates at 100BaseT speed only, then 10BaseT Ethernet cards won't work at all. (On the other hand, all 100BaseT Ethernet cards work with either 10BaseT or 100BaseT hubs.)

The moral: If you find auto-sensing, 10/100BaseT Ethernet cards (NICs) at almost the same price as 10BaseT cards, buy them, even if all you have is a 10BaseT hub. Later, if you upgrade to a 100BaseT hub (when the price drops, as all computer device prices do), you won't have to buy and reinstall your Ethernet cards.

Phone Line Networks

Instead of going to the trouble of wiring your home with Ethernet cables, you might consider using the wiring that's already *in* your house—telephone wiring. The phone wires in your walls have far more capacity than most people realize. The signal capacity of these wires far exceeds what's needed to have a telephone conversation or connect to the Internet. You can use this unused bandwidth for your network, without interfering with telephone or modem communications.

The networking cards you need for telephone-based network connections are slightly more expensive than Ethernet cards, and they operate at only one megabit/second—about 10 percent the speed of an Ethernet network. (Faster, and more expensive, phone-line networking cards, capable of operating at low-end Ethernet speeds, are on the way.) But you may not find that speed a drawback if you use your network only occasionally, or for only light duties like sharing a laser printer.

After you install the telephone-networking cards in your PCs, all you have to do is run telephone cable between the card and the nearest telephone wall jack.

Tip: If you put a two-for-one telephone adapter (line splitter) into the wall jack, you can connect your network to one jack, and your phone or modem to the other. If you have an external modem, you can even plug the telephone *into* the modem (which has a jack for this purpose) and then plug the *modem* into the wall adapter. Now you have a network, a modem, and a telephone hooked up simultaneously. (You can't make a modem and voice call simultaneously, but you *can* use the network even when using the modem or talking on the phone.)

Electrical Line Networks

Here's another way to connect your computers without rewiring the building: Use the power lines that are already in your walls. Unlike phone jacks, electrical outlets are usually available in every room in the house.

Creating an electrical line network takes only a few minutes, but there's a price to pay for all this ease. The communication between the computers is extremely slow, about 350 *kilo*bits per second—about one-third of the speed of the slowest telephone connection network.

Electrical line networks require two gizmos for each computer and printer on the network: a special adapter that plugs into an electrical outlet, and a cable that runs from that adapter to the parallel port (printer port) on the computer, or to the Centronics connector on the printer (with a special adapter).

For under $100, you can buy kits that include the equipment you need to create a two-computer, one-printer network. Hardware for additional computers or printers is usually less than $50 per machine.

Wireless (RF) Networks

Radio frequency (RF) wireless technology is also available for your network; it requires no cables at all. To create an RF network, you buy a special RF networking card, which has a little antenna that pokes out of your computer, or a little network box that connects to your PC's USB port. (One standard that's gaining ground quickly is called *Bluetooth* wireless technology; the card costs about $150 per PC.)

Computer placement has a great impact on the efficiency of RF networks; you may have to spend an afternoon shifting your PCs around until they can "hear" each other. A PC that seems to be disconnected from the network may need to be moved only slightly. Your computers must be placed in a relatively open area, too. Tucking a computer under a desk or close to a wall interferes with radio signals.

The computers don't have to be in the same room, but separating them by more than one room (or putting them on different floors) is pushing your luck. Big metal things, thick walls, or walls containing big metal things (such as pipes) can interfere with communication among the PCs, much to the disappointment of people who work in subways and meat lockers.

Top speed for this kind of wireless network is one megabit/second, about the same as telephone networking. But the speed declines if the computers are too far apart, or have too many walls, doors, or other physical impediments between them.

Installing Drivers

No matter which kind of networking cards you install, your next obligation is to install their software drivers. If you're lucky, the Plug and Play feature, or the installer that came with the card, takes care of this for you. If you weren't so lucky, see Chapter 13 for advice on what to do when Plug and Play fails.

The Home Networking Wizard

Once you've set up the networking equipment, you have to inform Windows Me about what you've been up to. You also have to configure your computers to share their files, folders, printers, modems, Internet connections, and so on. Fortunately, the new Windows Me Home Networking Wizard handles this duty for you.

To launch the wizard, double-click the My Network Places icon on your desktop, and then double-click the Home Networking Wizard icon in the window that opens. (Alternatively, you can chose Start→Programs→Accessories→Communications→ Home Networking Wizard.)

A welcome message appears; click Next.

Sharing your Internet connection

The next wizard window starts the process of setting up *Internet connection sharing,* which lets several PCs share the same Internet connection (see Figure 16-2).

If you've signed up for a cable modem or DSL line, connection sharing can save you big bucks; such an account costs about $40 per month for *one* machine. But even if you connect to the Internet by modem, connection sharing is still a great feature: It means that several PCs in the house or office can be using the Internet *simultaneously,* via a single phone call over one phone line.

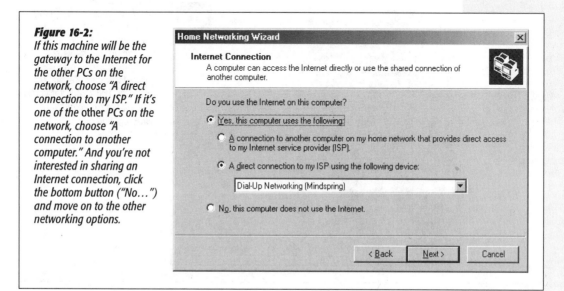

Figure 16-2:
If this machine will be the gateway to the Internet for the other PCs on the network, choose "A direct connection to my ISP." If it's one of the other PCs on the network, choose "A connection to another computer." And you're not interested in sharing an Internet connection, click the bottom button ("No...") and move on to the other networking options.

Here's how to proceed:

- **Skip connection sharing.** If sharing an Internet connection isn't the point of your networking efforts, click "No, this computer does not use the Internet" and click Next.

- **This is the computer with the connection.** If the computer you're using is the one connected to the Internet—that is, if it's the *host* computer—click "Yes, this computer uses the following," then "A direct connection." Then, from the drop-down menu, choose Dial-Up Networking (if it connects by modem) or the name of your networking card (if you have a cable modem or DSL).

Tip: If your DSL service is for *multiple fixed IP addresses,* then your computers can share the connection without having to choose one single computer as the "host."

- **This isn't the computer with the connection.** If you like the idea of sharing a PC's Internet connection, but the machine you're using now isn't the one with the connection (it's not the host), choose "A connection to another computer...."

Identifying the PC

No matter which connection-sharing setting you selected, click Next. On this wizard screen (Figure 16-3), you must give your PC its own, unique name—and specify the name of a workgroup (mini-network) that *isn't* unique. For example, if you have a desktop PC and a laptop, you might give them names like *Portegé* and *Millennia,* both of which are part of the workgroup called *MSHome.*

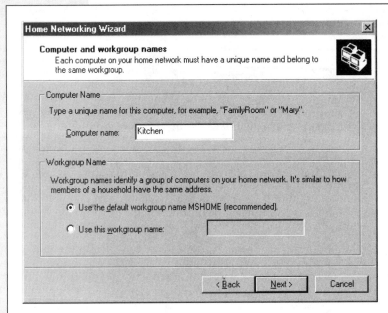

Figure 16-3:
Every computer on a Windows network (even big networks in corporations) must have a unique name. In addition, the network itself has a workgroup name. Windows Me proposes MSHOME, but you can call your little network whatever you like.

Note: Computer names and workgroup names are limited to 15 characters, and you're not allowed to use any kinds of slashes, the @ sign, commas, periods, or spaces.

Sharing folders and printers

Click Next. The next window (Figure 16-4) sets up file and printer sharing. This is the meat, the main course, of networking. When you share folders, you make all the files inside them available to any computer on the network. For example, suppose your computer is in the den—but at the moment, your daughter is using it to chat on AOL. Thanks to folder sharing, you can sit in front of the computer in the kitchen and open any files you've saved on the den computer. You can even send printouts from any PC on the network to any printer in the house.

To make things easier, Windows Me proposes sharing your My Documents folder. If that's the one you want to make public, turn on its checkbox, specify a password (if you like), and then click Next. (A password keeps the shared folder off-limits to people who don't know the password.)

Tip: If you don't specify a password, when you click the Next button, Windows Me urges you to create one. Click OK to make the message go away; you can always add a password to a shared folder later. In fact, if security isn't an issue on your network, skipping the password now will make your life a lot simpler in the months to come.

But you don't have to share My Documents (or *only* My Documents); after the wizard has done its duty, you'll be able to share any folders you want, whenever you want. Chapter 17 holds the step-by-step details.

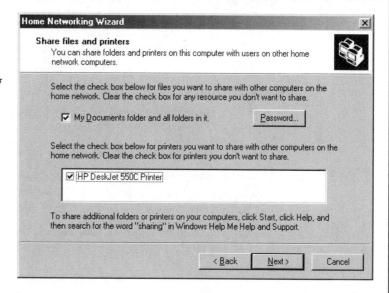

Figure 16-4:
Windows Me starts making the various components of your PC available to everyone else on the network, starting with your printer (if it finds one whose software has been installed) and the My Documents folder.

The wizard may also offer to share a My Shared Files folder, which the wizard creates either in your My Documents folder or in the C: drive→Windows→All Users folder.

Create a networking setup disk for other computers

The next window invites you to create a *home networking setup disk* for the other computers on your network. The wizard will copy a clone of itself onto a floppy disk that you can carry to the other PCs on your network (even if they're not running Windows Me). Because disk contains the very same Home Networking Wizard, it's a snap to configure those other machines for the network, even if they're Windows 95 or Word 98 machines. Take advantage of the free-disk offer; if you don't run the wizard on your other computers, you'll have to set up their networking settings manually, which is about as much fun as eating sand.

If you select the option to create the floppy disk and click Next, you're instructed to put a blank formatted disk in the floppy drive. Click Next again to create the disk, which takes only a moment or two. Then eject the disk; for best results, label it for easy identification.

Click Finish on the wizard window. Windows shuffles some files around, and may ask you to insert the Windows Me CD. Finally, Windows instructs you to restart your computer. When your machine reboots, it's a card-carrying member of your own personal network.

Installing the Networking Wizard on other computers

Having only one network-ready PC presents you with the problem of the first telephone owner: Who can you call?

Fortunately, the floppy disk you created is an easy-to-use tool for configuring the other computers on your network. Insert the disk in the floppy drive, open the My Computer icon on your desktop, double-click the floppy-drive icon, and then double-click the Setup.exe icon.

The now-familiar Home Networking Wizard now begins to walk you through each window, answering questions and making selections. Follow precisely the same steps described on the preceding pages. (But this time, of course, you don't need to create a network setup floppy disk.) When it's all over, each PC you've visited is ready for network action.

Testing the Network

After all of this setup, here's how you can find out whether or not the gods are smiling on your new network:

1. **Double-click the My Network Places desktop icon.**

   If you're performing this test on a machine running Windows 95 or 98, the icon is called Network Neighborhood instead. (All three generations of Windows can "see" each other and work joyously side-by-side on the same network.)

   The network window opens. The icons inside depend on which Windows version you're using, but one is always called Entire Network.

2. **Double-click Entire Network.**

   Now the window shows an icon representing your workgroup, called MSHome (or whatever you named it when you ran the wizard). If you don't see any icons in the window, click "View the entire contents of the folder."

3. **Double-click the Workgroup icon.**

   When the workgroup window opens, you should, at last, see an icon for the computer you're using, bearing whatever name you gave it (see Figure 16-5). You may also see icons for the other machines on the network, but that's a topic for the next chapter.

Figure 16-5:
This computer shows up in the window named for the workgroup (in this case the unimaginative but useful name "Workgroup"). After you set up shared folders on all the computers on the network, this window will display all the computers, disks, and folders available to you.

If you don't see the icon for your computer, something has gone wrong. Check to see that:

- Your cables are properly seated.

- Your Ethernet hub (if any) is plugged in.

- Your networking card is working. To do so, right-click My Computer; choose Properties from the shortcut menu; then click the Device Manager tab. Look for an error icon next to your networking card's name (see Chapter 13 for more on the Device Manager).

If you don't find a problem, rerun the Home Networking Wizard. If that doesn't work, you'll have to call Microsoft or your PC company for help.

Using Your Network

After you've installed your networking cards, connected the cables, and run the Home Networking Wizard (see Chapter 16), the fun begins. This chapter highlights a few of the ways in which network convenience can change your life: sharing folders and files, sharing a printer, and sharing a single Internet connection among all the machines on the network.

Note: If you're like many people, your network may include only one Windows Me PC, along with a Windows 95 or 98 computer or two. That's perfectly OK; all of these machines can participate as equals in this party. This chapter points out whatever differences you may find in the procedures.

Sharing Files, Disks, and Printers

Sharing the files, folders, disks, and printers among the PCs on a network is amazingly convenient. Once you've tried it, you'll wonder how anyone with more than one computer ever lived with individual, detached computers. For example, you can share any of these computer resources:

- **Files and folders.** No matter what PC you're using on the network, you can open and work on the files and folders on any *other* PC (if you've been given permission to do so).

- **Disks.** In fact, from anywhere on the network, you can work with the files on any *disks* attached to any PC. (This usually means hard drives. Technically, you can also share CD-ROMs, floppies, Zip disks, Jaz disks, and so on. But the moment you eject the disk, whatever was on it is no longer accessible.)

- **Printers.** No matter which PC you're using, you can send printouts to any printer connected to any computer on the network. (Pity the *non*-networked families or offices where there's only one good printer to go around: These people spend their lives carrying files on a floppy disk to the computer that's attached to the printer. There's even a name for this kind of "networking:" *sneakernet*.)

So that computer professionals won't go quietly insane repeatedly saying "files, folders, disks, and printers" when discussing networking, they use the collective term *resources*. And once they've made one of these resources available to the network, they call it a *shared resource*—or just *share* for short. (You'll see the term *share* used in Microsoft's own dialog boxes and help screens, too.)

You share something the same way whether it's a drive, folder, or printer: Highlight its icon, turn on sharing, type a name for the share, and adjust its settings. After that, anyone else on the network can see icons for the resources you've shared by double-clicking the My Network Places icon (Windows Me) or Network Neighborhood icon (Windows 95/98) on the desktop, or by using Windows Explorer.

Step 1: Finding the Icon to Share

The first step in sharing a resource, making it available to the network, is to locate its icon. For example:

- **Disk drives.** You can share any kind of disk; hard drive, floppy drive, CD-ROM drive, Zip, and so on. When you make a disk available to the network, you also make available every folder *on* it.

  To locate the icon of the disk you want to share, double-click the My Computer icon on your desktop. You'll see icons for all the drives on your system, as shown in Figure 17-1.

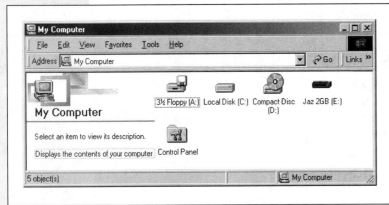

Figure 17-1:
All the drives attached to your computer appear in the My Computer window. This PC has a large removable drive (Jaz), which is useful for backing up and storing big files. Sharing the Jaz drive lets you do all these things on every PC without having to buy and install another Jaz drive for each one.

- **Folders.** Sharing folders has distinct advantages over sharing an entire drive. By sharing only a folder or two, you can keep *most* of the stuff on your hard drive private, out of view from curious network comrades. Furthermore, sharing only a folder or two makes it easier for them to find files you've made available, since they don't have to root through your drive looking for the appropriate folder.

To specify the folder you want to share, locate its icon using either Windows Explorer (page 88) or the My Computer icon (page 86).

• **Printer Shares.** Choose Start→Settings→Printers to open the Printers window, which has an icon for each printer connected to this computer. (See Chapter 12 for more information on printer icons.)

Step 2: Turning on Sharing

After you've located the icon of the drive, folder, or printer you want to share, proceed like this:

1. **Right-click the icon to be shared; from the shortcut menu, choose Sharing.**

    The Sharing tab of the Properties dialog box opens. (The shortcut menu includes the Sharing command only if you've set up the computer for networking, as described in the previous chapter.)

2. **Click Shared As (see Figure 17-2).**

    The other options in the dialog box spring to life.

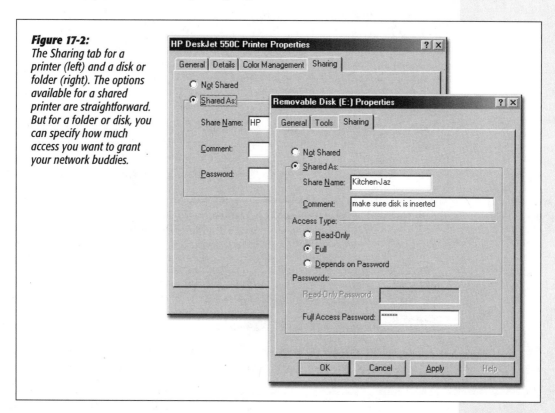

Figure 17-2:
The Sharing tab for a printer (left) and a disk or folder (right). The options available for a shared printer are straightforward. But for a folder or disk, you can specify how much access you want to grant your network buddies.

If you were to simply click OK at this point, you would make this resource available to everyone on the network. But before leaving the dialog box, take a moment to survey the identification and security options.

Step 3: Configuring Shares

The settings you're about to make can limit your colleagues' access to your shared disk, folder, or printer over the network. Note, however, that *you* will continue to have full and unfettered access (when you're at your PC); the changes you're about to make affect this resource's availability only to *other* people on the network.

Naming a share

As shown in Figure 17-2, you can choose a name for the resource you're sharing. This is the name other people will see when they open their My Network Places or Network Neighborhood desktop icons. Make this name as helpful as you can within the 12-letter length limit. For example, you may want to name the kitchen computer's hard drive *C-in-Kitchen.* (You can't use punctuation other than hyphens. Avoiding spaces, especially in printer names, will save you grief in the long run.) Similarly, naming a removable drive *Kitchen-Jaz* is a better description than the name Windows proposes (which is nothing more than a drive letter). Printers also benefit from helpful names, such as *NewLaser* instead of *HPLJ6P.*

You can use the Comment field to type up to 48 characters of additional information (*Jaz Drive with 2GB capacity* or *Pink paper in the tray at all times*, for example). But remember that other people on the network won't see your comments unless they switch their My Network Places or Network Neighborhood windows into Details View (by choosing View→Details).

Access Type

When you make a folder or disk available to the network, you don't necessarily give your co-workers permission to run wild, trashing your files, renaming things at random, and painting mustaches onto your JPEG family photos. Using the Access Type controls, you can restrict their vandalistic impulses like this:

- **Read-Only.** Turn on Read-Only for a "look, don't touch" policy. Other people on the network will be allowed to open and read what's inside this disk or folder, but won't be able to save changes, rename anything, delete anything, or deposit any new files.

Note: Other people on the network can *copy* folders and files from a Read-Only folder or disk onto their own computers. From there, they can do whatever they like to your files. But they can't copy the changed files back to your shared folder or disk.

- **Full.** Full access gives your network friends the right to do whatever they want to your files and folders, exactly as though they were sitting at your computer.

- **Depends on Password.** When you turn on this option, Windows treats the disk or folder as *either* Read-Only or Full, depending on the password a network citizen types in when trying to access it. That is, you can issue one password to, say, your spouse or partner (which gives full access), and another to all the less trustworthy members of the network. (You can even password-protect a printer, although it doesn't make much sense except in corporations where the expensive color laser printer costs $1.50 per sheet.)

If you select this option, the pair of text boxes at the bottom of the window becomes available (Read-Only Password and Full Access Password). As usual, Windows doesn't actually show you what you type here; only asterisks show up, to prevent somebody from peeking over your shoulder to learn the password. When you click OK, you'll be asked to type the passwords again to rule out typos.

Tip: Don't forget to provide the passwords to the other people using your network. Find some secret way to present the password in writing. (Leaving a note on the monitor doesn't qualify as *secret*.) If you don't put the password in writing, you'll spend a lot of time answering the same question over and over: "What was that password again?"

On the other hand, Windows Me passwords provide little actual security; if you truly can't trust your household or office comrades, Windows 2000 might be a better system.

Figure 17-3:
The My Computer and Printers windows show shared resources on this computer. You can tell which resources you've shared in your system because their icons change, as shown here. A hand cradles the icon to indicate that this object (drive, folder, or printer) is shared. This special icon provides an instant reference for the shares that have been configured on a computer.

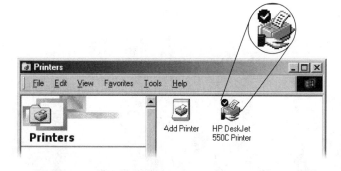

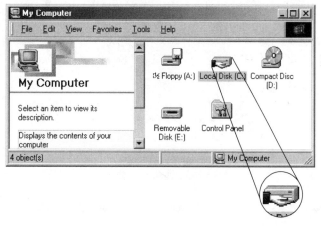

Saving the shared resource

When you're finished setting up the sharing options, click OK. As shown in Figure 17-3, the icon changes for the resource you just shared.

Tricks and Tips for Shares

As you survey your network domain, consider these variations on the sharing theme:

Share once and forget it

If security isn't a big deal on your network (because it's just you or a couple of family members, for example), you'll save time and headache by sharing your entire hard drive. You won't have to turn on sharing for every new folder you create.

Tracking activity with Net Watcher

To see who's connected to what on your PC (and for how long), choose Start→ Programs→Accessories→System Tools→Net Watcher. This handy utility shows you exactly what's been going on right under your nose.

Hiding folders

If a certain folder on your hard drive is really private, type a $ symbol at the end of its name. For example, if you name a certain folder MyNovel$, it won't show up in anybody's My Network Places window. They won't even know that it exists. (But it will be visible to other network PCs if you shared the *disk* on which the folder sits.)

POWER USERS' CLINIC

Un-Hiding Hidden Folders

As sneaky and delightful as the hidden-folder trick is, it has a distinct drawback: *You* can't see your hidden folder over the network, either. But now suppose you want to use another computer on the network—the one in the kitchen, for example—to open something in your hidden MyNovel folder (which is upstairs in your office). Fortunately, you can do so—if you know the secret steps:

On the remote computer, choose Start→Run. In the Run dialog box, type the path of the hidden folder, using the format *ComputerName**FolderName.*

For example, enter *kitchen**mynovel$* to get to the hidden folder called MyNovel$ on the PC called Kitchen. (Capitalization doesn't matter, and don't forget the dollar sign.) Then click OK to open a window showing the contents of your hidden folder.

This path format (including the double-backslash before the PC name and a single backslash before a folder name) is called the Universal Naming Convention (UNC). It was devised to let network geeks open various folders on networked machines without having to use the My Network Places (or Network Neighborhood) icon on the desktop.

Create family shares

If your network is designed for family use, you might consider creating and sharing a special, unprotected folder on one of the PCs. Use this folder for documents that everyone should see, as though it's an electronic family bulletin board. In fact, if you create a shared folder inside for each family member, you've created an electronic mailbox system. When you write a note to Mom, save it in that folder. She'll be able to get to it no matter what computer in the house she's using.

Sharing Files, Disks, and Printers

UP TO SPEED

Tips for Passwords

The problem with password-protecting shared disks and folders is that you have to keep track of them, and so does everyone else on the network. The permutations and combinations of passwords (this folder, that disk, Read-Only, Full Access...) can become frightening to contemplate. Eventually, you'll need a system of tracking who's entitled to what password, which password works for which share, and so on. In many cases, the result is a snowstorm of little scraps of paper. When they all end up in the kitchen junk drawer, available to the world, your password system is no longer very effective.

In other words, use passwords in moderation. For example, to keep certain folders for the household grown-ups' exclusive use, assign the *same* password to every shared resource on every PC. Give that password only to the adults.

If somebody forgets a password, by the way, there's no way to figure it out. Looking at the Sharing tab of the drive, folder, or printer (see Figure 17-2) doesn't help; you'll see only asterisks. You have no choice but to assign a new password. Fortunately, doing so is fairly easy: On the computer that contains the shared resource, open the icon's Properties dialog box, delete the asterisks on the Sharing tab, type in a new password, and click OK.

Figure 17-4:
First double-click Entire Network (top); you see an icon representing your workgroup (second from top). Double-click this workgroup icon to view the icon for each PC (third from top). Double-click one of them to see whatever shared folders, disks, or printers are on it (bottom). (When you double-click one of the shares, you'll be asked for a password, if one was assigned.)

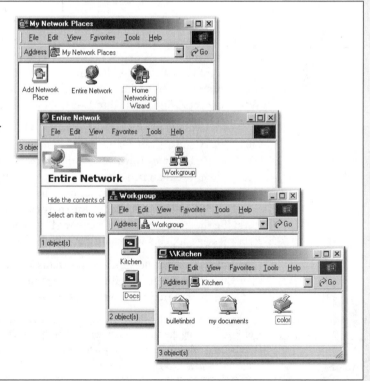

Accessing Other Computers

So far in this chapter, you've been reading from the point of view of the person doing the sharing. You've read the steps for preparing a PC for invasion by other people on the network. This section details how to be one of *them*—that is, how to connect to other PCs whose disks, folders, and printers have been shared.

Fortunately, doing so is extremely easy. All you have to do is open the icon that's sitting on the desktop at the left side of your screen. It's called My Network Places (in Windows Me) or Network Neighborhood (Windows 95/98). You may hear these special windows generically called *network browsers*.

Using My Network Places

The very first time you double-click the My Network Places icon on your desktop, you see the three icons shown in Figure 17-4 (top left). To see what's on the other networked machines, you have to double-click at least four times, also as shown in Figure 17-4.

Tip: If you're looking at a window full of shared icons (at bottom in Figure 17-4, for example) when somebody else on the network removes or adds shared icons, you won't see any change in this window until you press F5. That keystroke tells Windows Me to check the shared resources again and refresh the icon list.

Automatic shortcuts

Suppose you've just connected to another machine on the network and opened a document on one of its shared folders. As a favor, Windows Me automatically places a new icon for that folder in the My Network Places window, on the premise that you'll want to return to that folder. By putting this folder's icon directly in the My Network Places window (Figure 17-5), Windows saves you all of the usual double-clicking (Entire Network→Workgroup→target computer→shared folder).

That's a very considerate feature. Unfortunately, over time, the My Network Places window may become crowded with the icons of folders you've opened—especially if you have more than two computers on your network. Eventually, you may find it hard to find a particular folder among the dozens. (Furthermore, these are only shortcuts. If somebody deletes or un-shares a shared folder somewhere on the network, the shortcut in your My Network Places window stops working. Not even an error message appears when you double-click it.)

Fortunately, you can delete these shortcuts without another thought by dragging them directly to the Recycle Bin. Feel free to delete those that don't work, that represent folders you rarely visit, or that are simply getting in your way.

Tip: If you're using the multiple-user feature described in Chapter 14, any icon deletions you perform here "belong" only to your profile. The others who use this PC will still see the full assortment of shared icons and will have to do their own pruning.

Add Network Places icons manually

The Add Network Place icon lets you create shortcut icons for shared folders on the network—or even folders *not* on the network, such as those on corporate intranets or *FTP sites* (private, password-protected sets of folders on the Internet).

Double-clicking the Add Network Place icon launches a wizard (see Figure 17-5). Into the first text box, you can type any of these network addresses:

- **\\ComputerName\ShareName.** This format (called the Universal Naming Convention) lets you specify a shared folder on the network. For example, if you want to open the share named FamilyBiz on the computer named Dad, enter *\\dad\familybiz*. Capitalization doesn't matter.

- **\\ComputerName\ShareName\Filename.** You can create a My Network Places icon for a *file* somewhere on the network, too (not just a folder). For example, to open a document called Budget.xls, which is in a folder called Finances on the computer named Dad, enter *\\dad\finances\budget.xls*. (Remember that you're specifying the share name, which isn't necessarily the same as the folder name. If you get an error message when you try to add a folder or file to your Network Places window, this distinction may be at the heart of the problem.)

- **http://website/folder.** To see what's in a folder called Customers on a company Web site called BigBiz.com, enter *http://bigbiz.com/customers*. (You can't just type in any old Web address; it has to be a Web site that's been specifically designed to serve as a "folder" containing files.)

- **ftp://ftp.website/folder.** This is the address format for FTP sites. For example, if you want to use a file in a folder named Bids on a company site named WeBuyStuff.com, enter *ftp://ftp.webuystuff.com/bids*.

Figure 17-5:
Enter the location of the folder or file for which you want to create a shortcut in your My Network Places window. If you enter a location that's on the Internet instead of your network, the wizard launches your browser and connects to the Internet (if you've configured your PC to do so; see page 230).

What happens when you click Next depends on the kind of address you specified. If it was an FTP site, you're asked for a password; if you specified a folder or filename, the wizard proposes a name for it (which you're welcome to change).

Click Finish to complete the creation of your network shortcut, which now appears in the My Network Places window. To save you a step, the wizard also connects to, and opens, the corresponding folder.

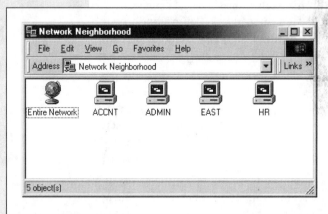

Figure 17-6:
This network has four computers. The Entire Network icon lets you drill down from the workgroup to the computers, exactly as in Windows Me's My Network Places. But because you see the networked PCs immediately, there's little reason to do so.

Using Network Neighborhood

On PCs running Windows 95 and Windows 98, you won't find a My Network Places icon on the desktop. Instead, you get its ancestor: Network Neighborhood.

When you open Network Neighborhood, Windows displays an icon in the window for each computer it finds on the network (see Figure 17-6), along with an Entire

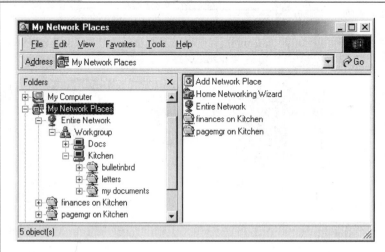

Figure 17-7:
The advantage of using Windows Explorer to look over your network is that you can simultaneously access folders and files on your local computer from this window, making it easier to copy files between the computers.

Network icon. You're spared the Windows Me step of having to burrow through a Workgroup icon to find the PC icons. Otherwise, however, the idea is the same: just double-click a computer's icon to see the shared disks, folders, and printers attached to it. (Once again, you may have to type in the correct password before you're given access.)

Using Windows Explorer

Instead of using the Network Places or Network Neighborhood icon on the desktop, some people prefer to survey the network landscape using Windows Explorer. This trick works in Windows Me, Windows 95, and Windows 98. (See page 88 for details on opening Windows Explorer.)

The left pane of the Windows Explorer window lists an icon for My Network Places or Network Neighborhood. As shown in Figure 17-7, you can click the + button to see a list of the computers and shared resources on them.

Mapping Shares to Drive Letters

If the networking bug has really bitten you, you may want to consider the advanced technique called *mapping shares*. Using this trick, you can assign a *letter* to a particular shared disk or folder on the network. You can give your FamilyStuff folder the letter F: and the Jaz drive in the kitchen the letter J:, just as your hard drive is called C: and your floppy drive is A:.

Doing so confers two benefits. First, these disks and folders now appear directly in the My Computer window. Getting to them is much faster now, because you're saved several layers of double-clicking required by the My Network Places window. Second, when you choose File→Open from within one of your applications, you'll be able to jump directly to a particular shared folder by typing its letter, instead of having to double-click, ever deeper, through the icons in the Open File dialog box (see page 124).

To map a drive letter to a disk or folder, open My Network Places, Network Neighborhood, or Windows Explorer to find the icon for the shared item. Then proceed like this:

1. **Right-click the shared disk or folder icon. From the shortcut menu, choose Map Network Drive.**

   If you don't see the Map Network Drive command, you're probably clicking a disk or folder that hasn't been shared. (You can't right-click a *shortcut* in the My Network Places window, either—only the actual disk or folder icon.)

2. **Select a drive letter to map to this share (see Figure 17-8).**

   Windows proposes the next available drive letter for your computer, but you can select any unused letter you like.

3. **To make this letter assignment "stick," turn on "Reconnect at logon."**

If you don't use this option, Windows will forget this assignment the next time you turn on the computer.

4. **Click OK.**

A window opens to display the contents of the folder or disk. If you don't want to work with any files at the moment, just close the window.

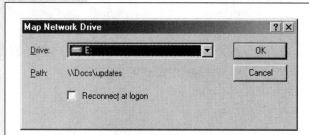

Figure 17-8:
The "Reconnect at logon" option tells Windows to locate the share and map this drive letter to it every time you start your computer.

Working With Network Files

Now that you know how to open shared drives and folders from across the network, you can start using the files you find there. Fortunately, there's nothing much to it:

At the Desktop

When you're working at the desktop, you can double-click icons to open them, drag them to the Recycle Bin, make copies of them, and otherwise manipulate them exactly as though they were icons on your own hard drive. Chapter 4 contains much more detail on manipulating files. (Of course, if you were given only Read-Only access, as described earlier in this chapter, you have less freedom.)

Tip: There's one significant difference between working with "local" icons and those that sit elsewhere on the network: When you delete a file from another computer on the network, you can't use the Recycle Bin, since it won't accept files dragged from other machines. Instead, highlight a file's icon and then press the Del key.

Inside Applications

When you're working in the program, opening files that sit elsewhere on the network requires only a couple of extra steps:

1. **From within the program, choose File→Open.**

The Open File dialog box (see page 124) appears.

2. **From the Look In drop-down menu, choose My Network Places.**

If you're using Windows 95 or 98, choose Network Neighborhood instead.

Either way, you get a list of the icons that would normally appear in the My Network Places (or Network Neighborhood) window, as shown in Figure 17-9.

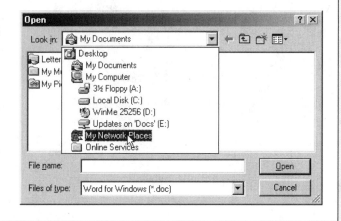

Figure 17-9:
If you mapped a drive letter to a folder, you'll see it listed here in the Open File dialog box, just as though it's a disk drive on your own computer. Mapping a shared folder or disk to a drive letter like this saves you a lot of navigating when you want to open a frequently used share on the network.

3. **Double-click your way to the folder containing the file you want to use.**

In Windows Me, open the shortcut for the folder you want, if it appears; otherwise, open Entire Network, then Workgroup, then the PC you want, then the drive and folder you want. In Windows 95/98, just double-click the computer, drive, and folder.

WORKAROUND WORKSHOP

Automatic Reconnections of Mapped Shares Can Be Tricky

If you select "Reconnect at logon" when mapping a shared disk or folder to a letter, the order in which you start your computers becomes important. The PC containing the shared disk or folder should boot before the computer that refers to it as, say, drive K:. That way, when the second computer searches for "drive K:" on the network, its quest will be successful.

On the other hand, this guideline presents a seemingly insurmountable problem if you have two computers on the network, and each of them maps drive letters to folders or disks on the other.

Workaround #1: When a computer can't find a shared folder or disk, it shows you an error message. It says that the permanent connection is not available and asks if you

want to reconnect the next time you start the computer. Click Yes.

Then, after all the computers have started up, open My Computer or Windows Explorer. You can see the mapped drive, but there's a red X mark under the icon. Ignore the X. Just double-click the icon; the shared folder or disk opens normally (because the other machine is now available), and the red X goes away.

Workaround #2: Choose Start→Settings→Control Panel. Open the Network Control Panel. In the scrolling list, double-click the Client for Microsoft Networks icon, turn on Quick Logon, click OK, and click OK again. From now on, Windows Me won't reconnect to the mapped drives until you actually double-click their icons.

---

4. **Double-click the file you want to use.**

The file opens. You can work on the document just as if it were sitting on your own computer.

At this point, using the File→Save command saves your changes to the original file, wherever it was on the network (unless you were given Read-Only access, of course). If you choose File→Save As and then choose a different location in the "Look in:" box, you can save a copy of the file onto your own PC.

Network Printing

Another excellent justification for creating a small network is that all of the PCs can share a single printer. Or, if you've bought several printers—say, a high-speed laser printer for one computer, a color printer for another—everyone on the network can use whichever printer is appropriate to the document he's printing.

Sharing Printers

To make a printer available to the entire network, make sure that it's working properly with the computer it's attached to (see Chapter 12). You probably don't even have to share it (see page 360); the Home Networking Wizard generally shares every printer it finds automatically.

Tip: You can tell if a printer is being shared just by looking at its icon. Choose Start→Settings→Printers; a shared printer looks as though there's a tiny hand cradling its icon, as shown in Figure 17-3.

Installing Printer Drivers via Network

Unfortunately, just because a printer has been shared doesn't necessarily mean that you can send printouts to it from other PCs. Those computers, too, require installation of that printer's driver software, just as though they were physically attached to the printer. Windows Me offers several methods for installing these drivers.

Netcrawler: Automatic printer installation

If all of the computers on the network are running Windows Me, you lucked out: You don't have to take any steps at all. Once every 15 minutes, an ingenious, behind-the-scenes Windows Me new feature called Netcrawler searches your network in search of correctly installed printer drivers. If it finds such drivers, Netcrawler silently installs them on all *other* Windows Me machines on the network. It even puts an icon for that printer in the Start→Settings→Printers window of every one of those computers.

Note: If you don't see your printer's icon in the Printers window (and it's been at least 15 minutes since you installed the software on one PC), you must have a Netcrawler-incompatible printer model. In that case, read on.

Using the network browser window to install printers

If Netcrawler doesn't seem to be able to find your printer, or if not all of the machines on your network are running Windows Me, you can try another time-saving feature: the Connect (or Install) command. It goes like this:

Start by opening the network browser on your desktop (My Network Places or Network Neighborhood). Locate and open the icon for the PC to which the printer is directly connected.

When the computer's window opens, you should see an icon for the shared printer. Right-click the icon and, from the shortcut menu, choose Connect (Windows Me) or Install (Windows 95/98). Most of the time, Windows takes over from here, automatically installing the drivers. (You may be asked to insert your Windows CD.)

Using the Add Printer Wizard

If you have a very old, very new, or very obscure printer model, even the Network Places/Network Neighborhood method described above may not succeed in installing your printer drivers. In that case, you may have to use the Add Printer Wizard:

1. **Choose Start→Settings→Printers.**

    The Printers window opens.

2. **Double-click the Add Printer icon.**

    The Add Printer Wizard opens with a welcoming message. Click Next to get started.

3. **Select Network Printer, and then click Next.**

    The wizard needs to know where to find the printer on the network. If you know the printer's path, you can type it now (in the format *ComputerName*\ *PrinterShareName)*; otherwise, click Browse to open the Browse for Printer window shown in Figure 17-10.

Figure 17-10:
This is the Browse for Printer window in Windows Me. "Expand" the computer and select the printer. Then click OK.

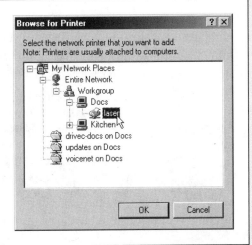

4. **Click Yes or No to indicate whether you ever print from MS-DOS applications, then click Next.**

   Some MS-DOS software applications can only send printouts to an LPT port, and not directly to a network printer. This option redirects all such printer output to the network printer.

5. **Enter a name for this printer. Specify whether or not you'd like it to be the default (primary) printer for this computer.**

   Windows proposes the printer's official name, but you can enter a friendlier name, if you like.

6. **Select the option to print a test page.**

   The test page is the only way to make sure the installation went smoothly. If the test page doesn't print, or prints incorrectly, consult Chapter 12 to learn how to troubleshoot printer installations.

Now you have a printer, even if your PC doesn't. Your software programs don't know or care where the printer is; Windows automatically directs your programs' printouts across the network to the physical printer, wherever it may be.

Internet Connection Sharing (ICS)

As noted in the previous chapter, Internet connection sharing (ICS) can save you a lot of money if one of your PCs is blessed with a cable modem or DSL connection. Thanks to ICS, the other computers on your network can enjoy the same always-online, high-speed access without your having to pay another $40 a month for each. And if you use a standard dial-up modem, ICS means that everybody in the house can be surfing the Internet at the same time, over the same phone-line connection. For many frazzled PC owners in single- or even dual-phone-line households, this feature alone justifies the installation of Windows Me.

The premise of ICS is simple: Suppose the PC in the upstairs office has the cable modem (or the phone jack). You sit down in front of the PC in the kitchen, which is part of the same network. When you launch your Web browser or email program to go online, the PC in the *office* dials or connects; you surf in the kitchen *via* the upstairs PC.

If the office PC is turned off, nobody else in the house can go online; on the other hand, if somebody is already using the office PC to surf the Internet, she won't even be aware that you're piggybacking on her connection simultaneously.

Making Dial-Up Sharing Work

If the office PC—henceforth called the *host* computer—is connected to a cable modem or DSL line, you can skip this discussion. If it connects via dial-up modem, however, you'll probably want to take a few extra configuration steps to prevent driving everyone else on the network crazy.

For example, Windows Me assumes that you want the host computer to be online constantly, all day long, so that it'll be ready when anyone else on the network tries to go online. As a result, the host computer tries to dial the Internet the instant it's turned on—and if the call gets disconnected, it redials automatically. (These phenomena occur regardless of the settings you established when you set up Dial-Up Networking, as described in Chapter 10.)

Unfortunately, having the host computer insist on connecting to your ISP 24 hours a day can have a dramatic negative effect on your life. For example, its modem is now tying up the household phone line all day long. Furthermore, most ISPs limit you to a certain number of hours of connection time each month—100 hours, for example. If you exceed that number, you're charged more money. Your connection-sharing PC, if left undisciplined, could rack up astronomical bills (and even get your ISP account canceled).

Fortunately, it's easy enough to give Internet connection sharing some behavior-modification therapy, so that it won't insist on being online all day long. Using the following steps, you can set things up so that the host computer will dial the Internet automatically, but only when another PC on the network is "trying" to go online:

1. **Choose Start→Settings→Dial-Up Networking.**

   The Dial-Up Networking window opens.

2. **Right-click your ISP connection icon; choose Properties from the shortcut menu.**

   The Properties dialog box for the connection opens.

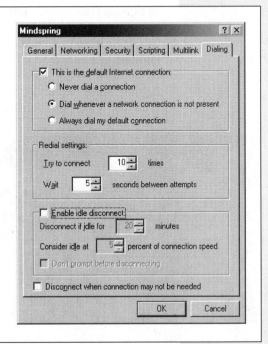

Figure 17-11:
The Home Networking Wizard may have established your connection icon with some inconvenient settings. If the host PC insists on being online at all hours, this is where you can set it straight. (If your kid insists on being online at all hours, that's another book.)

3. **Click the Dialing tab.**

The dialog box shows the settings that have been established by the Home Networking wizard (see Figure 17-11).

4. **Select "This is the default Internet connection."**

This option is important only if you've created *several* Dial-Up Networking connections; you're telling your PC to use the one you've just right-clicked.

5. **Turn on "Always dial my default connection."**

This step tells Windows Me to dial automatically whenever someone on the network tries to use an email, Web browser, or other Internet program. (If you forget this step, then whoever's trying to use the PC in the kitchen will get nothing but an error message when she tries to go online, to the effect that no connection to the Internet exists. If you're using the office [host] PC at the time, the next thing you'll hear is a shout from the kitchen: "Yo! Could you please connect us?!")

By doing so, you also turn off "Dial whenever a network connection is not present," which is what makes Windows try to stay online continuously.

6. **Click OK.**

The dialog box closes, and the new settings are in effect.

Troubleshooting Connection Problems

Unfortunately, it's not unheard of to have problems using Internet connection sharing even when the host computer has successfully connected to the Internet. This section provides some solutions.

Your lease wasn't renewed

Way, way behind the scenes, in the technical underbrush of your network, the client computers must ask the host computer for what's called a *lease* for an Internet connection. The lease lasts 24 hours and then must be renewed; otherwise, the client computer can't contact the host.

TROUBLESHOOTING MOMENT

Browsers Give up Early

If you open your Web browser on a *client* computer (that is, not the one with the Internet connection), the host computer dials. Unfortunately, dialing and connecting take time; before the host computer has finished making the connection, your Web browser may already have reported that the Web page can't be opened. Similarly, your email program may report that "the server isn't available," simply because it took an especially long time for the host computer to make the connection.

In either case, simply wait a moment and then try again: in your Web browser, click the Refresh button; in the email program, click the Send/Receive button again. This time, your PC should find the connection and succeed in getting online.

This lease-renewal business ordinarily takes place invisibly and automatically. When the time comes, the client computer simply asks for a renewed lease and gets one, instantly.

But suppose your 24-hour lease happens to expire when the host computer is turned off. In the case, your PC has no way to request a renewal, and it won't be able to go online via the host, even after the host computer is back on.

This is a long and technical way of saying that, if your routine is to turn off your computers every night, the *sequence* in which you turn them on again is important. Turn on the host computer before the others on the network. By the time the other PCs start up, their "landlord" is on and ready to issue new leases on Internet life.

POWER USERS' CLINIC

Investigating an Expired Lease

If your client computer's Internet-connection-sharing lease expires, you don't get any intelligent notification. Instead, you just get error messages when you try to access a Web site or check your email.

Finding out if an expired lease is causing the problem takes a bit of snooping using the MS-DOS prompt. (Before you begin, make sure the host computer is turned on.)

Start by opening an MS-DOS command prompt window by choosing Start→Programs→Accessories→MS-DOS Prompt (in Windows Me). (In earlier Windows versions, choose Start→Programs→MS-DOS Prompt.)

Type *winipcfg* and press Enter; the IP Configuration dialog box opens. Click More info. Now the IP Configuration dialog box expands. If the Lease Expires field is empty, your lease has expired. You've just found out why your PC can't use the host's connection.

If that's the case, make sure that the Adapter drop-down menu correctly identifies your networking card. To request a new lease, click Release All, then click Renew All, click OK, type *exit*, and then press Enter.

Your client computer should be back in business—at least until the next time.

Problems playing computer games

Most multi-player Internet games require a clean, direct connection. The Internet connection-sharing feature itself is what causes glitches (such as system hangs when you select a game room, game rooms that appear empty, other players' inability to see you, and so on).

The only way to play these Internet games is to disable ICS, as described on page 379, and work from the host computer.

NetMeeting doesn't work

If NetMeeting's whiteboard or chat-room features don't work, or you can't even enter the meeting, you've found your culprit. NetMeeting, like Internet games, requires a clean, direct connection. Here again, the solution is to turn off Internet connection sharing (see page 379) when you want to participate in a NetMeeting. (See the end of Chapter 11 for more on this program.)

The host computer dials out to ISP for no reason

You're sitting there at the host computer working on a spreadsheet, when suddenly the PC dials the Internet. Nobody on your network was even thinking about going online. Bewildered, you disconnect—but then your PC dials again a few minutes later, as though haunted.

You're witnessing the efforts of the AutoUpdate feature (see page 116). In an effort to keep Windows Me up-to-date, AutoUpdate is taking it upon itself to check the Internet for the latest Microsoft bug fixes.

If this behavior bothers you, you can turn off AutoUpdate (on *every* computer) by choosing Start→Settings→Control Panel to open the Control Panel window. Double-click the Automatic Updates icon, and then select "Turn off automatic updating."

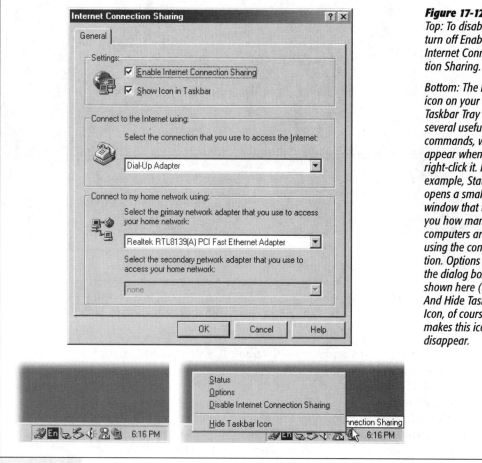

Figure 17-12:
Top: To disable ICS, turn off Enable Internet Connection Sharing.

Bottom: The ICS icon on your Taskbar Tray has several useful commands, which appear when you right-click it. For example, Status opens a small window that tells you how many computers are using the connection. Options opens the dialog box shown here (top). And Hide Taskbar Icon, of course, makes this icon disappear.

Temporarily turning off Internet connection sharing

To disable ICS, check your Taskbar Tray for the presence of an ICS icon, as shown at bottom in Figure 17-12. If you see this icon, right-click it and choose Disable Internet Connection Sharing. If you *don't* have an ICS icon on your Taskbar Tray, you can put one there like this:

1. **Choose Start→Settings→Control Panel. In the Control Panel window, double-click the Internet Options icon.**

   The Internet Properties dialog box opens.

2. **Click the Connections tab, then click the Sharing button.**

   You have a Sharing button only if, when using the Home Networking Wizard, you indicated that this is the host computer (the one with the Internet connection). The Internet Connection Sharing dialog box shown at top in Figure 17-12 opens.

3. **Turn on "Show Icon in Taskbar," then click OK.**

   Windows prompts you to restart the machine. When it reboots, you'll see the Internet Connection Sharing icon on your Tray (Figure 17-12, bottom).

GEM IN THE ROUGH

Two-Computer Ethernet–and Direct Cable Connections

If you want to network only two computers, you can do so without having to buy and set up a hub.

All you need is a special cable called a *crossover cable*, which can connect two computers directly. It costs about $10 at your local computer store or online shop; just run the cable directly from one networking card to the other. Everything else in this chapter works exactly as though you had purchased a hub and were using a "real" Ethernet network.

There's another way to connect two machines, too—one that doesn't even require Ethernet cards: *direct connections*. You can create this kind of miniature homemade network only if (a) the computers are close to each other, (b) they both have parallel ports, and (c) you've bought a high-speed DirectParallel cable (*www.lpt.com*).

To begin, use the Add/Remove Programs control panel (page 185) to install the Windows component called Direct Cable Connection on each PC.

Now choose Start→Programs→Accessories→Communications→Direct Cable Connection. A wizard appears, ask-

ing if the computer you're using will be the *host* (the machine whose files will be shared) or the *guest* (the one that will be accessing shared resources on the other machine). Choose Host, and then click Next.

On the next wizard screen, specify the port you're using to connect the machines (from the list of unused serial, parallel, or infrared ports). Click Parallel. Plug in the cable, if you haven't already; click Next, then Finish. The host computer starts "listening" for the guest to visit it.

Repeat all of this on the other machine, this time designating it the Guest.

Once the two machines are connected by cable, you can open the My Network Places icon on the guest machine; you'll see the shared folders, disks, and printers, just as though they were connected via "real" network.

Thereafter, whenever you want to repeat this procedure, just run the Direct Cable Connection Wizard on each machine to establish the connection.

Part Six:
Appendixes

6

Installing Windows Me

In the old days, few words could strike greater raw, quivering terror into mortal hearts than these: *installing Windows*. Anyone who had ever used a PC knew what that little project entailed: Sitting down Saturday morning with the Windows CD and a cup of coffee, beginning a journey into the unknown that finally ended Tuesday afternoon—and, too often, produced a PC whose features didn't quite work anymore.

Fortunately, Microsoft decided that a drastically improved installation process would be one of the key new features of Windows Me. For example, the Windows Me installation routine is now what Microsoft calls a "silent install." That is, while the installer chugs away, you won't be asked to make decisions, identify hardware, restart the computer, or do anything, in fact, other than read the ads for Windows Me that fill your screen. The Windows installer does everything else automatically.

That doesn't necessarily mean that the installation will go perfectly for you and everybody you know, especially if you're upgrading an existing PC that you've tricked out with shareware, off-brand add-on equipment, and so on. But odds certainly are that the Windows Me installation will go more smoothly than the installation of previous Windows versions.

Tip: If your computer came with Windows Me already installed, congratulations. You can skip this appendix.

System Requirements

To run Windows Me, your computer must have, at minimum, a processor that operates at 150 MHz, 32 megabytes of RAM, and 500 MB of empty disk space. Higher
numbers for these statistics, of course, make Windows Me run better and faster.

Upgrading from Windows 95 or 98

The Windows Me installer can install the new Windows version right on top of
Windows 95 or 98. This process doesn't disturb any of your files or documents; in
fact, it even preserves your fonts, networking and Internet settings, and other preference settings.

Here's the ritual:

Prepare Your System

Before you start, run down this checklist of safety steps:

1. **Run ScanDisk to make sure your drive is healthy.**

   Windows Me runs ScanDisk during installation, but only an abridged version
   that can't actually fix any problems it finds. Running the ScanDisk version that's
   already on your Windows 95 or 98 machine, therefore, is a better preparatory
   step.

2. **Run a virus scan to make sure your system is clean.**

   Antivirus software interferes with all installations, not just Windows. Therefore,
   after the virus check, turn off the virus software.

3. **Decompress your hard drives, if you had compressed them.**

   You can't install Windows Me onto a compressed drive.

4. **Empty the Recycle Bin to reclaim disk space.**

5. **Back up all your important files.**

   Installing Windows is extremely unlikely to disturb your documents and other
   data files, but knowing that you have a recent backup will make the installation
   less stressful.

6. **Quit all running programs; disconnect from the Internet.**

7. **Find your old Windows CD and your Windows Me serial number.**

   If you bought the Windows Me Upgrade kit, the installer will ask you to insert
   your Windows 95 or 98 CD or floppy disks to prove that you are, in fact, a legiti-
   mate owner of the previous Windows version.

   As for the serial number: You'll be asked to type it in whether you bought the
   Windows Me upgrade kit or the full Windows Me kit. You'll find this long "product key" password on the back of the Windows Me CD case.

Read or Print the Help Files

Microsoft provides a lot of information, including specific hints for certain hardware brands, in the text files on the Windows Me CD. Printing these documents before the installation is a great idea, so that you can consult them if problems arise during installation.

Unfortunately, as soon as you insert the CD, the Windows installer launches. The solution is to click Cancel (if a message appears offering to upgrade your system). Then click the Browse This CD icon. Now you're taken to the desktop, where a window appears showing the folders and files on the Windows Me CD-ROM.

Double-click the "add-ons" folder to open it; double-click the Document folder to open *it*. The "guide" folder contains a concise, Microsoft Word-format document that's as close as Microsoft comes to an instruction manual; the "textfile" folder contains an assortment of text-based help files. Open them, read them, and, if you think it might be helpful during the installation, print these documents.

Install Windows Me

To run the Windows Me installer, eject its CD (if necessary) and then re-insert it. The installation program starts automatically. (If it doesn't, you must have turned off the AutoRun feature. In that case, double-click My Computer, double-click the icon for your CD-ROM drive, and then double-click the file *Setup.exe* to start the installer.)

If the installer asks you if you'd like to upgrade, click Yes. Then the Windows Millennium Edition Setup Wizard welcomes you; click Next. From this point on, the installer runs on autopilot. It will ask you for help five times, so that you can:

1. **Promise to uphold the Microsoft law.**

   That is, you must agree to the software license agreement that appears on the screen (by clicking "I accept the Agreement").

2. **Enter the key code for your copy of Windows Me.**

   This lengthy serial number appears on a sticker on the back of the Windows Me CD case.

GEM IN THE ROUGH

Secrets of the Software License Agreement

Few people bother to read the Agreement, but you'll find some howlers if you do. For example, it says that you're not advised to use Windows Me in "nuclear facilities, aircraft navigation, direct life-support machines, or weapons systems," and that when you use the Internet games feature described in Chapter 7, your PC will send information about your PC to Microsoft, which you give the company permission to use.

And then, in all capitals, it says that there is no warranty for "QUIET ENJOYMENT."

Librarians: You've been warned.

Tip: You don't need to type the hyphens in the product-key serial number. In fact, you don't even need to Tab or click from one text box to the next; just keep typing letters and numbers in a continuous stream. Your numbers jump to the next text box when the previous one is full.

3. **Indicate whether or not you want Windows Me to keep a copy of your earlier Windows version ("Save System Files") as a backup.**

   If you click Yes, you'll next be asked to choose the drive on which you want to save the old system files.

   This "Save System Files" feature is a great safety net: If you don't fall madly in love with Windows Me, or if it turns out to be incompatible with some game or piece of hardware, you'll be able to uninstall it later and return to your Windows 95 or 98 installation. Here's how to proceed, once you've made up your mind:

   If you decide to keep Windows Me: Open the Add/Remove Programs control panel described on the next page. Click "Delete Windows Millennium Uninstall information," then click Add/Remove. You've just deleted your older operating system, reclaiming about 200 MB of disk space in the process.

   If you decide to ditch Windows Me: Open the Add/Remove Programs control panel described the next page. Click "Uninstall Windows Me," then click Add/Remove. You've just returned to Windows 95 or 98.

4. **Create an emergency startup floppy disk.**

   During the installation, Windows Me offers to create an emergency startup floppy disk. By all means, find and insert a blank floppy disk; such an emergency startup disk can be worth its weight in gold if, someday, your hard drive calls in sick and won't start up the machine. (And the startup floppy Windows Me builds for you is far more powerful and useful than in previous Windows versions.)

Note: A few Windows utilities require free updaters to be compatible with Windows Me: Solomon AntiVirus 7.70, Norton Internet Security, GoBack versions lower than 2.1.5.0, and so on. If it finds one of these on your PC, the Windows Me installer will halt installation and advise you to uninstall the offending program.

Following these four queries (and a request to click a Finish button thereafter), the installer leaves you alone and does its duty unattended, which takes about half an hour and includes restarting your computer a couple of times. During this process, you'll see an "Estimated time remaining" counter at the left side of the screen, and a readout at the lower-left corner that tells you what the installer is doing.

If the installer encounters a problem, you'll see an error message; to troubleshoot, consult the text files you printed, call Microsoft for help, or try the installation again.

When the installation is over, you'll see a glitzy, TV-style advertisement for the new features in Windows Me. (If the Stop and Close buttons don't work, you can press Alt+F4 to bail out.) When it's over, you're finally ready to start work.

Wrapping up Loose Ends

After Windows Me is installed, you have a couple of chores: First, set the date and time as described on page 188.

Second, if you didn't upgrade from Windows 95 or 98, Windows Me may have set your screen to a gigantic, zoomed-in resolution like 640 by 400 pixels (screen dots), which almost certainly needs adjustment. Visit your Display control panel applet (page 188) to adjust this setting.

Tip: If you're used to Windows 95 or 98, you may be disconcerted to find that Microsoft has moved the command to open Windows Explorer; it's been banished to the Start→Programs→Accessories submenu. Fortunately, you can move it back to the Programs menu—or anywhere on the Start menu you want it to be—by following the instructions on page 47.

POWER USERS' CLINIC

Installing Windows Me from Your Hard Drive

If you have a lot of free hard drive space, consider copying the "win9x" folder of the Windows Me CD to your hard drive before installing Windows Me.

Then open this folder (which is now on your hard drive) and double-click *setup.exe*. (Or, if you're installing from MS-DOS, type *setup.exe* and press Enter.)

Installing Windows Me from the hard drive rather than the CD-ROM offers two advantages. First, the installation goes much faster, because your hard drive is faster than your CD-ROM drive.

Second, when the Windows Plug and Play feature tries to find the driver for some new piece of equipment you're installing, you won't be prompted to find and insert the original Windows Me CD, as you might otherwise. Instead, Windows will find whatever files it needs right there, ready to roll, on your hard drive.

Adding and Removing Windows Components

Not every Windows Me software feature gets copied to your hard drive by its installer. Plenty of second-tier programs and features are left behind on the CD, awaiting the day you decide you need them. They lurk in two places: the Add/Remove Programs control panel and the "add-ons" folder.

The Add/Remove Programs Control Panel

Windows Me maintains a master list that reveals which software components you have and haven't yet installed. To see this list, choose Start→Settings→Control Panel. When the Control Panel window opens, double-click the Add/Remove Programs icon. Click the Windows Setup tab, and continue as described on page 185.

For example, the following are some of the components that a fresh Windows Me installation doesn't include, but that you may find useful. (The category of the Add/Remove Programs applet that contains each of these items follows in parentheses.)

- **Additional wallpaper, screen-saver choices, and sounds.** Install them if you crave additional variety. (Accessories, Multimedia.)

- **Clipboard Viewer.** A handy program that lets you see and manipulate whatever you've most recently copied to the Windows Clipboard (see page 126). (System Tools.)

- **Character Map.** Here's another extremely useful program, described on page 146. (System Tools.)

- **Net Watcher, System Monitor, System Resource Meter.** Technical tools for monitoring the status of your PC and network. (System Tools.)

- **WinPop.** An extremely useful utility that lets you look at, and even create, Zip files right at the desktop. (Most files that you download from the Web or from email arrive compressed in Zip format, and must be opened with a utility like this one before you can use them.)

- **WebTV for Windows.** This program has its own category here; it lets you watch TV on your PC, as described on page 174.

POWER USERS' CLINIC

The Clean Windows Me Install

Microsoft thinks it's doing you a favor by designing the Windows Me installer to upgrade your existing Windows installation, without disturbing any of your settings, fonts, preferences, drivers, and so on. But that's not *always* what you want. What if, for example, you're looking forward to installing Windows Me precisely because your existing Windows installation is a mess? What if several things haven't been working right, or you haven't been able to get on the Internet, or your scanner doesn't work? The last thing you want to do is to pass along those problems to the next generation of Windows.

In these extreme cases, you may want to start over completely—to wipe your hard drive clean, to erase your computer, to take it back to its factory-fresh condition—and then to install a virginal, perfect copy of Windows Millennium. Doing this is called performing a *clean install,* and it's not for the faint of heart.

Before you begin, you must have a PC with a working hard drive; a Windows emergency startup disk (page 186); and, if you bought the Windows Me Upgrade CD, your original, earlier Windows-version CD. And for goodness' sake, back

up all your files! The clean-install process *erases your hard drive completely.*

Now you're ready to begin. Insert the emergency floppy, and then start up the computer. When the startup menu appears, choose "with CD-ROM support."

Now the computer shows you the DOS prompt, which looks like a little > bracket. If you're absolutely positive you want to erase your hard drive, type *format c:* (if that's your drive letter) and then press Enter. Confirm your drastic decision by pressing Y for Yes. Eventually, you'll be asked to provide a name for the newly erased hard drive; do so, and then press Enter.

At the next command prompt, switch DOS's attention to your CD-ROM drive by typing *d:* (or whatever your CD-ROM's drive letter is) and then pressing Enter. Then type *setup* and press Enter again.

Instructions on the screen now guide you through the rest of the installation. You may be asked for your serial number, to insert your old Windows CD, or to provide a name and password (you can leave the password blank).

- **Multilanguage Support.** This category contains the fonts and software components Windows needs to display written Albanian, Bulgarian, and any of 17 other languages (when your system has appropriate applications or is showing appropriate Web sites).

On the other hand, if you'd like to reclaim some hard drive space, you can use the Add/Remove Programs program to *remove* some nonessential Windows files, including wallpaper, sounds, screen savers, and so on. Just turn off the corresponding checkboxes, click OK, and then agree to restart your machine.

The "add-ons" Folder

If you click the Browse This CD button on the Windows Me CD's welcome screen, or if you open the CD via the My Computer→CD-ROM icon, you'll find several folders in the CD's main window. One of them, called simply *add-ons,* contains a handful of meaty bonus morsels, such as a Document folder containing a miniature Windows Me user's guide.

The most useful add-on here is Backup, described (with installation instructions) in Chapter 15.

Windows Me, Menu by Menu

A menu bar tops every Windows desktop window and almost every application window. Along this menu bar, of course, are the names of the menus that, when clicked, produce lists of the commands available to you. Menus are a great invention, especially when compared with the DOSsish requirement to *memorize* every conceivable command.

Most menu bars have a menu named File on the extreme left side, and Help is always the last menu on the right. What comes between depends on the program you're using. This appendix covers the menus in the Windows Me desktop windows.

Tip: You can choose almost any Windows Me menu command entirely from the keyboard; the necessary keystrokes are described in this appendix. (If you open a submenu that doesn't bear the telltale keystroke-hint underlines, press the arrow keys to highlight the command you want, and then Enter to trigger it.)

If you open a menu and then change your mind, press the Esc key to close the menu.

File Menu

Most of these commands operate on a *selection*—that is, you're supposed to highlight an icon, or several icons, before using the menu. It's worth noting, too, that the File menu *changes* depending what you've highlighted; for example, the Print command appears only if you've highlighted a document.

Note: Certain software installations may add other commands to your File menu.

Open

Opens a highlighted document, program, folder, or disk into a window, exactly as though you had double-clicked its icon. *Keyboard equivalent:* Enter.

Print

Sends the highlighted document to your printer, after first opening the necessary application (such as your word processor) and offering you the Print dialog box, where you can specify, for example, how many copies you want. *Keyboard equivalent:* Alt+F, P.

Explore

Opens Windows Explorer, which shows you what's in the highlighted disk or folder in the Explorer two-pane format (see page 88). This command is available only if the selected icon is a drive or a folder. *Keyboard equivalent:* Alt+F, X.

Search

Opens a Search window that's ready to look in the selected drive or folder (the Search command isn't available if you select a file). See page 28 for more on the Search command. *Keyboard equivalent:* F3.

Sharing

This command (available only for folders and disks) opens the Sharing tab of the icon's Properties dialog box. As described in Chapter 17, this dialog box is exclusively for people with networks; it lets you make a folder or disk available to other people on the network. *Keyboard equivalent:* Alt+F, H.

Send To

This command (for files and folders) offers submenu commands that move or copy the highlighted icon(s) to the desktop, to a floppy disk, to the My Documents folder, and so on. *Keyboard equivalent:* Alt+F, E.

New

This command's submenu lets you create a new folder, shortcut, text file, or other new document, depending on the programs you've installed. (For example, if you have Microsoft Office installed, you'll find a New→Microsoft Word Document command here.) *Keyboard equivalent:* Alt+F, W.

Create Shortcut

Creates a *shortcut* to the selected icon. (See page 101 for more on shortcuts.) If you've highlighted a folder or document icon, the shortcut appears in the same window as the original icon; at this point, you haven't accomplished much. To make it useful, drag the shortcut to, for example, the desktop or the Quick Launch toolbar.

If the selected icon is a drive, Windows Me displays a message that says: "Windows cannot create a shortcut here. Do you want the shortcut to be placed on the desktop instead?" Click Yes. *Keyboard equivalent:* Alt+F, S.

Delete

Moves the highlighted folder or file to the Recycle Bin (page 98), after first requesting confirmation. *Keyboard equivalent:* Delete.

Rename

Opens an editing box for the name of the highlighted icon. *Keyboard equivalent:* F2.

Properties

Opens the Properties dialog box for the highlighted icon. Folder and file properties display creation-date and modification-date information; disks display information about available and used space, along with a Tools tab that lets you open the disk-maintenance tools described in Chapter 15. If you've set up a network (Chapter 16), disk and folder Properties dialog boxes may also offer a Sharing tab. *Keyboard equivalent:* Alt+Enter.

Close

Closes the window, just as though you'd clicked the X in the upper-right corner of the window (or double-clicked the icon in the upper-left corner). *Keyboard equivalent:* Alt+F4.

Edit Menu

When you work in, say, your word processor, you use the Edit menu quite a bit—its Cut, Copy, and Paste commands are very useful for moving bits of text. At the desktop, these commands operate on icons, providing an easy way for you to move files and folders from one window or disk to another.

Figure B-1:
Click the + button to "expand" your drive's contents, so that you can choose a destination folder for the icon you're moving or copying. You can create a new folder inside the selected folder by clicking the New Folder button.

Undo

Reverses the last action you performed. The name of the command changes to reflect what you've just done: Undo Delete, Undo Rename, and so on. (Alas, there's no Undo Print feature.) *Keyboard equivalent:* Ctrl+Z.

Cut, Copy, Paste, Paste Shortcut

These commands let you move or copy files or folders from one window to another, as described on page 94. (The Paste Shortcut command offers yet another method of creating a shortcut icon.) Keyboard equivalents: Ctrl+C (for Copy), Ctrl+X (for Cut), Ctrl+V (for Paste), Alt+E, S (for Paste Shortcut).

Copy (or Move) to Folder

If the Cut/Paste and Copy/Paste routines for moving or copying a file or folder to a different window aren't your cup of tea, you can use these commands instead. When you choose either command, a dialog box opens so you can select a destination folder (see Figure B-1). Keyboard equivalents: Alt+E, F (for Copy to Folder), Alt+E, V (for Move to Folder).

Select All

Highlights all of the icons in the open window (or, if no window is open, on the desktop). Windows applies any subsequent command (Copy, Delete, Print, or whatever) to all of them at once.

If you're editing an icon's name, and your cursor is blinking in the renaming rectangle, this command highlights the entire filename instead. *Keyboard equivalent:* Ctrl+A.

Invert Selection

If there are 50 icons in a folder, and you want to highlight 49 of them, don't bother trying to click and Shift-click all 49. Instead, use this trick: Click the one icon (or, with the Shift key pressed, click the handful of icons) you *don't* want. Then choose Edit→Invert Selection. Windows highlights the icons that weren't selected, and vice versa. *Keyboard equivalent:* Alt+E, I.

View Menu

The commands in the View menu apply only to the active desktop window: the one that's open and in front of all the others.

Toolbars

This command offers a submenu of toolbars you can add to the top of the window. For details on these toolbars and their functions, see page 79. *Keyboard equivalent:* Alt+V, T.

Status Bar

Makes the status bar appear or disappear at the bottom of the window. The status bar displays information about the contents of the current window, or the selection you've made inside of it. (It may say, for example, "3 object(s) selected" or "Type: Microsoft Word Document.") *Keyboard equivalent:* Alt+V, B.

Explorer Bar

Splits the window, creating a new left-side pane. In this special panel, you can summon your choice of extra information; make your choice using the View→Explorer Bar submenu. The choices are:

- **Search.** Lets you enter criteria for searching your system (see page 28).

- **Favorites.** Shows a list of your favorite Internet sites for one-click access (see page 125).

- **History.** Shows a list of Web sites and desktop folders you've had open recently. Click an item to return to the same place.

- **Folders.** Turns any window into a Windows Explorer-like view, with a folder hierarchy on the left side, folder contents on the right.

- **Tips.** Offers a new Windows Me tip every day (at the bottom of the window, not the left side).

Keyboard equivalent: Alt+V, E.

Large Icons, Small Icons, List, Details, Thumbnails

These commands let you view the files in a window as *icons* (which you move by dragging freely), as a *list* (a neat list view that's automatically sorted), or as *thumbnails* (large, "pillowed" buttons that reveal what's in graphics files). Page 63 begins a complete description of these views and their relative advantages.

Arrange Icons, Line Up Icons

These commands are both useful for tidying up a window that's filled with file icons.

If you choose View→Line Up Icons (available in icon views only), all icons in the window jump to the closest positions on the invisible underlying grid. This is a temporary status, however—as soon as you drag icons around, or add more icons to the window, the newly moved icons wind up just as sloppily positioned as before you used the command. *Keyboard equivalent:* Alt+V, U.

If you choose View→Arrange Icons, on the other hand, all icons in the window snap to the invisible grid *and* sort themselves according to your choice from the submenu (by size, name, date, and so on). Use this method to place the icons as close as possible to each other within the window, rounding up any strays. (In a list view, these commands simply sort the list according to the criterion you specify in the submenu.) *Keyboard equivalent:* Alt+V, I.

Tip: Both of these commands reorganize the icons in the window at this moment. Moving or adding icons in the window means you'll wind up with icons out of order again. If you'd rather have all icons remain sorted and clustered, also turn on View→Arrange Icons→Auto Arrange. Now any icons you drag jump into grid alignment when you release the mouse. (You can drag icons around freely only when you choose Auto Arrange again to turn it off.)

Choose Columns

In a list view, Windows shows the details of each file in Name, Size, Type, and Modified columns. But using this command, you can choose from an enormous list of additional columns that you'd like displayed (in the frontmost window): Company Name, Product Version, Sender Name, and so on. You can also specify how wide you'd like each column to be, and (using the Move Up and Move Down buttons) where you'd like it to appear in the left-to-right order.

Customize This Folder

This command launches a wizard that walks you through the process of changing the folder window's background (such as the identifying text and graphics that appear on the left side of the window). *Keyboard equivalent:* Alt+V, C.

Go To

This command's submenu lets you move forward or backward through desktop windows you've recently opened, much like the Back and Forward buttons in your Web browser. (The View→Go To→Home Page launches your Web browser, connects to the Internet, and takes you to the page you've designated as your home page.)

Keyboard equivalents: Backspace (for Go To→Back), Alt+right arrow (for Go To→Forward), Alt+V, O, U (for Up One Level), Alt+Home (for Home Page), Windows key+D (for Desktop).

Refresh

Updates the contents of the window. Use this command if you've just cut, pasted, or deleted icons, and the window doesn't reflect the changes. *Keyboard equivalent:* F5.

Favorites Menu

The Favorites menu shows the list of Web pages you've "bookmarked" when using Internet Explorer (see page 125) *and* desktop windows you've designated as Favorites to which you'd like quick access.

Add to Favorites

Adds the currently open Web page or desktop window to the Favorites list. *Keyboard equivalent:* Alt+A, A.

Organize Favorites

Opens the window shown in Figure B-2. Here, you can edit your Favorites list in several ways:

- **Rearrange them** by dragging your Favorites items up or down in the right-side list.

Tip: Windows can sort your Favorites alphabetically, but not in the Organize Favorites dialog box. Instead, right-click any item *in the Favorites menu itself* and choose Sort by Name from the shortcut menu.

Figure B-2:
Click a folder to see what's in it. Drag a Favorites item up or down the list to rearrange it; drag it onto a folder icon to file it away into a subcategory. Click its name once to read, in the lower-left panel, about its origin and when you last looked at it.

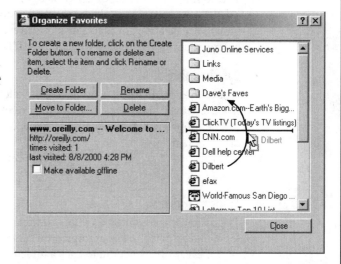

- **Delete or rename one** by clicking its name and then clicking Delete.

- **Organize them into folders.** For example, you may want a folder for all the favorite folders on your PC, another folder for all the Internet sites related to cooking, and another folder for all the Internet sites you visit to get help on computing.

  Click Create Folder to add a new, empty folder to the right-side list; type a name for it and then press Enter. Then file a Favorites listing away by dragging it onto the folder icon (see Figure B-2).

Keyboard equivalent: Alt+A, O.

Favorites List

Choose a name from this list to open the desktop window, or visit the Web site, in question. If you choose a folder name, a submenu lists all of the windows or Web pages you filed in that "folder," as described in the preceding paragraphs.

Tools Menu

This menu offers a handful of leftover commands that didn't quite belong in any of the other menus.

Map Network Drive

This command, exclusively for people on a network, lets you assign a drive letter to a folder to which you've connected over the network. For details on drive mapping, see page 369. *Keyboard equivalent:* Alt+T, N.

Disconnect Network Drive

This command, also just for networked people, summons a dialog box that lets you *delete* a drive mapping you've established using the Map Network Drive command. (You're not deleting any actual disk or drive; only its appearance in your My Computer window.) *Keyboard equivalent:* Alt+T, D.

Synchronize

Synchronize, in Microsoft-ese, means "copy files so both computers contain the identical contents." Using the Briefcase, for example, you can ensure that your laptop and desktop computers contain the same, updated files (see page 339 for details). Synchronizing also means updating the Web pages you've told Internet Explorer that you want to read when you're not online, a trick described on page 250. *Keyboard equivalent:* Alt+T, S.

Folder Options

The dialog box summoned by this command lets you change several global desktop–window options. For example, you can specify that you want a new window to appear every time you double-click a folder (instead of the uni-window approach); that you want one click, not two, to open a folder; and so on. You can read about these settings in detail starting on page 72. *Keyboard equivalent:* Alt+T, O.

Help Menu

This menu has two commands: Help Topics, which opens the Windows Me help system discussed in Chapter 5; and About Windows, which tells you how much memory Windows is using.

Index

Colophon

Due to a wrist ailment you really don't want to hear about, the author wrote the chapters of this book by voice, using Dragon Naturally Speaking on a Micron PC. The book was created in Microsoft Word 2000, whose revision-tracking feature made life far easier as drafts were circulated from author to technical and copy editors. TechSmith Software's SnagIt (*www.techsmith.com*) was used to capture illustrations; Adobe Photoshop and Macromedia Freehand were called in as required for touching them up.

The book was designed and laid out in Adobe PageMaker 6.5 on a Power Mac 8500 and Power Mac G3. The fonts used include Formata (as the sans-serif family) and Minion (as the serif body face). The index was created using EZ Index, a shareware indexing program by John Holder, available at *www.northcoast.com/~jvholder.* The book was then generated as an Adobe Acrobat PDF file for proofreading, indexing, and final transmission to the printing plant.

O'REILLY WOULD LIKE TO HEAR FROM YOU

Which book did this card come from?

_____

Where did you buy this book?
- ❑ Bookstore
- ❑ Direct from O'Reilly
- ❑ Bundled with hardware/software
- ❑ Computer Store
- ❑ Class/seminar
- ❑ Other _____

What operating system do you use?
- ❑ UNIX
- ❑ Windows NT
- ❑ Macintosh
- ❑ PC(Windows/DOS)
- ❑ Other _____

What is your job description?
- ❑ System Administrator
- ❑ Network Administrator
- ❑ Web Developer
- ❑ Programmer
- ❑ Educator/Teacher
- ❑ Other _____

❑ Please send me O'Reilly's catalog, containing a complete listing of O'Reilly books and software.

Name _____ Company/Organization _____

Address _____

City _____ State _____ Zip/Postal Code _____ Country _____

Telephone _____ Internet or other email address (specify network) _____

Nineteenth century wood engraving
of a bear from the O'Reilly &
Associates Nutshell Handbook®
Using & Managing UUCP.

BUSINESS REPLY MAIL

FIRST CLASS MAIL   PERMIT NO. 80   SEBASTOPOL, CA

Postage will be paid by addressee

O'Reilly & Associates, Inc.
101 Morris Street
Sebastopol, CA 95472-9902